Round off to the nearest whole!

Ken-ichi Sakura

It's the fourth volume! Look how far we've come! I thought things might get a little less hectic after four volumes. But the truth is, I'm still going flat-out every day, just like I did for volume I. However, thanks to the help of my assistants, I'm now able to take out the trash in the morning. Heh heh heh...

Ken-ichi Sakura's manga debut was *Fabre Tanteiki*, which was published in a special edition of *Monthly Shonen Jump* in 2000. Serialization of *Dragon Drive* began in the March 2001 issue of *Monthly Shonen Jump* and the hugely successful series has inspired video games and an animated TV show. Sakura's latest title, *Kotokuri*, began running in the March 2006 issue of *Monthly Shonen Jump*. *Dragon Drive* and *Kotokuri* have both become tremendously popular in Japan because of Sakura's unique sense of humor and dynamic portrayal of feisty teen characters.

DRAGON DRIVE

DRAGON DRIVE
VOLUME 4

The SHONEN JUMP Manga Edition

STORY AND ART BY
KEN-ICHI SAKURA

Translation/Martin Hunt, HC Language Solutions, Inc.
English Adaptation/Ian Reid, HC Language Solutions, Inc.
Touch-up Art & Lettering/Jim Keefe
Design/Sam Elzway
Editor/Shaenon K. Garrity

Editor in Chief, Books/Alvin Lu
Editor in Chief, Magazines/Marc Weidenbaum
VP of Publishing Licensing/Rika Inouye
VP of Sales/Gonzalo Ferreyra
Sr. VP of Marketing/Liza Coppola
Publisher/Hyoe Narita

Printed in the U.S.A.

Published by VIZ Media, LLC
P.O. Box 77010
San Francisco, CA 94107

SHONEN JUMP Manga Edition
10 9 8 7 6 5 4 3 2 1
First printing, October 2007

www.viz.com

THE WORLD'S
MOST POPULAR MANGA

www.shonenjump.com

SHONEN JUMP MANGA EDITION

DRAGON DRIVE

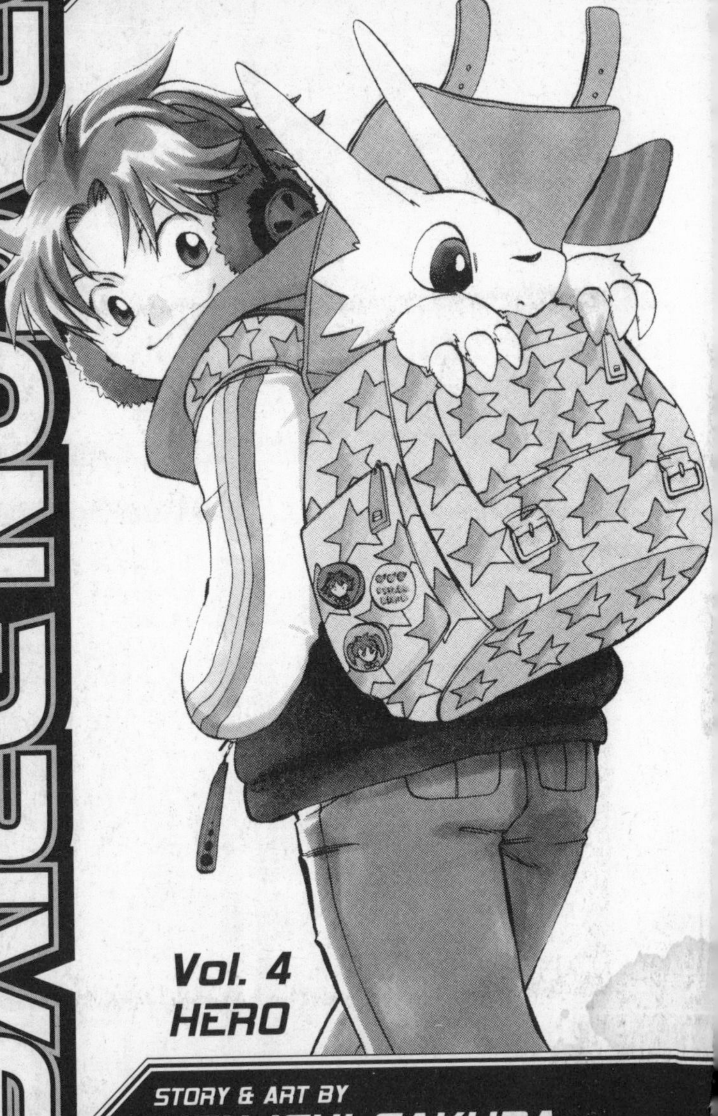

Vol. 4
HERO

STORY & ART BY

KEN-ICHI SAKURA

IN COLLABORATION WITH BANDAI • CHAN'S • ORG

CHARACTERS

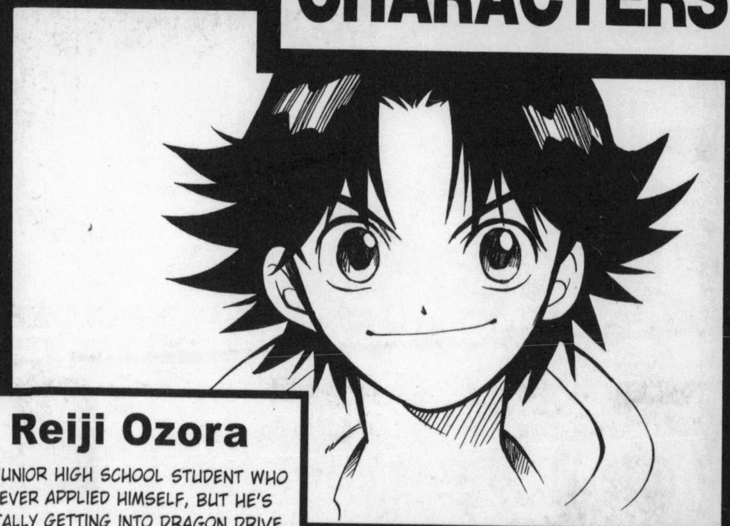

Reiji Ozora

A JUNIOR HIGH SCHOOL STUDENT WHO NEVER APPLIED HIMSELF, BUT HE'S TOTALLY GETTING INTO DRAGON DRIVE.

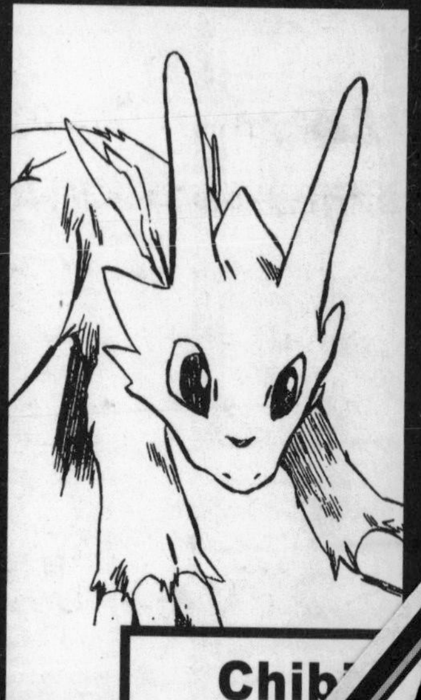

Chib

REIJI'S D
PARTNER. I
KNOWN A

Maiko Yukino

SHE'S ALWAYS GETTING TICKED OFF BY HER UNRELIABLE CHILDHOOD PAL REIJI, BUT SHE SECRETLY CARES ABOUT HIM.

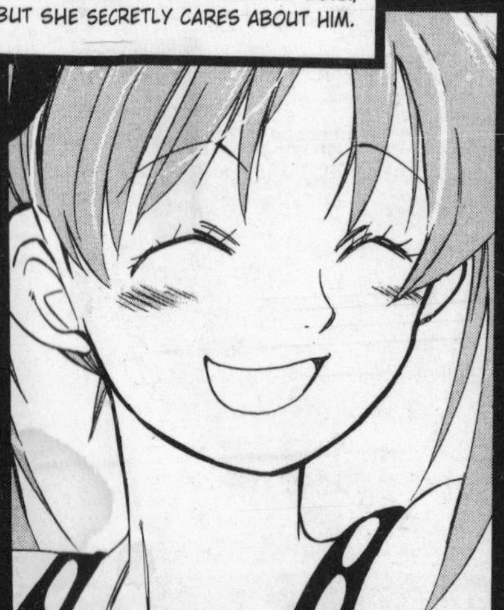

Daisuke Hagiwara

HE'S CONVINCED THAT REIJI IS HIS RIVAL FOR MAIKO'S AFFECTIONS.

Rokkaku

A REAL TOUGH GUY WHO LIKES TO PARTY! HE RECENTLY JOINED UP WITH REIJI TO FIGHT IN THE DRAGONIC HEAVEN TOURNAMENT.

Meguru

A MYSTERIOUS GIRL WHO BROUGHT REIJI AND FRIENDS TO RIKYU.

STORY

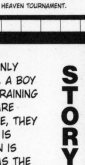

DRAGON DRIVE IS A VIRTUAL REALITY GAME THAT ONLY KIDS CAN PLAY. THE THRILL OF THE GAME GRIPS REIJI, A BOY WHO WAS NEVER REALLY GOOD AT ANYTHING. WHILE TRAINING IN A SPECIAL ROOM ONE DAY, REIJI AND HIS FRIENDS ARE WHISKED AWAY TO RIKYU, AN ALTERNATE EARTH. THERE, THEY LEARN THAT RI-ON, THE ORGANIZATION RUNNING D.D., IS PLOTTING TO CONQUER BOTH RIKYU AND EARTH. RI-ON IS USING CHILDREN TO GET THE JINRYU STONE, WHICH HAS THE POWER TO CONTROL DRAGONS. TO SAVE HIS HOME PLANET, AS WELL AS THE ONE HE HAS JUST DISCOVERED, REIJI JOINS ROKKAKU TO ENTER THE DRAGONIC HEAVEN COMPETITION IN RIKYU, IN THE HOPES OF WINNING THE JINRYU STONE. THE FIERCE BATTLE FOR THE STONE IS JUST ABOUT TO ENTER ITS MAIN PHASE...

Vol. 4 HERO
CONTENTS

DRAGON DRIVE

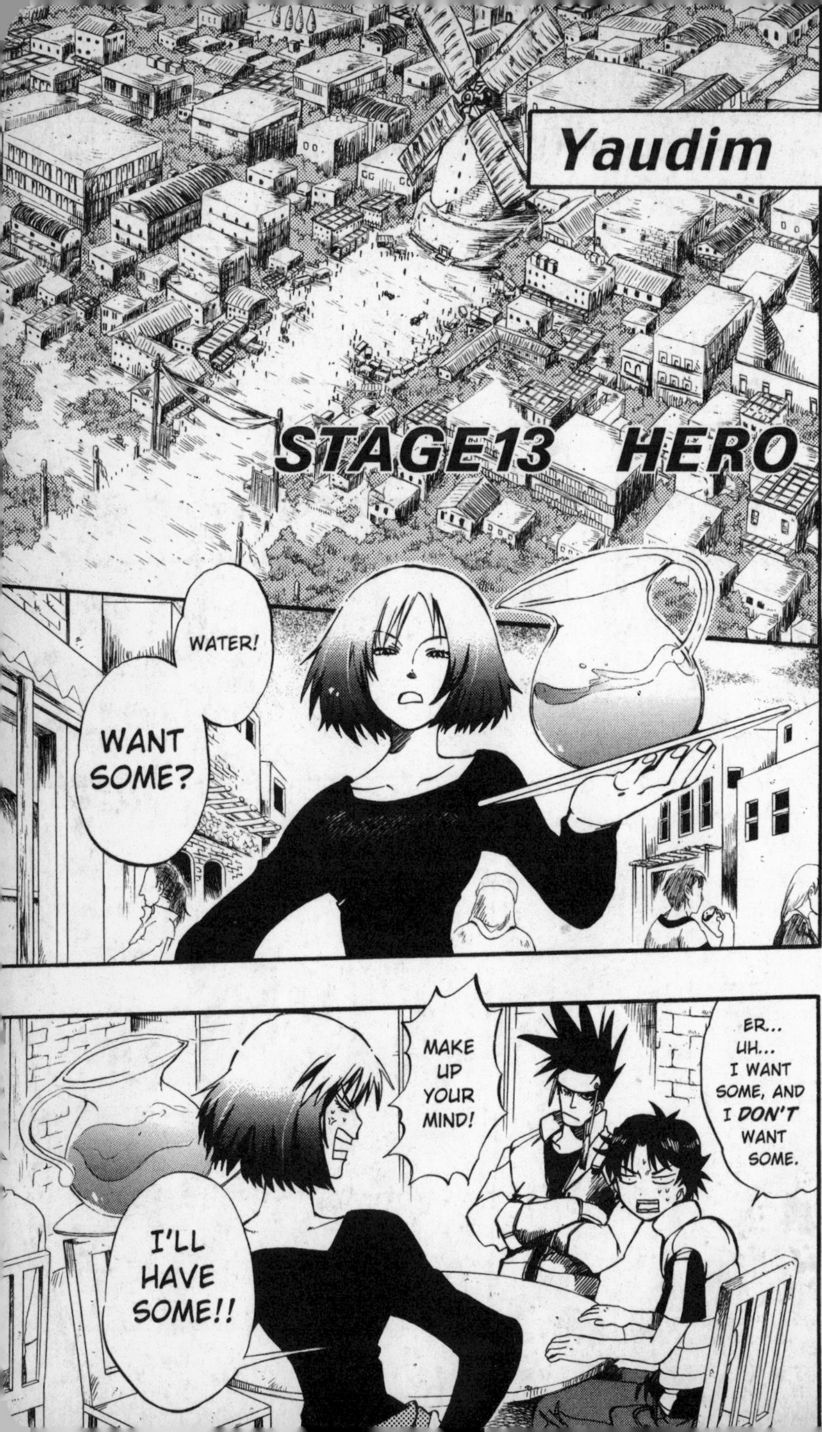
Yaudim
STAGE13 HERO
WATER!
WANT SOME?
ER... UH... I WANT SOME, AND I *DON'T* WANT SOME.
MAKE UP YOUR MIND!
I'LL HAVE SOME!!

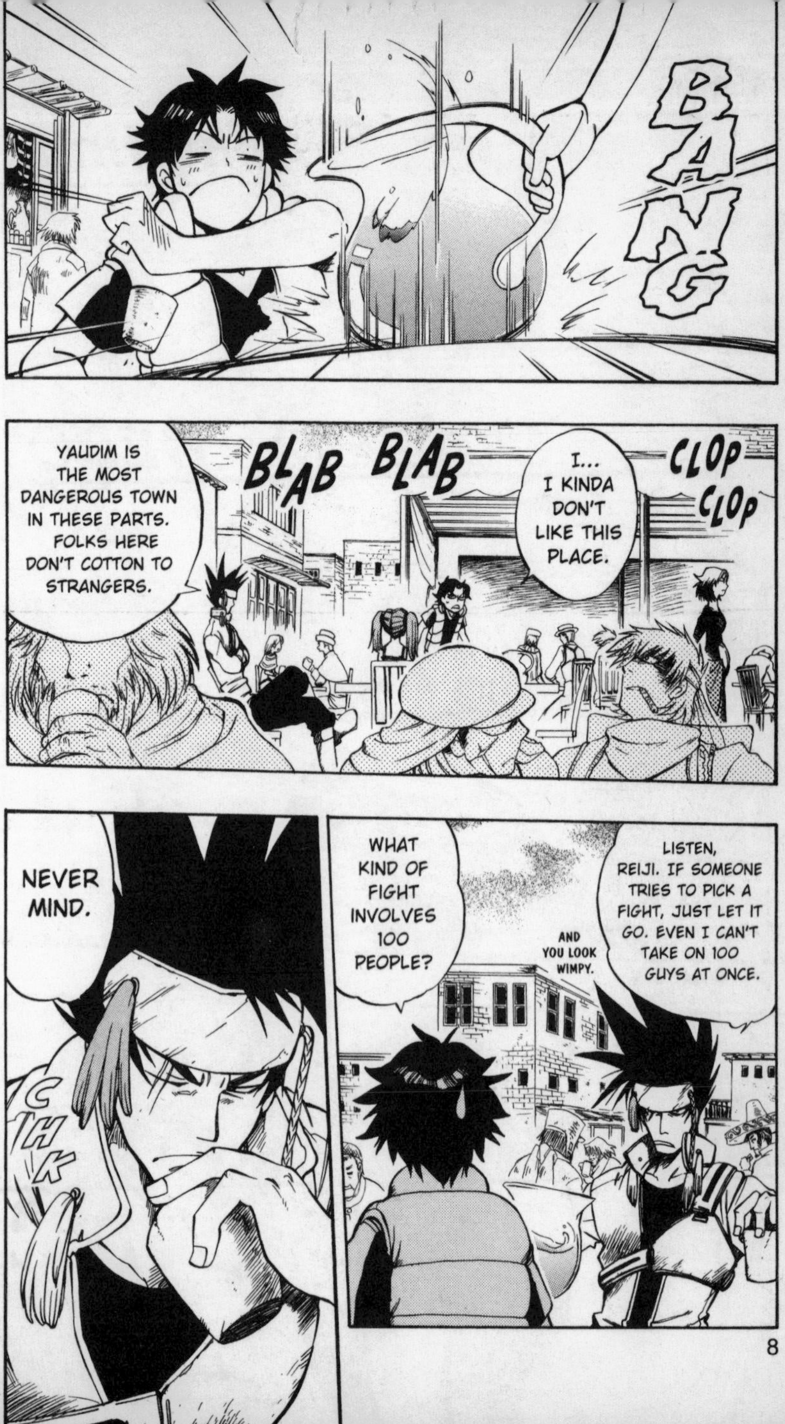
BANG
CLOP CLOP
I... I KINDA DON'T LIKE THIS PLACE.
BLAB BLAB
YAUDIM IS THE MOST DANGEROUS TOWN IN THESE PARTS. FOLKS HERE DON'T COTTON TO STRANGERS.
LISTEN, REIJI. IF SOMEONE TRIES TO PICK A FIGHT, JUST LET IT GO. EVEN I CAN'T TAKE ON 100 GUYS AT ONCE.
AND YOU LOOK WIMPY.
WHAT KIND OF FIGHT INVOLVES 100 PEOPLE?
NEVER MIND.
CHK

READ THIS WAY

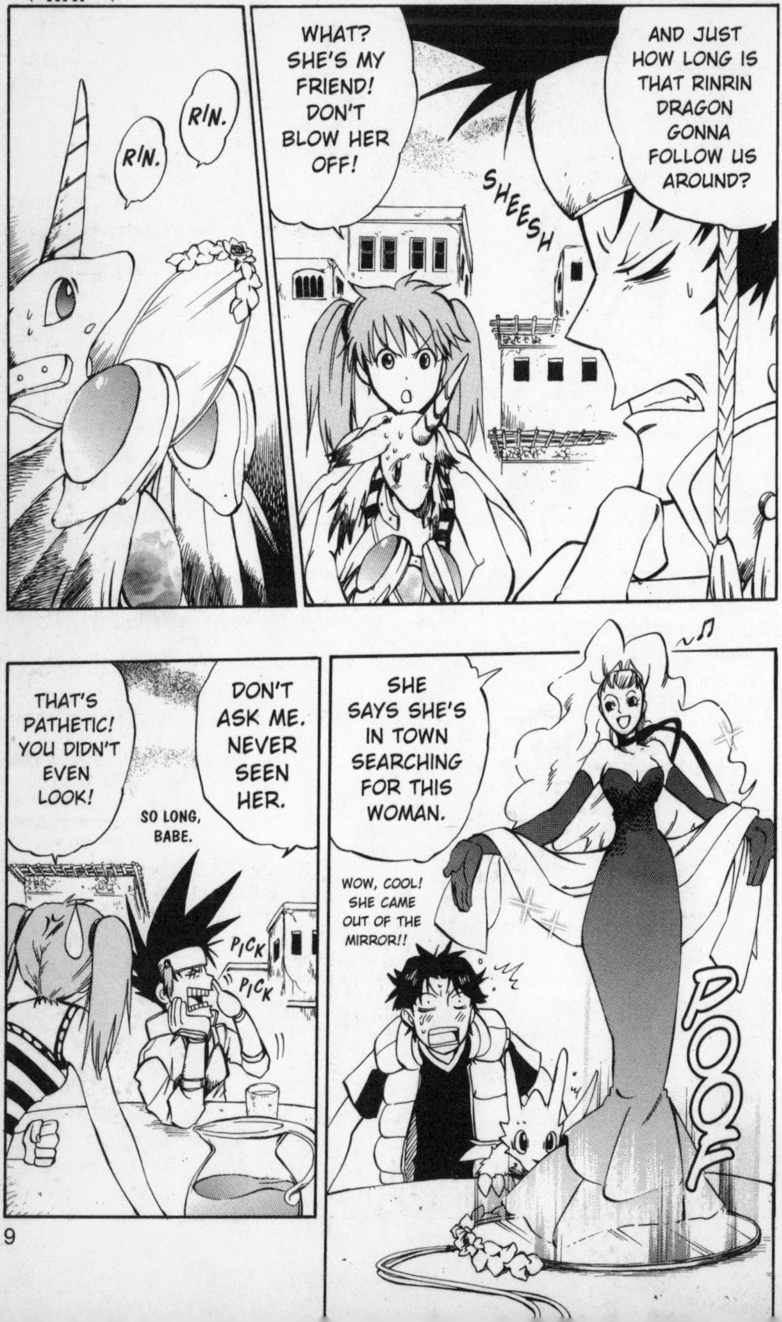
AND JUST HOW LONG IS THAT RINRIN DRAGON GONNA FOLLOW US AROUND?
SHEESH
WHAT? SHE'S MY FRIEND! DON'T BLOW HER OFF!
RIN.
RIN.
SHE SAYS SHE'S IN TOWN SEARCHING FOR THIS WOMAN.
WOW, COOL! SHE CAME OUT OF THE MIRROR!!
POOF
DON'T ASK ME. NEVER SEEN HER.
THAT'S PATHETIC! YOU DIDN'T EVEN LOOK!
SO LONG, BABE.
PICK
PICK

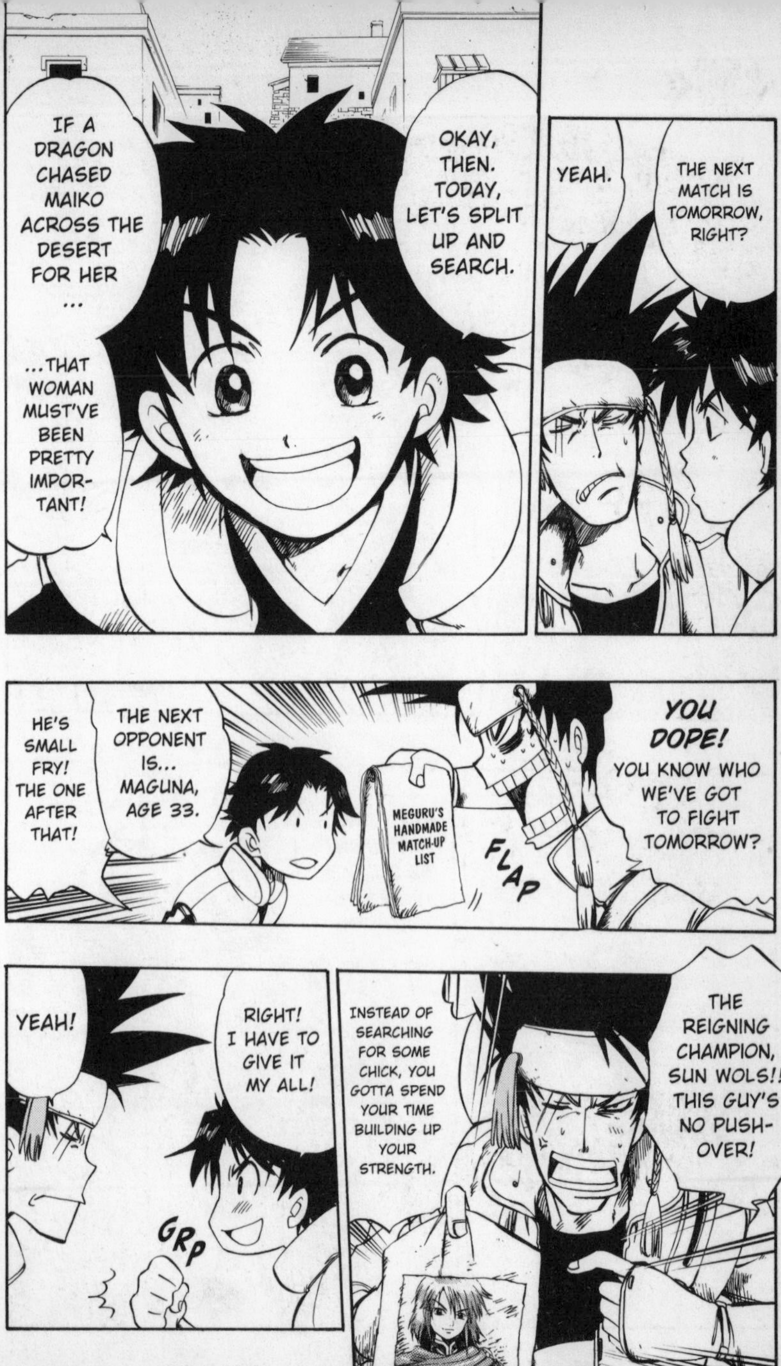
THE NEXT MATCH IS TOMORROW, RIGHT?
YEAH.
OKAY, THEN. TODAY, LET'S SPLIT UP AND SEARCH.
IF A DRAGON CHASED MAIKO ACROSS THE DESERT FOR HER ...
...THAT WOMAN MUST'VE BEEN PRETTY IMPOR-TANT!
YOU DOPE! YOU KNOW WHO WE'VE GOT TO FIGHT TOMORROW?
FLAP
MEGURU'S HANDMADE MATCH-UP LIST
THE NEXT OPPONENT IS... MAGUNA, AGE 33.
HE'S SMALL FRY! THE ONE AFTER THAT!
THE REIGNING CHAMPION, SUN WOLS!! THIS GUY'S NO PUSH-OVER!
INSTEAD OF SEARCHING FOR SOME CHICK, YOU GOTTA SPEND YOUR TIME BUILDING UP YOUR STRENGTH.
RIGHT! I HAVE TO GIVE IT MY ALL!
GRP
YEAH!

READ THIS WAY

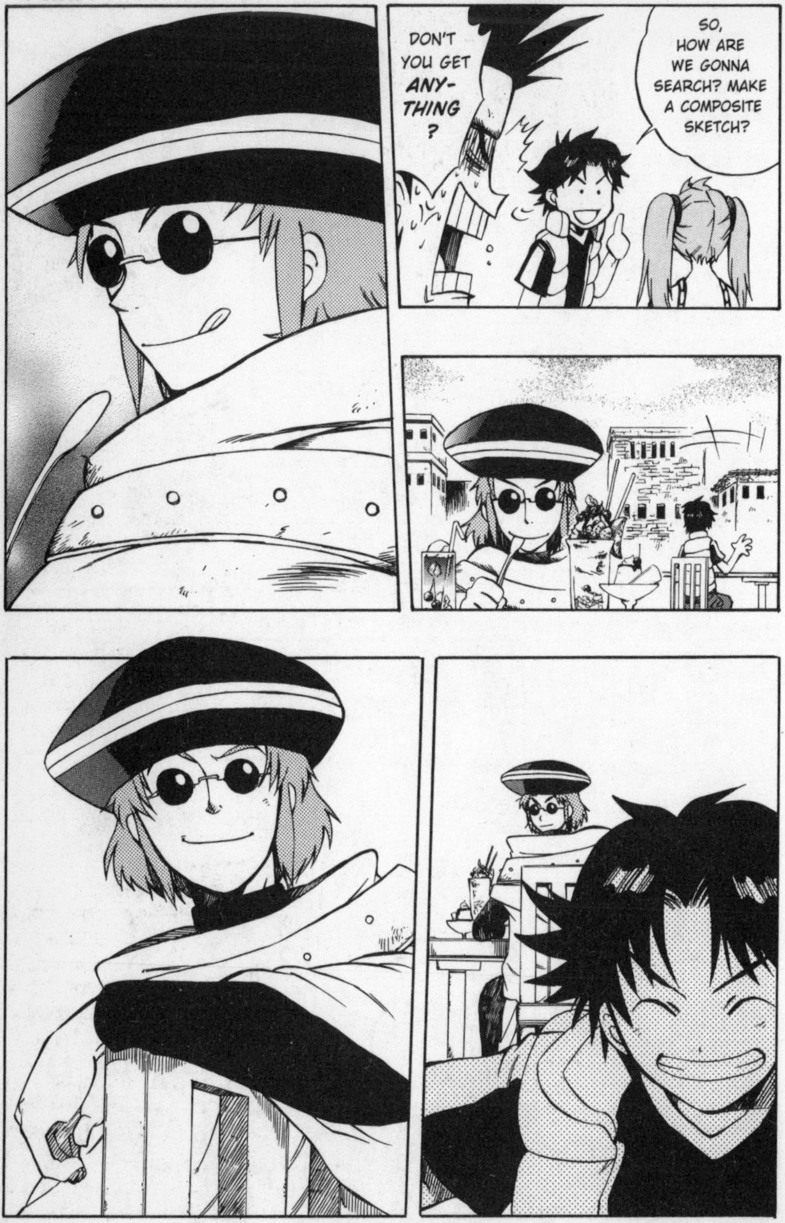
SO, HOW ARE WE GONNA SEARCH? MAKE A COMPOSITE SKETCH?
DON'T YOU GET **ANYTHING**?

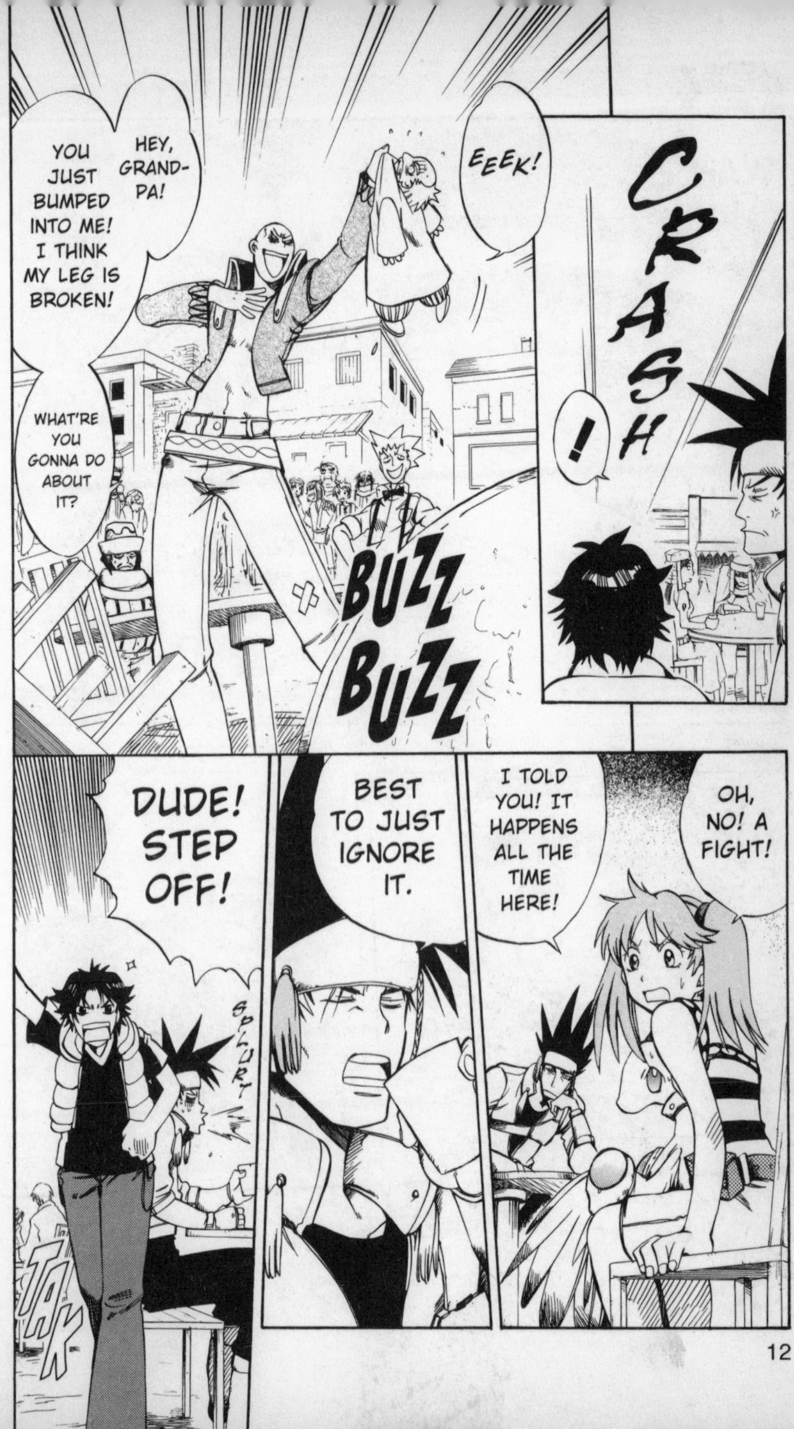
CRASH
!
EEEK!
HEY, GRANDPA!
YOU JUST BUMPED INTO ME! I THINK MY LEG IS BROKEN!
WHAT'RE YOU GONNA DO ABOUT IT?
BUZZ BUZZ
OH, NO! A FIGHT!
I TOLD YOU! IT HAPPENS ALL THE TIME HERE!
BEST TO JUST IGNORE IT.
DUDE! STEP OFF!
SPLURT
TAK

READ THIS WAY

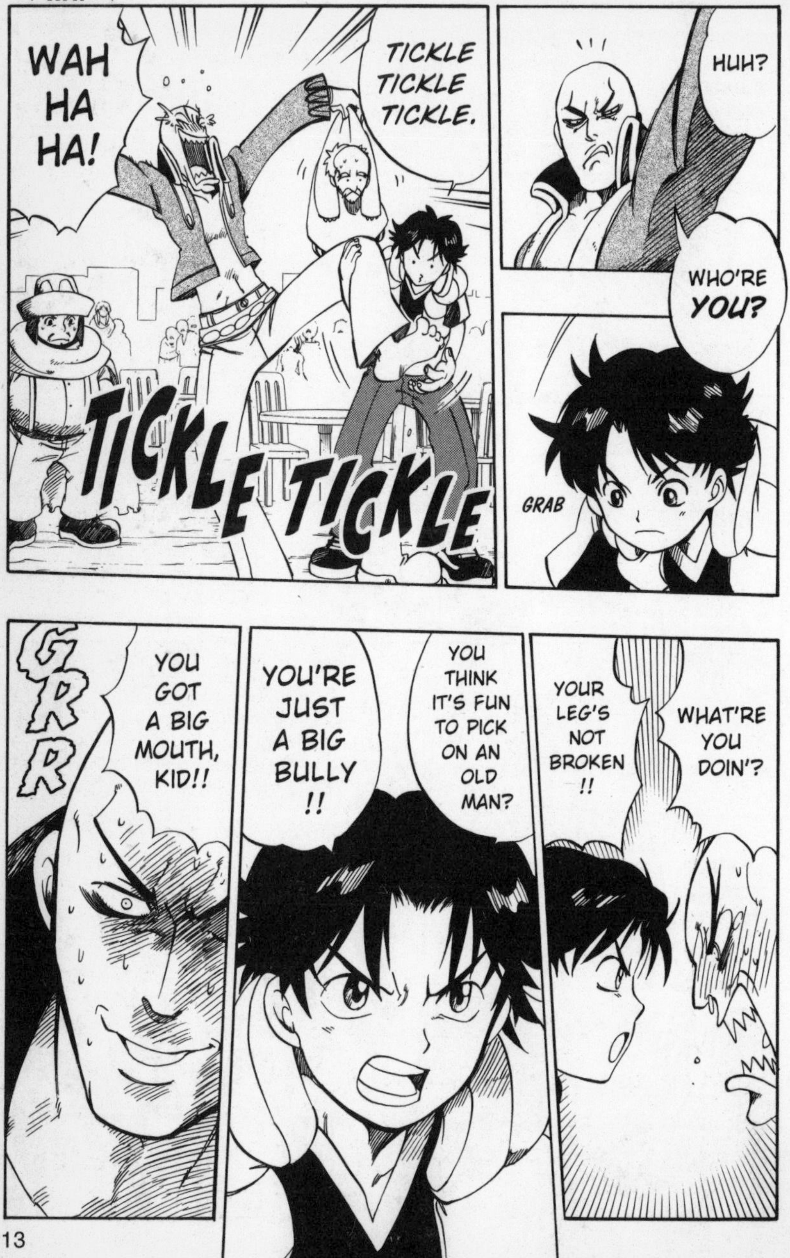
HUH?
WHO'RE YOU?
GRAB
TICKLE TICKLE TICKLE.
WAH HA HA!
TICKLE TICKLE
WHAT'RE YOU DOIN'?
YOUR LEG'S NOT BROKEN !!
YOU THINK IT'S FUN TO PICK ON AN OLD MAN?
YOU'RE JUST A BIG BULLY !!
YOU GOT A BIG MOUTH, KID!!
GRR

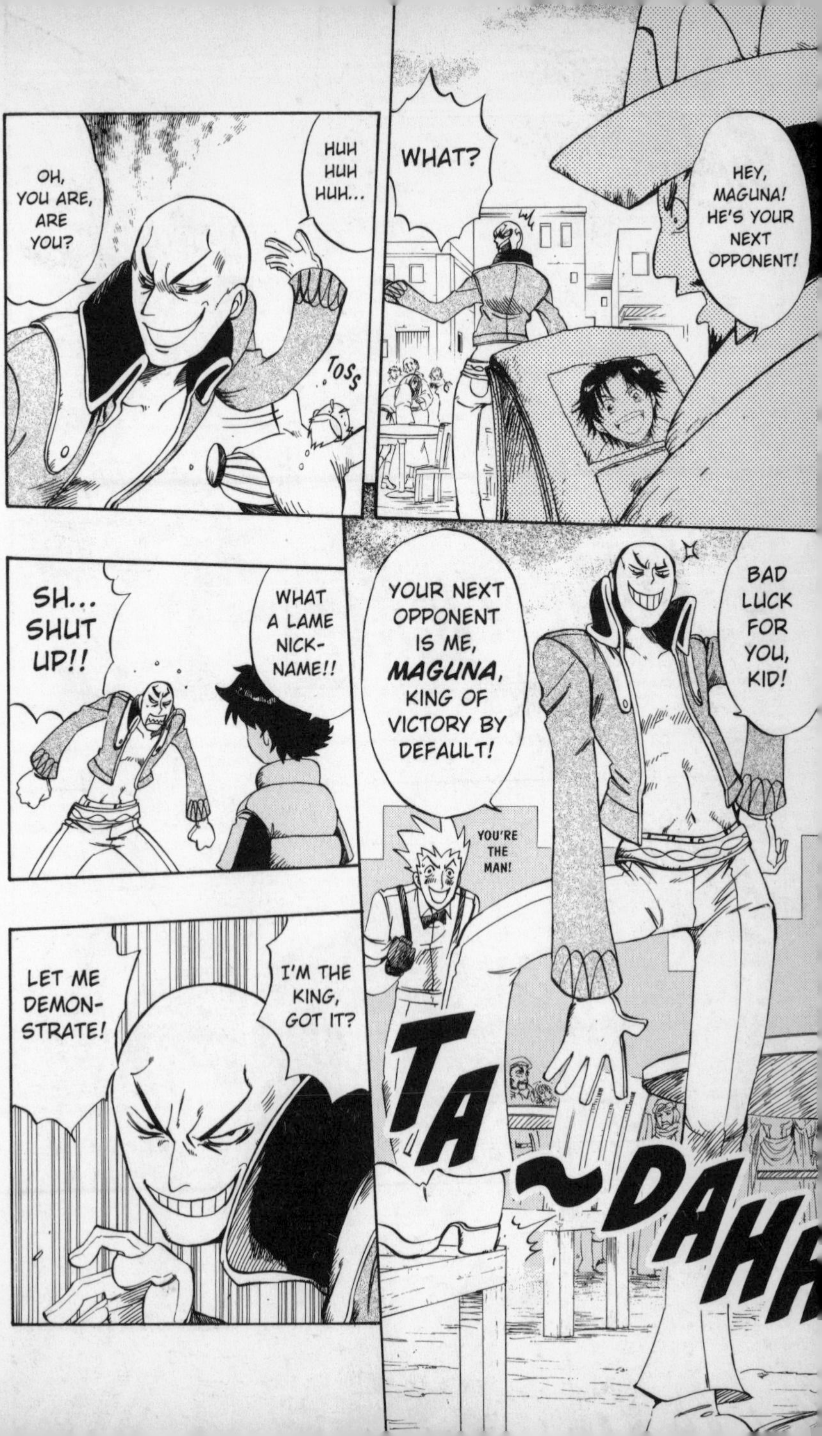
HEY, MAGUNA! HE'S YOUR NEXT OPPONENT!
WHAT?
HUH HUH HUH...
OH, YOU ARE, ARE YOU?
TOSS
BAD LUCK FOR YOU, KID!
YOUR NEXT OPPONENT IS ME, **MAGUNA**, KING OF VICTORY BY DEFAULT!
YOU'RE THE MAN!
TA ~DAH
WHAT A LAME NICK-NAME!!
SH... SHUT UP!!
I'M THE KING, GOT IT?
LET ME DEMON-STRATE!

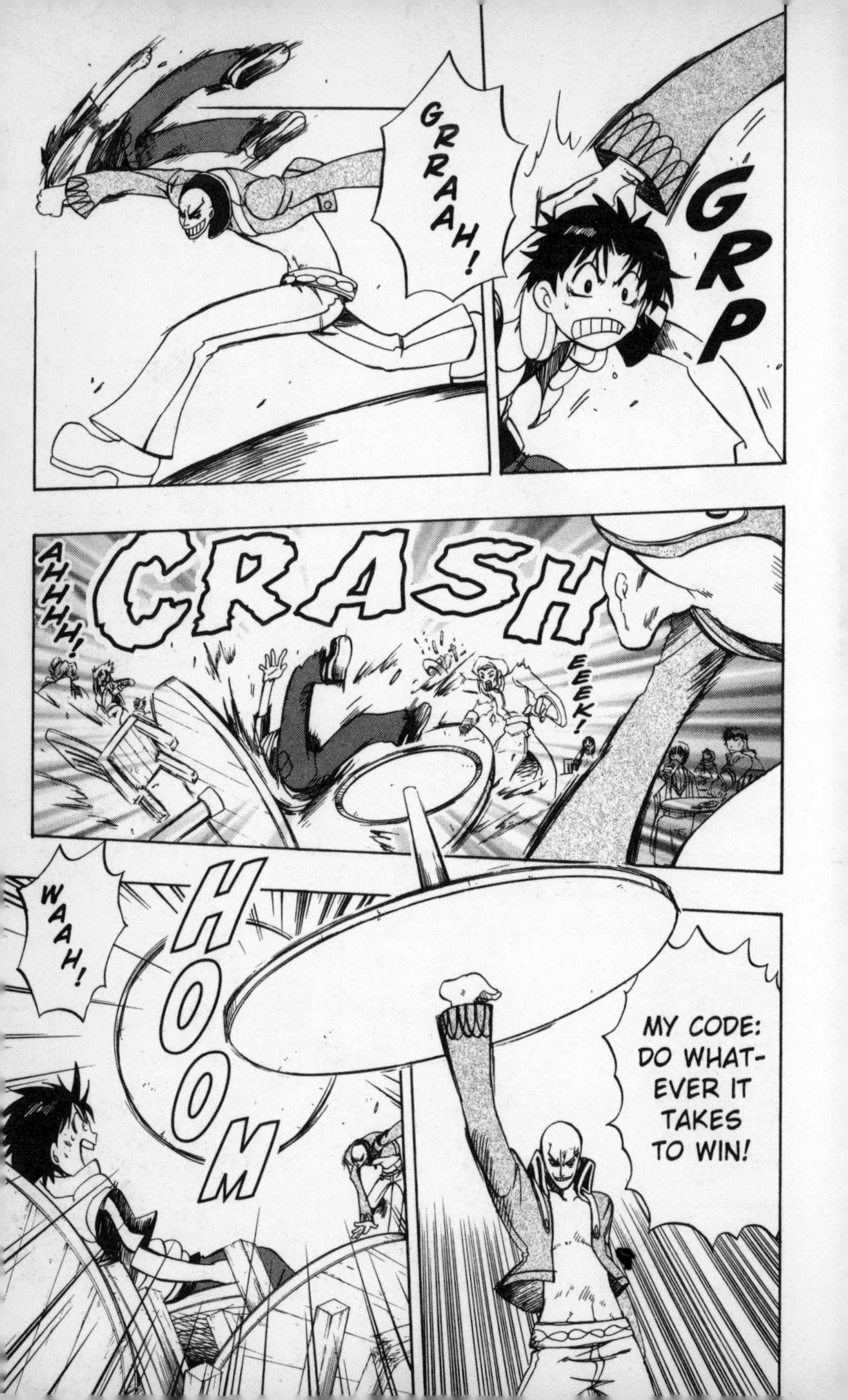
GRP
GRRAAH!
CRASH
EEEK!
AHHHH!
MY CODE: DO WHATEVER IT TAKES TO WIN!
HOOOM
WAAH!

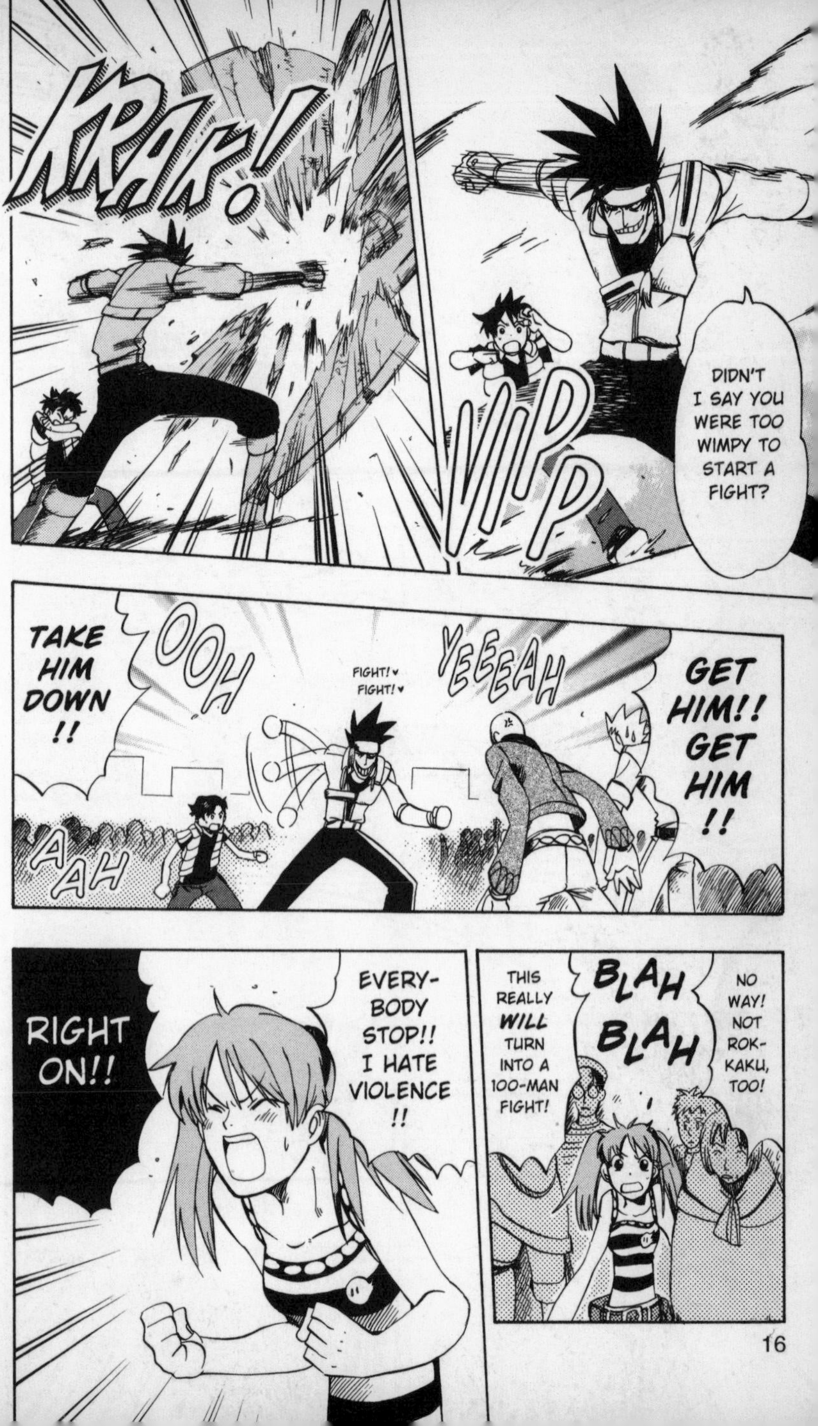

DIDN'T I SAY YOU WERE TOO WIMPY TO START A FIGHT?
VIPP
KRAK!
GET HIM!! GET HIM!!
YEEEAH
FIGHT!♥ FIGHT!♥
OOH
TAKE HIM DOWN!!
AAH
NO WAY! NOT ROKAKU, TOO!
BLAH BLAH
THIS REALLY **WILL** TURN INTO A 100-MAN FIGHT!
EVERYBODY STOP!! I HATE VIOLENCE!!
RIGHT ON!!

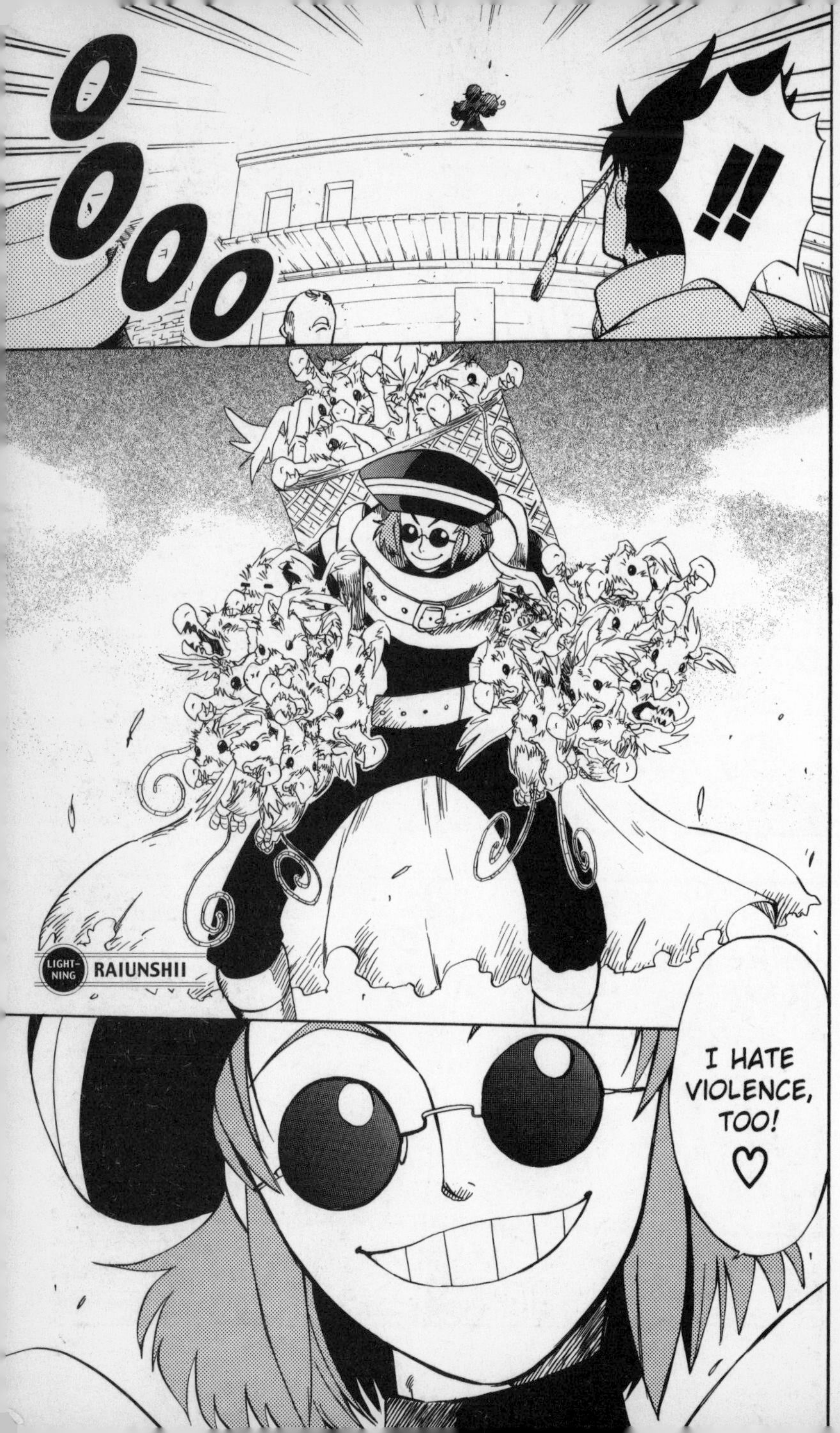
!!
OOOOO
LIGHTNING RAIUNSHII
I HATE VIOLENCE, TOO! ♡

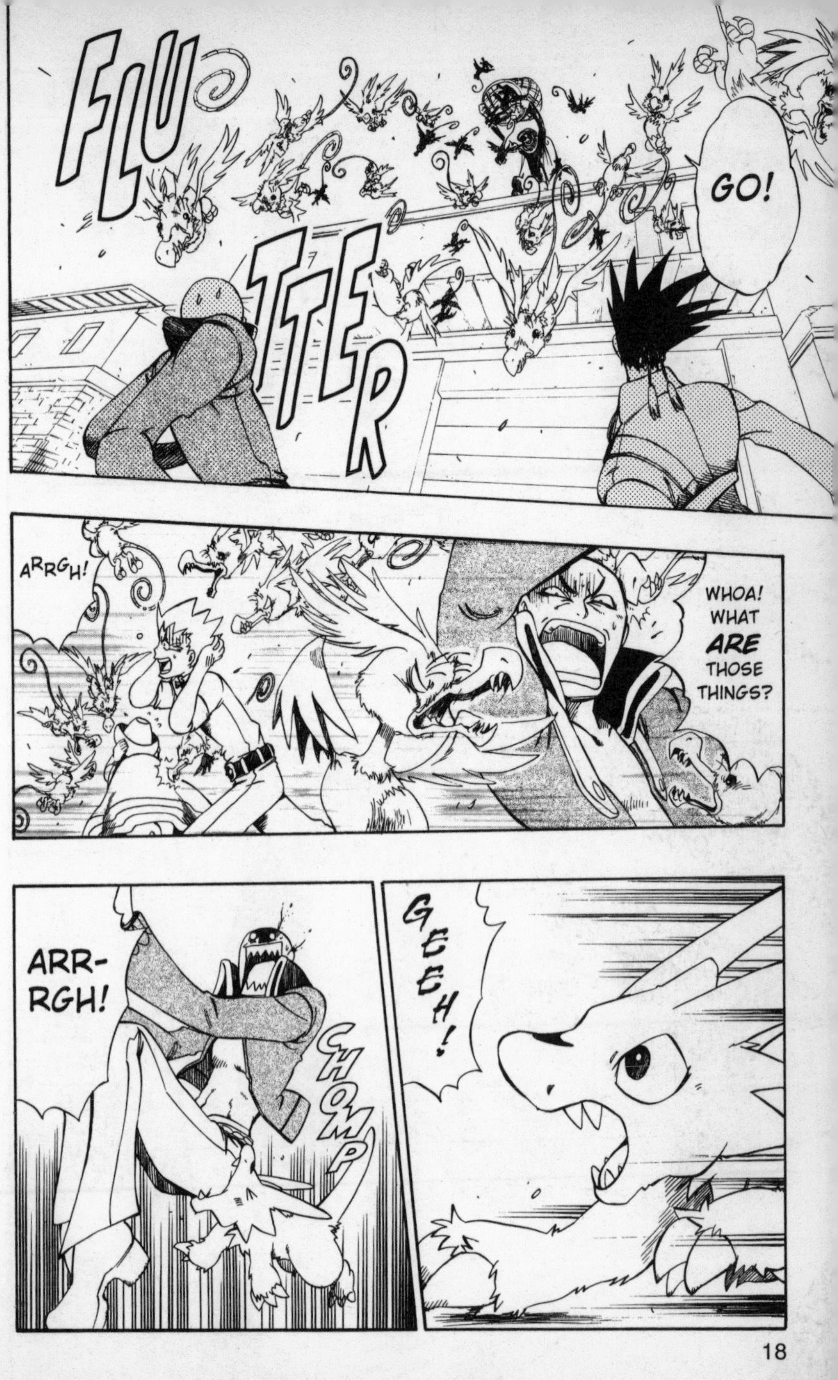
GO!
FLUTTER
WHOA! WHAT **ARE** THOSE THINGS?
ARRGH!
GEEH!
ARR-RGH!
CHOMP

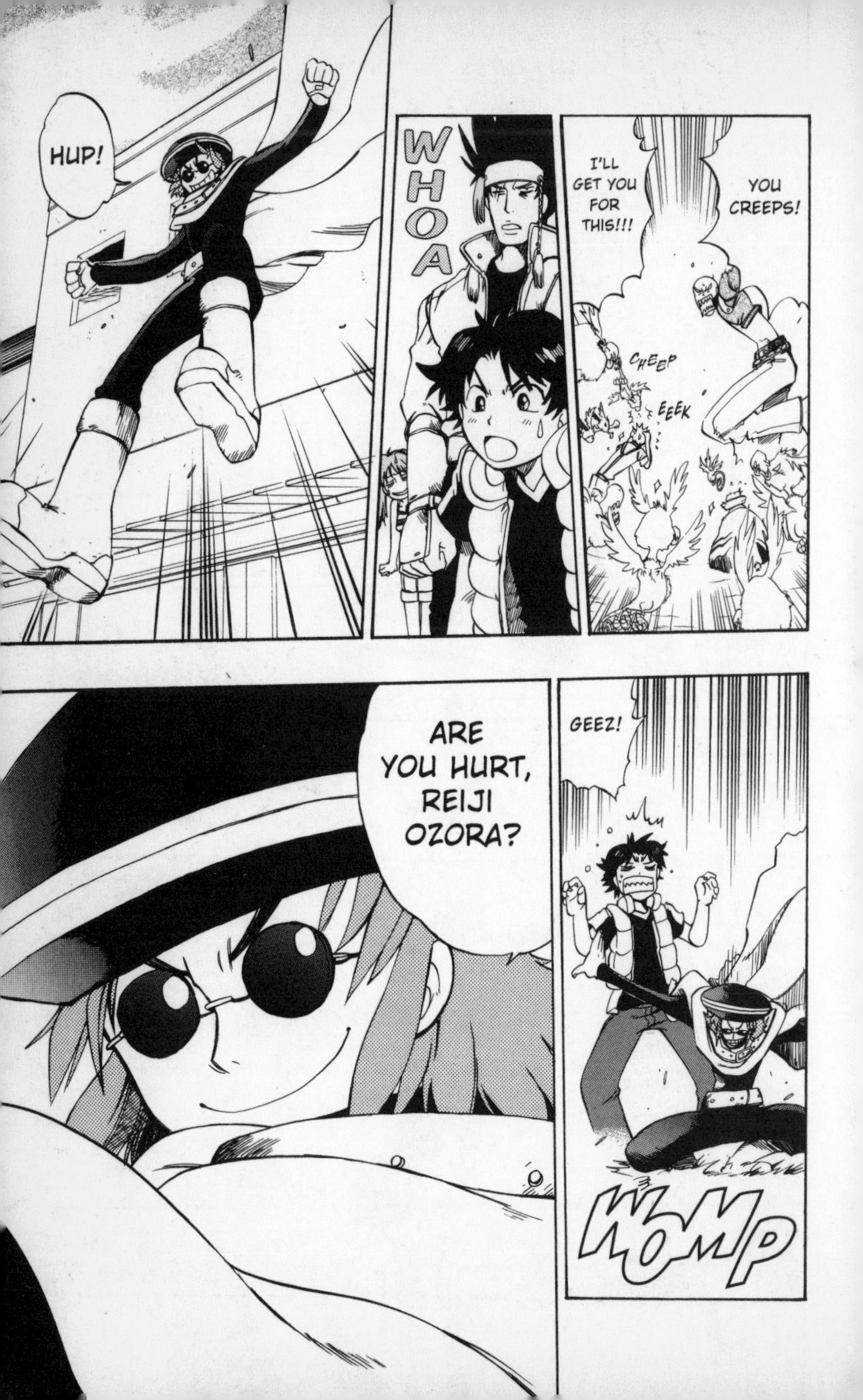
YOU CREEPS!
I'LL GET YOU FOR THIS!!!
CHEEP
EEEK
WHOA
HUP!
GEEZ!
WOMP
ARE YOU HURT, REIJI OZORA?

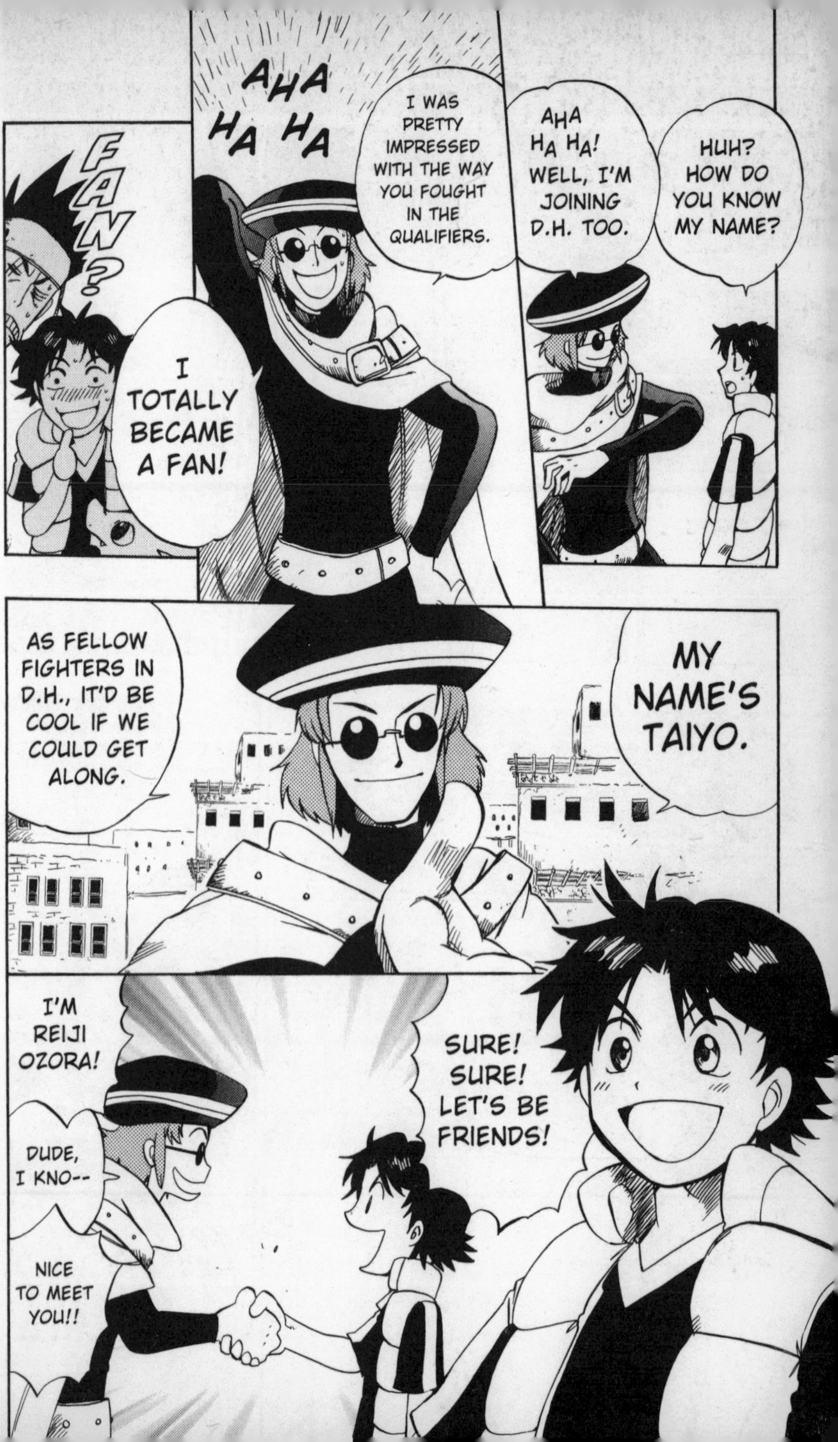
HUH? HOW DO YOU KNOW MY NAME?
AHA HA HA! WELL, I'M JOINING D.H. TOO.
AHA HA HA HA
I WAS PRETTY IMPRESSED WITH THE WAY YOU FOUGHT IN THE QUALIFIERS.
I TOTALLY BECAME A FAN!
FAN?
MY NAME'S TAIYO.
AS FELLOW FIGHTERS IN D.H., IT'D BE COOL IF WE COULD GET ALONG.
SURE! SURE! LET'S BE FRIENDS!
I'M REIJI OZORA!
DUDE, I KNO--
NICE TO MEET YOU!!

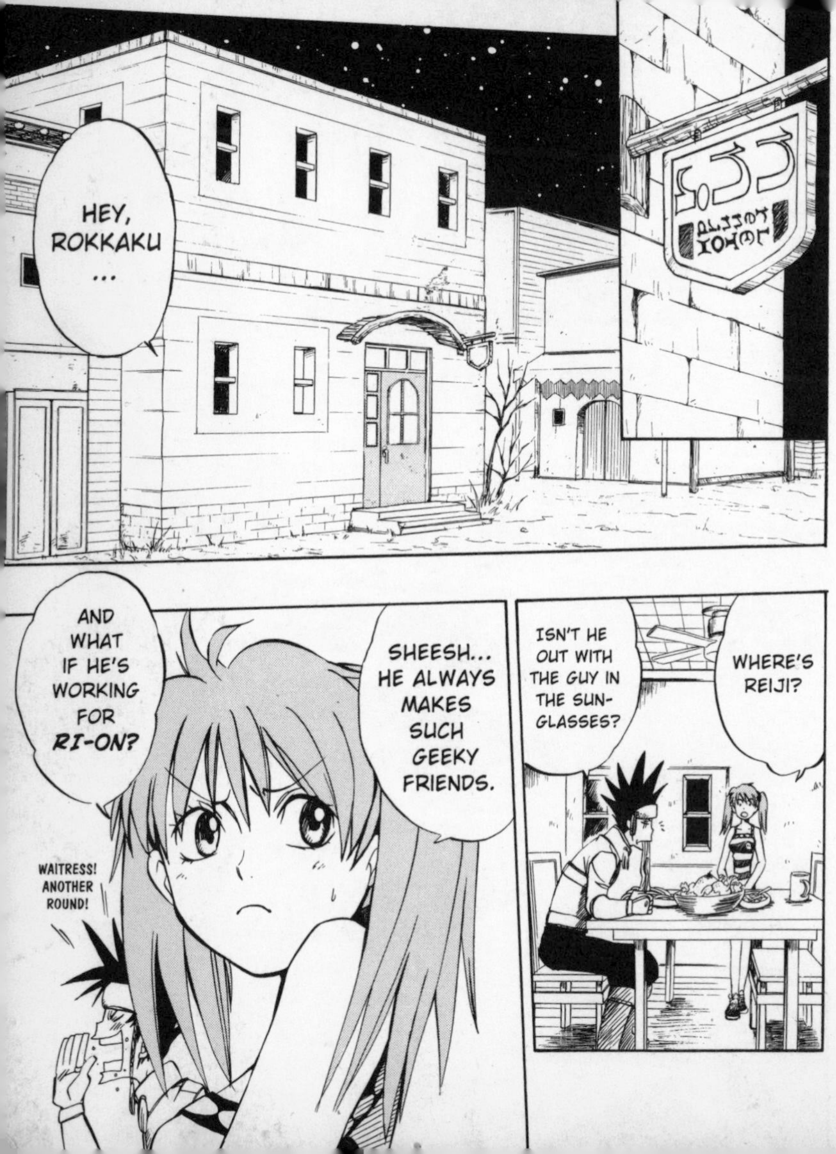
HEY, ROKKAKU...
WHERE'S REIJI?
ISN'T HE OUT WITH THE GUY IN THE SUN-GLASSES?
SHEESH... HE ALWAYS MAKES SUCH GEEKY FRIENDS.
AND WHAT IF HE'S WORKING FOR *RI-ON*?
WAITRESS! ANOTHER ROUND!

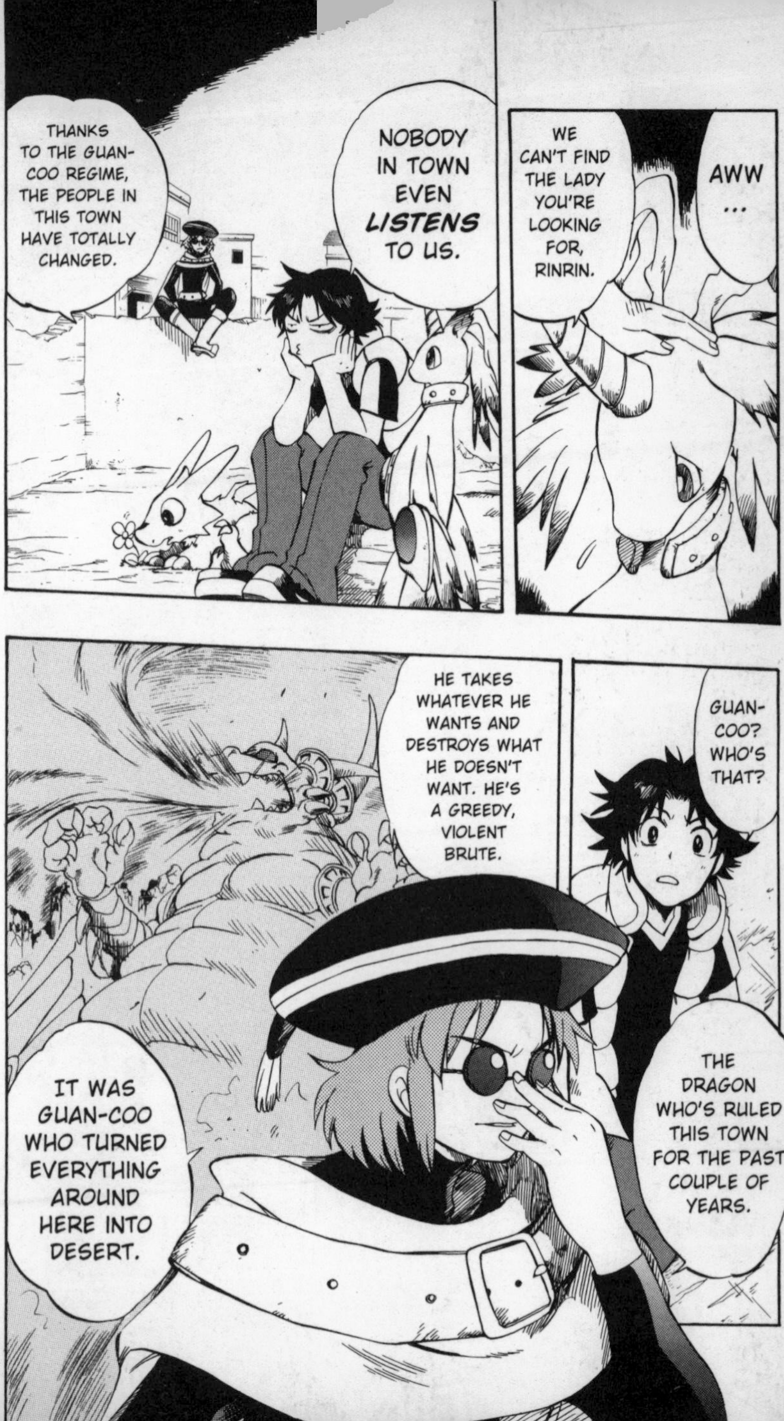
AWW ...
WE CAN'T FIND THE LADY YOU'RE LOOKING FOR, RINRIN.
NOBODY IN TOWN EVEN *LISTENS* TO US.
THANKS TO THE GUAN-COO REGIME, THE PEOPLE IN THIS TOWN HAVE TOTALLY CHANGED.
GUAN-COO? WHO'S THAT?
THE DRAGON WHO'S RULED THIS TOWN FOR THE PAST COUPLE OF YEARS.
HE TAKES WHATEVER HE WANTS AND DESTROYS WHAT HE DOESN'T WANT. HE'S A GREEDY, VIOLENT BRUTE.
IT WAS GUAN-COO WHO TURNED EVERYTHING AROUND HERE INTO DESERT.

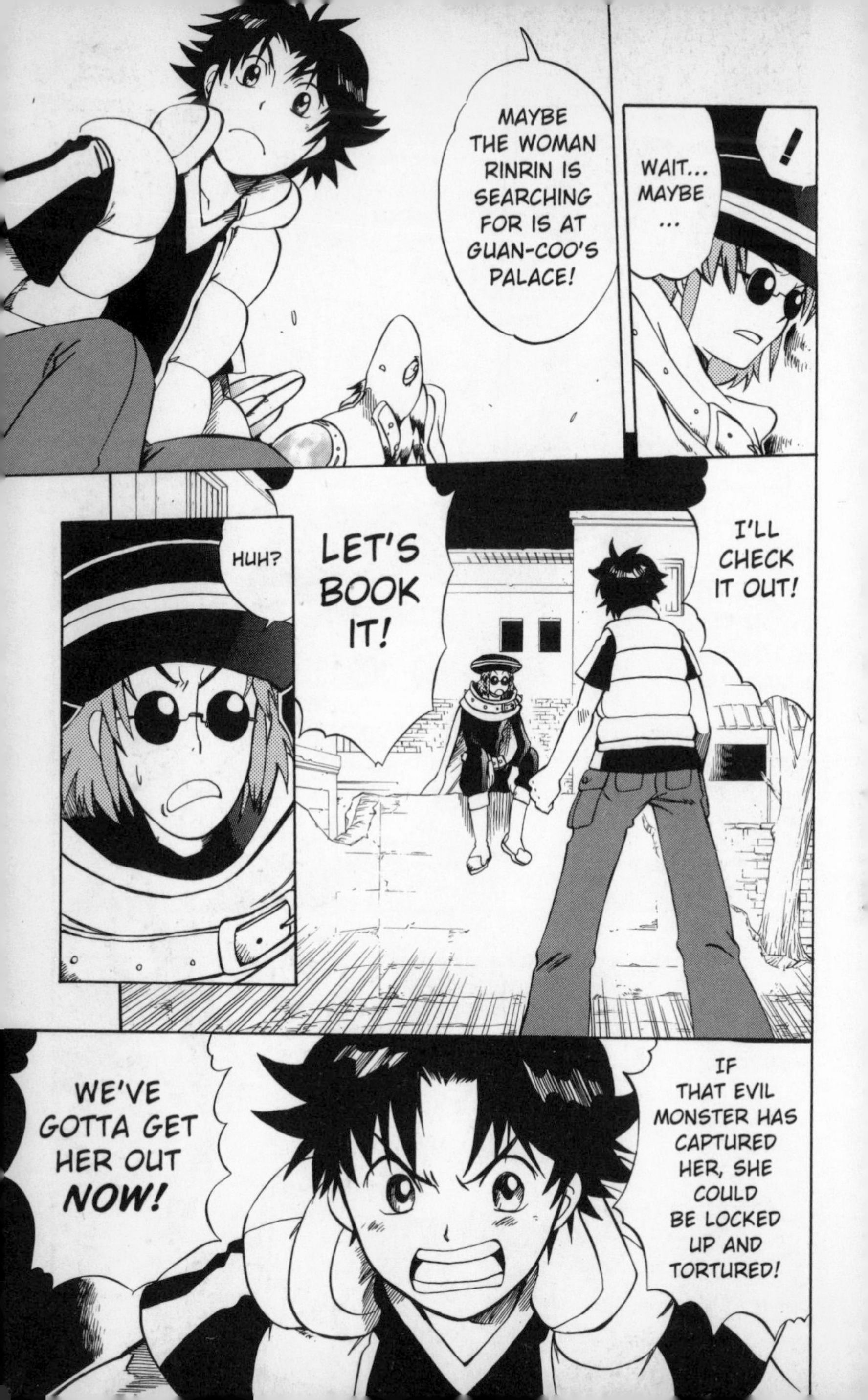
!
WAIT... MAYBE ...
MAYBE THE WOMAN RINRIN IS SEARCHING FOR IS AT GUAN-COO'S PALACE!
I'LL CHECK IT OUT!
LET'S BOOK IT!
HUH?
IF THAT EVIL MONSTER HAS CAPTURED HER, SHE COULD BE LOCKED UP AND TORTURED!
WE'VE GOTTA GET HER OUT NOW!

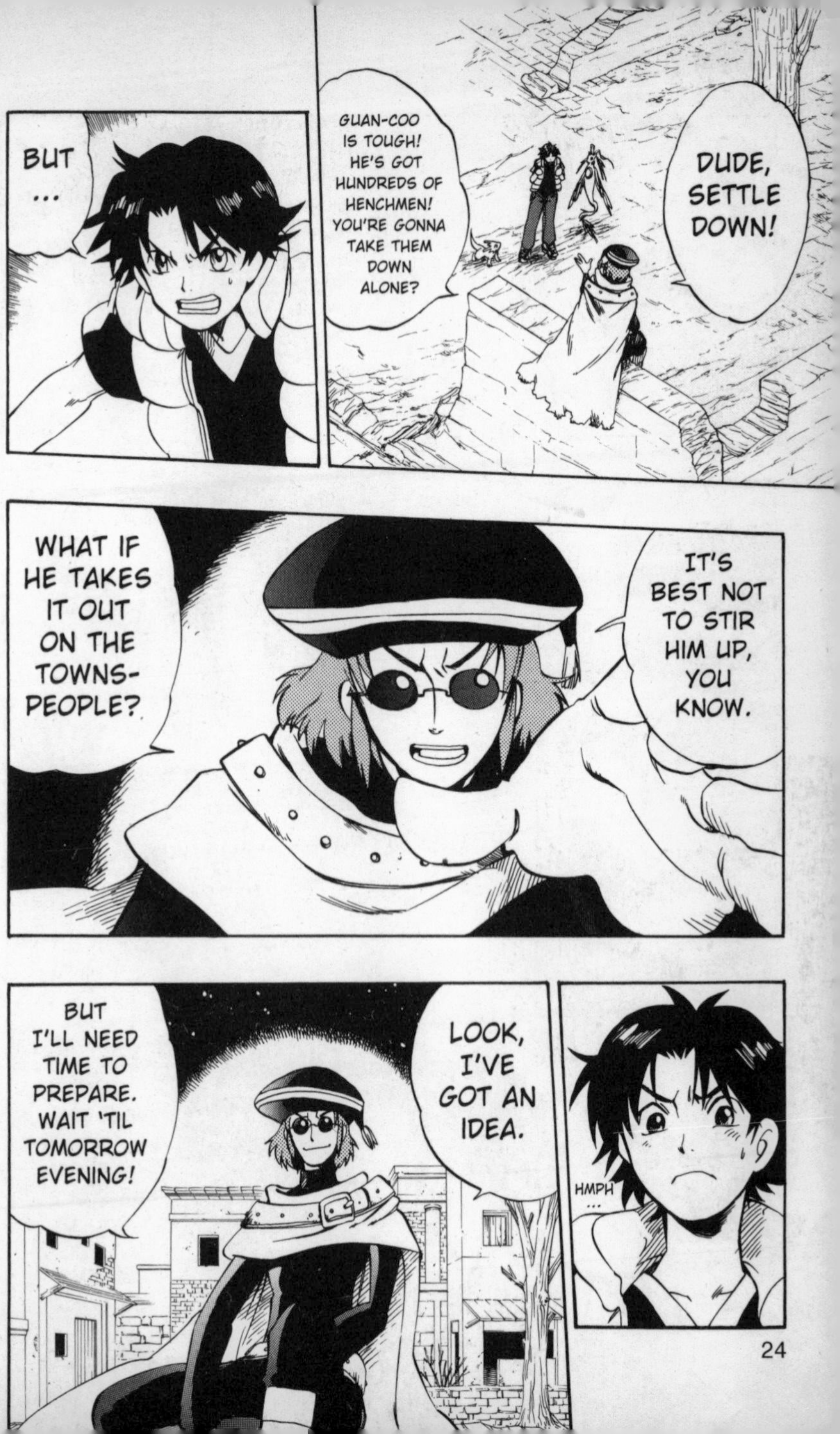
DUDE, SETTLE DOWN!
GUAN-COO IS TOUGH! HE'S GOT HUNDREDS OF HENCHMEN! YOU'RE GONNA TAKE THEM DOWN ALONE?
BUT ...
IT'S BEST NOT TO STIR HIM UP, YOU KNOW.
WHAT IF HE TAKES IT OUT ON THE TOWNS-PEOPLE?
HMPH ...
LOOK, I'VE GOT AN IDEA.
BUT I'LL NEED TIME TO PREPARE. WAIT 'TIL TOMORROW EVENING!

READ THIS WAY

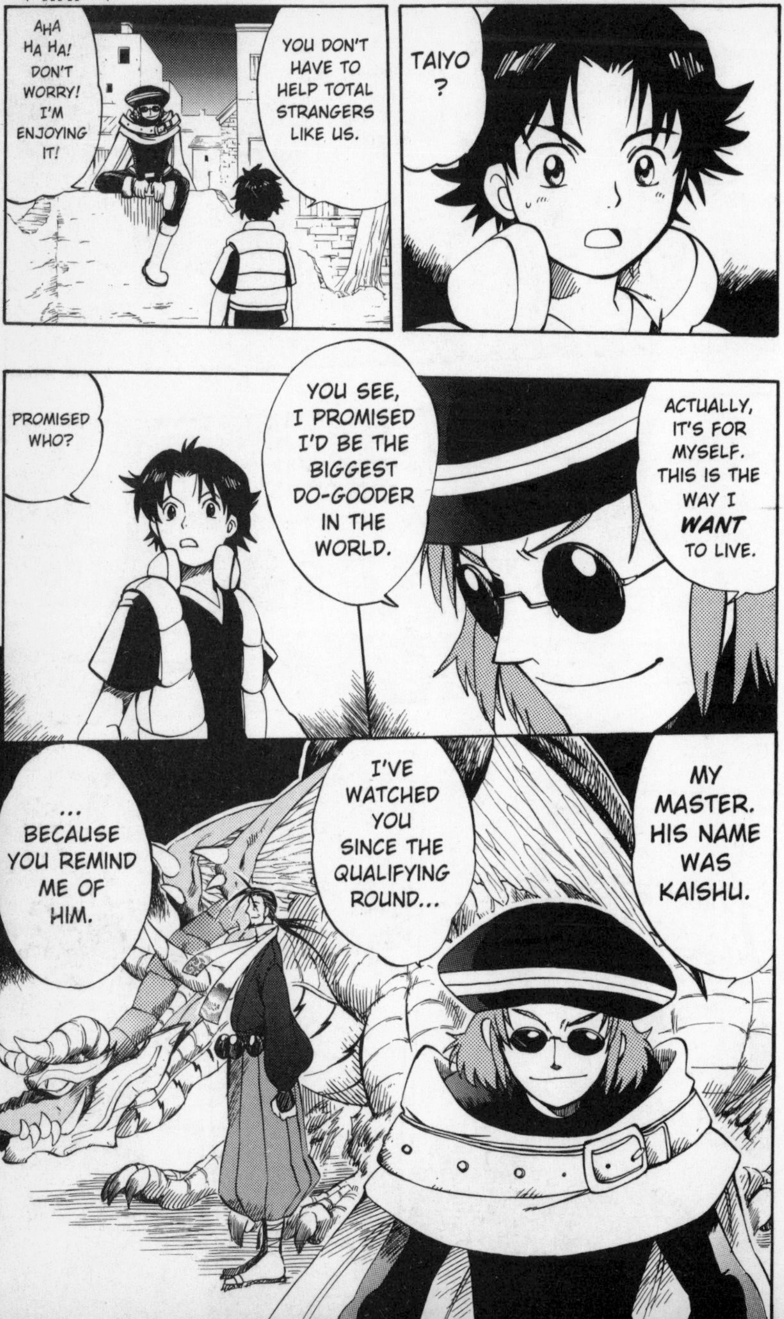
TAIYO ?
YOU DON'T HAVE TO HELP TOTAL STRANGERS LIKE US.
AHA HA HA! DON'T WORRY! I'M ENJOYING IT!
ACTUALLY, IT'S FOR MYSELF. THIS IS THE WAY I *WANT* TO LIVE.
YOU SEE, I PROMISED I'D BE THE BIGGEST DO-GOODER IN THE WORLD.
PROMISED WHO?
MY MASTER. HIS NAME WAS KAISHU.
I'VE WATCHED YOU SINCE THE QUALIFYING ROUND...
... BECAUSE YOU REMIND ME OF HIM.

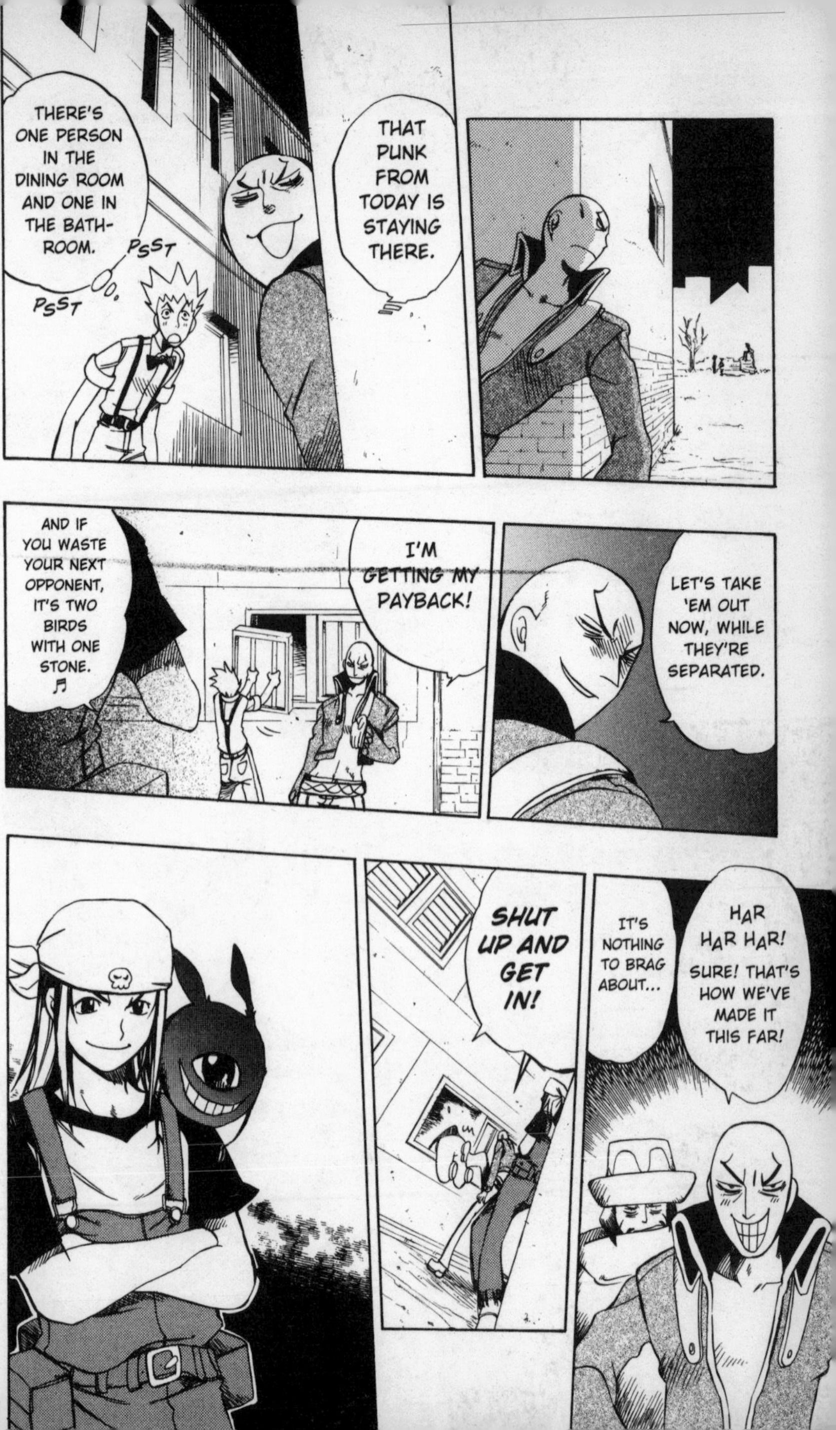
THAT PUNK FROM TODAY IS STAYING THERE.
THERE'S ONE PERSON IN THE DINING ROOM AND ONE IN THE BATH-ROOM.
PSST
PSST
LET'S TAKE 'EM OUT NOW, WHILE THEY'RE SEPARATED.
I'M GETTING MY PAYBACK!
AND IF YOU WASTE YOUR NEXT OPPONENT, IT'S TWO BIRDS WITH ONE STONE. ♬
HAR HAR HAR! SURE! THAT'S HOW WE'VE MADE IT THIS FAR!
IT'S NOTHING TO BRAG ABOUT...
SHUT UP AND GET IN!

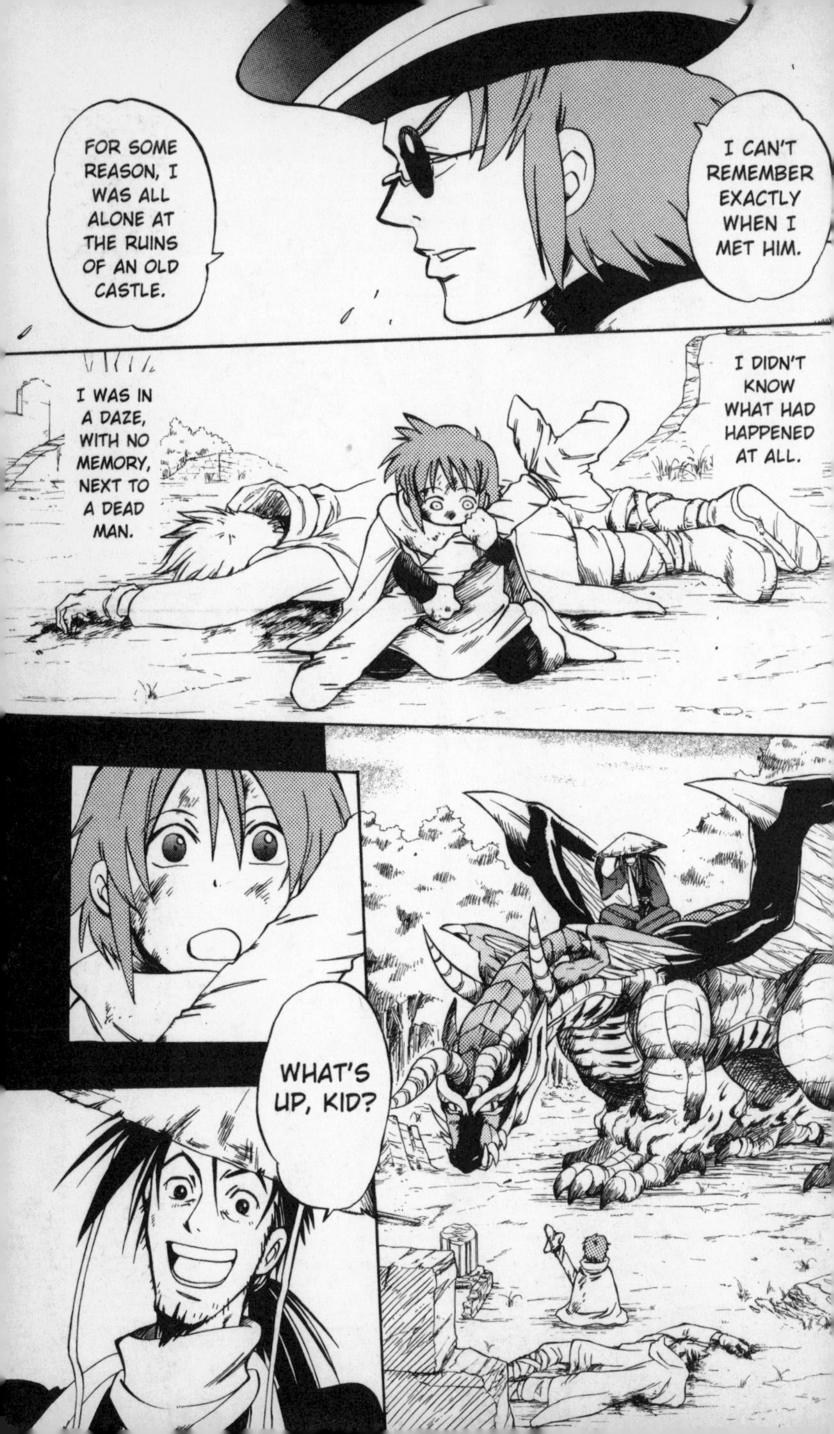
I CAN'T REMEMBER EXACTLY WHEN I MET HIM.
FOR SOME REASON, I WAS ALL ALONE AT THE RUINS OF AN OLD CASTLE.
I DIDN'T KNOW WHAT HAD HAPPENED AT ALL.
I WAS IN A DAZE, WITH NO MEMORY, NEXT TO A DEAD MAN.
WHAT'S UP, KID?

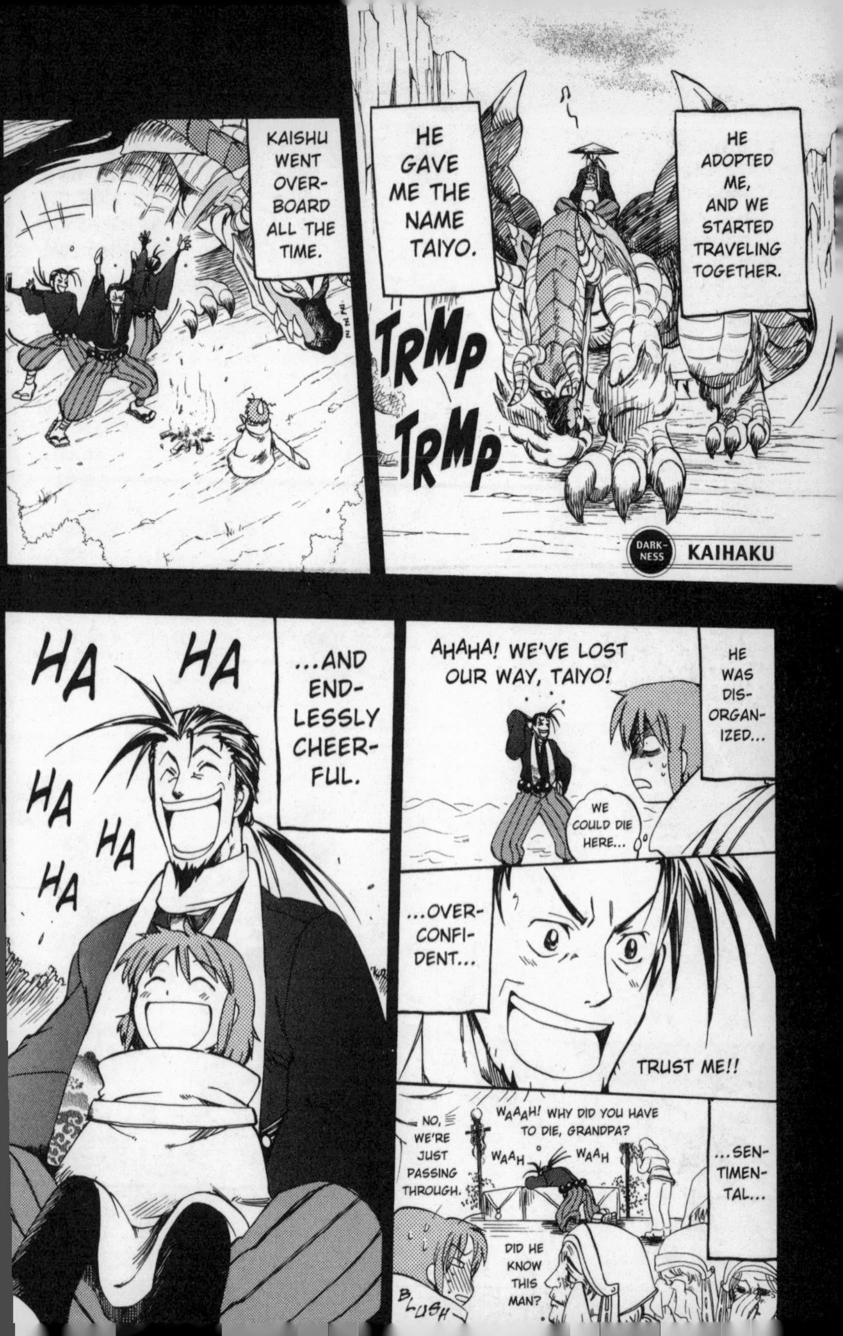
HE ADOPTED ME, AND WE STARTED TRAVELING TOGETHER.
HE GAVE ME THE NAME TAIYO.
TRMP
TRMP
DARKNESS
KAIHAKU
KAISHU WENT OVERBOARD ALL THE TIME.
HE WAS DISORGANIZED...
AHAHA! WE'VE LOST OUR WAY, TAIYO!
WE COULD DIE HERE...
...OVERCONFIDENT...
TRUST ME!!
...SENTIMENTAL...
WAAAH! WHY DID YOU HAVE TO DIE, GRANDPA?
WAAH
WAAH
NO, WE'RE JUST PASSING THROUGH.
DID HE KNOW THIS MAN?
BLUSH
...AND ENDLESSLY CHEERFUL.
HA HA
HA HA
HA

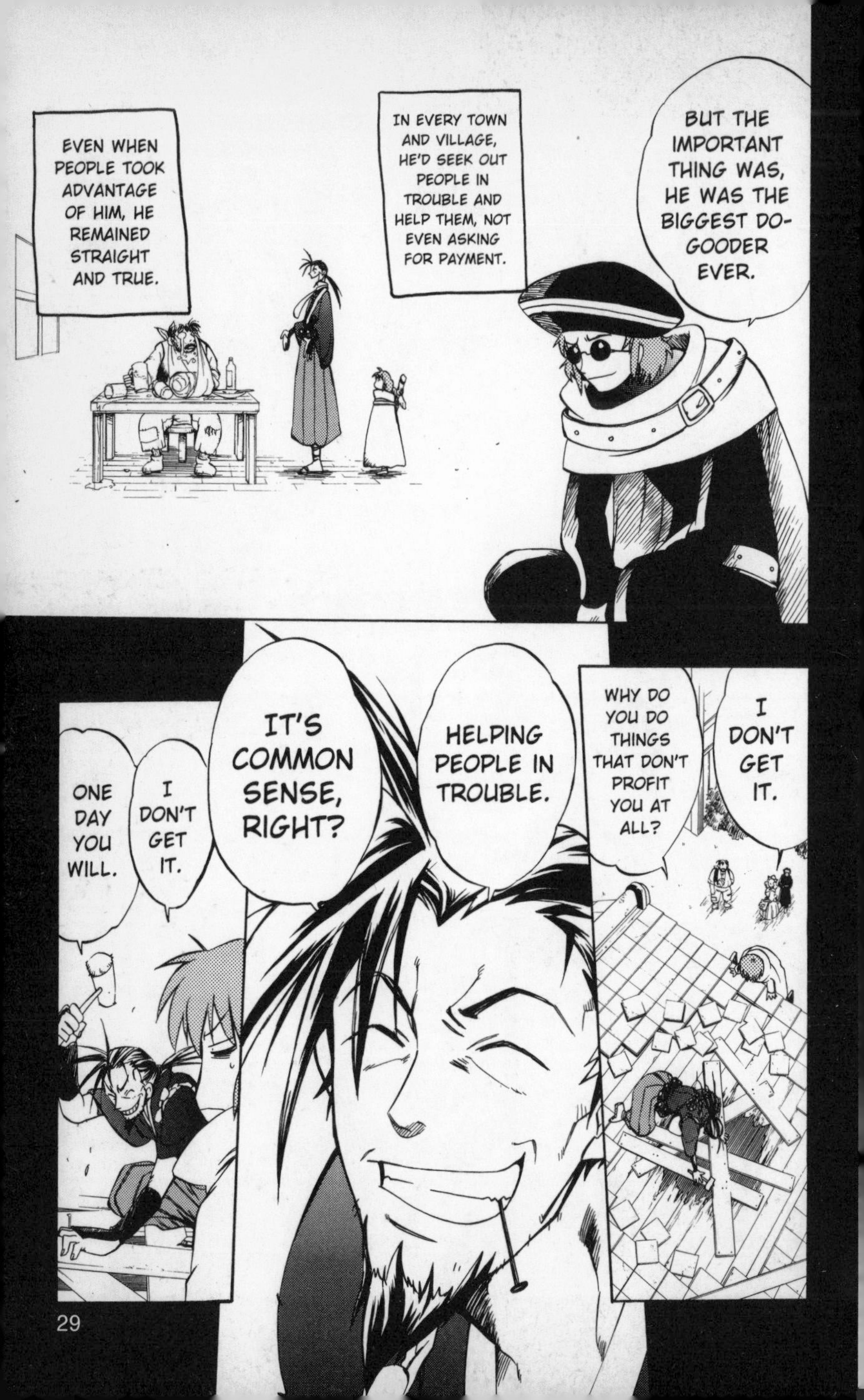
BUT THE IMPORTANT THING WAS, HE WAS THE BIGGEST DO-GOODER EVER.
IN EVERY TOWN AND VILLAGE, HE'D SEEK OUT PEOPLE IN TROUBLE AND HELP THEM, NOT EVEN ASKING FOR PAYMENT.
EVEN WHEN PEOPLE TOOK ADVANTAGE OF HIM, HE REMAINED STRAIGHT AND TRUE.
I DON'T GET IT.
WHY DO YOU DO THINGS THAT DON'T PROFIT YOU AT ALL?
HELPING PEOPLE IN TROUBLE.
IT'S COMMON SENSE, RIGHT?
I DON'T GET IT.
ONE DAY YOU WILL.

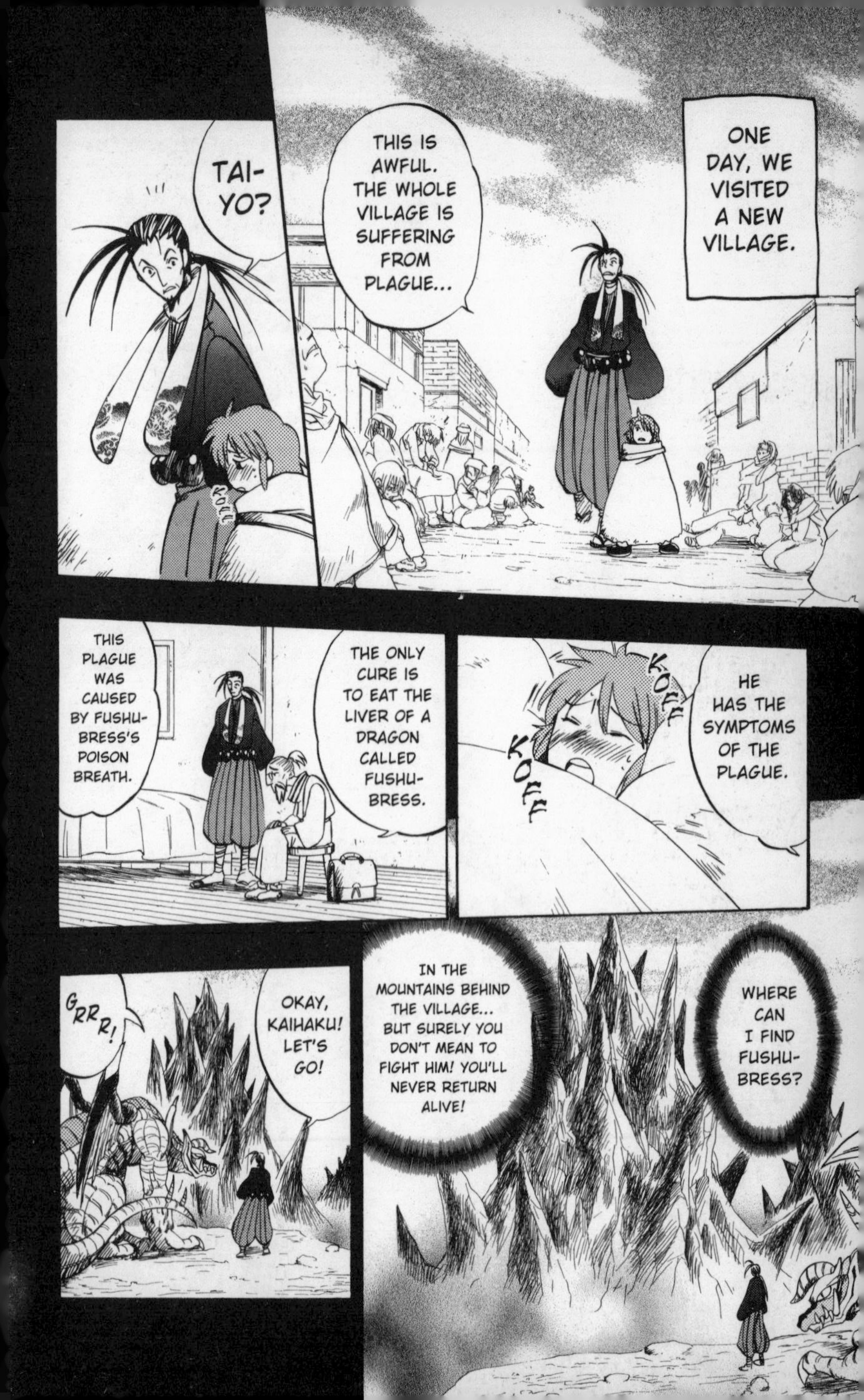
ONE DAY, WE VISITED A NEW VILLAGE.
THIS IS AWFUL. THE WHOLE VILLAGE IS SUFFERING FROM PLAGUE...
TAI-YO?
KOFF
KOFF
KOFF
HE HAS THE SYMPTOMS OF THE PLAGUE.
THE ONLY CURE IS TO EAT THE LIVER OF A DRAGON CALLED FUSHU-BRESS.
THIS PLAGUE WAS CAUSED BY FUSHU-BRESS'S POISON BREATH.
WHERE CAN I FIND FUSHU-BRESS?
IN THE MOUNTAINS BEHIND THE VILLAGE... BUT SURELY YOU DON'T MEAN TO FIGHT HIM! YOU'LL NEVER RETURN ALIVE!
OKAY, KAIHAKU! LET'S GO!
GRRR!

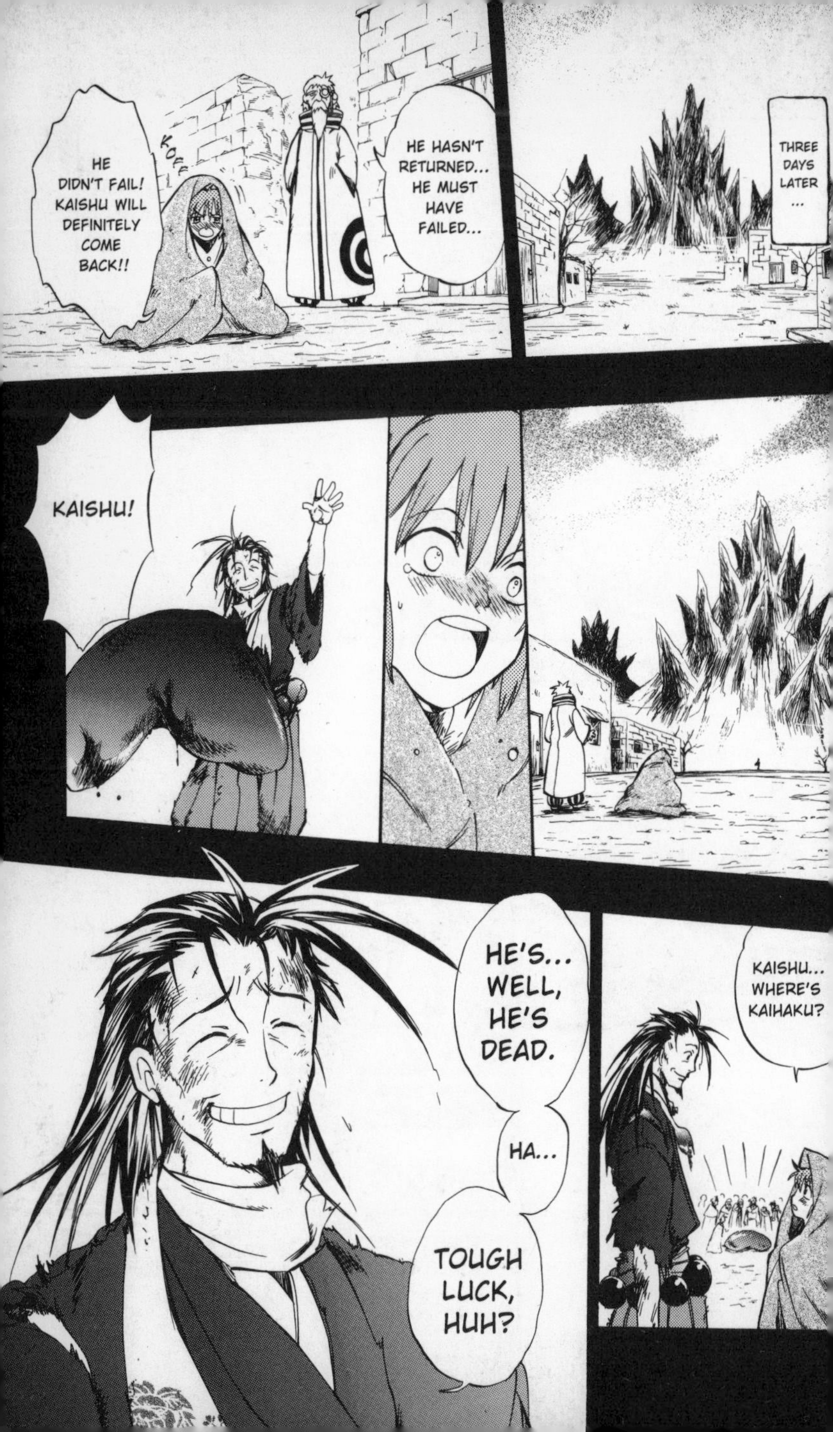
THREE DAYS LATER...
HE HASN'T RETURNED... HE MUST HAVE FAILED...
KOFF
HE DIDN'T FAIL! KAISHU WILL DEFINITELY COME BACK!!
KAISHU!
KAISHU... WHERE'S KAIHAKU?
HE'S... WELL, HE'S DEAD.
HA...
TOUGH LUCK, HUH?

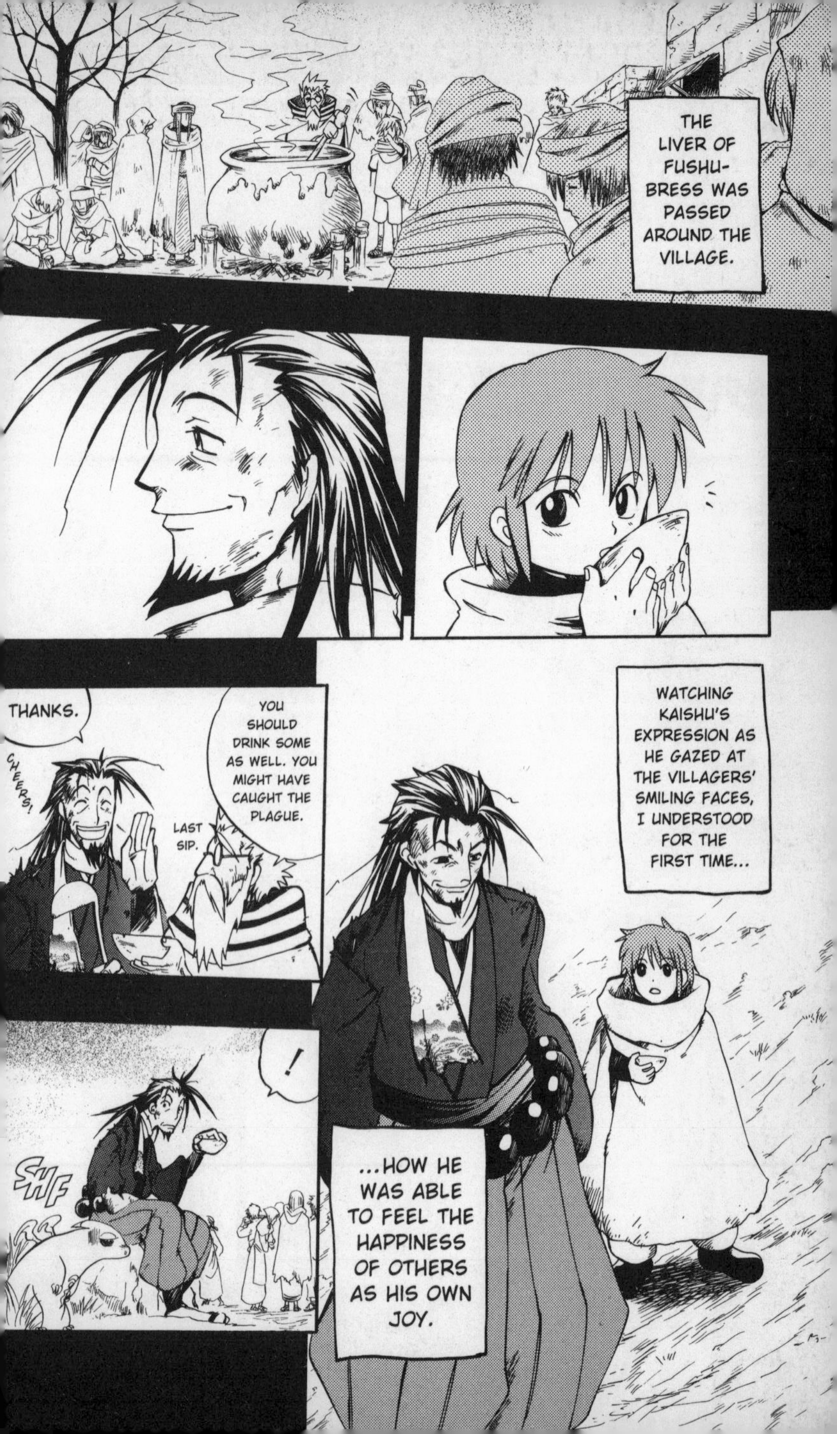
THE LIVER OF FUSHU-BRESS WAS PASSED AROUND THE VILLAGE.
WATCHING KAISHU'S EXPRESSION AS HE GAZED AT THE VILLAGERS' SMILING FACES, I UNDERSTOOD FOR THE FIRST TIME...
...HOW HE WAS ABLE TO FEEL THE HAPPINESS OF OTHERS AS HIS OWN JOY.
YOU SHOULD DRINK SOME AS WELL. YOU MIGHT HAVE CAUGHT THE PLAGUE.
THANKS.
LAST SIP.
CHEERS!
!
SHF

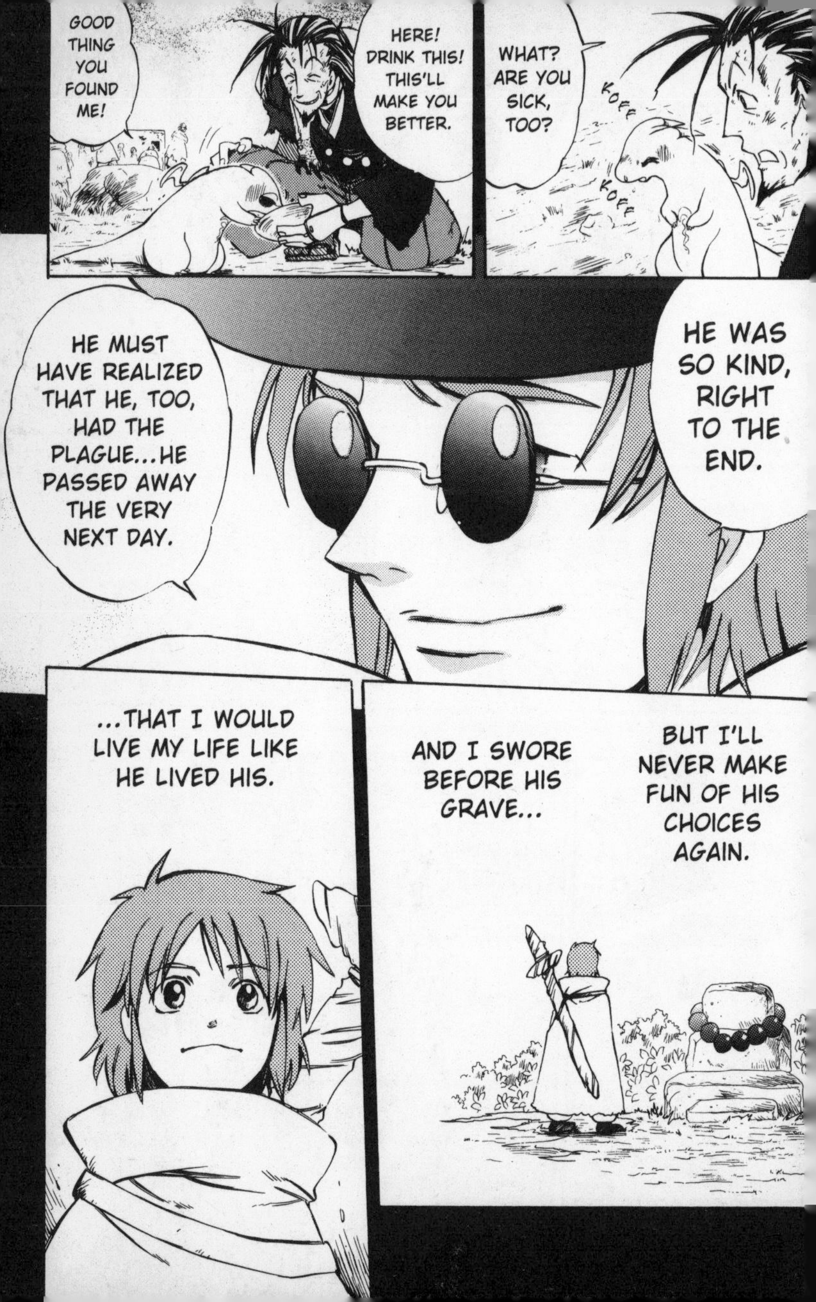
WHAT? ARE YOU SICK, TOO?
KOFF
KOFF
HERE! DRINK THIS! THIS'LL MAKE YOU BETTER.
GOOD THING YOU FOUND ME!
HE WAS SO KIND, RIGHT TO THE END.
HE MUST HAVE REALIZED THAT HE, TOO, HAD THE PLAGUE...HE PASSED AWAY THE VERY NEXT DAY.
BUT I'LL NEVER MAKE FUN OF HIS CHOICES AGAIN.
AND I SWORE BEFORE HIS GRAVE...
...THAT I WOULD LIVE MY LIFE LIKE HE LIVED HIS.

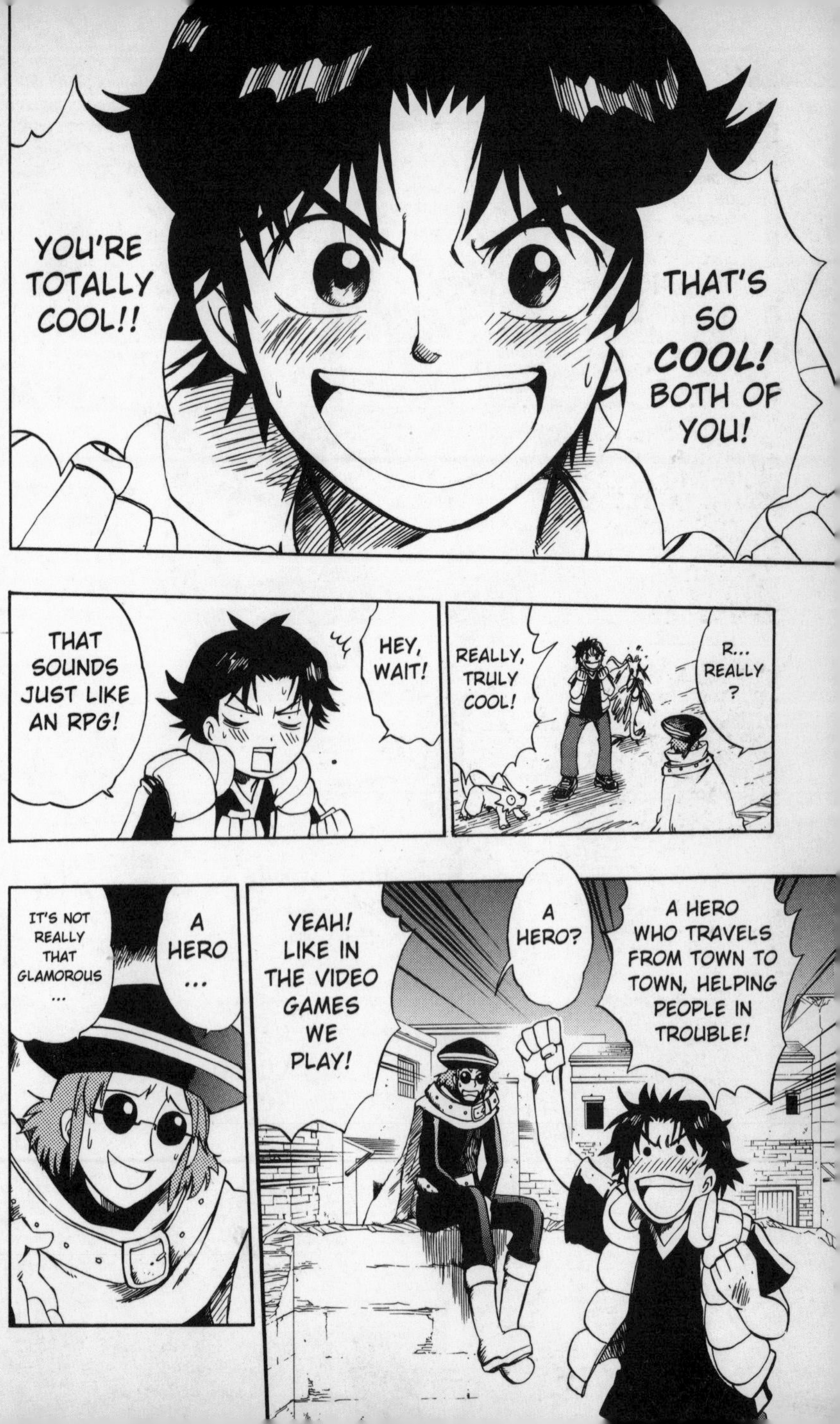
THAT'S SO COOL! BOTH OF YOU!
YOU'RE TOTALLY COOL!!
R... REALLY?
REALLY, TRULY COOL!
HEY, WAIT!
THAT SOUNDS JUST LIKE AN RPG!
A HERO WHO TRAVELS FROM TOWN TO TOWN, HELPING PEOPLE IN TROUBLE!
A HERO?
YEAH! LIKE IN THE VIDEO GAMES WE PLAY!
A HERO ...
IT'S NOT REALLY THAT GLAMOROUS ...

READ THIS WAY

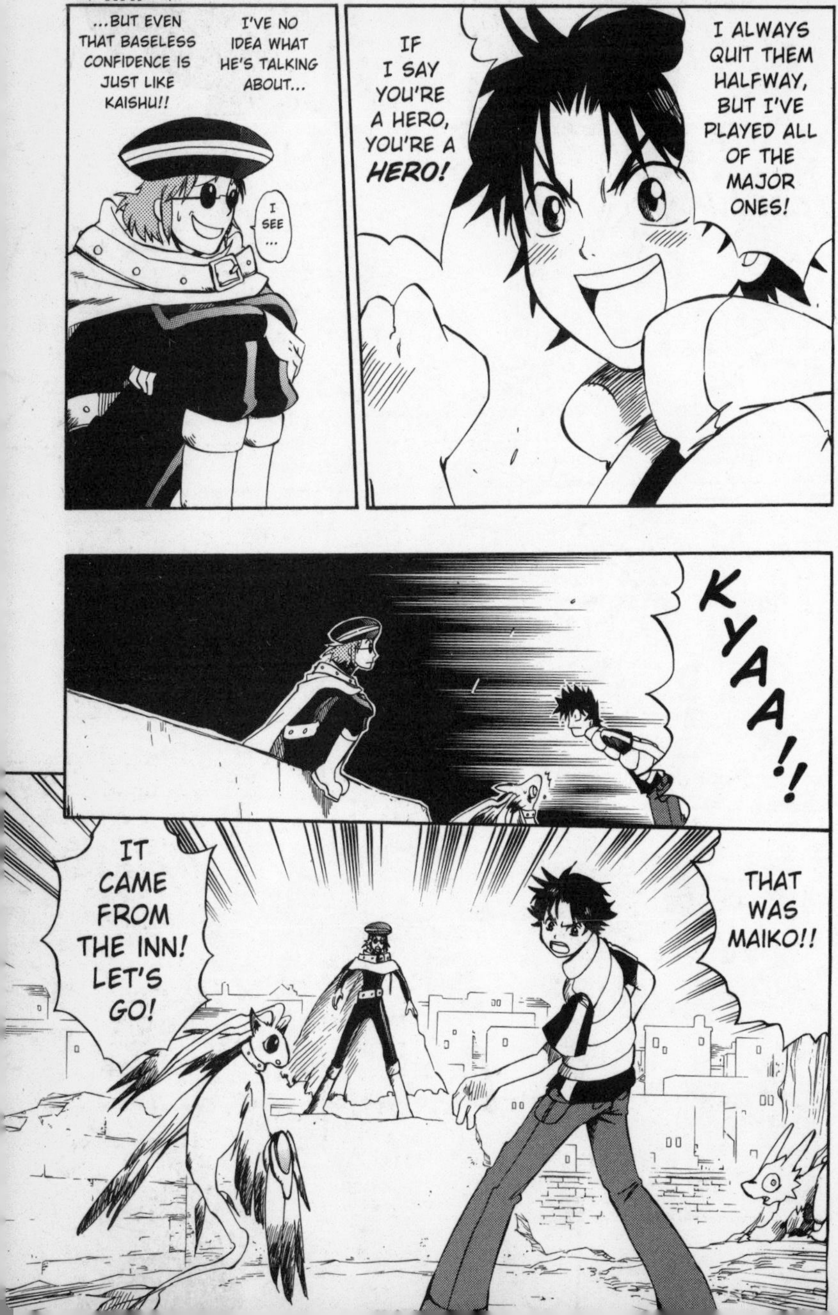
I ALWAYS QUIT THEM HALFWAY, BUT I'VE PLAYED ALL OF THE MAJOR ONES!
IF I SAY YOU'RE A HERO, YOU'RE A *HERO!*
I'VE NO IDEA WHAT HE'S TALKING ABOUT...
...BUT EVEN THAT BASELESS CONFIDENCE IS JUST LIKE KAISHU!!
I SEE...
KYAA!!
THAT WAS MAIKO!!
IT CAME FROM THE INN! LET'S GO!

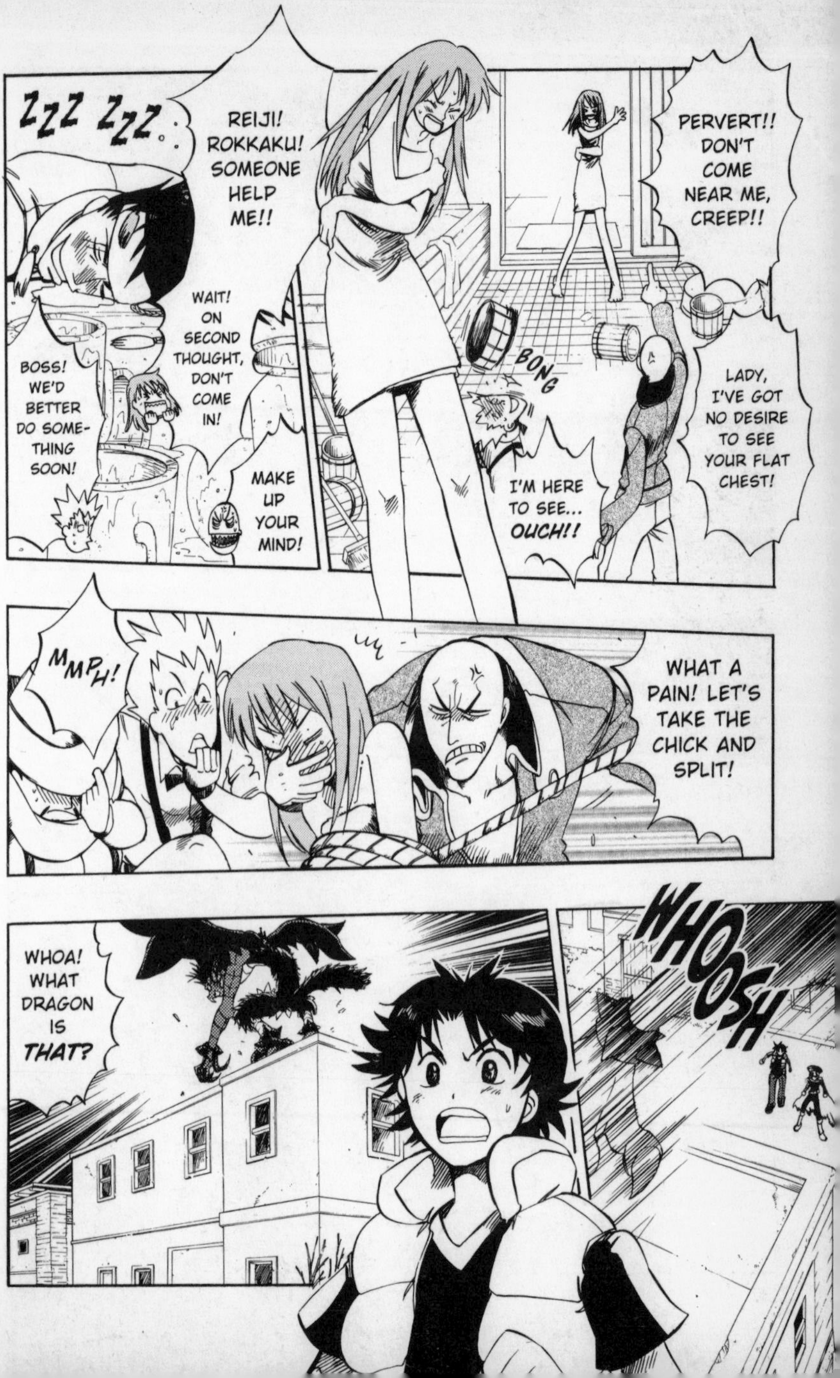
PERVERT!! DON'T COME NEAR ME, CREEP!!
LADY, I'VE GOT NO DESIRE TO SEE YOUR FLAT CHEST!
BONG
I'M HERE TO SEE... OUCH!!
REIJI! ROKKAKU! SOMEONE HELP ME!!
ZZZ ZZZ
WAIT! ON SECOND THOUGHT, DON'T COME IN!
MAKE UP YOUR MIND!
BOSS! WE'D BETTER DO SOME-THING SOON!
WHAT A PAIN! LET'S TAKE THE CHICK AND SPLIT!
MMPH!
WHOOSH
WHOA! WHAT DRAGON IS THAT?

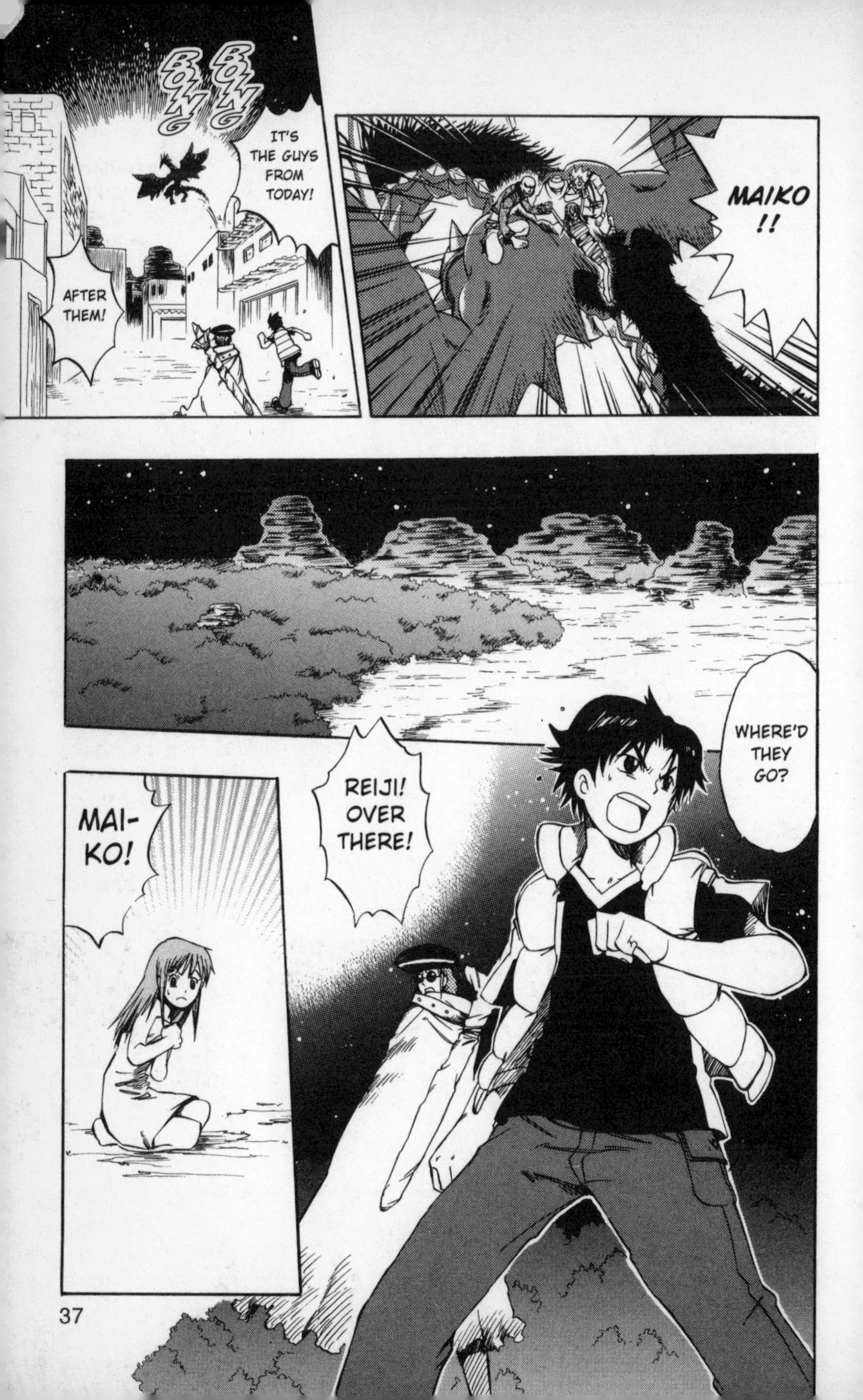
MAIKO !!
BOING BOING
IT'S THE GUYS FROM TODAY!
AFTER THEM!
WHERE'D THEY GO?
REIJI! OVER THERE!
MAI-KO!

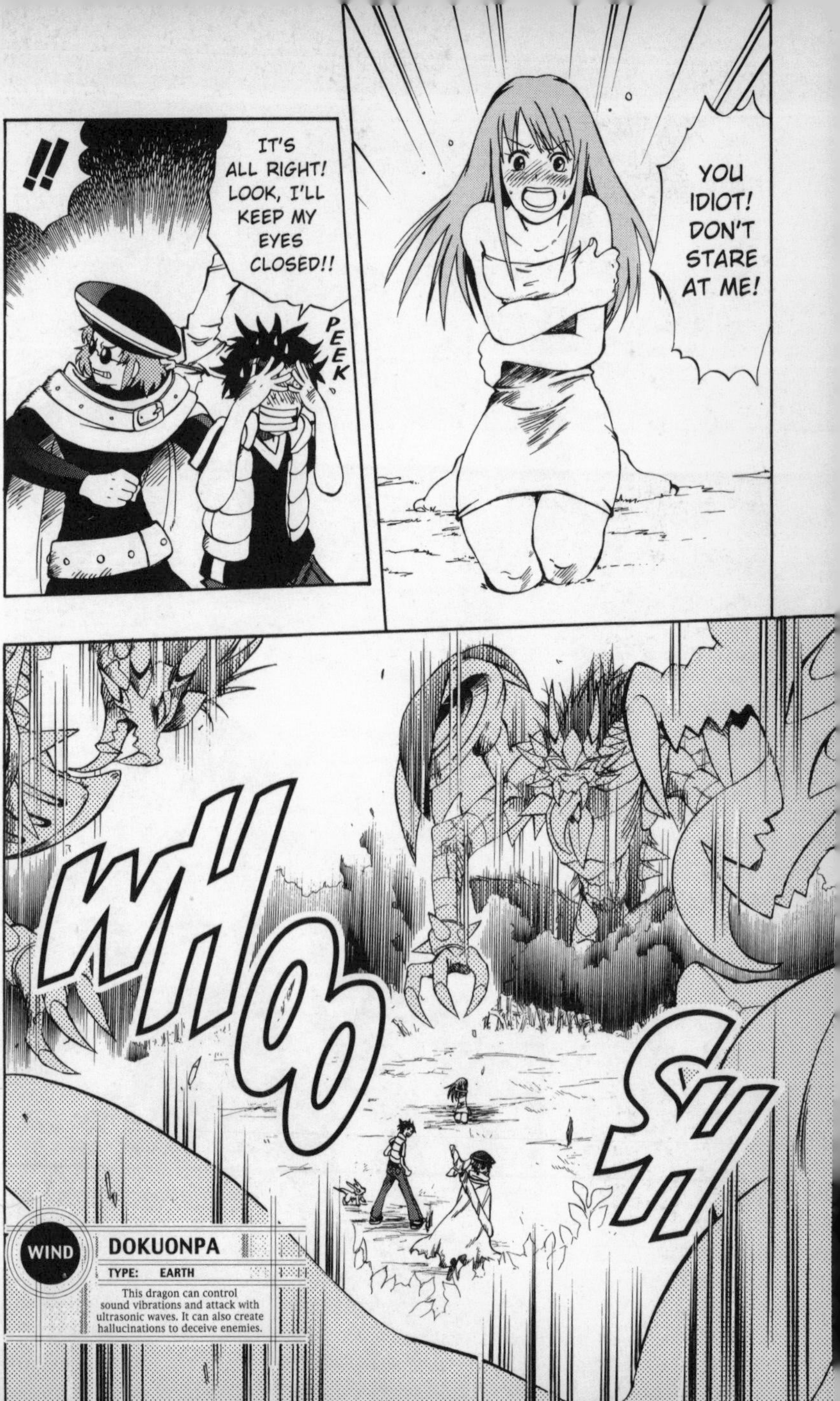
YOU IDIOT! DON'T STARE AT ME!
!!
IT'S ALL RIGHT! LOOK, I'LL KEEP MY EYES CLOSED!!
PEEK
WHOOSH
WIND
DOKUONPA
TYPE: EARTH
This dragon can control sound vibrations and attack with ultrasonic waves. It can also create hallucinations to deceive enemies.

READ THIS WAY

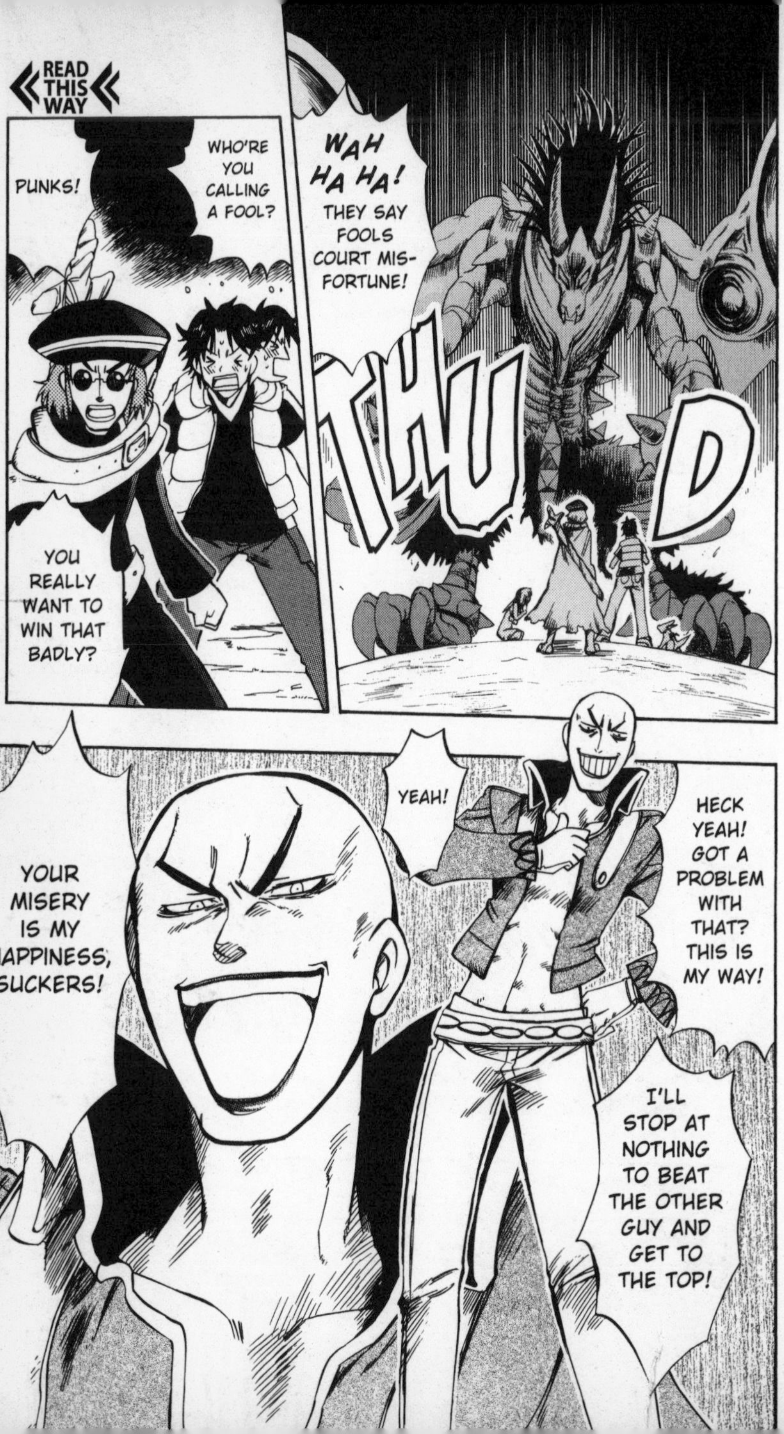
WAH HA HA! THEY SAY FOOLS COURT MISFORTUNE!
THUD
WHO'RE YOU CALLING A FOOL?
PUNKS!
YOU REALLY WANT TO WIN THAT BADLY?
HECK YEAH! GOT A PROBLEM WITH THAT? THIS IS MY WAY!
YEAH!
I'LL STOP AT NOTHING TO BEAT THE OTHER GUY AND GET TO THE TOP!
YOUR MISERY IS MY HAPPINESS, SUCKERS!

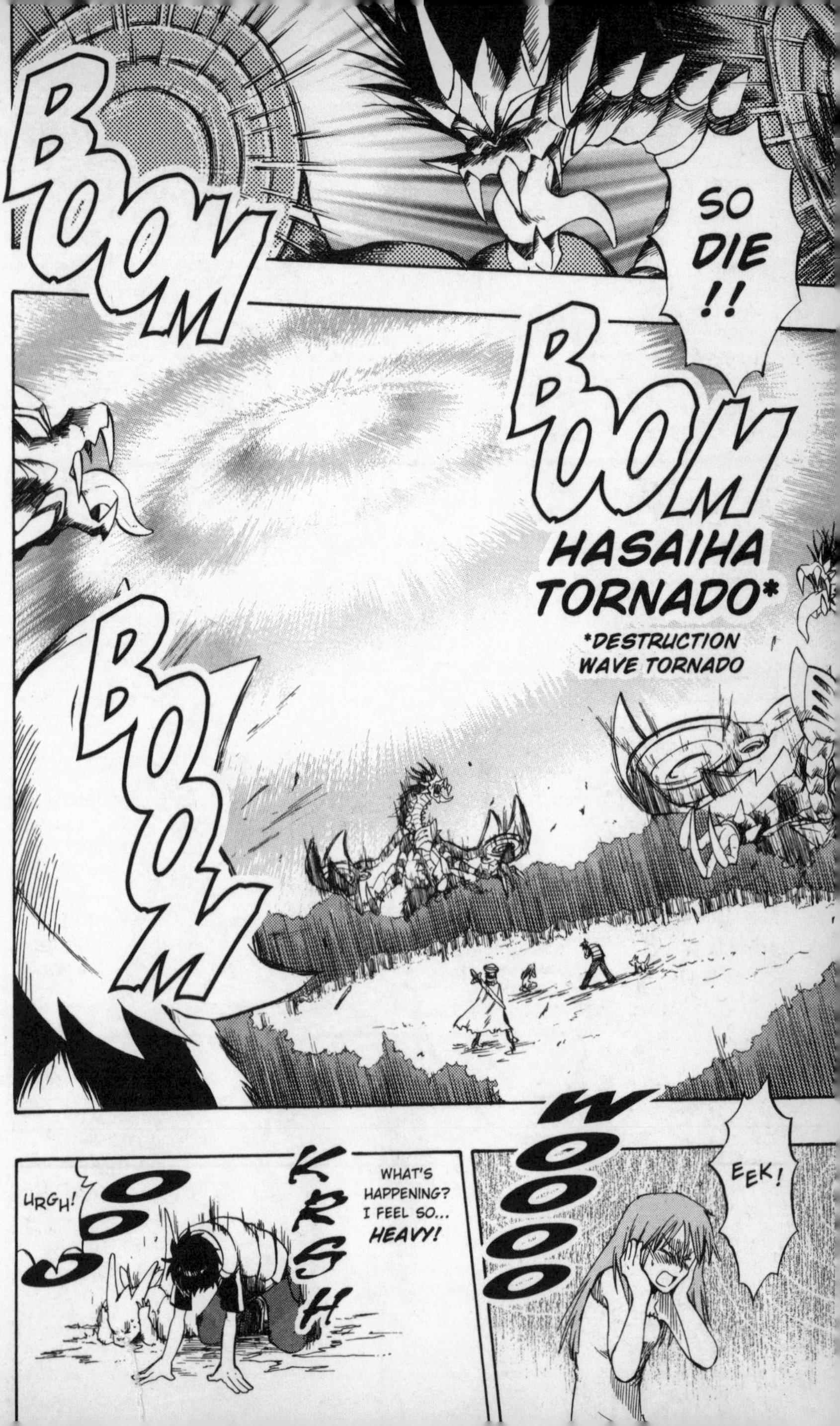
SO DIE!!
BOOOM
BOOOM
HASAIHA TORNADO*
*DESTRUCTION WAVE TORNADO
BOOOOM
EEK!
WOOOOO
KRSH
WHAT'S HAPPENING? I FEEL SO... HEAVY!
URGH!
OOOO

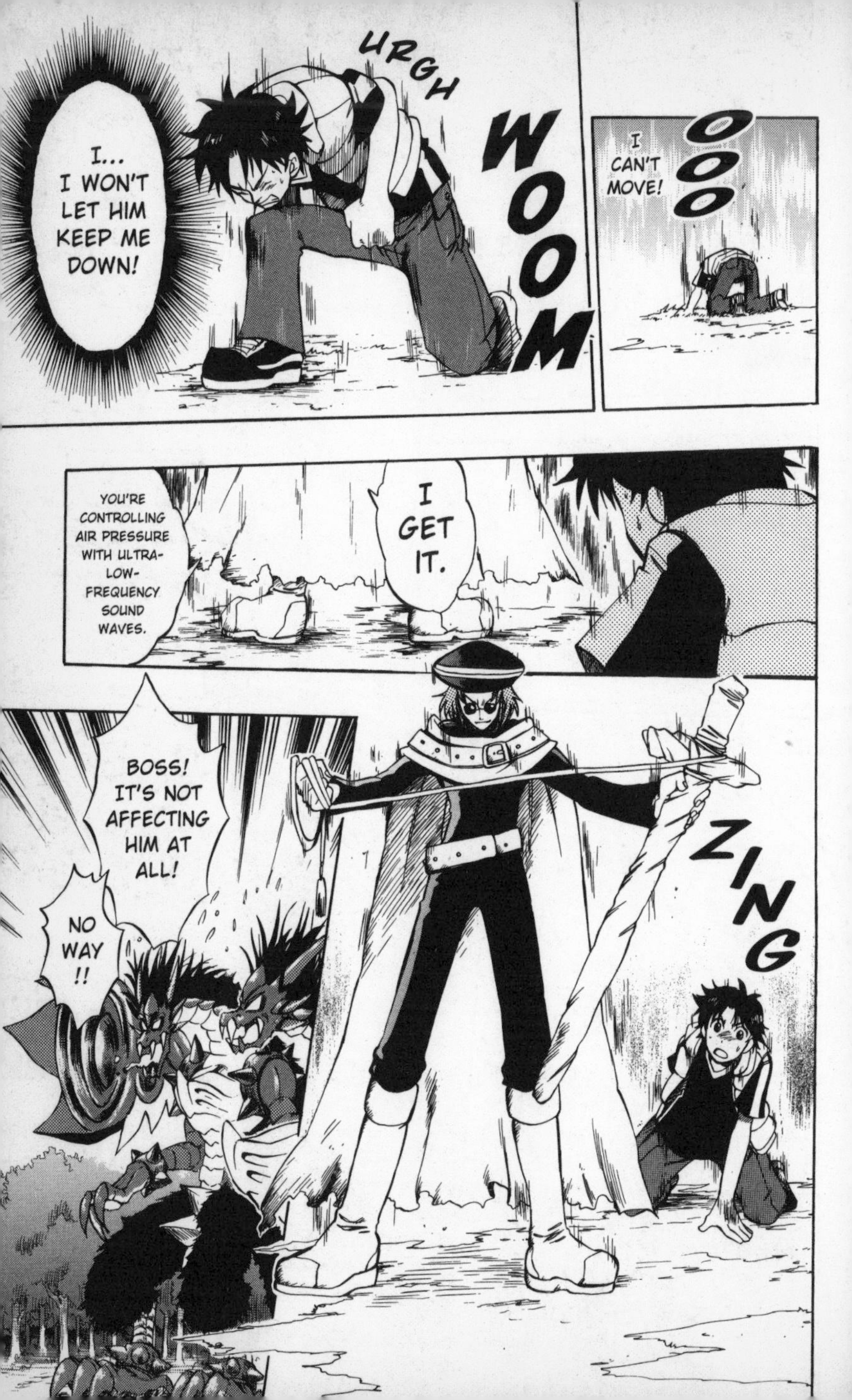
OOO
I CAN'T MOVE!
URGH
WOOM
I... I WON'T LET HIM KEEP ME DOWN!
I GET IT.
YOU'RE CONTROLLING AIR PRESSURE WITH ULTRA-LOW-FREQUENCY SOUND WAVES.
ZING
BOSS! IT'S NOT AFFECTING HIM AT ALL!
NO WAY !!

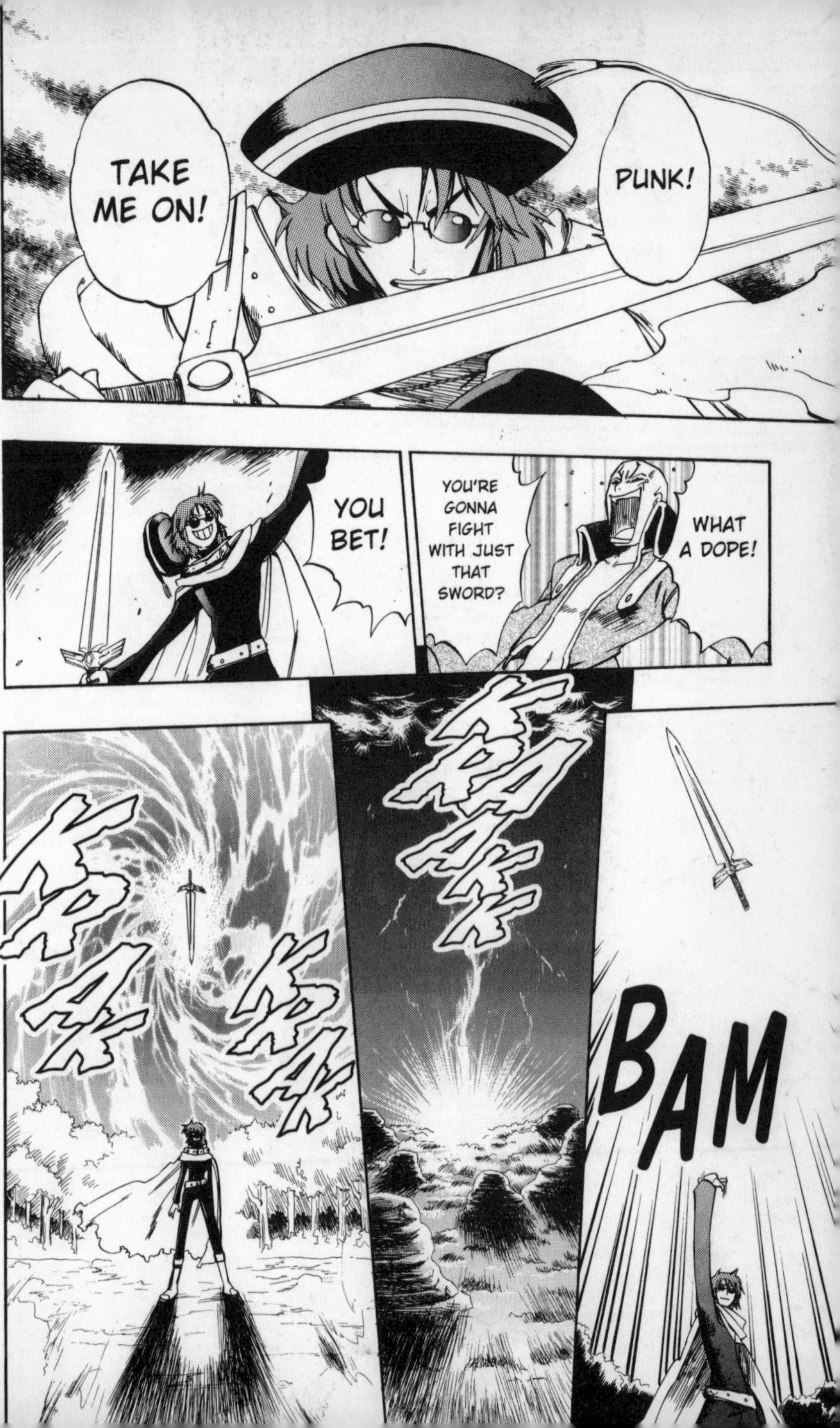
PUNK!
TAKE ME ON!
WHAT A DOPE!
YOU'RE GONNA FIGHT WITH JUST THAT SWORD?
YOU BET!
BAM
KRAAKK
KRAAK
KRAAK

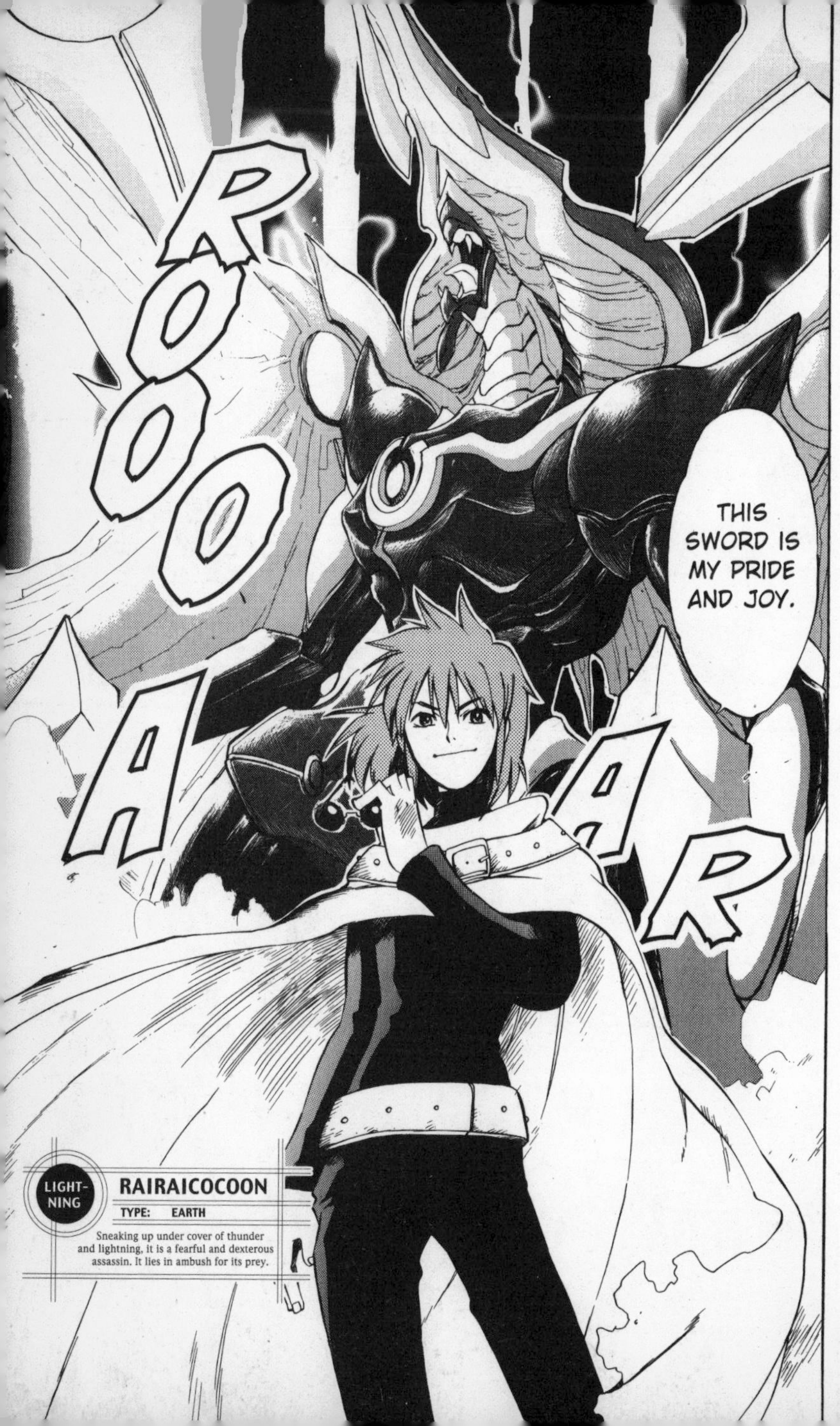
ROOOAAR
THIS SWORD IS MY PRIDE AND JOY.
LIGHT-NING
RAIRAICOCOON
TYPE: EARTH
Sneaking up under cover of thunder and lightning, it is a fearful and dexterous assassin. It lies in ambush for its prey.

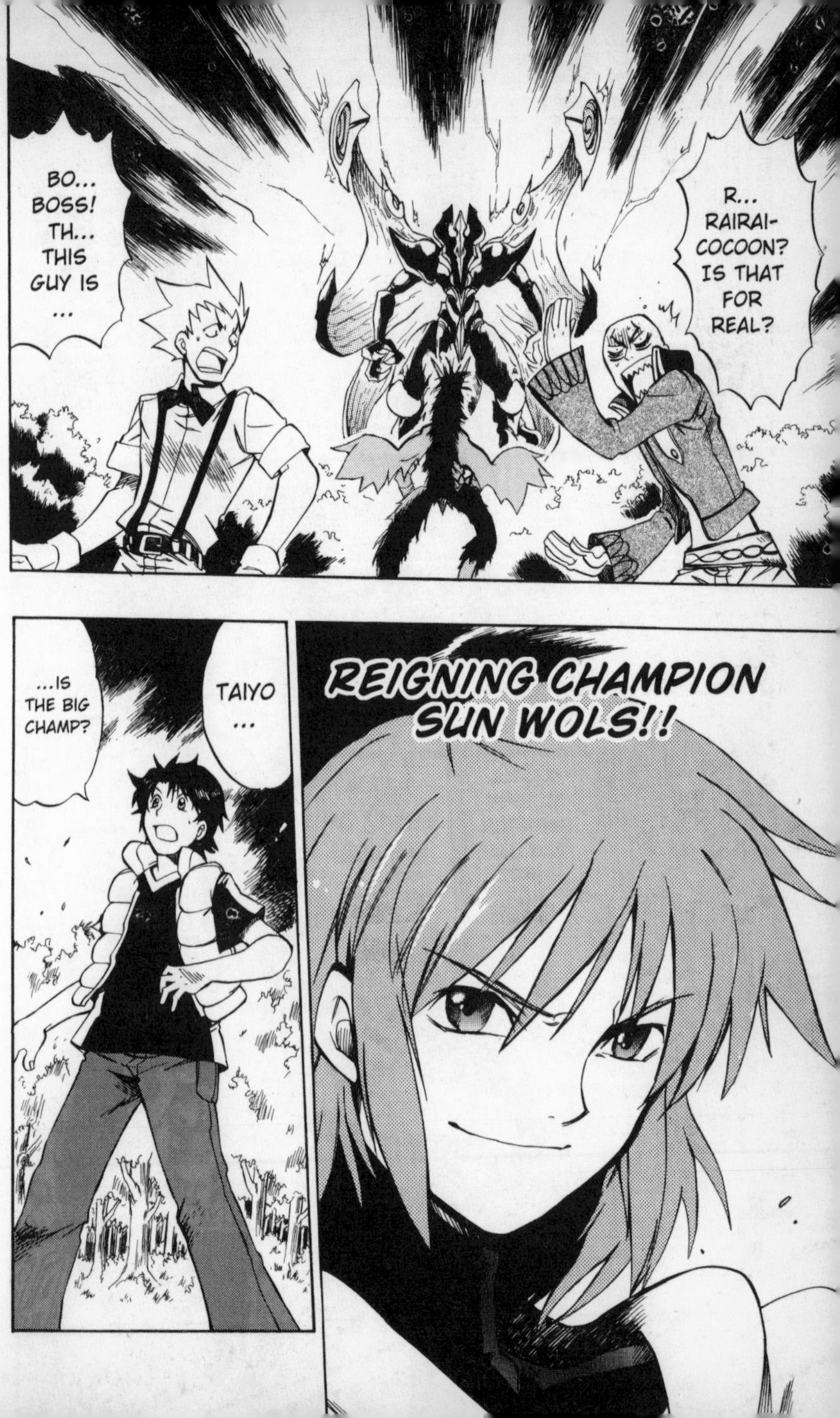
R... RAIRAI-COCOON? IS THAT FOR REAL?
BO... BOSS! TH... THIS GUY IS ...
REIGNING CHAMPION SUN WOLS!!
TAIYO ...
...IS THE BIG CHAMP?

READ THIS WAY

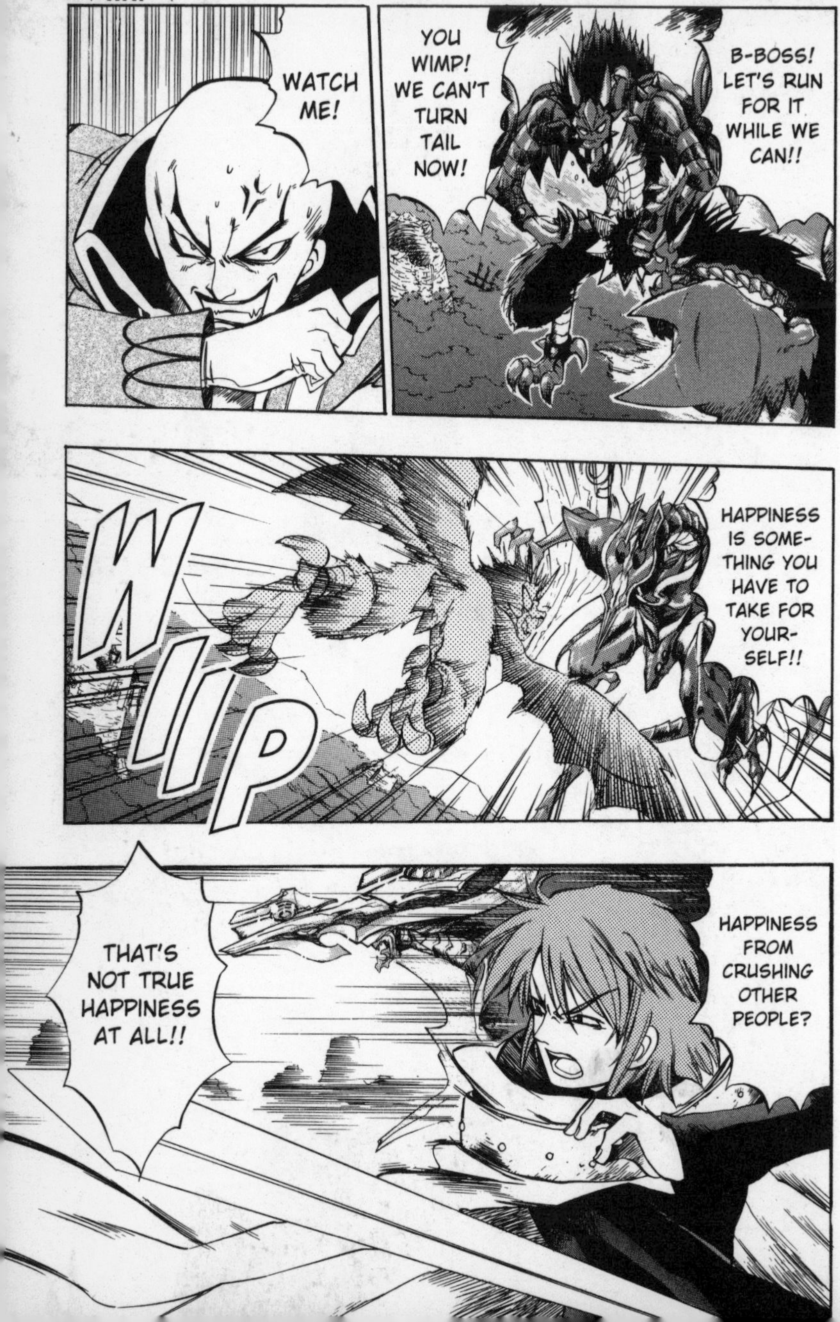

B-BOSS! LET'S RUN FOR IT WHILE WE CAN!!
YOU WIMP! WE CAN'T TURN TAIL NOW!
WATCH ME!
HAPPINESS IS SOME-THING YOU HAVE TO TAKE FOR YOUR-SELF!!
WHIP
HAPPINESS FROM CRUSHING OTHER PEOPLE?
THAT'S NOT TRUE HAPPINESS AT ALL!!

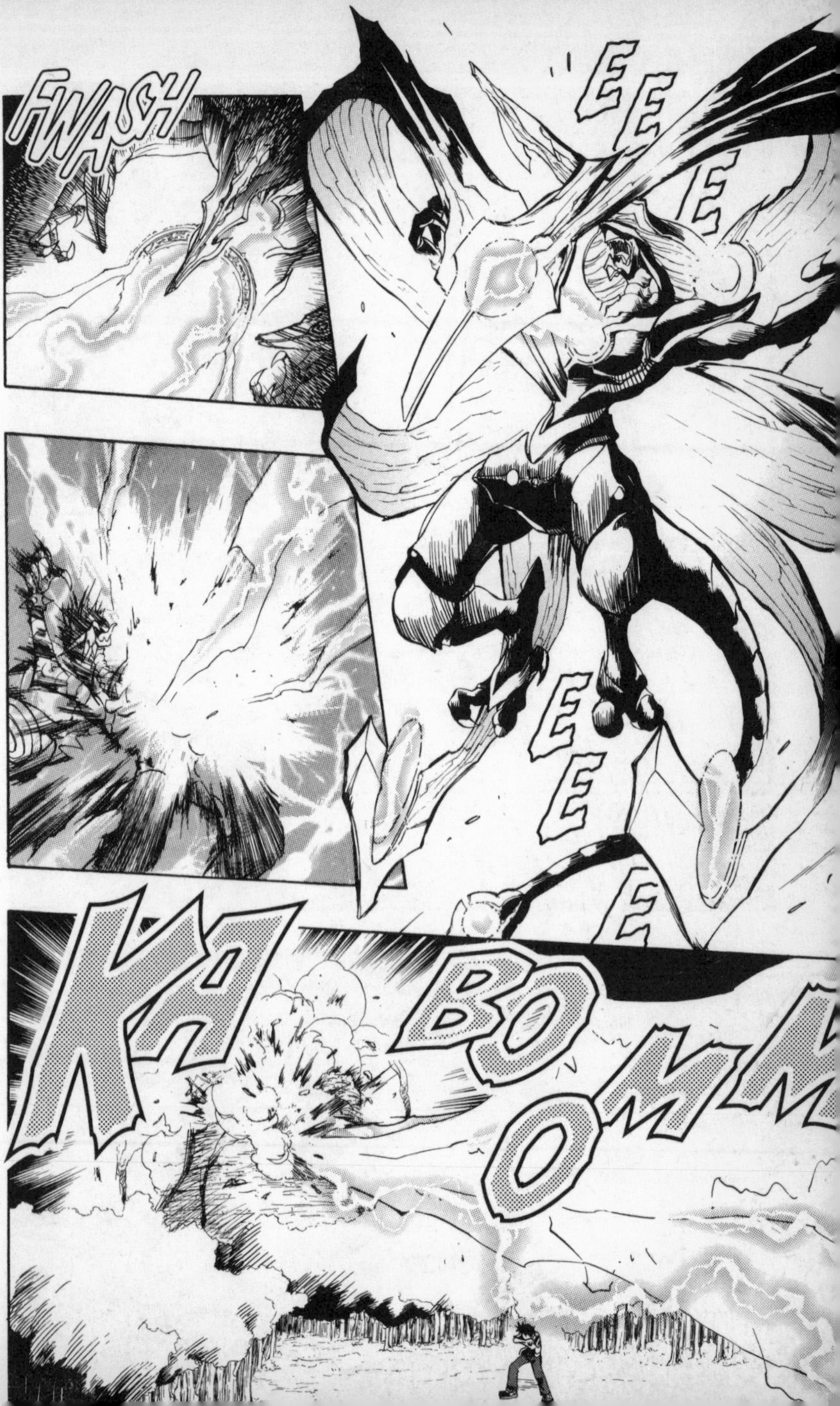
EEEE
EEE
FWASH
KABOOMMM

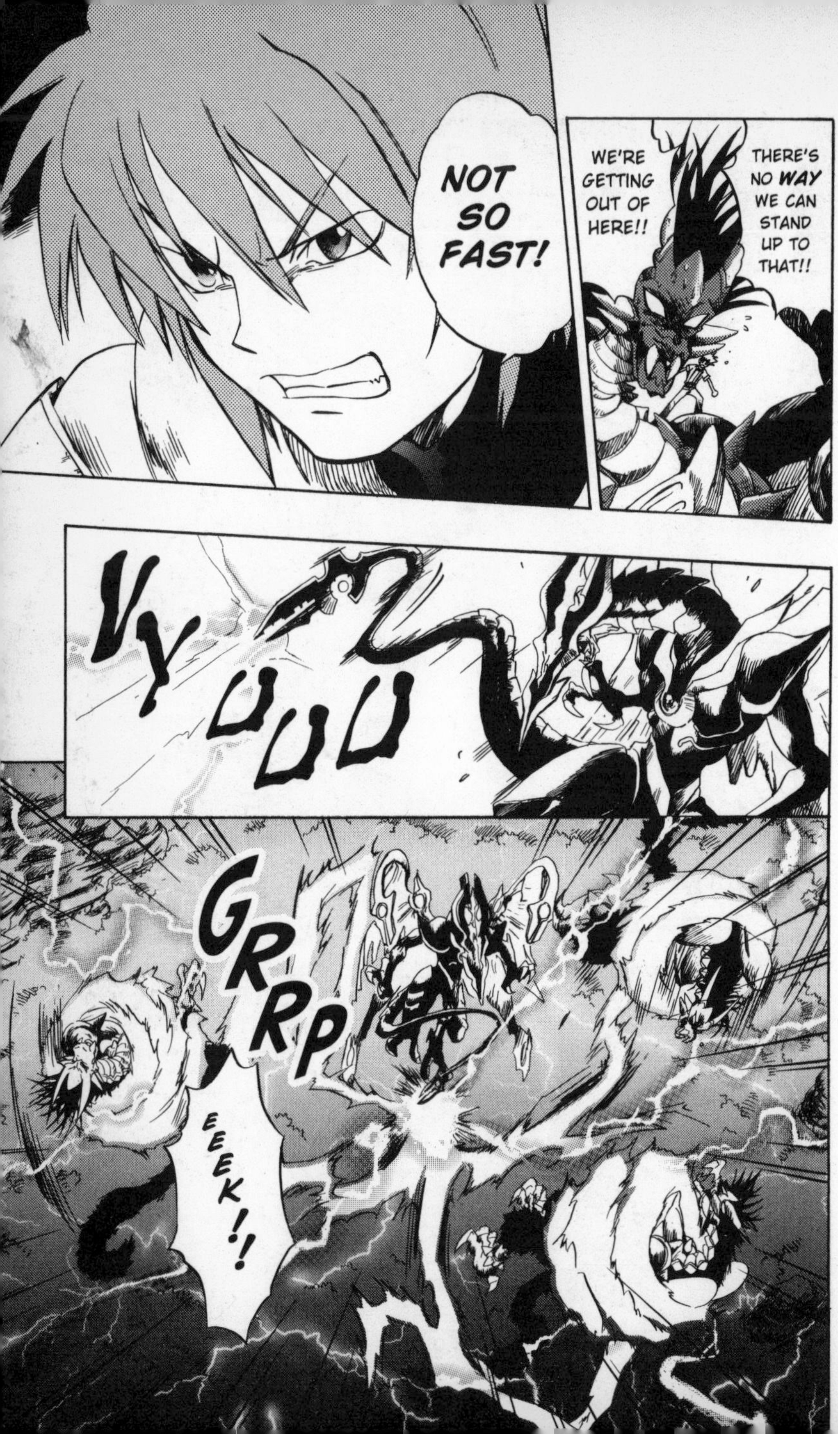
THERE'S NO **WAY** WE CAN STAND UP TO THAT!!
WE'RE GETTING OUT OF HERE!!
NOT SO FAST!
VYUUU
GRRP
EEEK!!

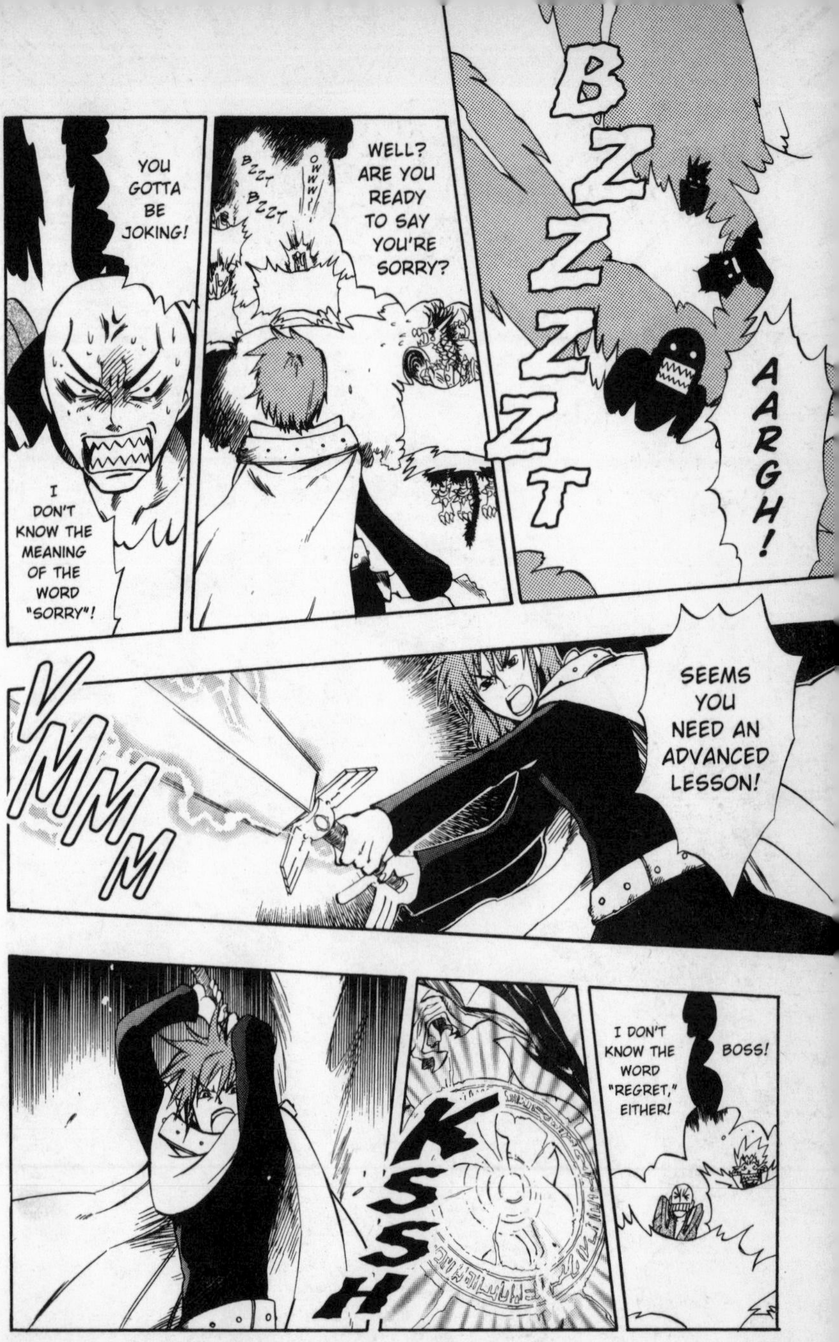
BZZZZT
AARGH!
WELL? ARE YOU READY TO SAY YOU'RE SORRY?
OWWW
BZZT BZZT
YOU GOTTA BE JOKING!
I DON'T KNOW THE MEANING OF THE WORD "SORRY"!
SEEMS YOU NEED AN ADVANCED LESSON!
VMMM
BOSS!
I DON'T KNOW THE WORD "REGRET," EITHER!
KSSH

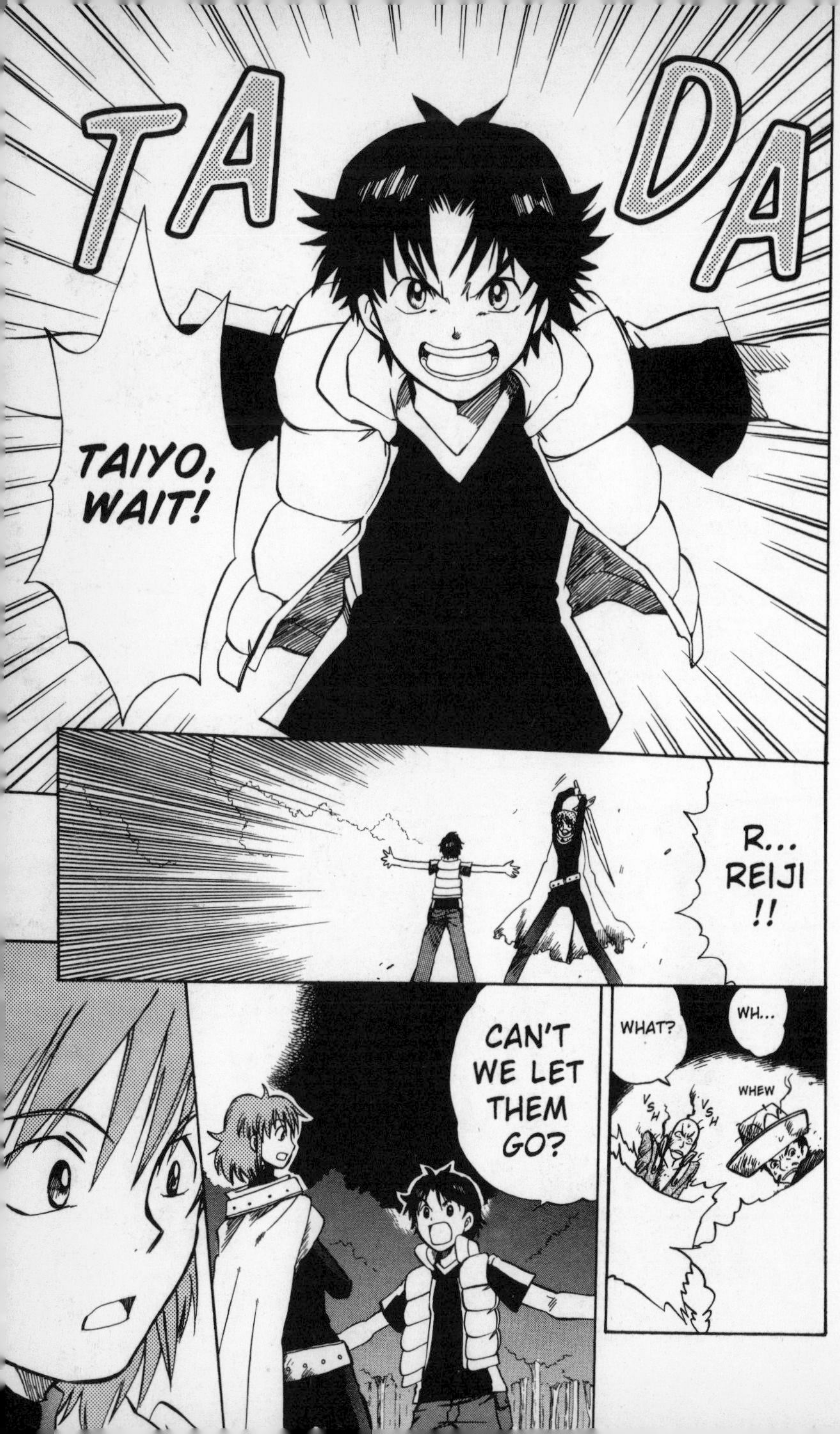
TA DA
TAIYO, WAIT!
R... REIJI!!
WH...
WHAT?
VSH VSH
WHEW
CAN'T WE LET THEM GO?

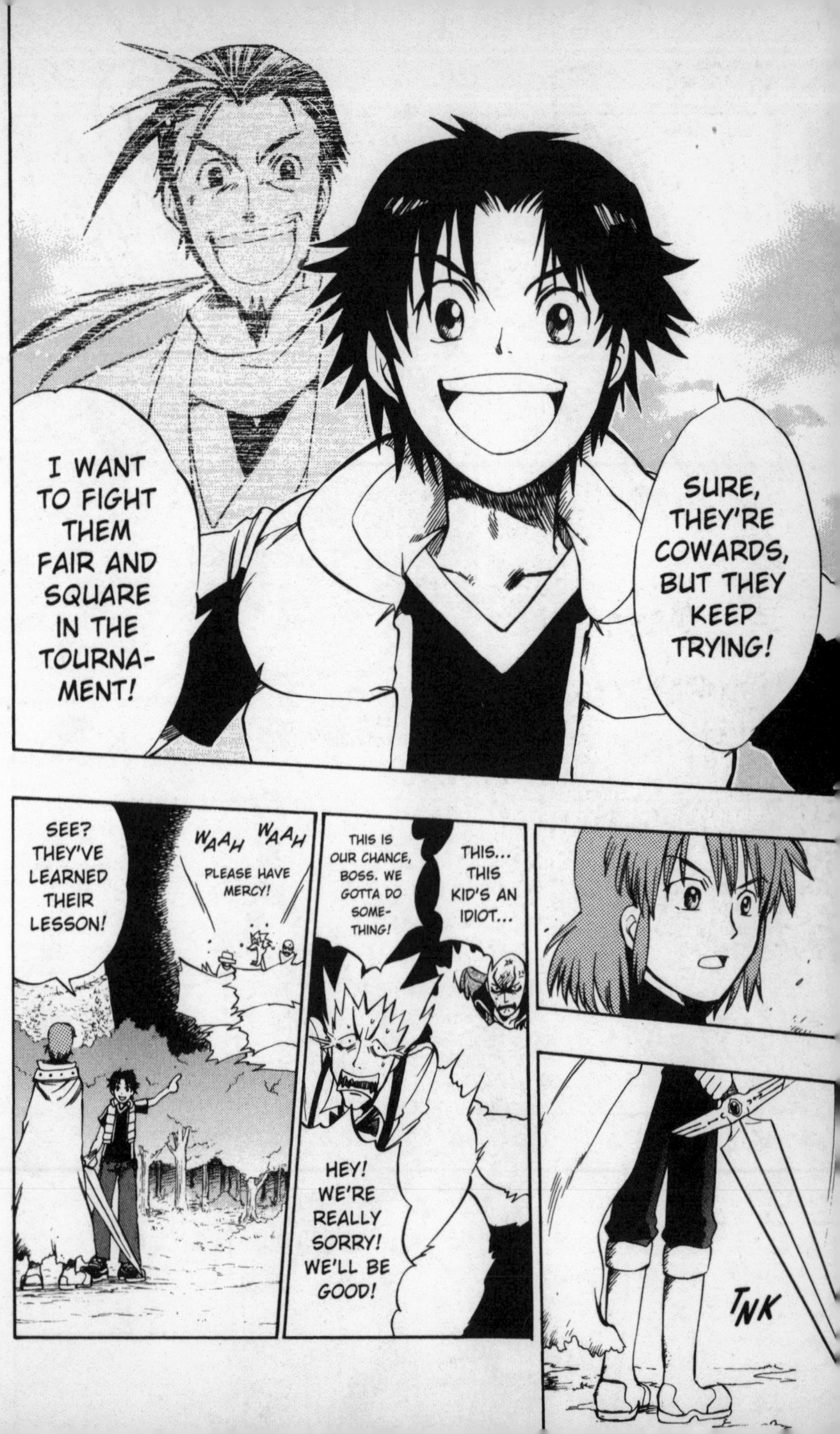
SURE, THEY'RE COWARDS, BUT THEY KEEP TRYING!
I WANT TO FIGHT THEM FAIR AND SQUARE IN THE TOURNA-MENT!
TNK
THIS... THIS KID'S AN IDIOT...
THIS IS OUR CHANCE, BOSS. WE GOTTA DO SOME-THING!
HEY! WE'RE REALLY SORRY! WE'LL BE GOOD!
WAAH WAAH
PLEASE HAVE MERCY!
SEE? THEY'VE LEARNED THEIR LESSON!

READ THIS WAY

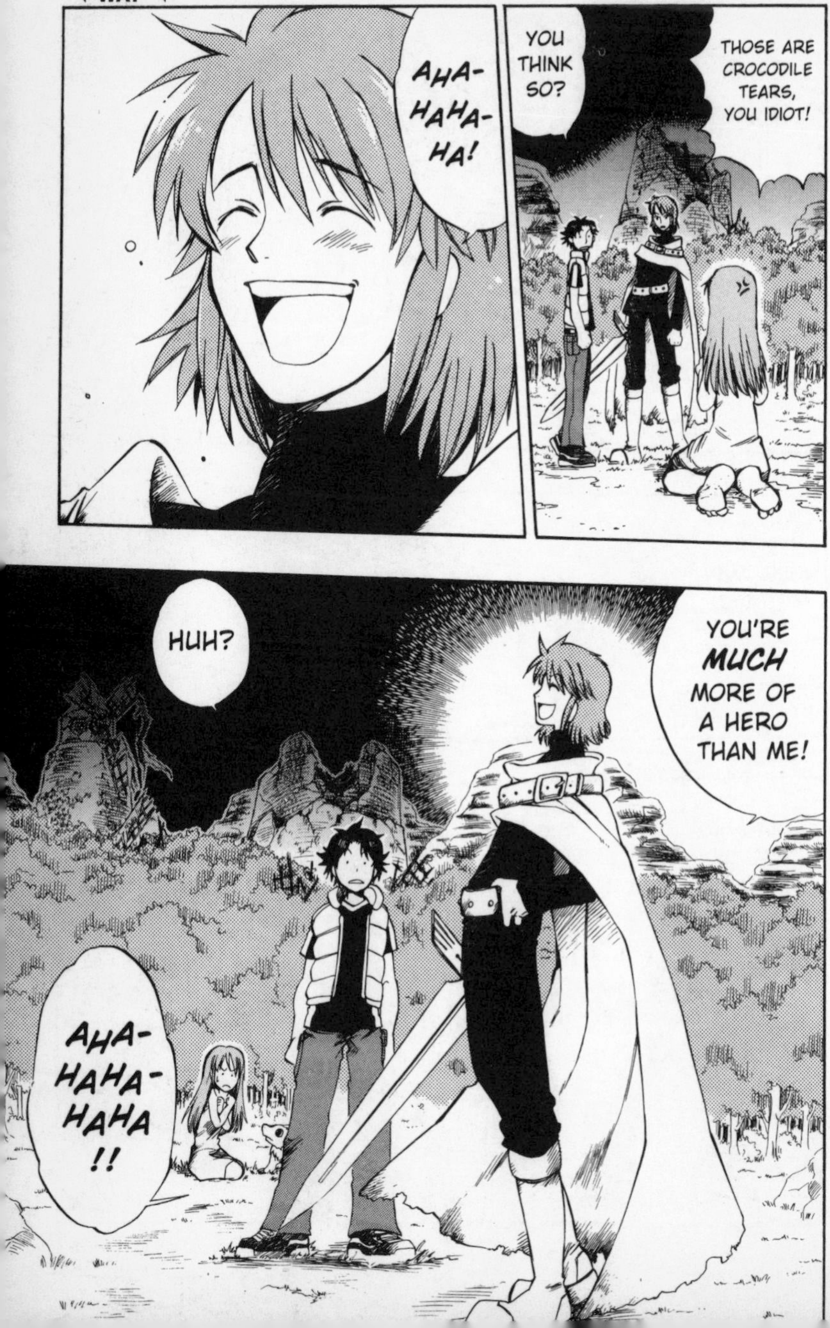
THOSE ARE CROCODILE TEARS, YOU IDIOT!
YOU THINK SO?
AHA-HAHAHA-HA!
YOU'RE MUCH MORE OF A HERO THAN ME!
HUH?
AHA-HAHAHA-HAHA!!

I'M LOOKING FORWARD TO TAKING YOU GUYS ON IN THE SECOND ROUND!
YEAH.
SO MAKE SURE YOU DON'T SLIP UP IN THE FIRST!
GRIP
WE CAN FIGHT FAIR AND SQUARE, TOO!
YEAH !!
BRR
WHAT'S THE MATTER NOW?
SUDDENLY, I'M ALL FIRED UP!

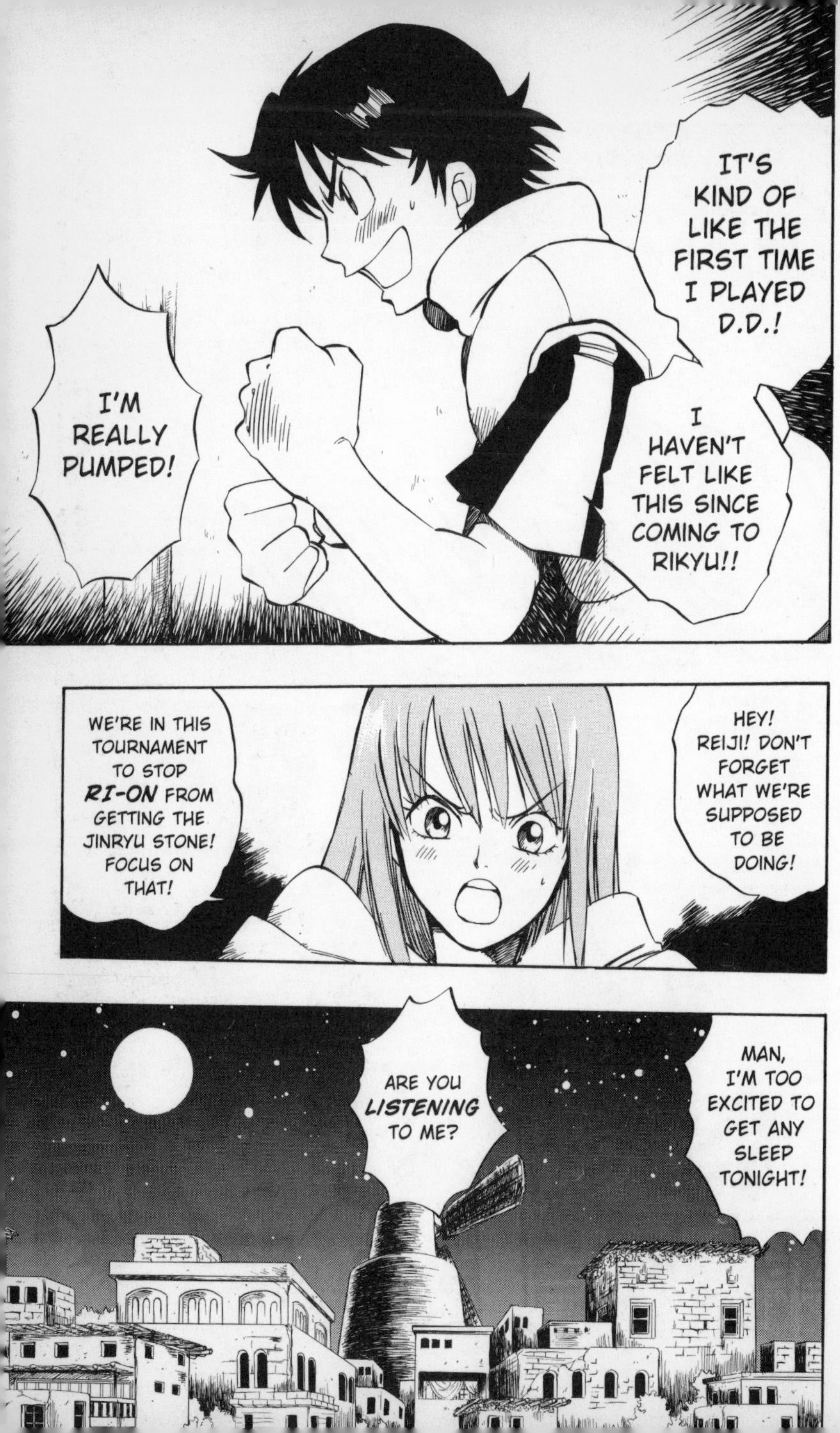
IT'S KIND OF LIKE THE FIRST TIME I PLAYED D.D.!
I HAVEN'T FELT LIKE THIS SINCE COMING TO RIKYU!!
I'M REALLY PUMPED!
HEY! REIJI! DON'T FORGET WHAT WE'RE SUPPOSED TO BE DOING!
WE'RE IN THIS TOURNAMENT TO STOP ***RI-ON*** FROM GETTING THE JINRYU STONE! FOCUS ON THAT!
MAN, I'M TOO EXCITED TO GET ANY SLEEP TONIGHT!
ARE YOU ***LISTENING*** TO ME?

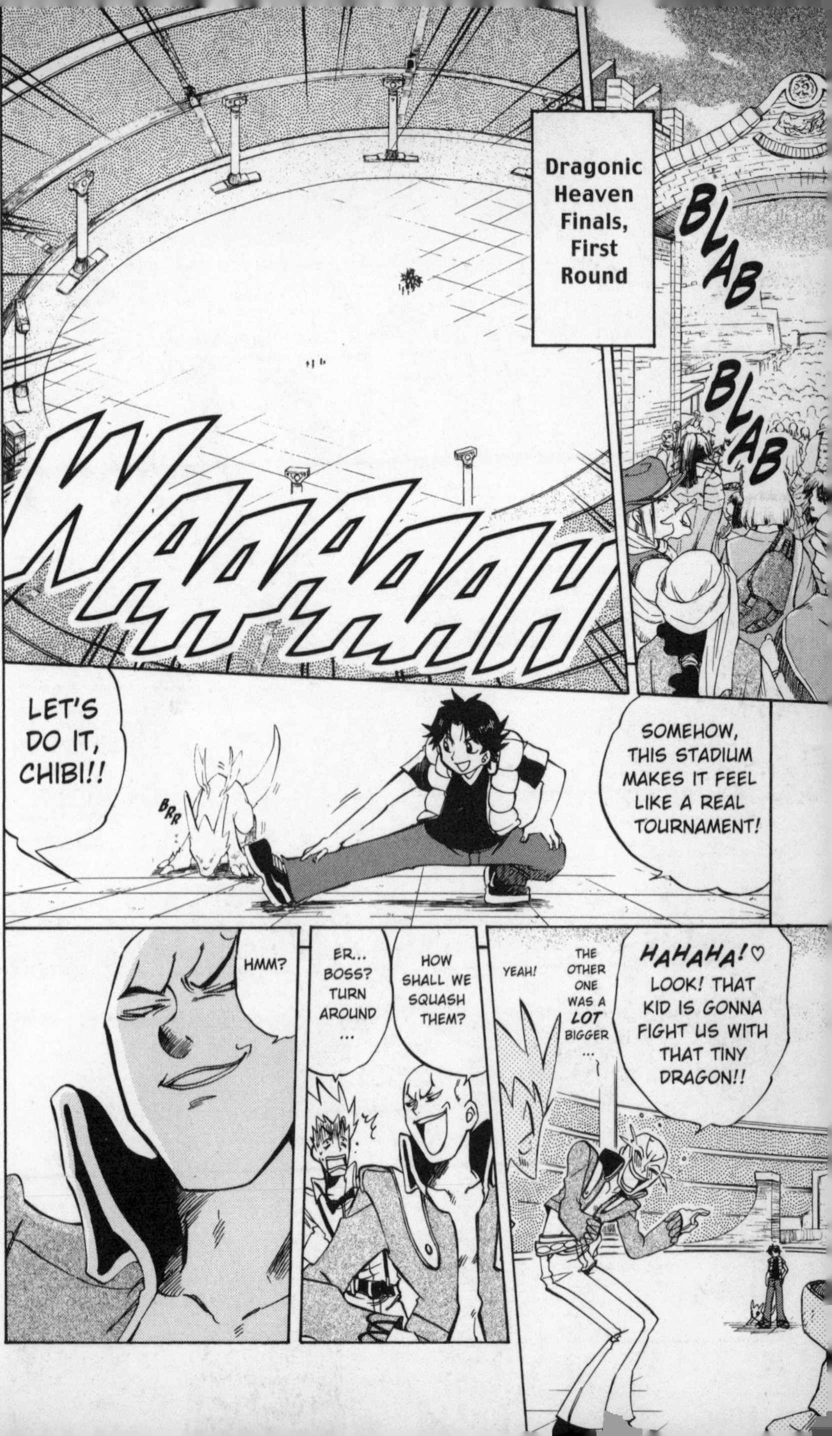
Dragonic Heaven Finals, First Round
BLAB BLAB
WAAAAAH
SOMEHOW, THIS STADIUM MAKES IT FEEL LIKE A REAL TOURNAMENT!
LET'S DO IT, CHIBI!!
BRR
HAHAHA! ♡ LOOK! THAT KID IS GONNA FIGHT US WITH THAT TINY DRAGON!!
THE OTHER ONE WAS A LOT BIGGER ...
YEAH!
HOW SHALL WE SQUASH THEM?
ER... BOSS? TURN AROUND ...
HMM?

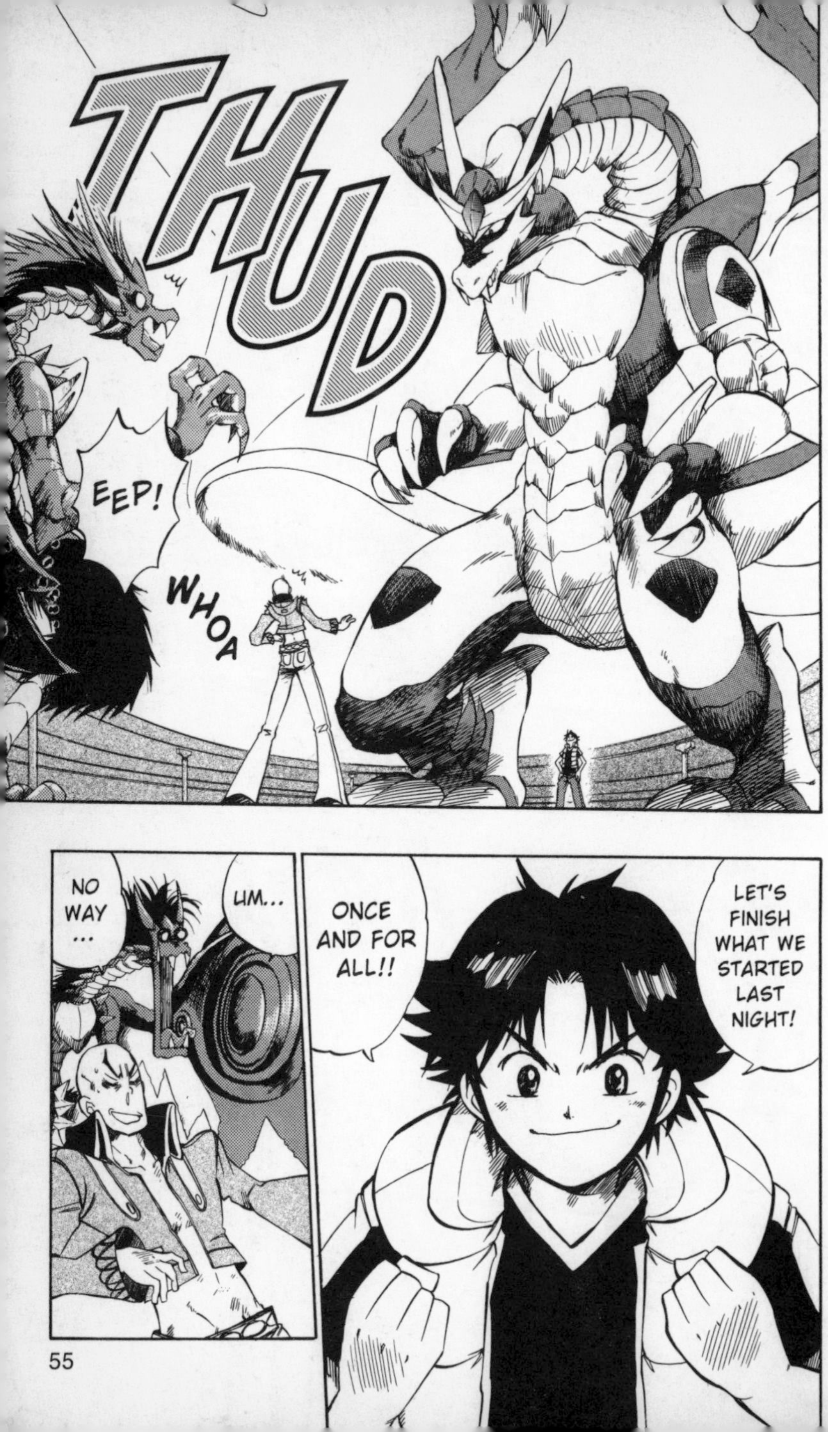
THUD
EEP!
WHOA
LET'S FINISH WHAT WE STARTED LAST NIGHT!
ONCE AND FOR ALL!!
UM...
NO WAY ...

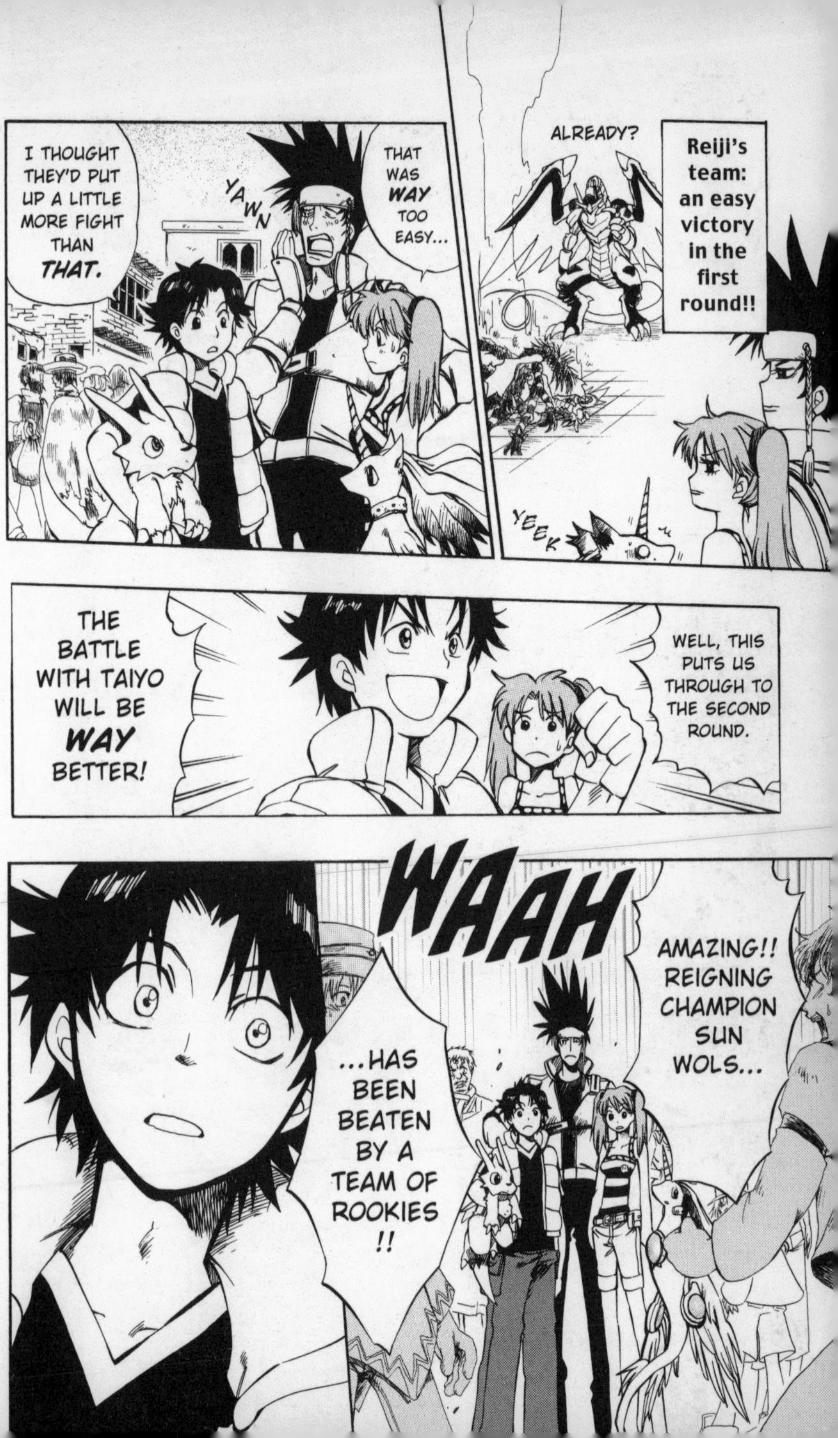
Reiji's team: an easy victory in the first round!!
ALREADY?
YEEK
THAT WAS WAY TOO EASY...
YAWN
I THOUGHT THEY'D PUT UP A LITTLE MORE FIGHT THAN THAT.
WELL, THIS PUTS US THROUGH TO THE SECOND ROUND.
THE BATTLE WITH TAIYO WILL BE WAY BETTER!
AMAZING!! REIGNING CHAMPION SUN WOLS...
WAAH
...HAS BEEN BEATEN BY A TEAM OF ROOKIES!!

READ THIS WAY

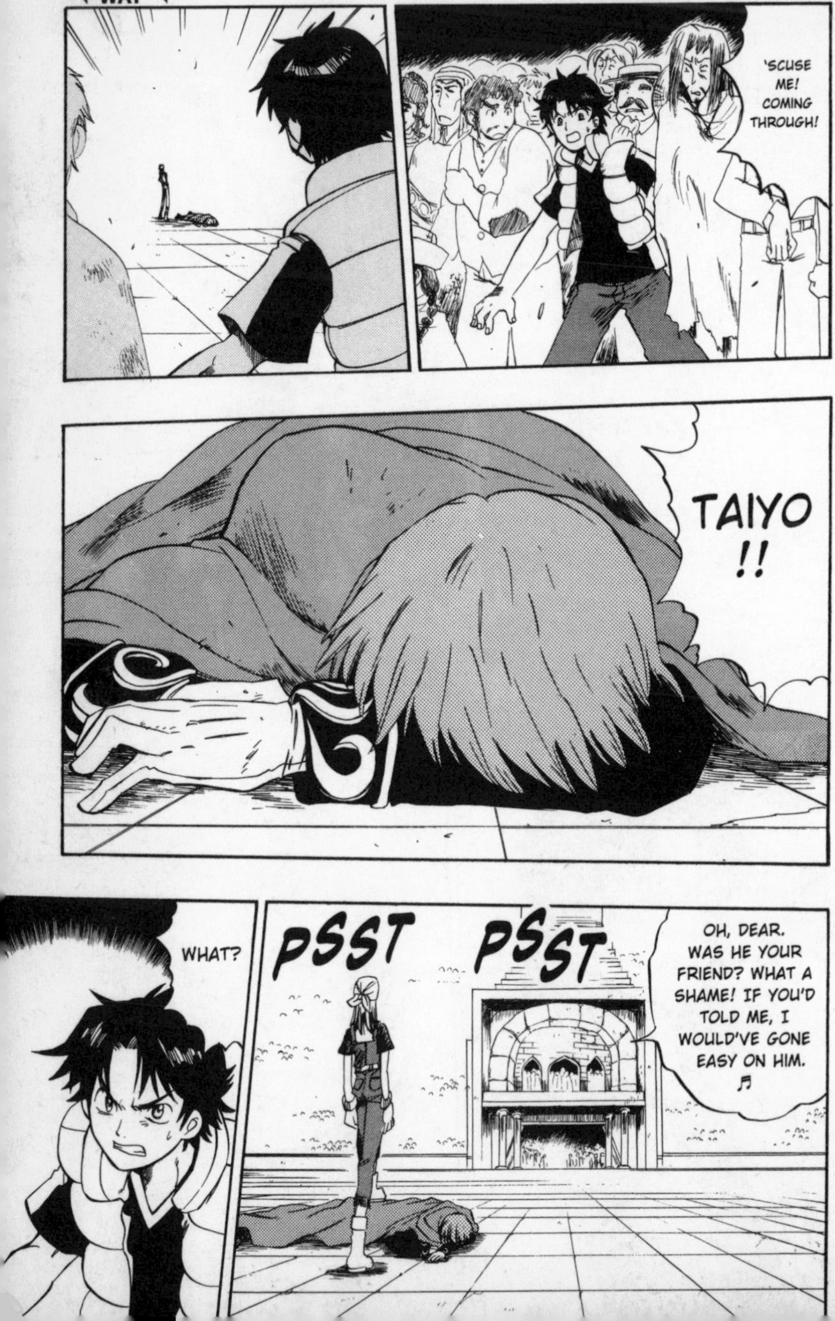
'SCUSE ME! COMING THROUGH!
TAIYO !!
PSST PSST
OH, DEAR. WAS HE YOUR FRIEND? WHAT A SHAME! IF YOU'D TOLD ME, I WOULD'VE GONE EASY ON HIM. ♬
WHAT?

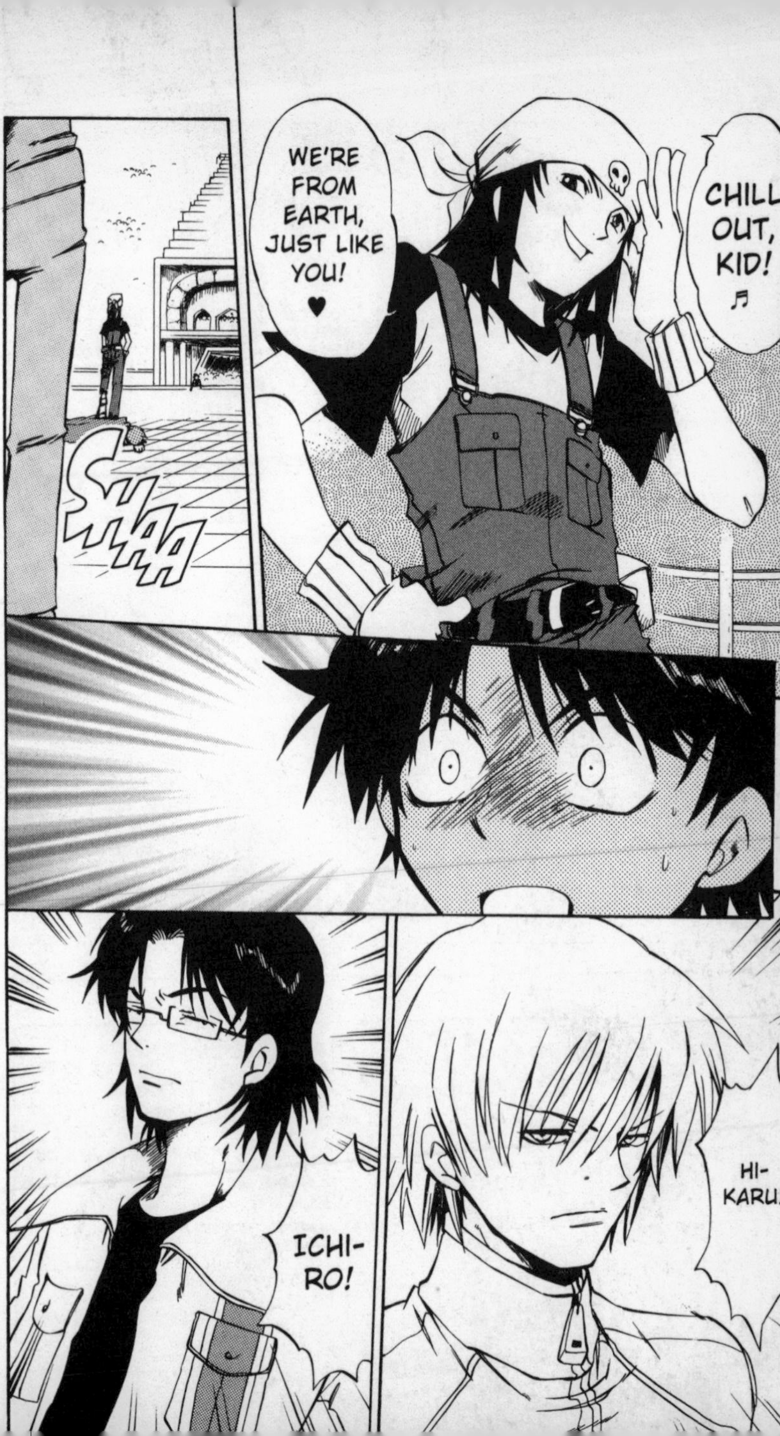
CHILL OUT, KID! ♫
WE'RE FROM EARTH, JUST LIKE YOU! ♥
SHAA
HI-KARU!
ICHI-RO!

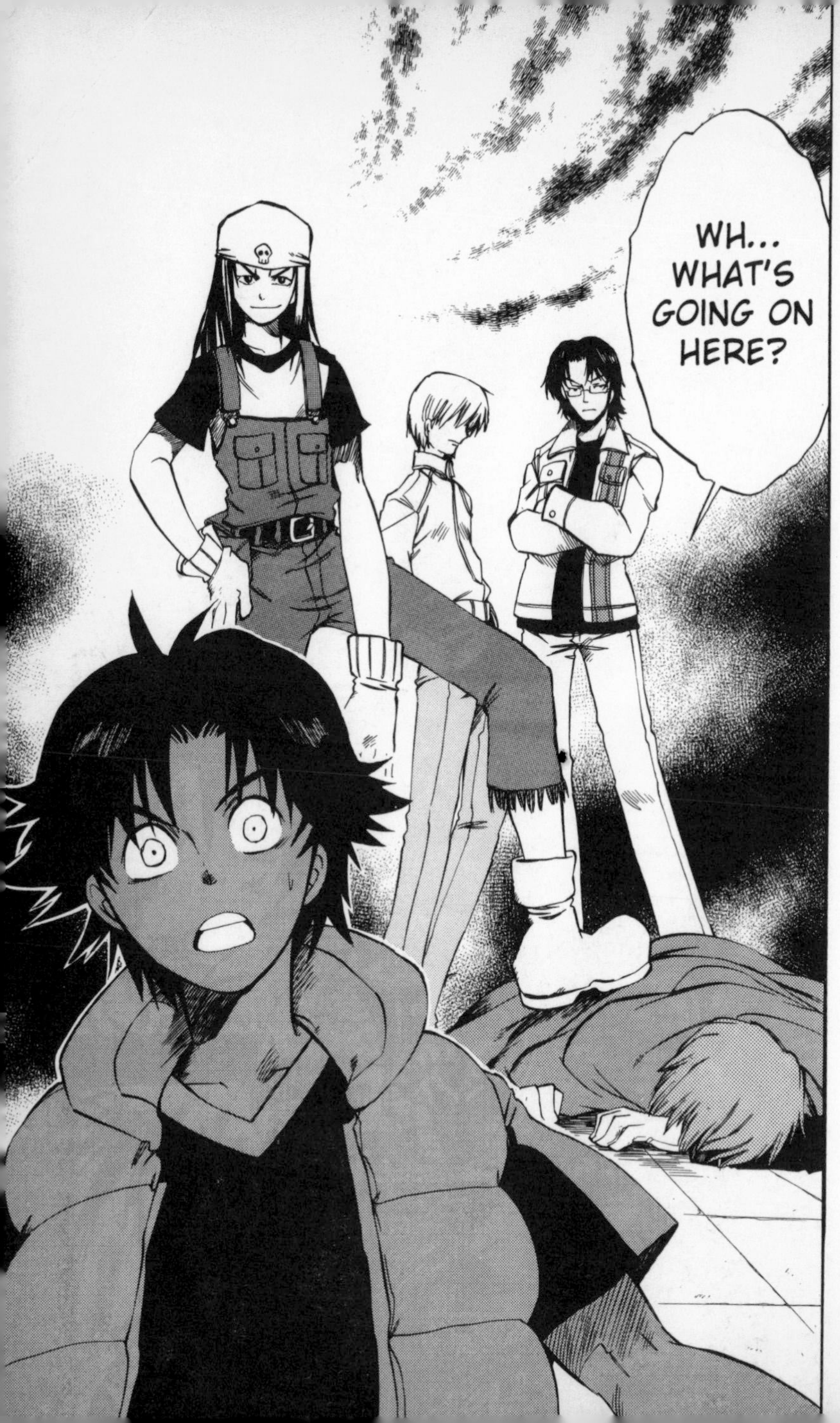
WH... WHAT'S GOING ON HERE?

RI-ON
TRIVIA

ALL ABOUT AGENT I.

OBJECTION!

HYSTERICAL.

BANG

ALWAYS HAS MENACE IN HIS EYES.

HMPH

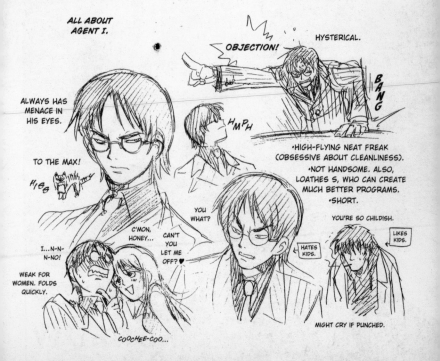

•HIGH-FLYING NEAT FREAK (OBSESSIVE ABOUT CLEANLINESS).
•NOT HANDSOME. ALSO, LOATHES S, WHO CAN CREATE MUCH BETTER PROGRAMS.
•SHORT.

TO THE MAX!

HISS

YOU WHAT?

YOU'RE SO CHILDISH.

C'MON, HONEY... CAN'T YOU LET ME OFF? ♥

LIKES KIDS.

I...N-N-N-NO!

HATES KIDS.

WEAK FOR WOMEN. FOLDS QUICKLY.

MIGHT CRY IF PUNCHED.

COOCHEE-COO...

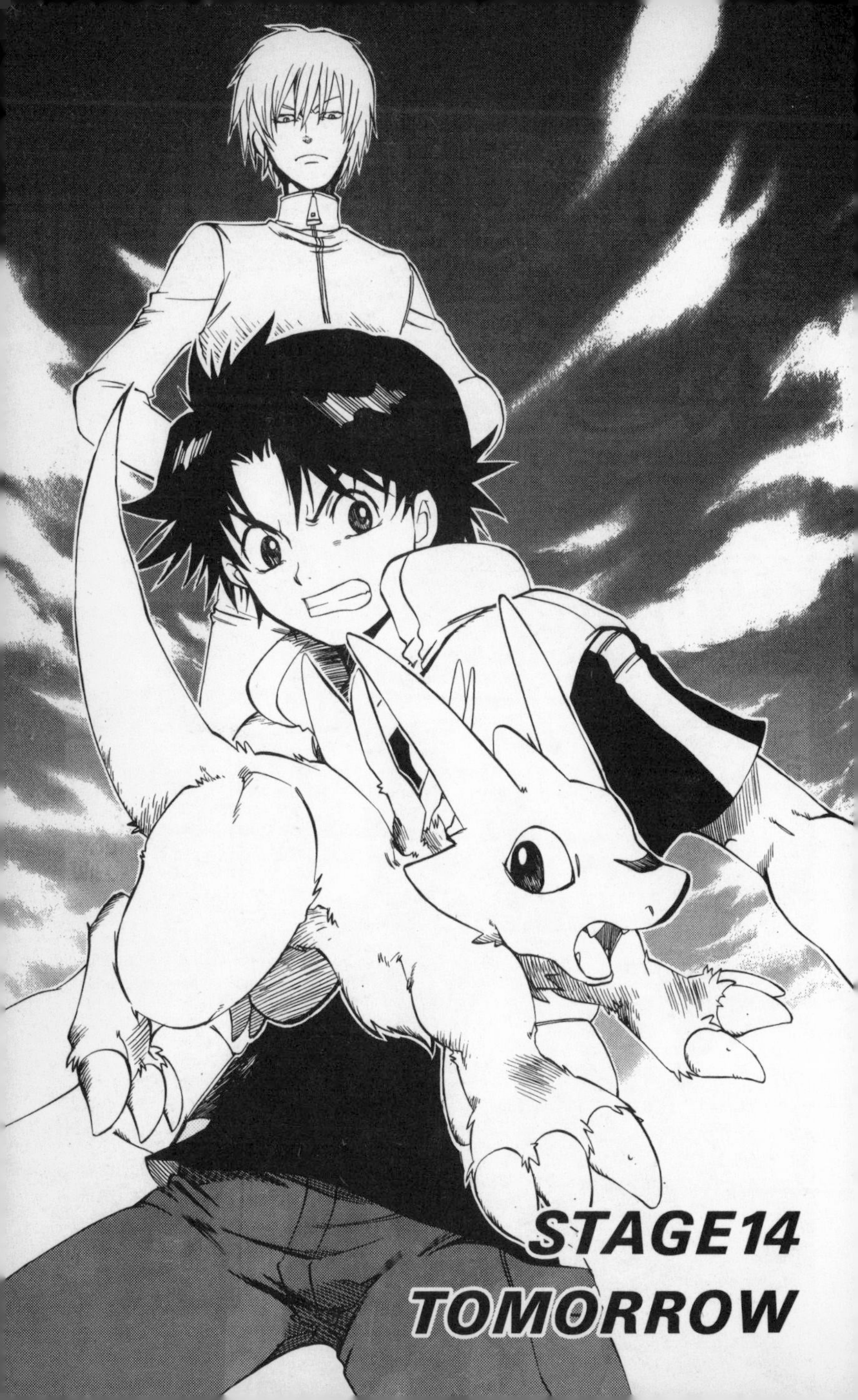
STAGE14
TOMORROW

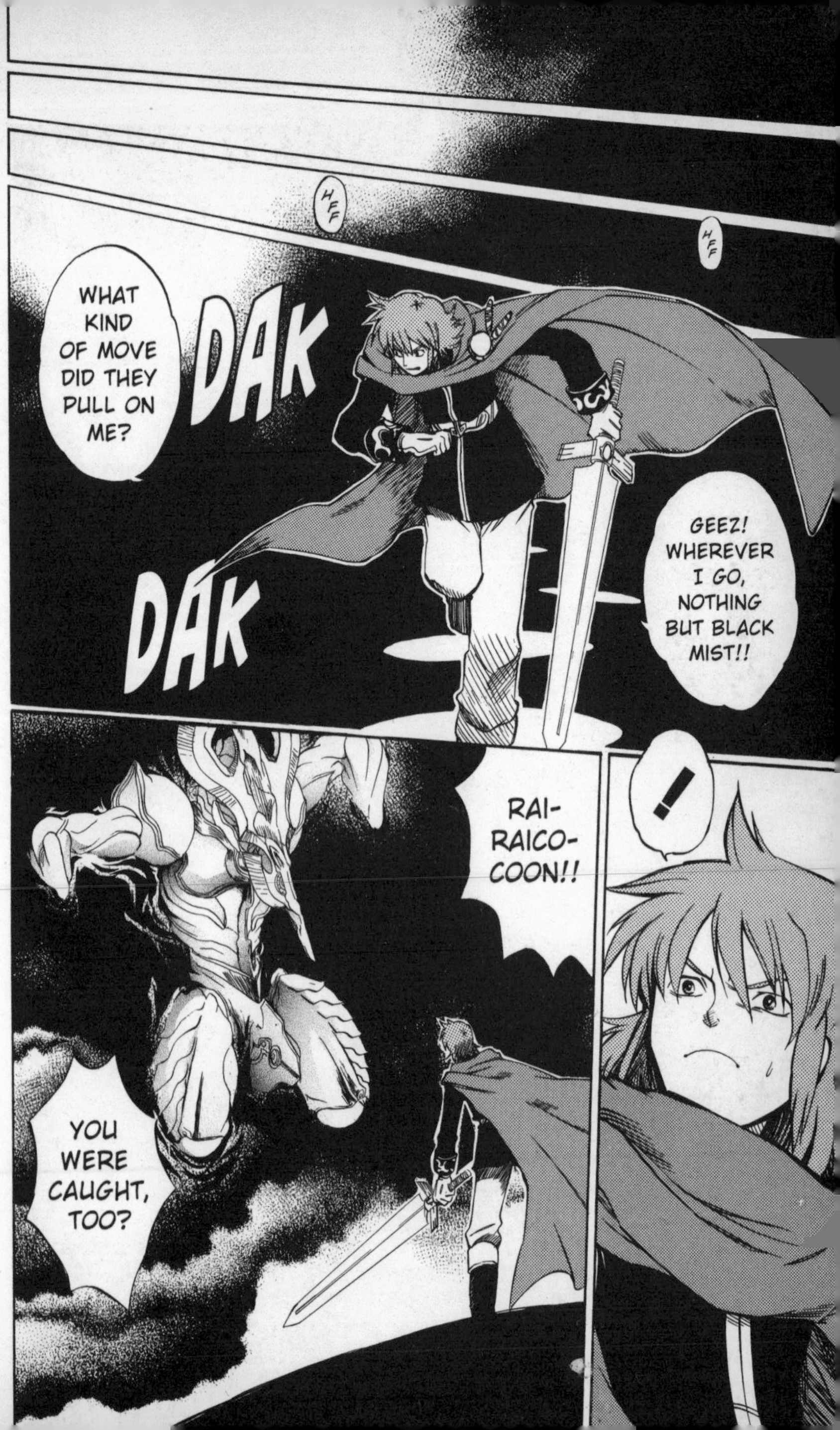
HFF
HFF
GEEZ! WHEREVER I GO, NOTHING BUT BLACK MIST!!
WHAT KIND OF MOVE DID THEY PULL ON ME?
DAK
DAK
!
RAI-RAICO-COON!!
YOU WERE CAUGHT, TOO?

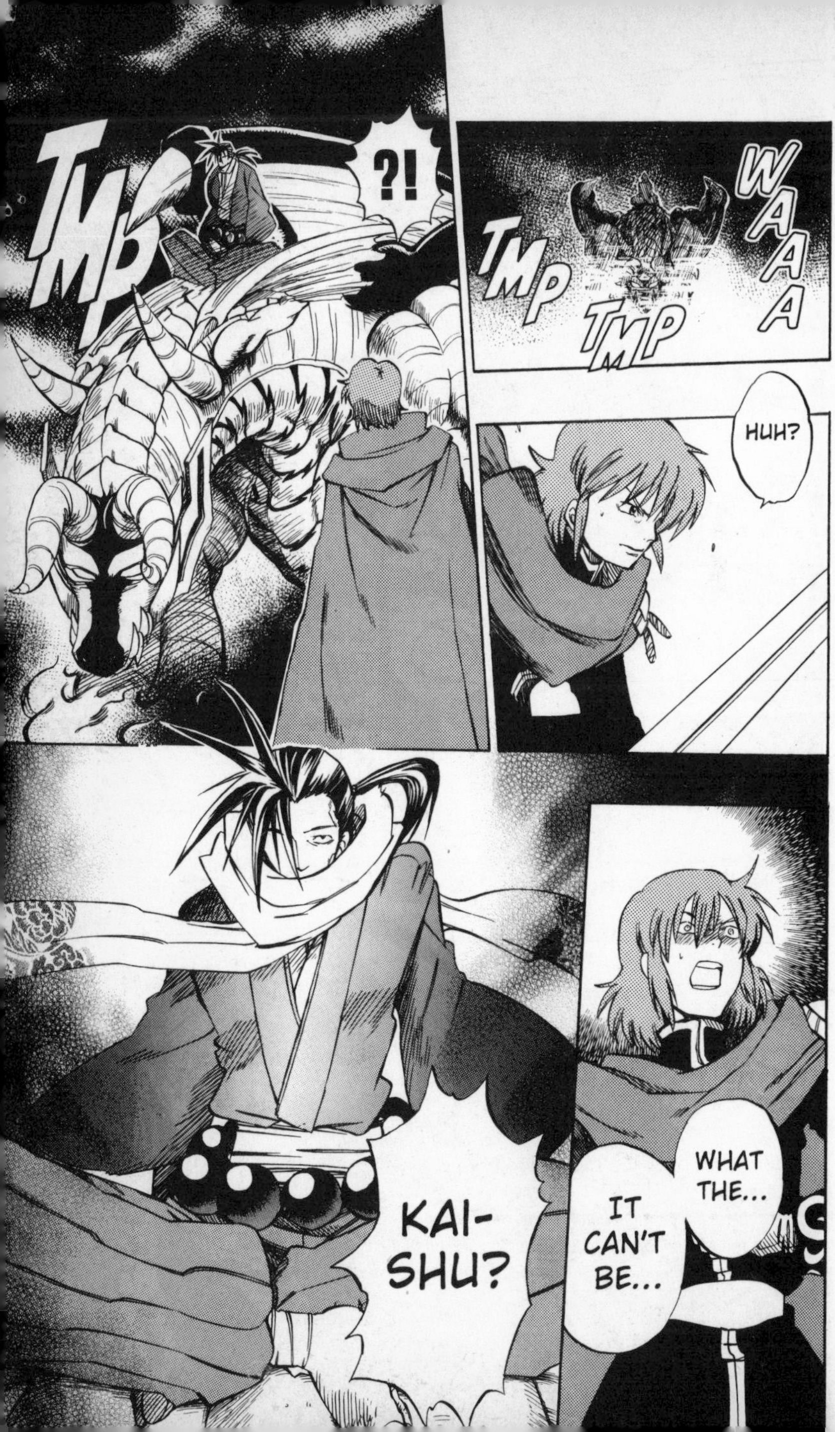
WAAAA
TMP
TMP
HUH?
?!
TMP
WHAT THE...
IT CAN'T BE...
KAI-SHU?

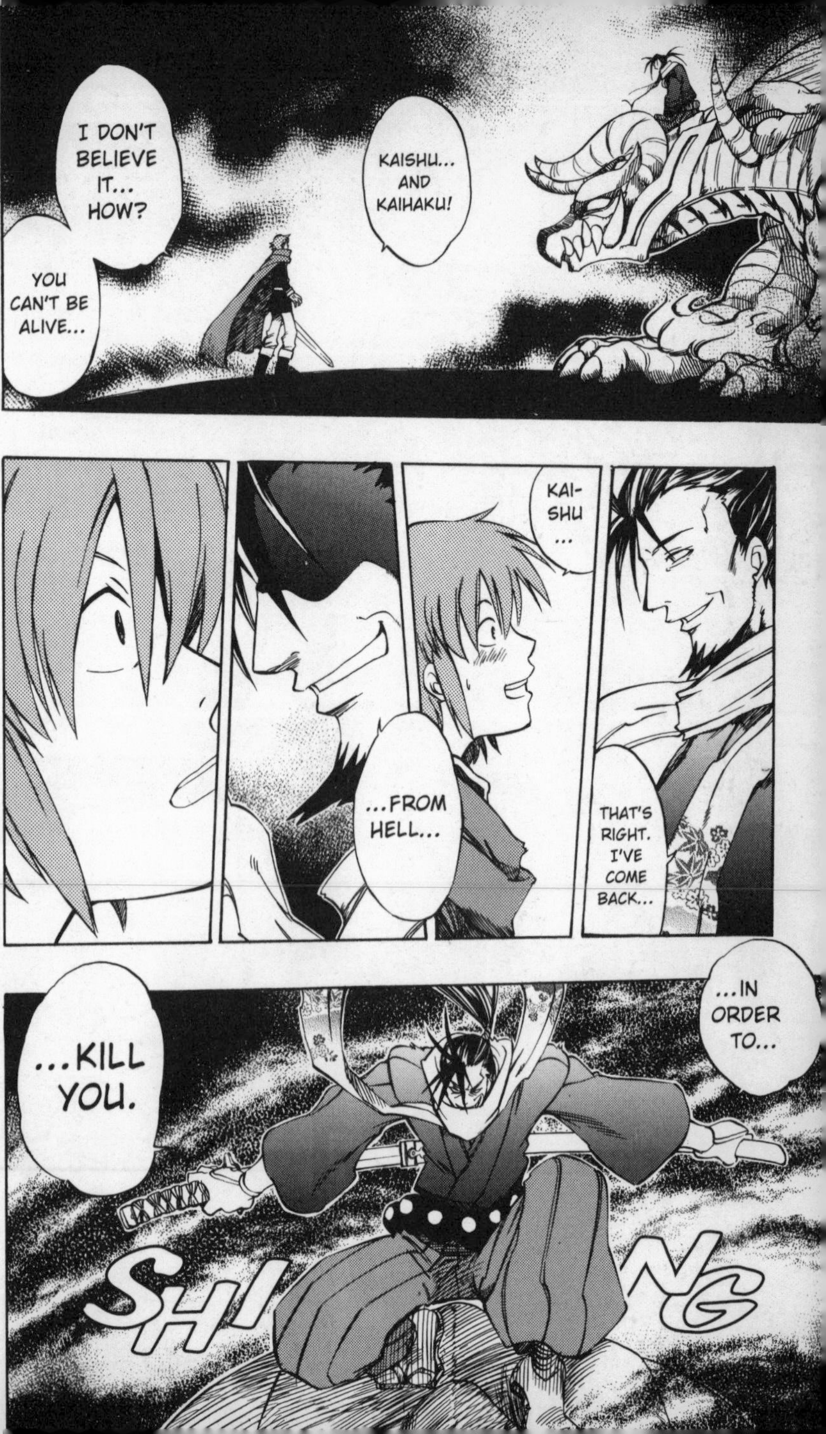
KAISHU... AND KAIHAKU!
I DON'T BELIEVE IT... HOW?
YOU CAN'T BE ALIVE...
THAT'S RIGHT. I'VE COME BACK...
KAI-SHU...
...FROM HELL...
...IN ORDER TO...
...KILL YOU.
SHI NG

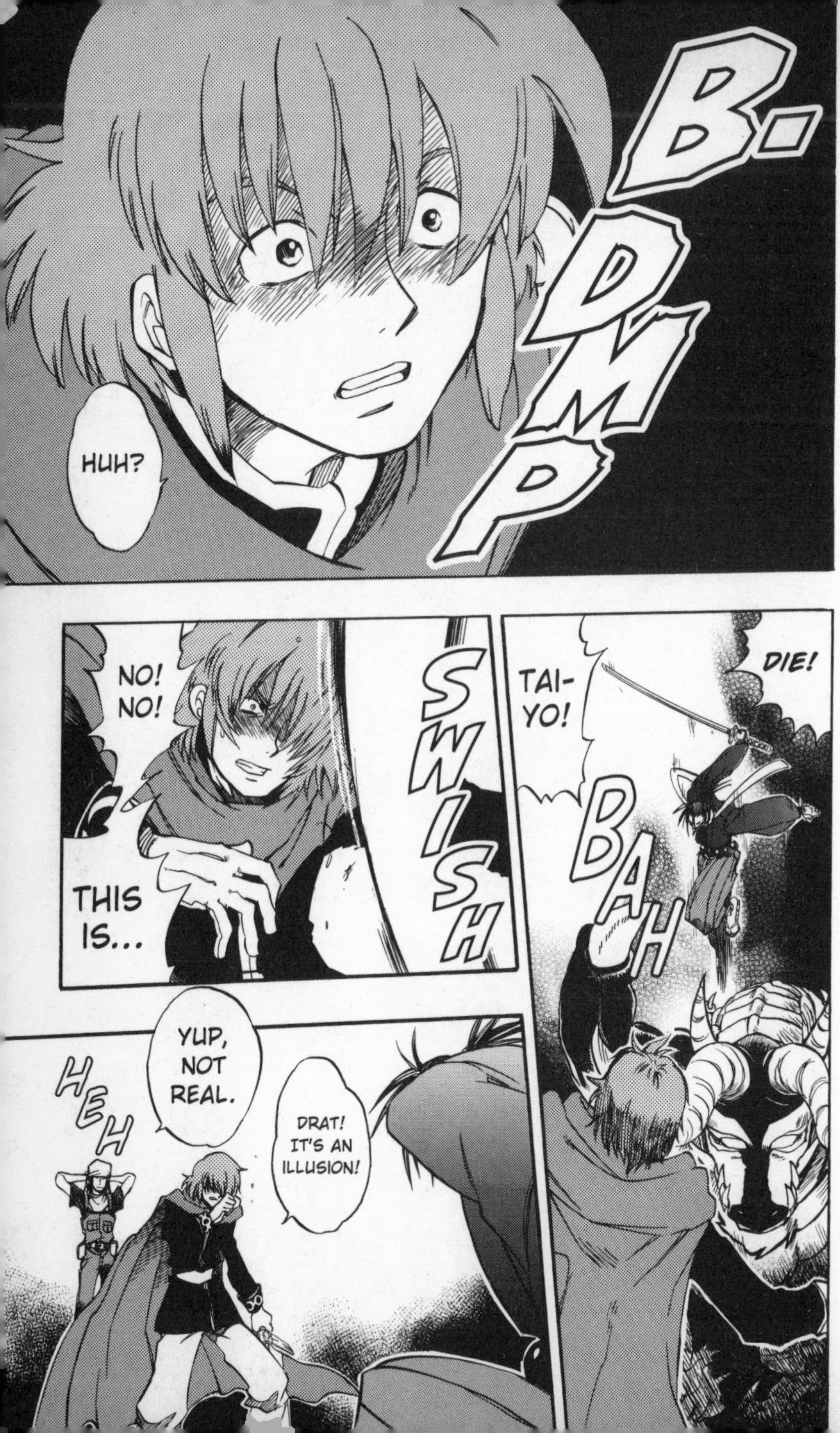
B. DMP
HUH?
DIE!
TAI-YO!
BAH
SWISH
NO! NO!
THIS IS...
DRAT! IT'S AN ILLUSION!
YUP, NOT REAL.
HEH

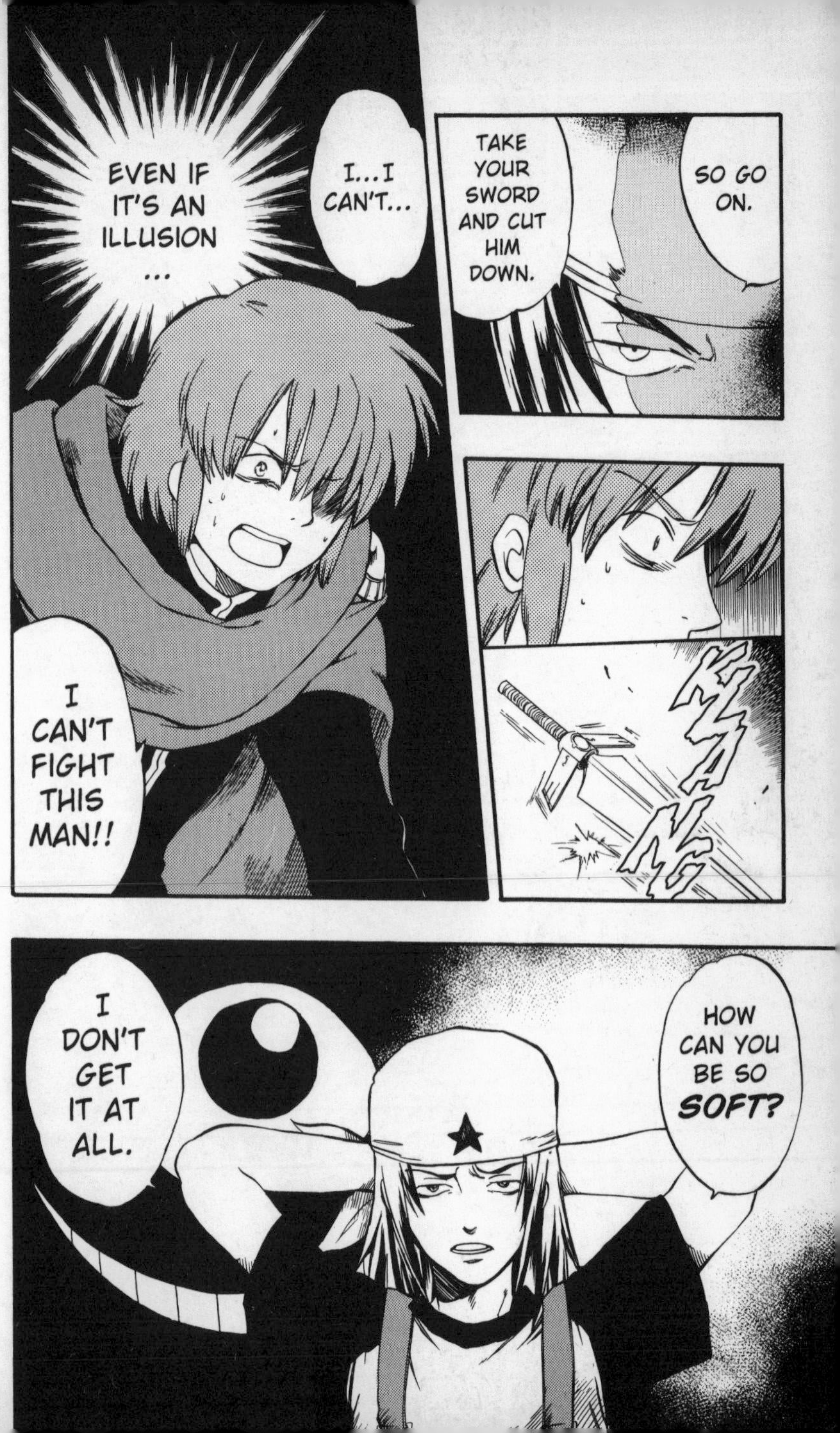
SO GO ON.
TAKE YOUR SWORD AND CUT HIM DOWN.
KLANG
I...I CAN'T...
EVEN IF IT'S AN ILLUSION ...
I CAN'T FIGHT THIS MAN!!
HOW CAN YOU BE SO SOFT?
I DON'T GET IT AT ALL.

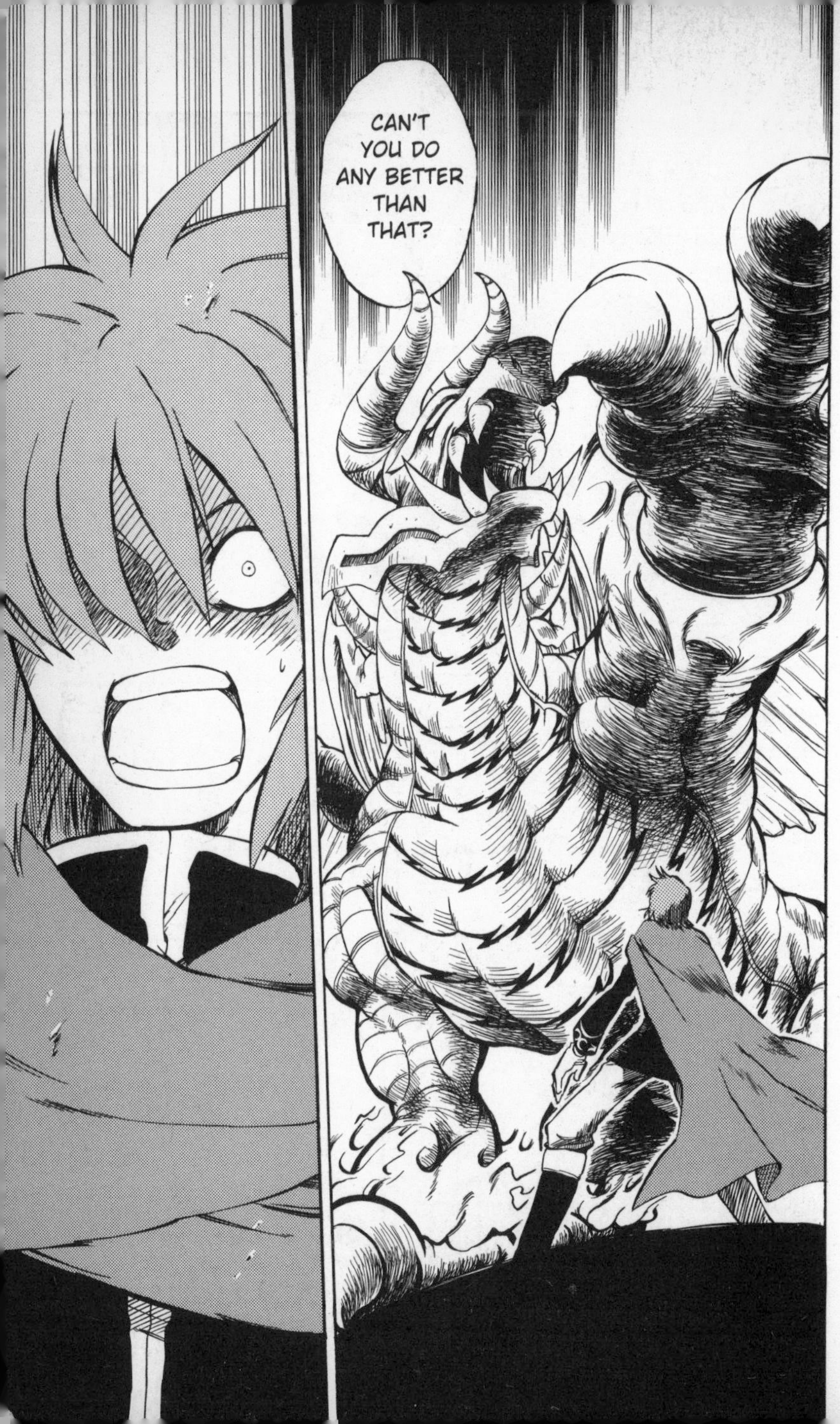
CAN'T YOU DO ANY BETTER THAN THAT?

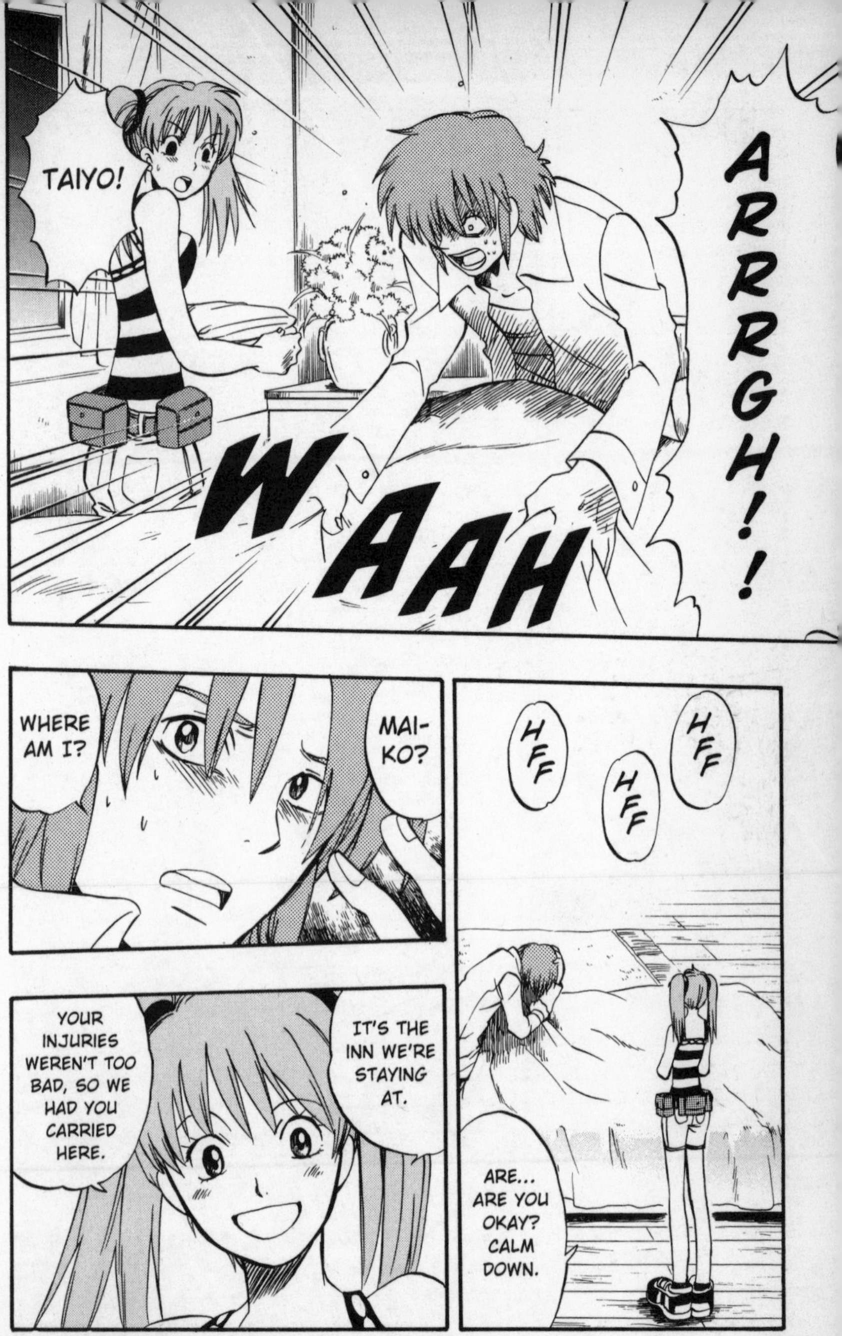
ARRRGH!!
WAAH
TAIYO!
HFF
HFF
HFF
ARE... ARE YOU OKAY? CALM DOWN.
MAI-KO?
WHERE AM I?
IT'S THE INN WE'RE STAYING AT.
YOUR INJURIES WEREN'T TOO BAD, SO WE HAD YOU CARRIED HERE.

READ THIS WAY

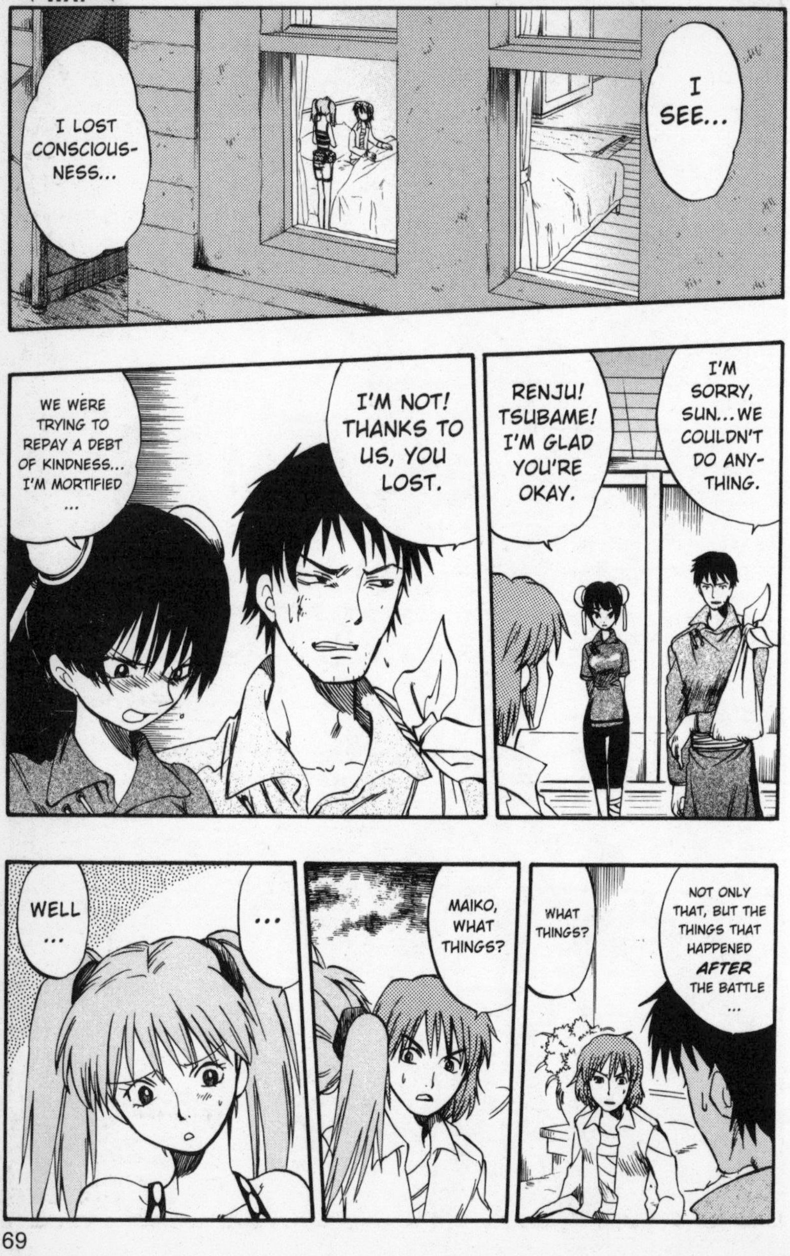
I SEE...
I LOST CONSCIOUS-NESS...
I'M SORRY, SUN...WE COULDN'T DO ANY-THING.
RENJU! TSUBAME! I'M GLAD YOU'RE OKAY.
I'M NOT! THANKS TO US, YOU LOST.
WE WERE TRYING TO REPAY A DEBT OF KINDNESS... I'M MORTIFIED ...
NOT ONLY THAT, BUT THE THINGS THAT HAPPENED AFTER THE BATTLE ...
WHAT THINGS?
MAIKO, WHAT THINGS?
...
WELL ...

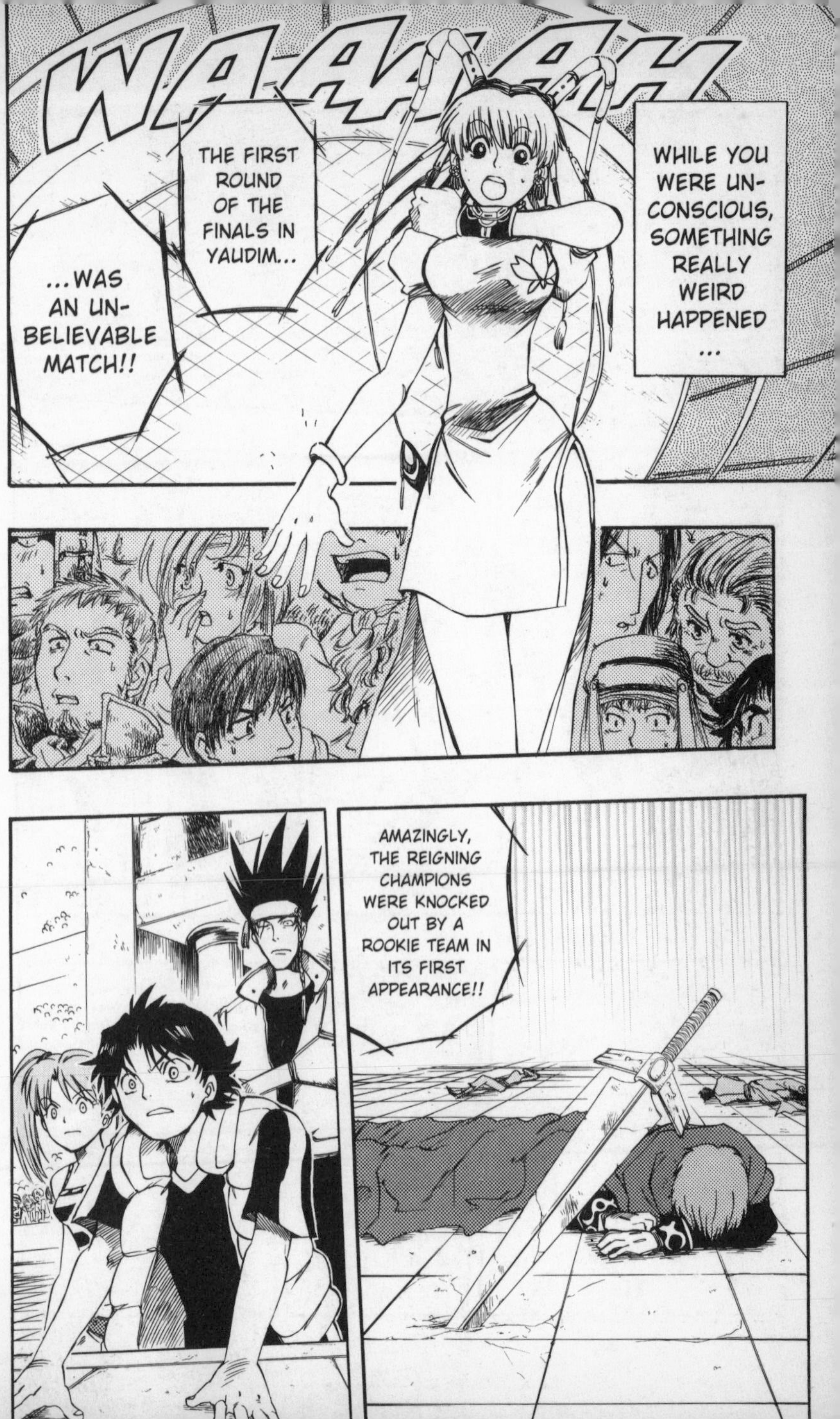
WAAAAH
WHILE YOU WERE UN-CONSCIOUS, SOMETHING REALLY WEIRD HAPPENED ...
THE FIRST ROUND OF THE FINALS IN YAUDIM...
...WAS AN UN-BELIEVABLE MATCH!!
AMAZINGLY, THE REIGNING CHAMPIONS WERE KNOCKED OUT BY A ROOKIE TEAM IN ITS FIRST APPEARANCE!!

READ THIS WAY

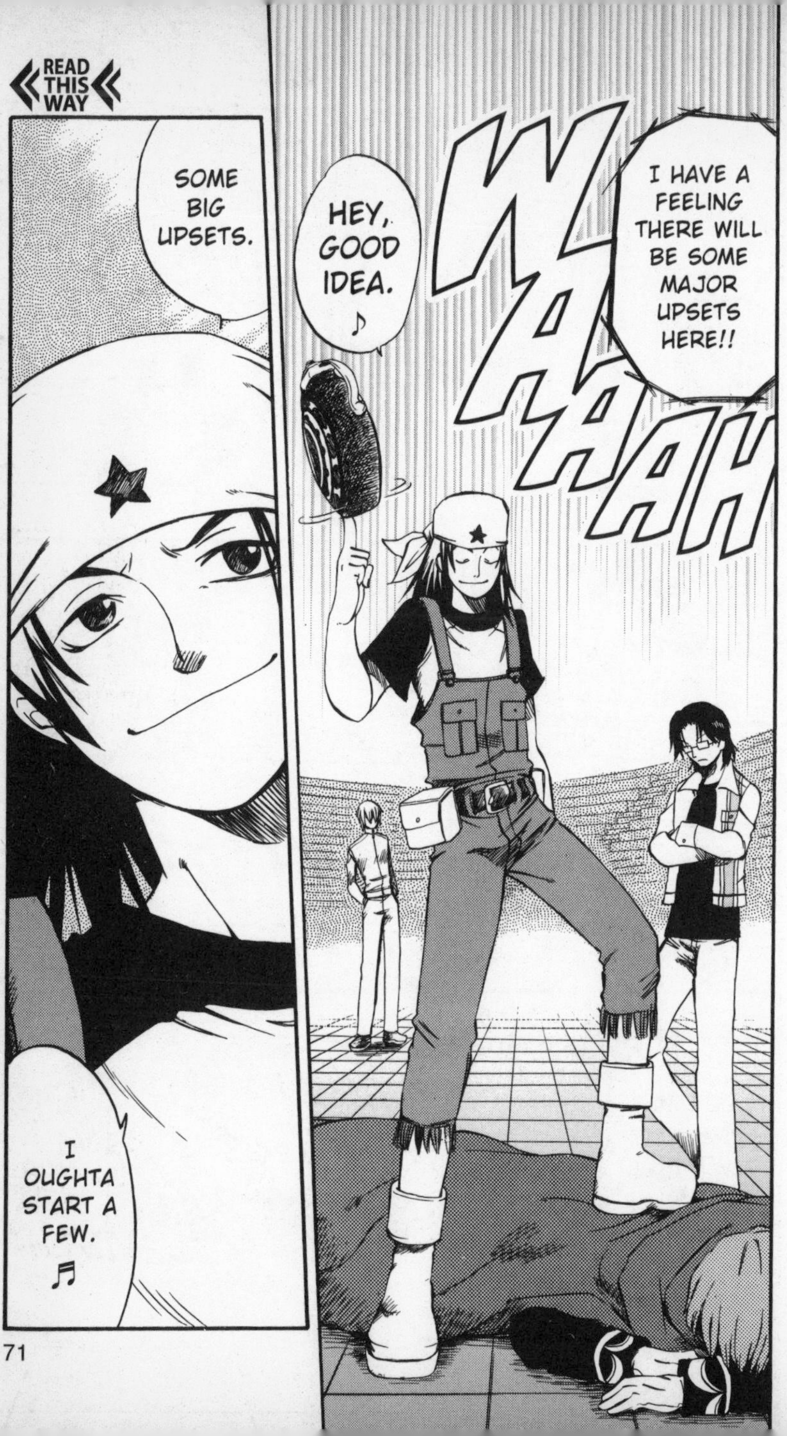
I HAVE A FEELING THERE WILL BE SOME MAJOR UPSETS HERE!!
WAHAHAH
HEY, GOOD IDEA. ♪
SOME BIG UPSETS.
I OUGHTA START A FEW. ♬

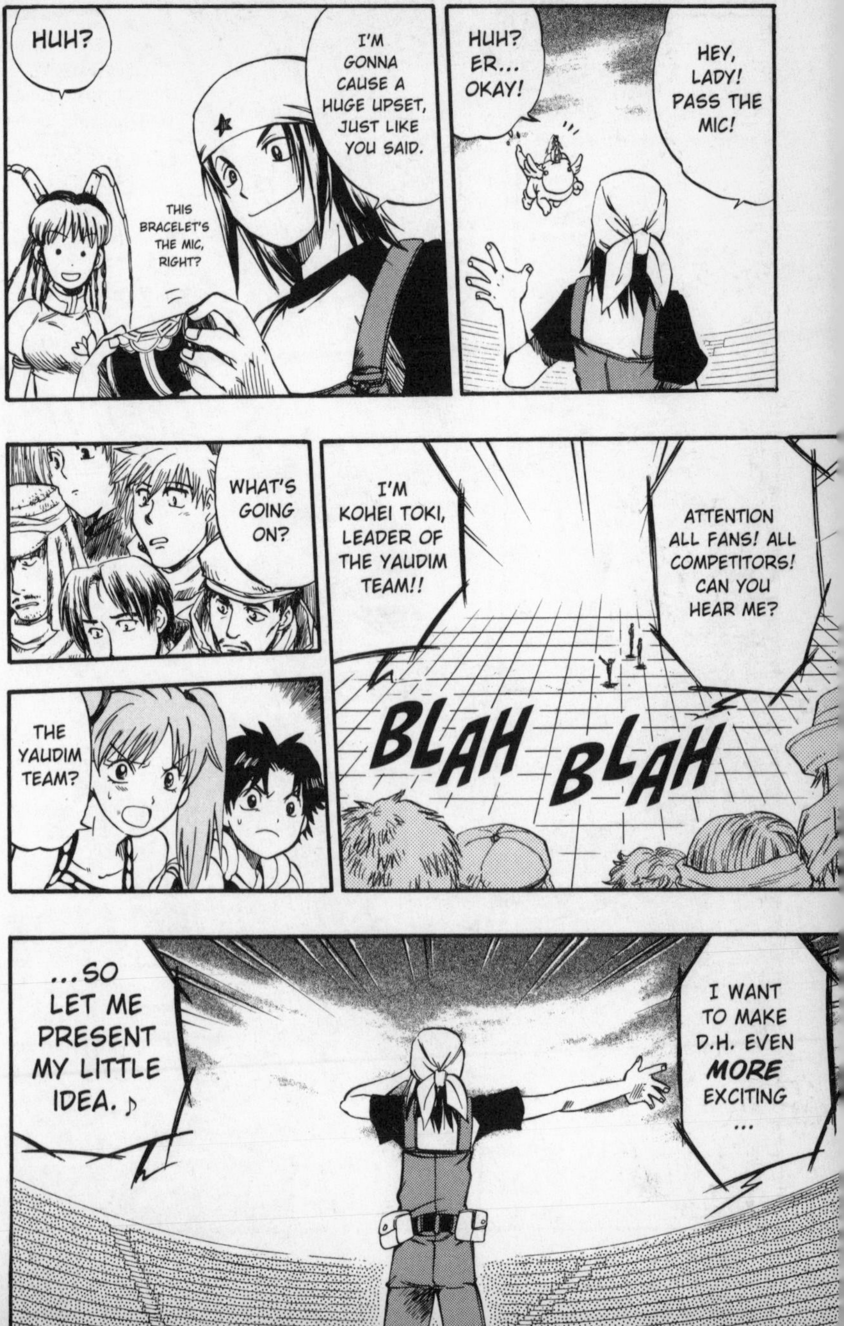
HEY, LADY! PASS THE MIC!
HUH? ER... OKAY!
I'M GONNA CAUSE A HUGE UPSET, JUST LIKE YOU SAID.
HUH?
THIS BRACELET'S THE MIC, RIGHT?
ATTENTION ALL FANS! ALL COMPETITORS! CAN YOU HEAR ME?
I'M KOHEI TOKI, LEADER OF THE YAUDIM TEAM!!
BLAH BLAH
WHAT'S GOING ON?
THE YAUDIM TEAM?
I WANT TO MAKE D.H. EVEN MORE EXCITING ...
...SO LET ME PRESENT MY LITTLE IDEA. ♪

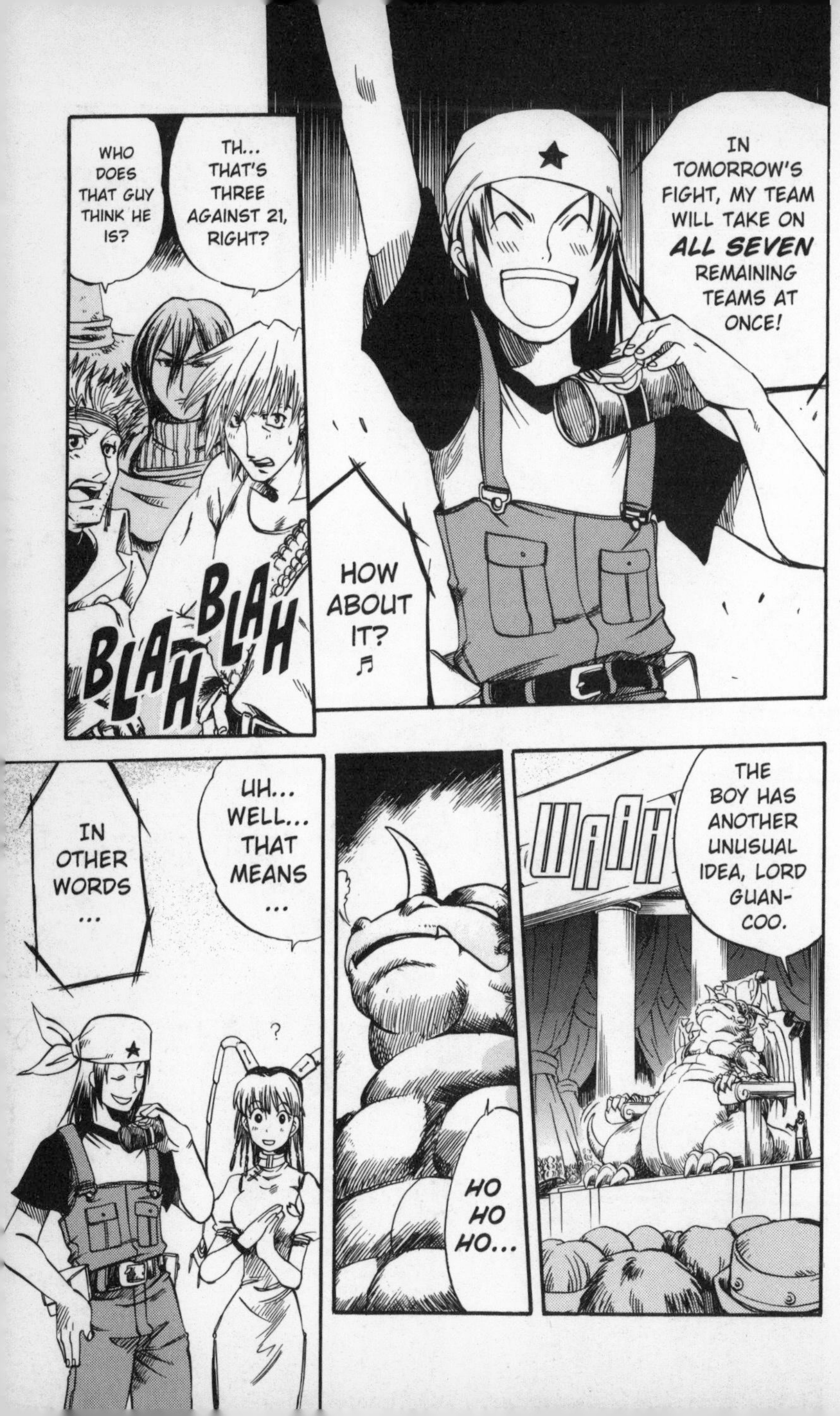
IN TOMORROW'S FIGHT, MY TEAM WILL TAKE ON **ALL SEVEN** REMAINING TEAMS AT ONCE!
HOW ABOUT IT? ♬
TH... THAT'S THREE AGAINST 21, RIGHT?
WHO DOES THAT GUY THINK HE IS?
BLAH BLAH BLAH
WAAAH
THE BOY HAS ANOTHER UNUSUAL IDEA, LORD GUAN-COO.
HO HO HO...
UH... WELL... THAT MEANS...
IN OTHER WORDS...
?

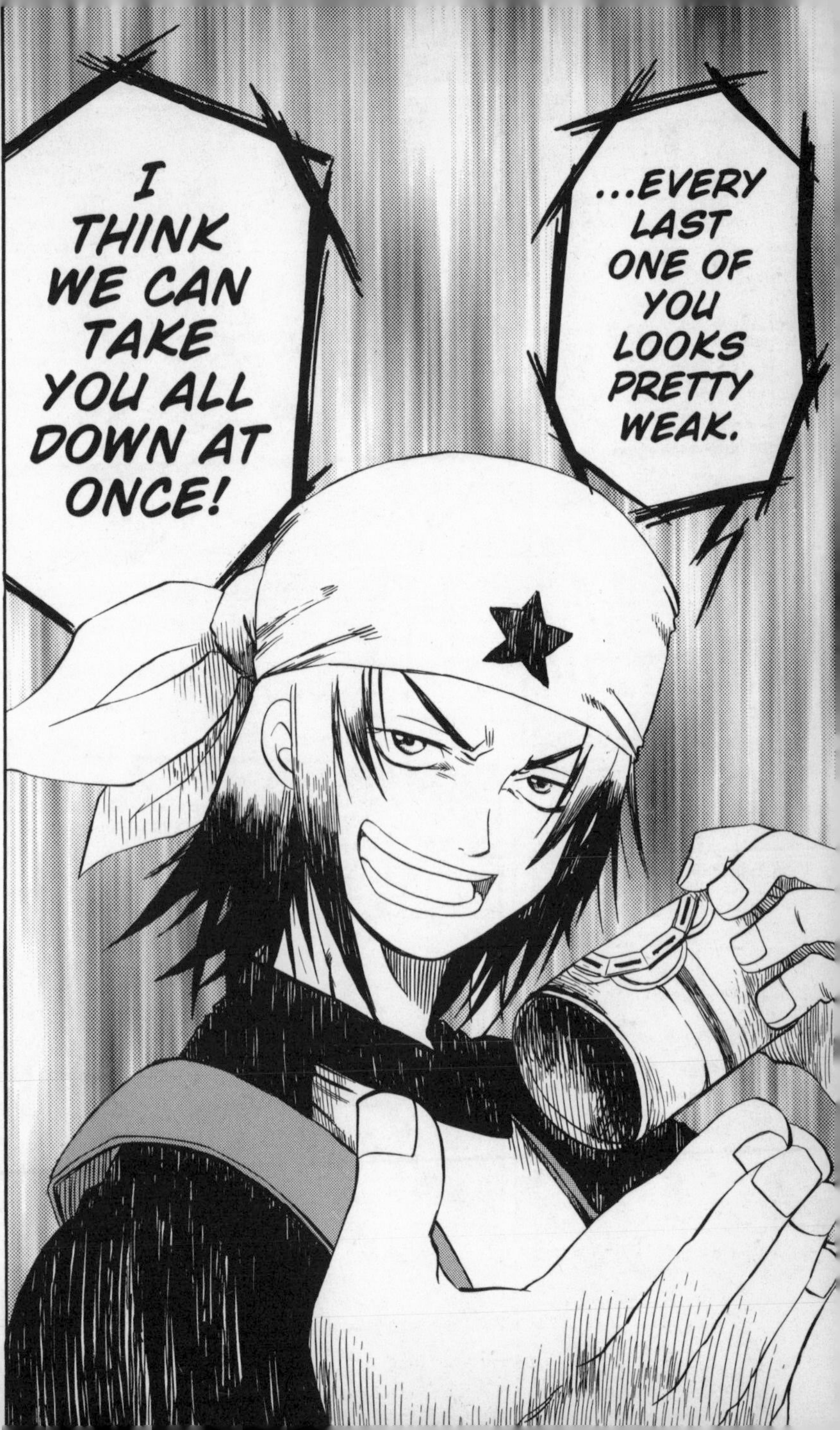
...EVERY LAST ONE OF YOU LOOKS PRETTY WEAK.
I THINK WE CAN TAKE YOU ALL DOWN AT ONCE!

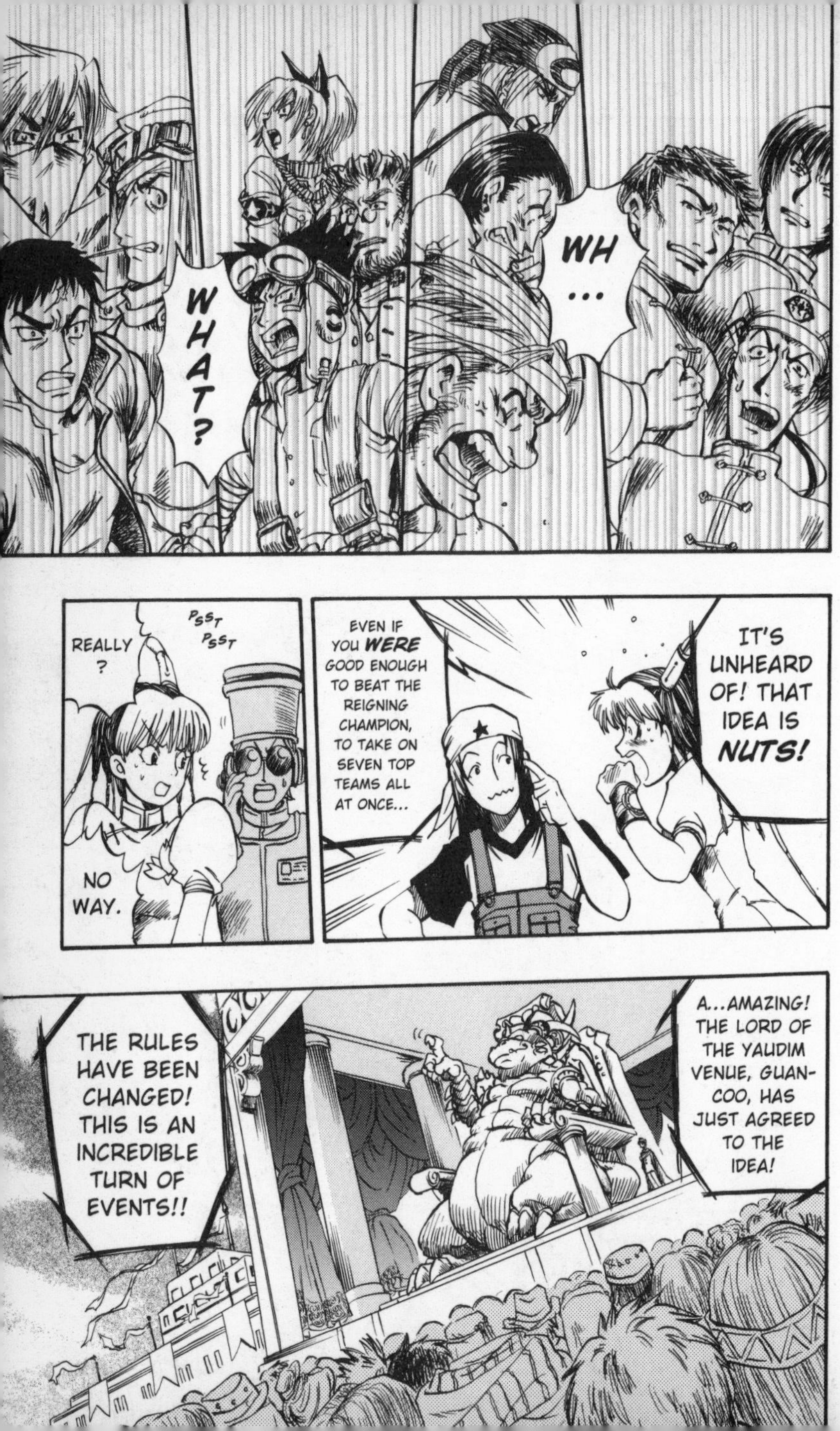
WH...
WHAT?
IT'S UNHEARD OF! THAT IDEA IS NUTS!
EVEN IF YOU WERE GOOD ENOUGH TO BEAT THE REIGNING CHAMPION, TO TAKE ON SEVEN TOP TEAMS ALL AT ONCE...
PSST PSST
REALLY?
NO WAY.
A...AMAZING! THE LORD OF THE YAUDIM VENUE, GUAN-COO, HAS JUST AGREED TO THE IDEA!
THE RULES HAVE BEEN CHANGED! THIS IS AN INCREDIBLE TURN OF EVENTS!!

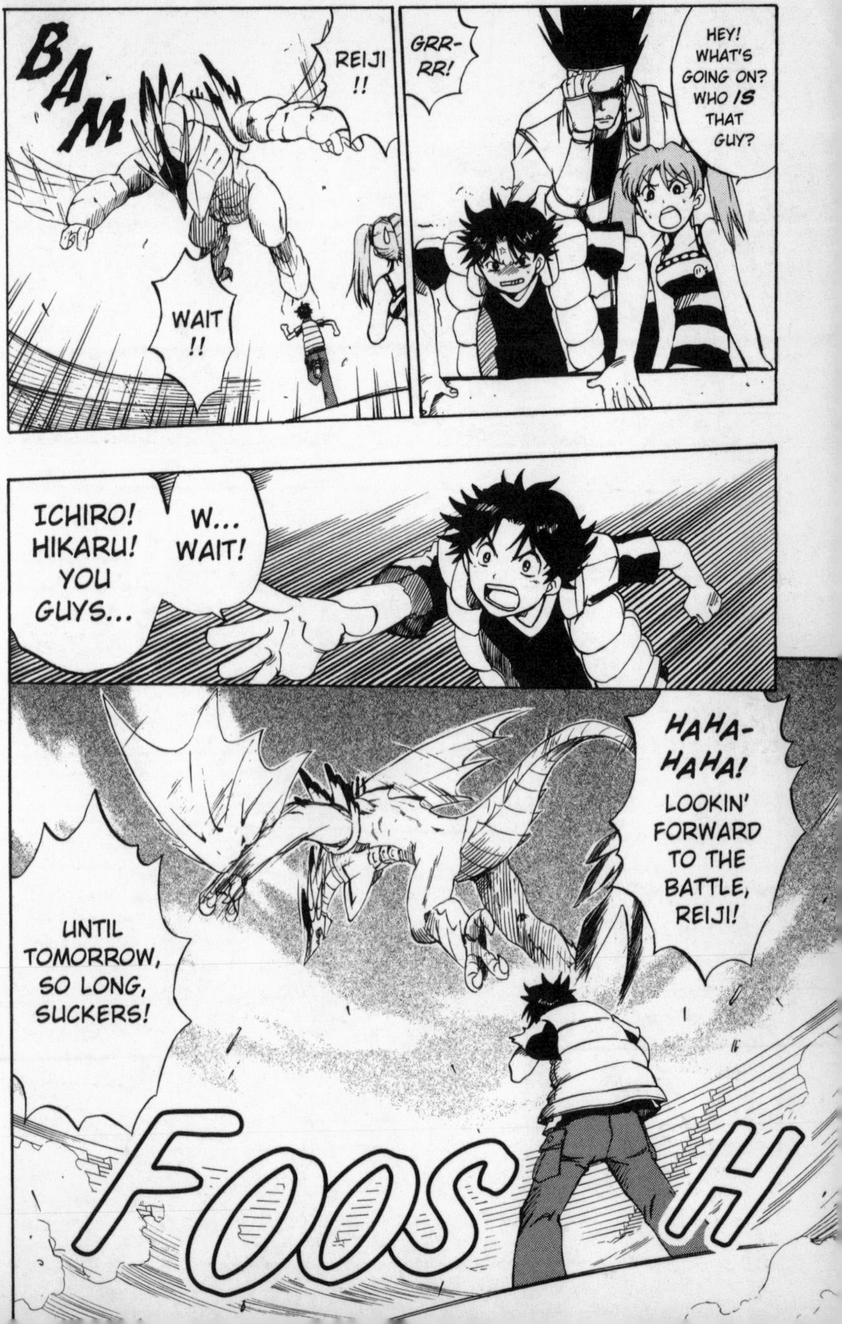
HEY! WHAT'S GOING ON? WHO *IS* THAT GUY?
GRR-RR!
REIJI !!
BAM
WAIT !!
W... WAIT!
ICHIRO! HIKARU! YOU GUYS...
HAHA-HAHA! LOOKIN' FORWARD TO THE BATTLE, REIJI!
UNTIL TOMORROW, SO LONG, SUCKERS!
FOOSH

READ THIS WAY

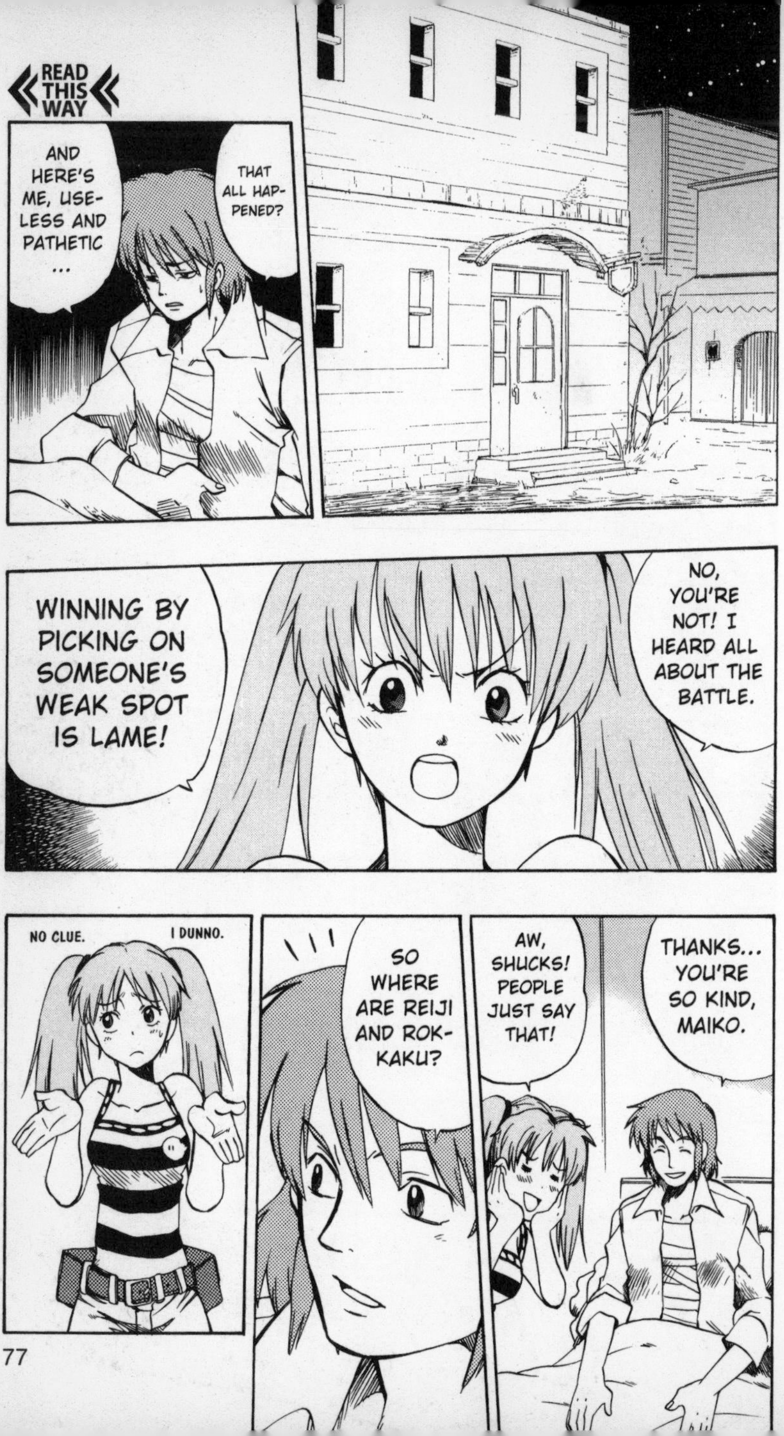
THAT ALL HAPPENED?
AND HERE'S ME, USELESS AND PATHETIC...
NO, YOU'RE NOT! I HEARD ALL ABOUT THE BATTLE.
WINNING BY PICKING ON SOMEONE'S WEAK SPOT IS LAME!
THANKS... YOU'RE SO KIND, MAIKO.
AW, SHUCKS! PEOPLE JUST SAY THAT!
SO WHERE ARE REIJI AND ROKKAKU?
I DUNNO.
NO CLUE.

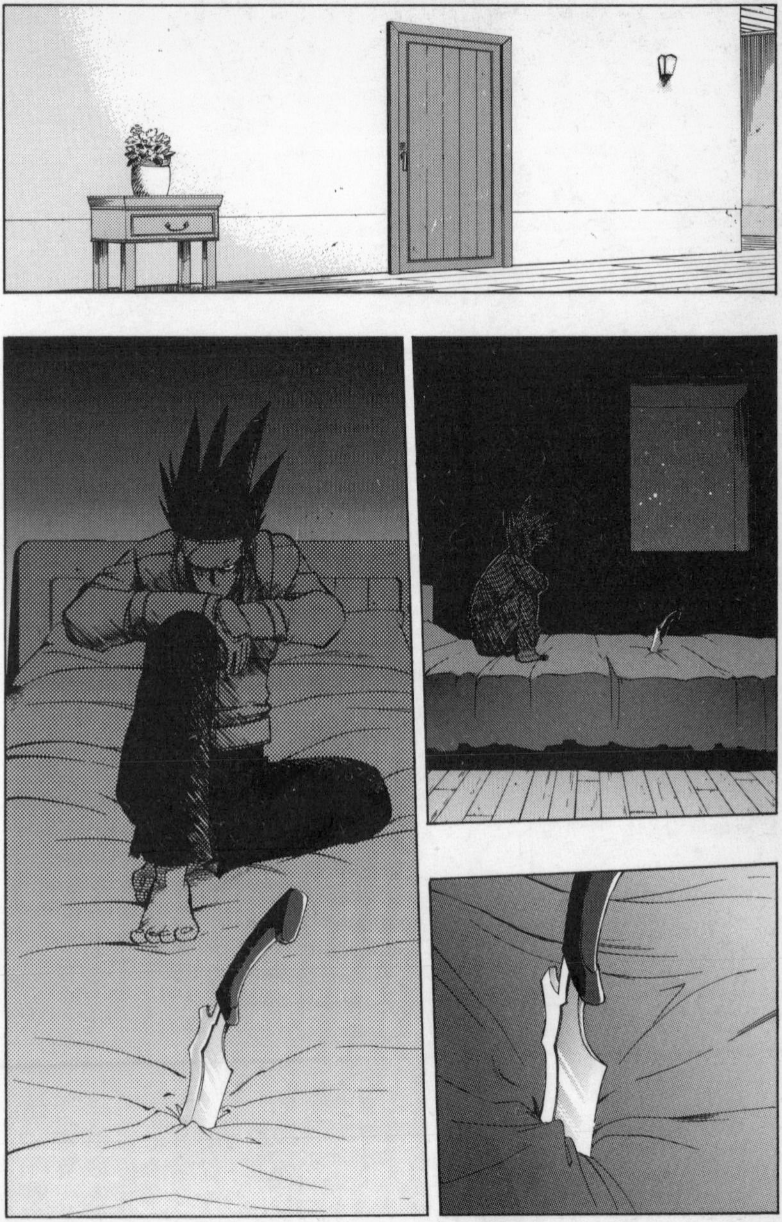

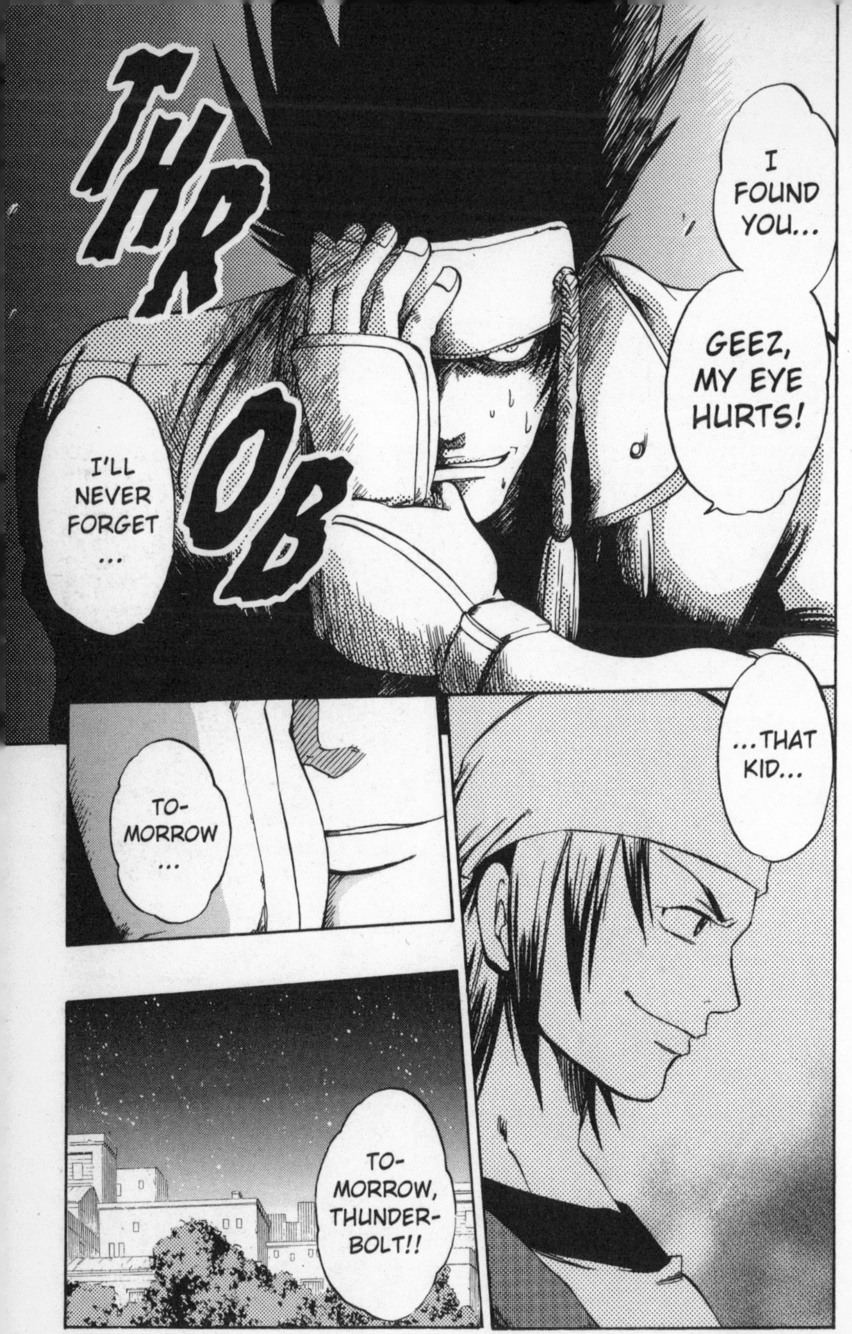
I FOUND YOU...
GEEZ, MY EYE HURTS!
THROB
I'LL NEVER FORGET...
...THAT KID...
TO-MORROW...
TO-MORROW, THUNDER-BOLT!!

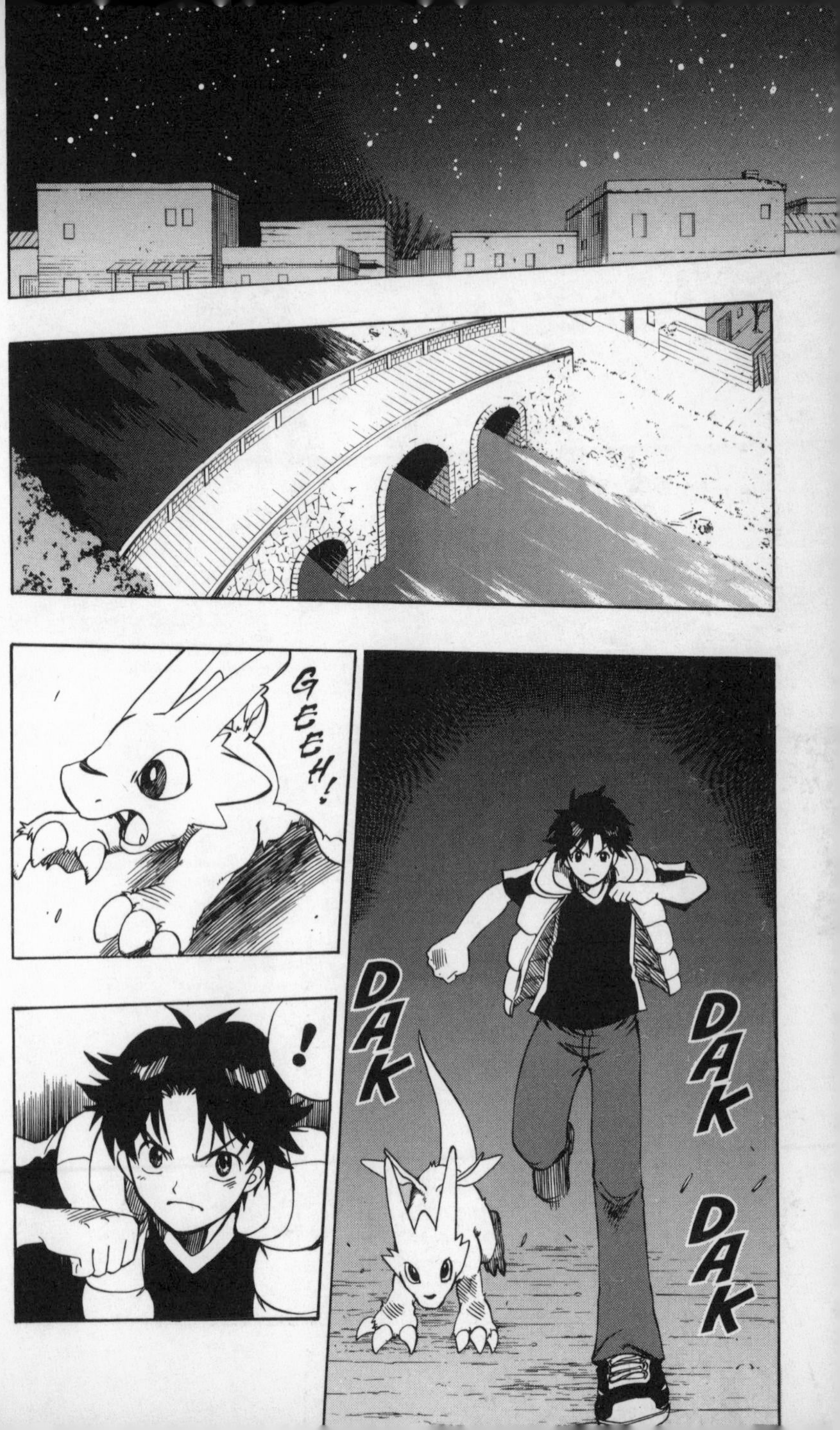
DAK
DAK
DAK
GECCH!
!

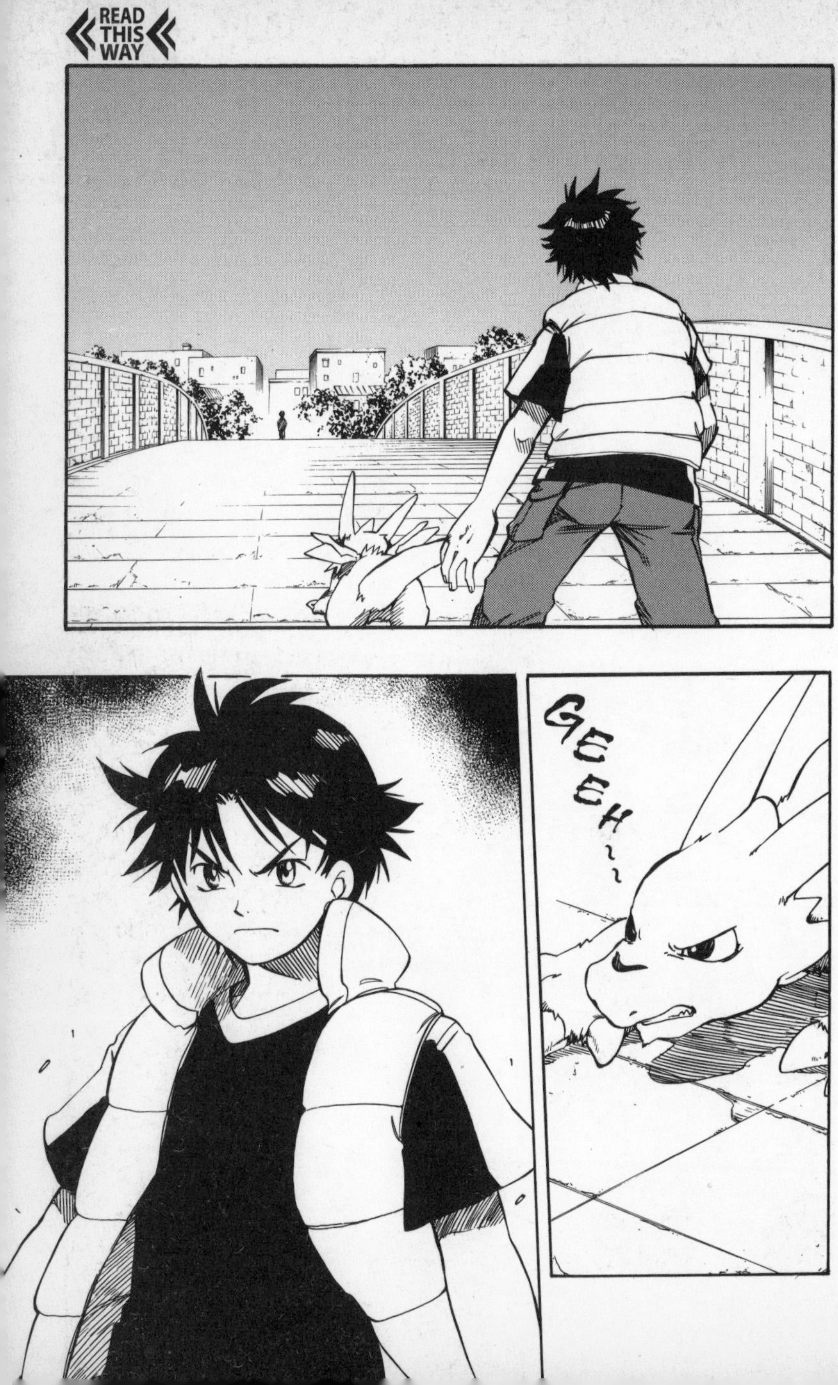
READ THIS WAY
GEEH~~

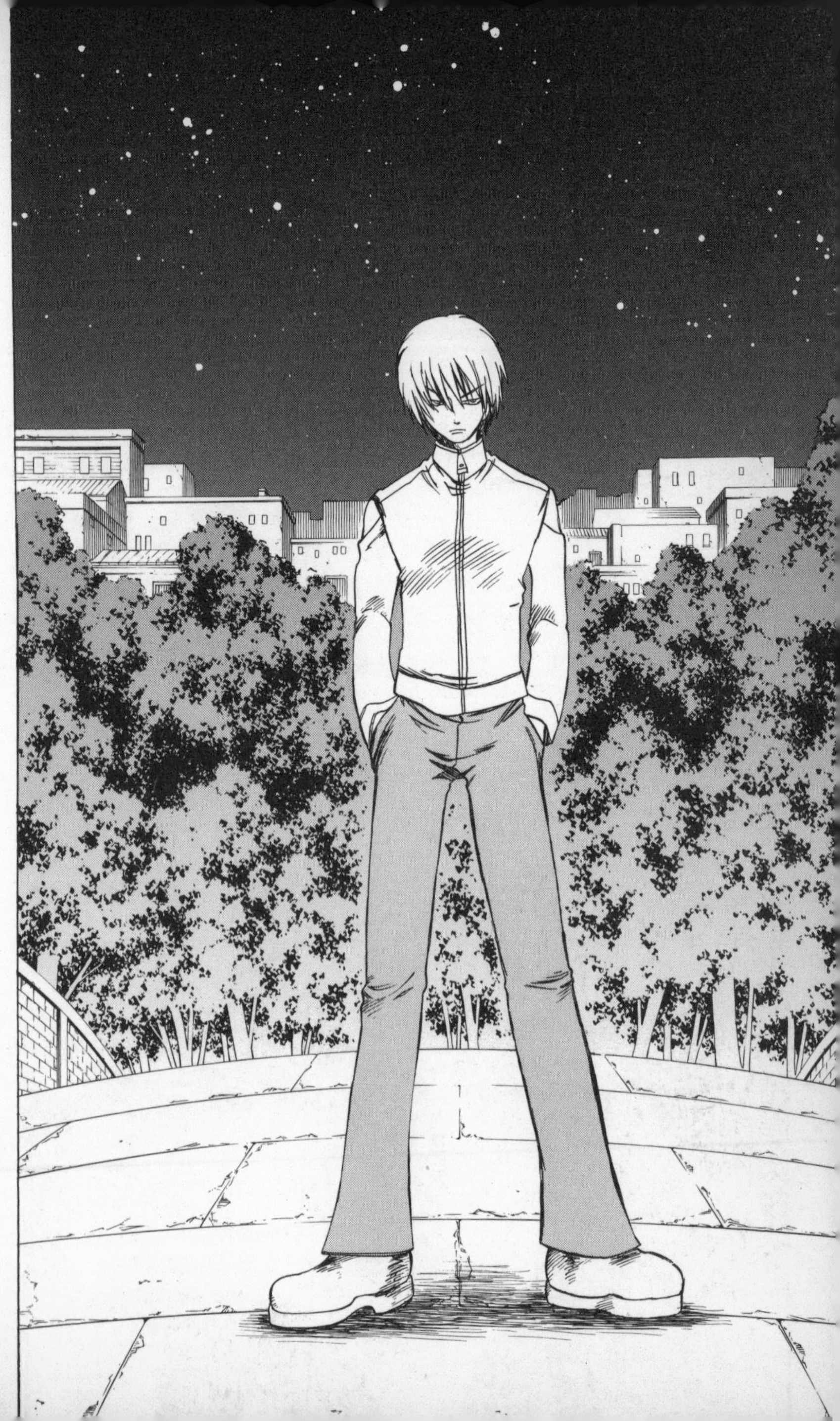

READ THIS WAY

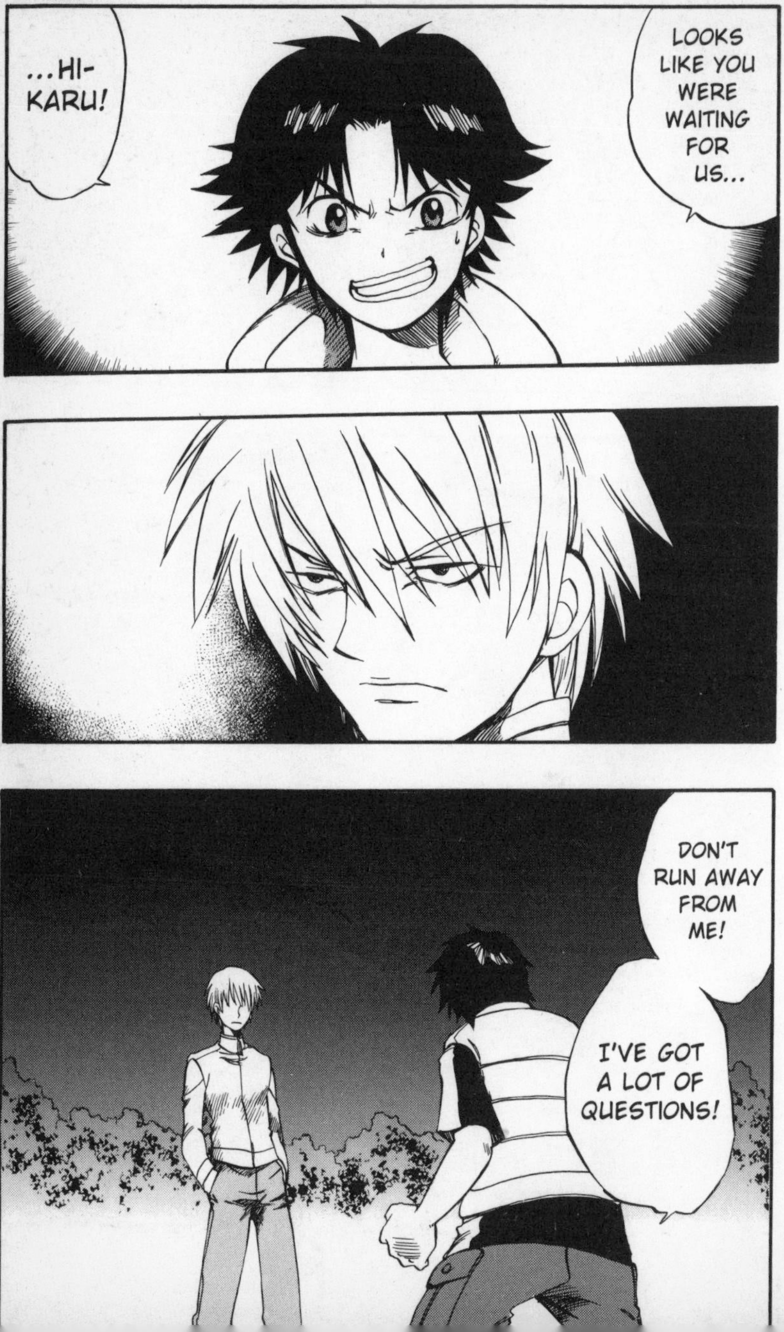
LOOKS LIKE YOU WERE WAITING FOR US...
...HI-KARU!
DON'T RUN AWAY FROM ME!
I'VE GOT A LOT OF QUESTIONS!

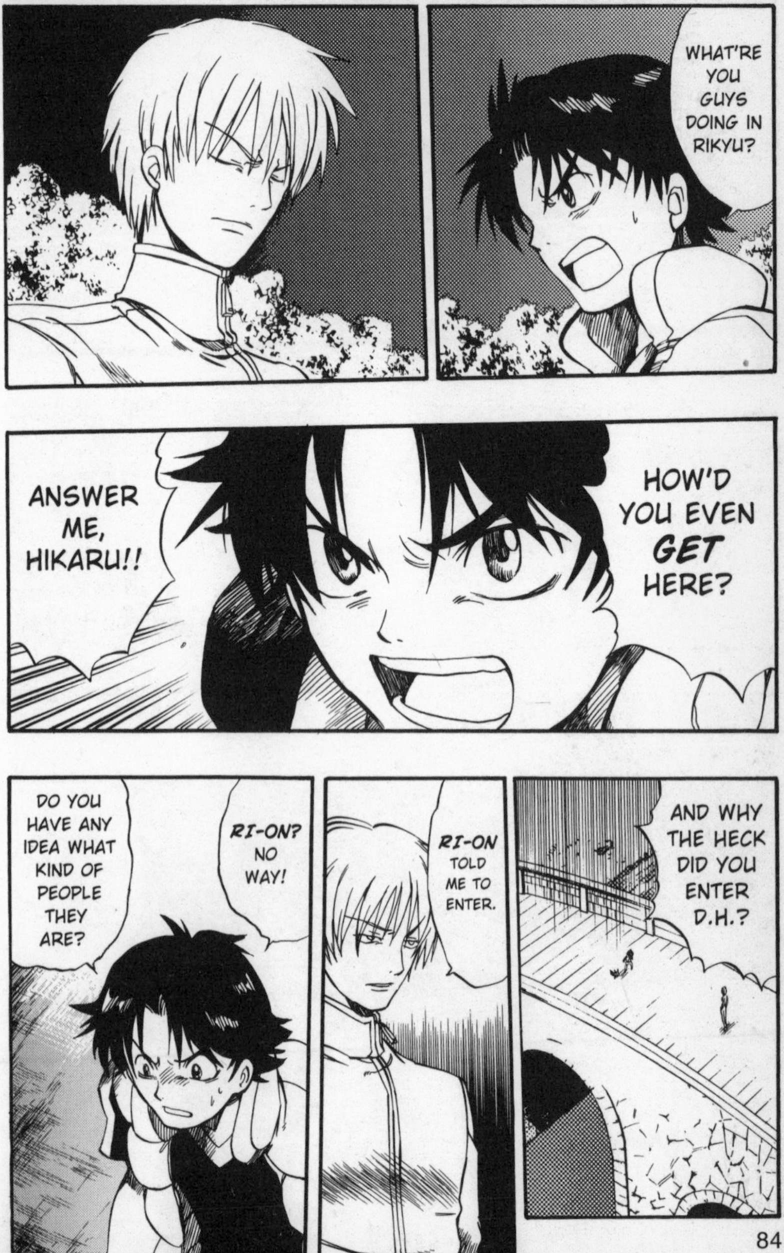
WHAT'RE YOU GUYS DOING IN RIKYU?
HOW'D YOU EVEN **GET** HERE?
ANSWER ME, HIKARU!!
AND WHY THE HECK DID YOU ENTER D.H.?
RI-ON TOLD ME TO ENTER.
RI-ON? NO WAY!
DO YOU HAVE ANY IDEA WHAT KIND OF PEOPLE THEY ARE?

READ THIS WAY

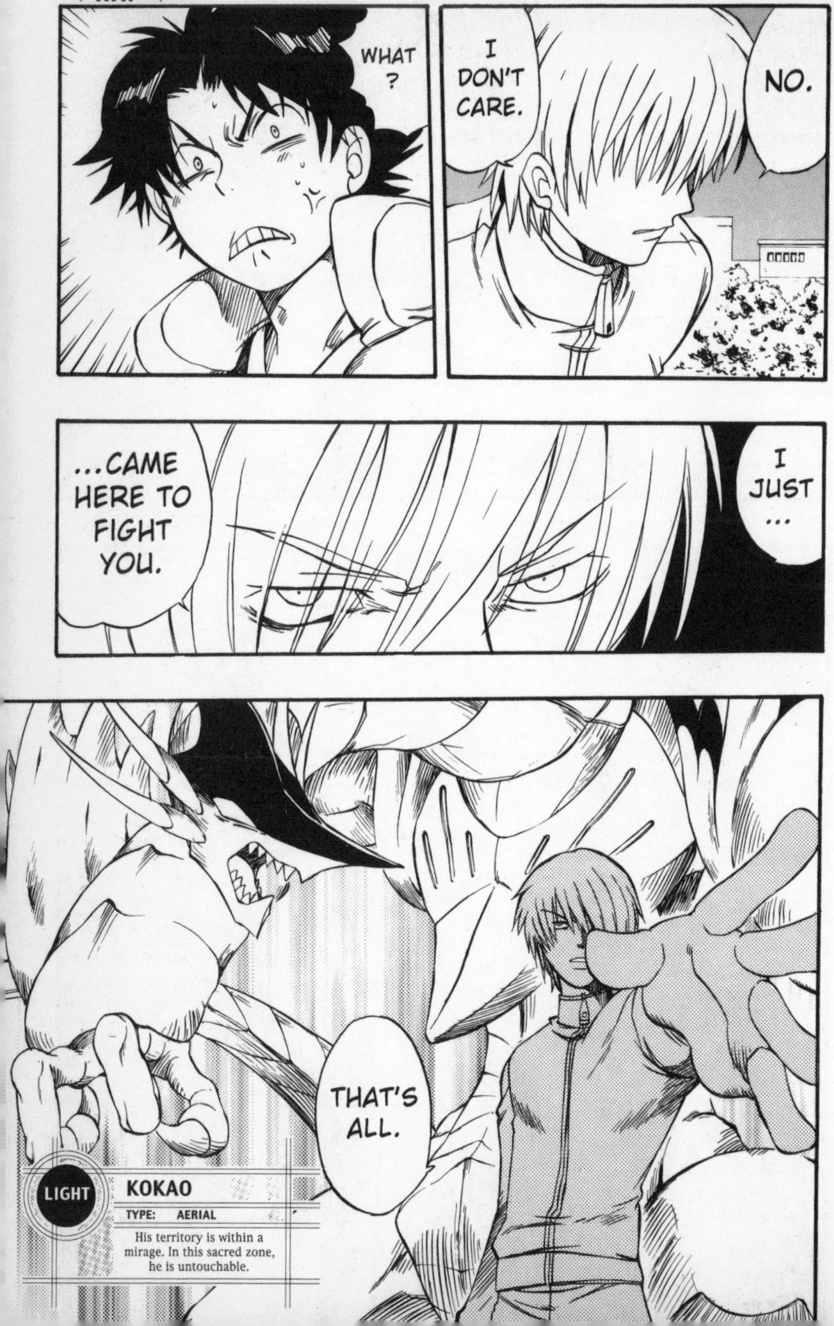
NO.
I DON'T CARE.
WHAT ?
I JUST ...
...CAME HERE TO FIGHT YOU.
THAT'S ALL.
LIGHT
KOKAO
TYPE: AERIAL
His territory is within a mirage. In this sacred zone, he is untouchable.

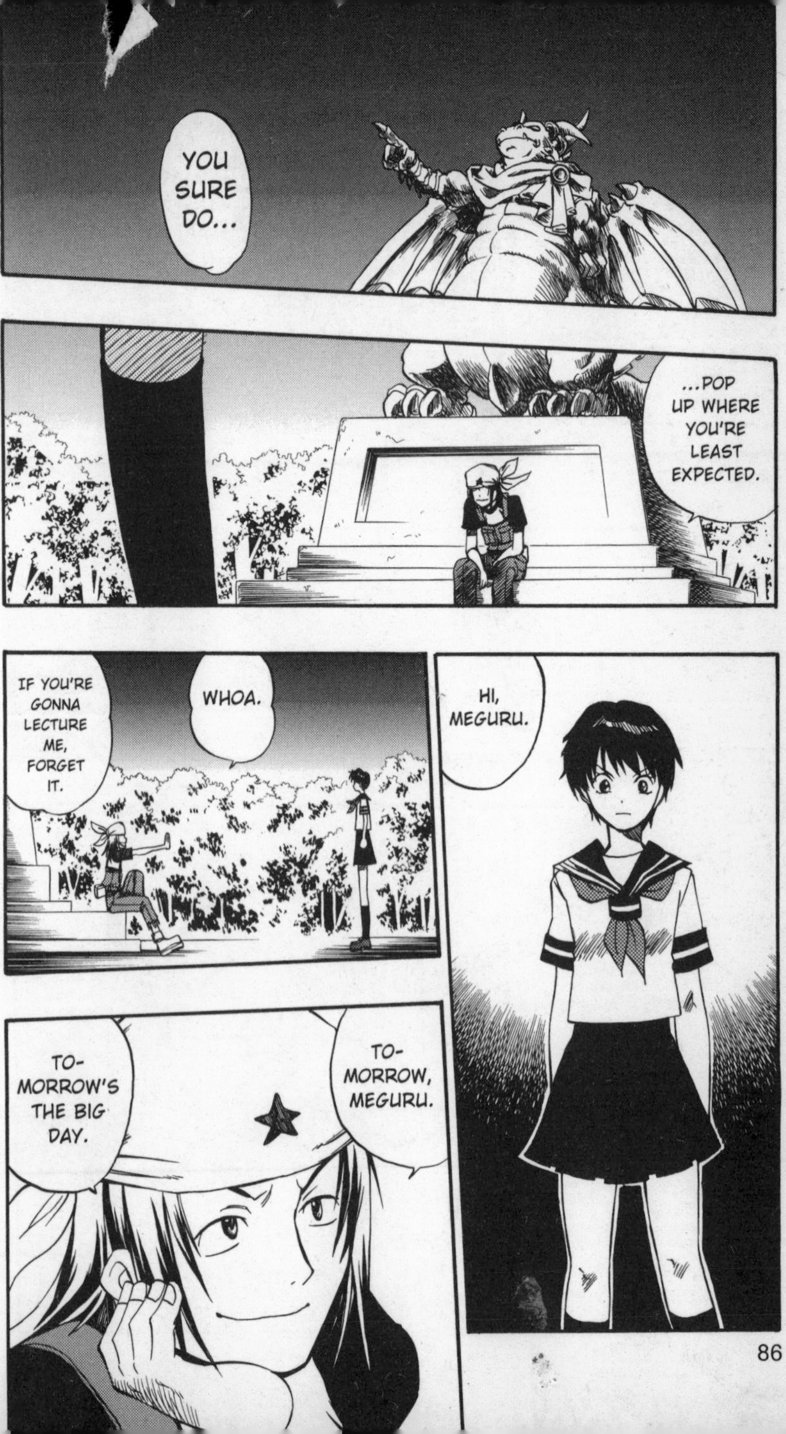
YOU SURE DO...
...POP UP WHERE YOU'RE LEAST EXPECTED.
HI, MEGURU.
WHOA.
IF YOU'RE GONNA LECTURE ME, FORGET IT.
TO-MORROW, MEGURU.
TO-MORROW'S THE BIG DAY.

READ THIS WAY

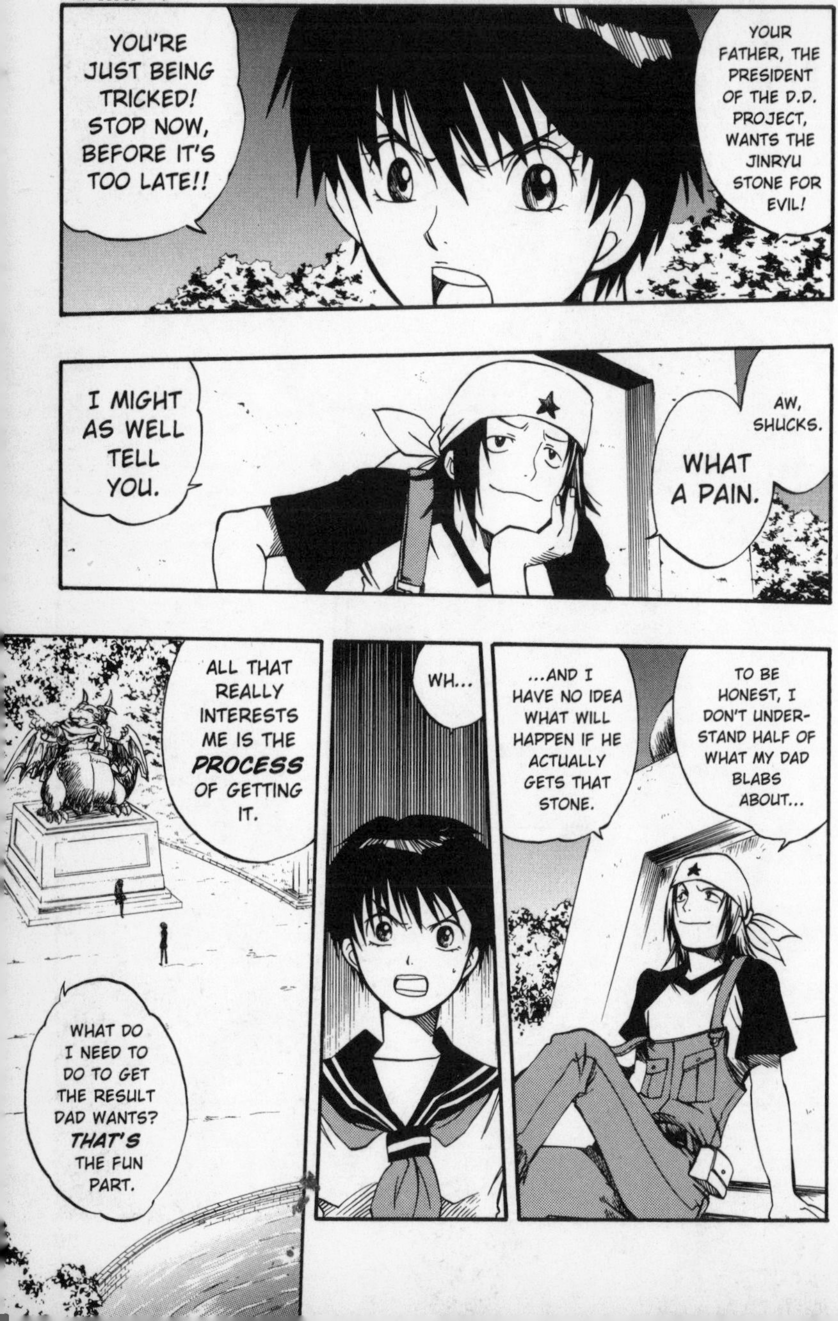
YOUR FATHER, THE PRESIDENT OF THE D.D. PROJECT, WANTS THE JINRYU STONE FOR EVIL!
YOU'RE JUST BEING TRICKED! STOP NOW, BEFORE IT'S TOO LATE!!
AW, SHUCKS.
WHAT A PAIN.
I MIGHT AS WELL TELL YOU.
TO BE HONEST, I DON'T UNDER-STAND HALF OF WHAT MY DAD BLABS ABOUT...
...AND I HAVE NO IDEA WHAT WILL HAPPEN IF HE ACTUALLY GETS THAT STONE.
WH...
ALL THAT REALLY INTERESTS ME IS THE ***PROCESS*** OF GETTING IT.
WHAT DO I NEED TO DO TO GET THE RESULT DAD WANTS? ***THAT'S*** THE FUN PART.

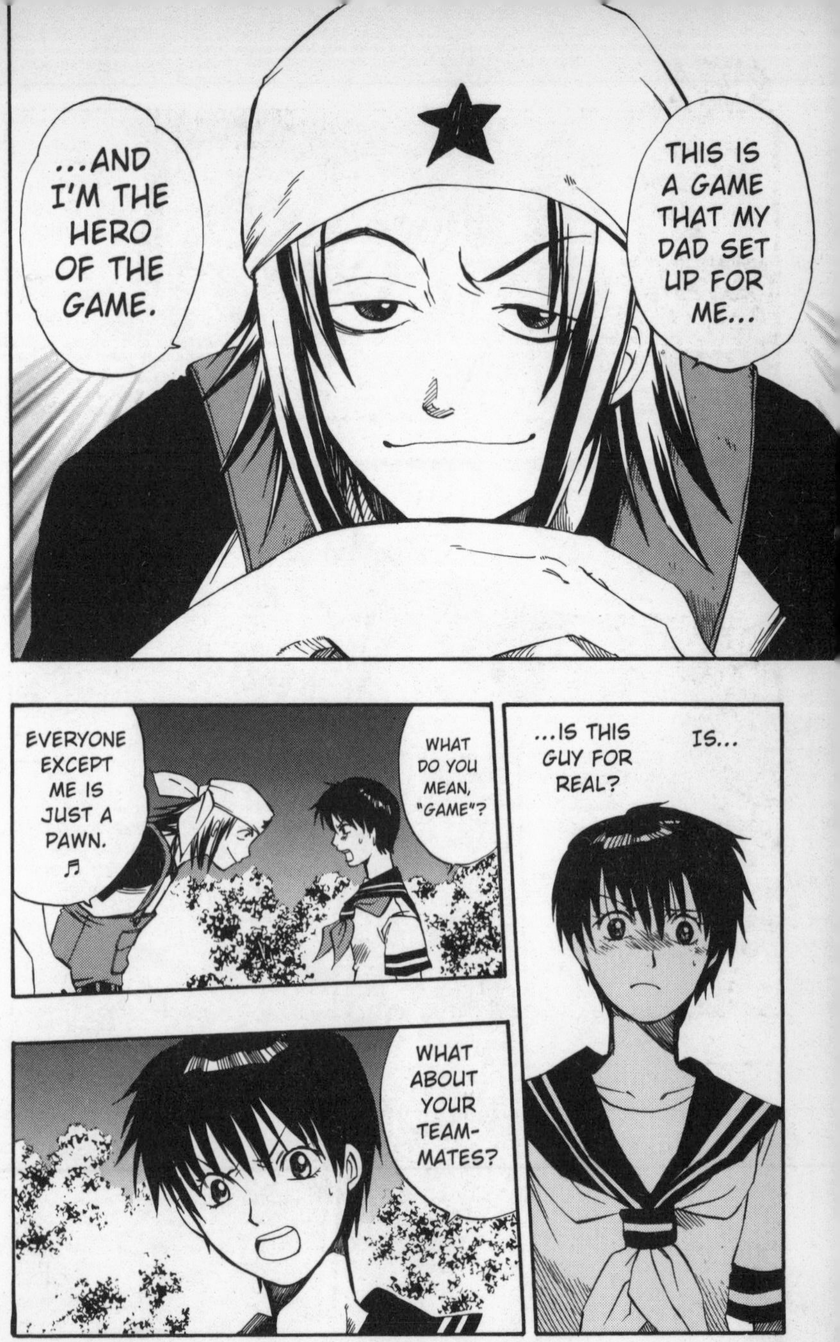
THIS IS A GAME THAT MY DAD SET UP FOR ME...
...AND I'M THE HERO OF THE GAME.
IS...
...IS THIS GUY FOR REAL?
WHAT DO YOU MEAN, "GAME"?
EVERYONE EXCEPT ME IS JUST A PAWN. ♬
WHAT ABOUT YOUR TEAM-MATES?

READ THIS WAY

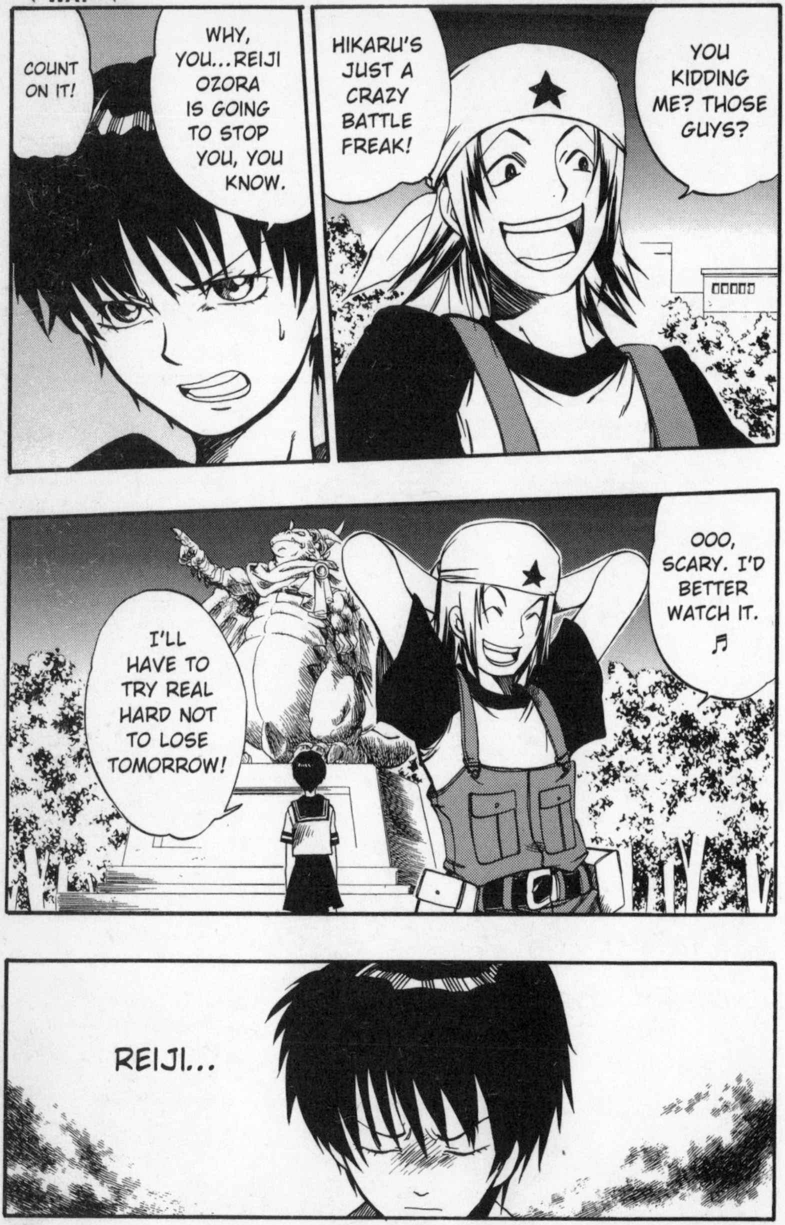
YOU KIDDING ME? THOSE GUYS?
HIKARU'S JUST A CRAZY BATTLE FREAK!
WHY, YOU...REIJI OZORA IS GOING TO STOP YOU, YOU KNOW.
COUNT ON IT!
OOO, SCARY. I'D BETTER WATCH IT. ♬
I'LL HAVE TO TRY REAL HARD NOT TO LOSE TOMORROW!
REIJI...

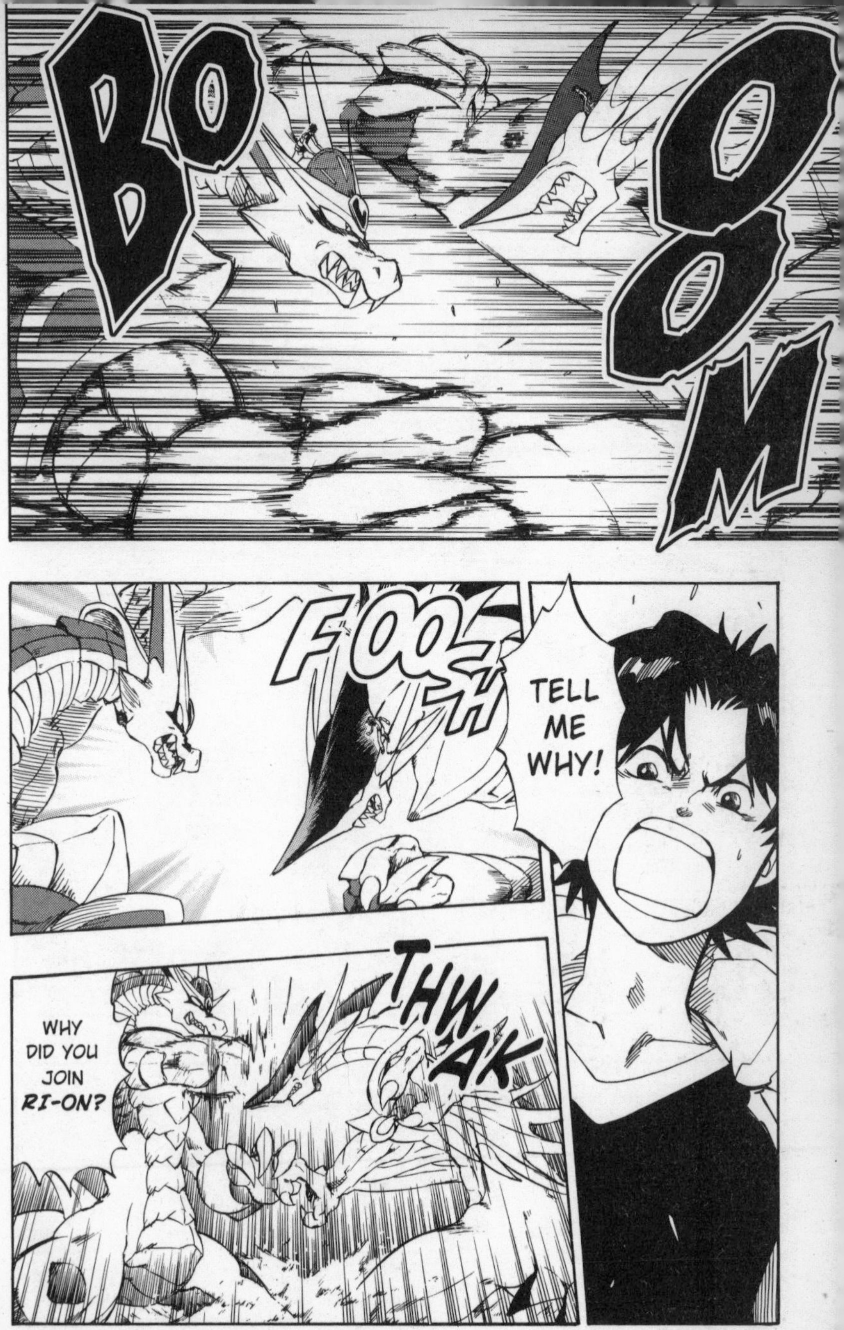
BOOOM
TELL ME WHY!
FOOSH
THWAK
WHY DID YOU JOIN RI-ON?

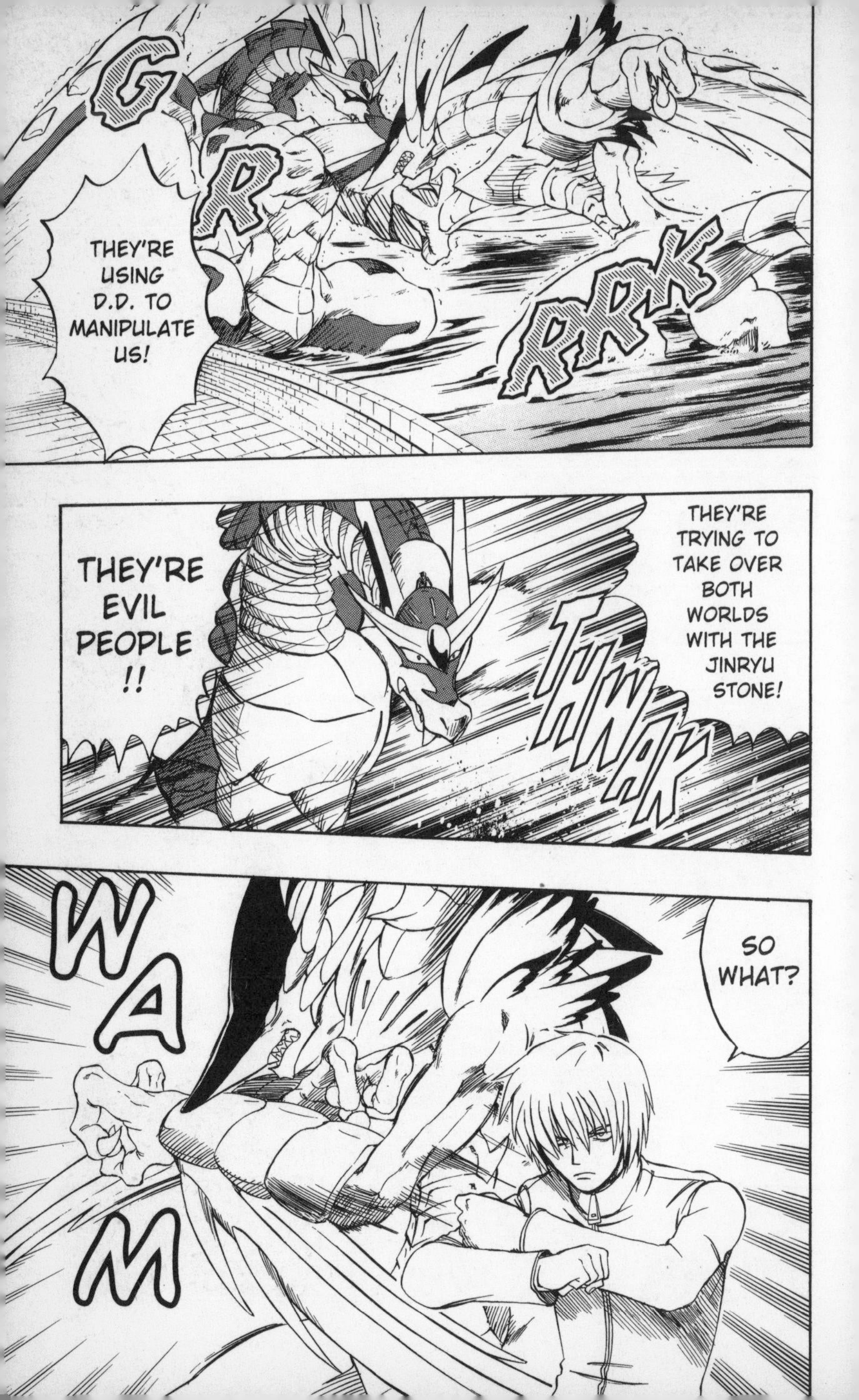
GR
RRRK
THEY'RE USING D.D. TO MANIPULATE US!
THEY'RE TRYING TO TAKE OVER BOTH WORLDS WITH THE JINRYU STONE!
THWAK
THEY'RE EVIL PEOPLE !!
SO WHAT?
WAM

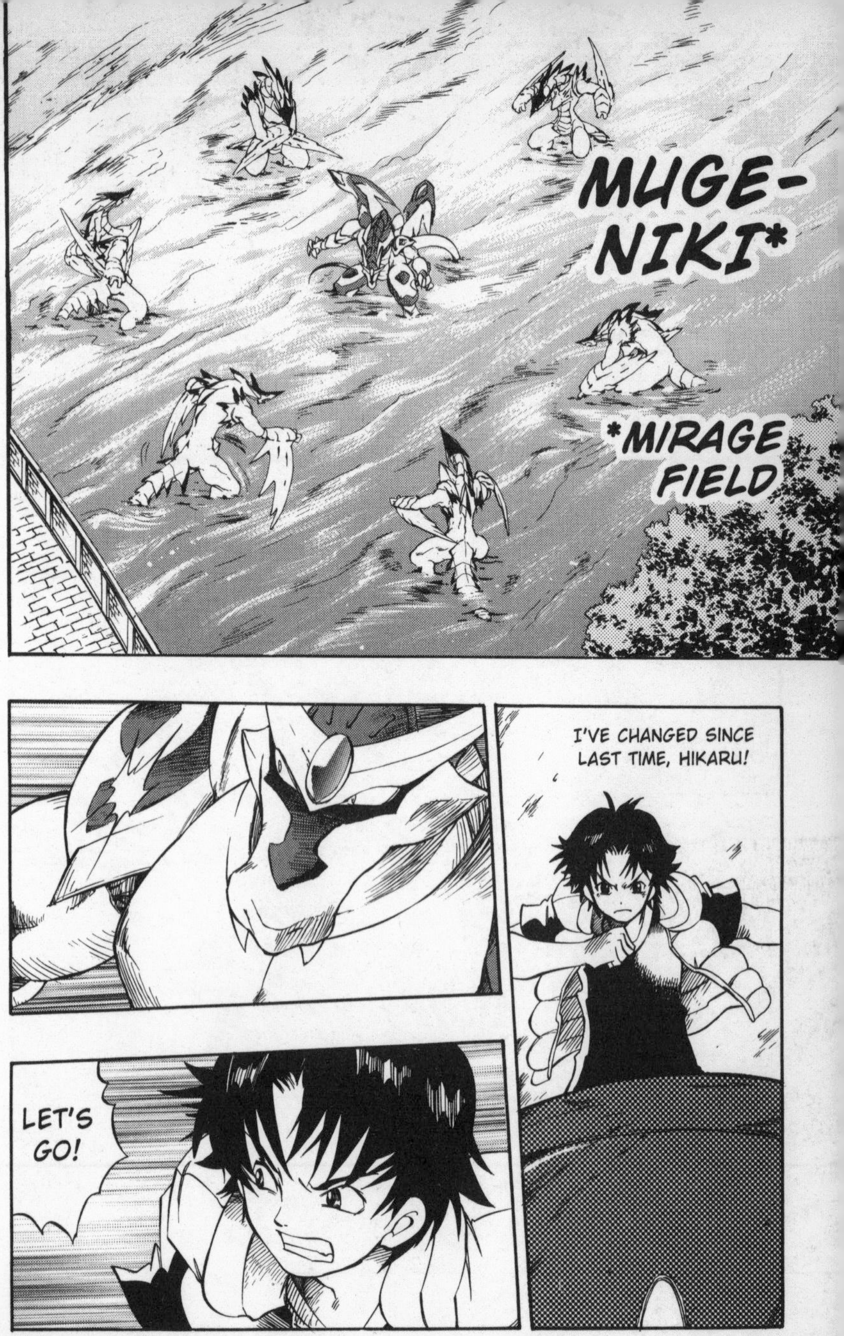
MUGE-NIKI*
*MIRAGE FIELD
I'VE CHANGED SINCE LAST TIME, HIKARU!
LET'S GO!

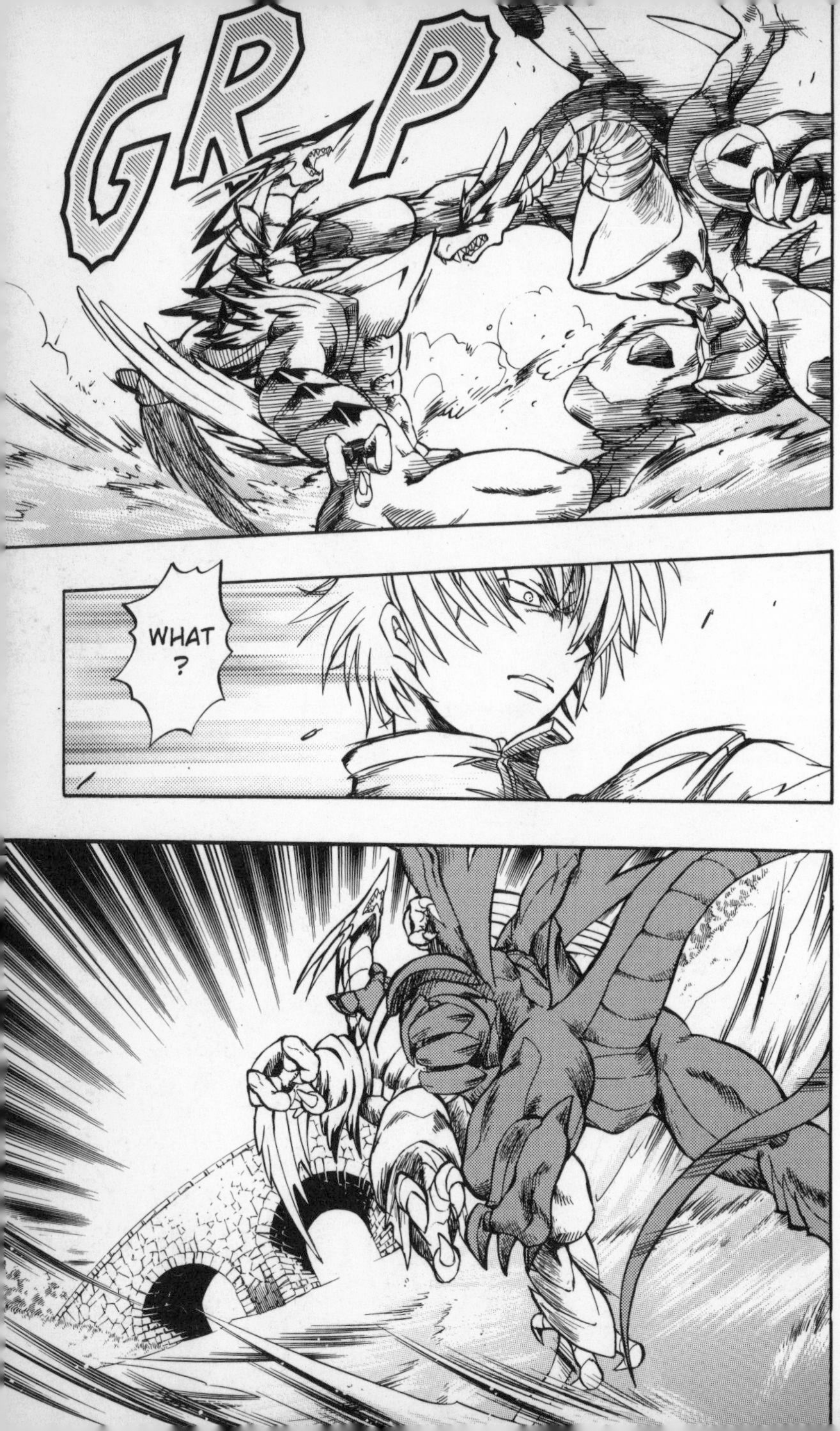
GRP
WHAT?

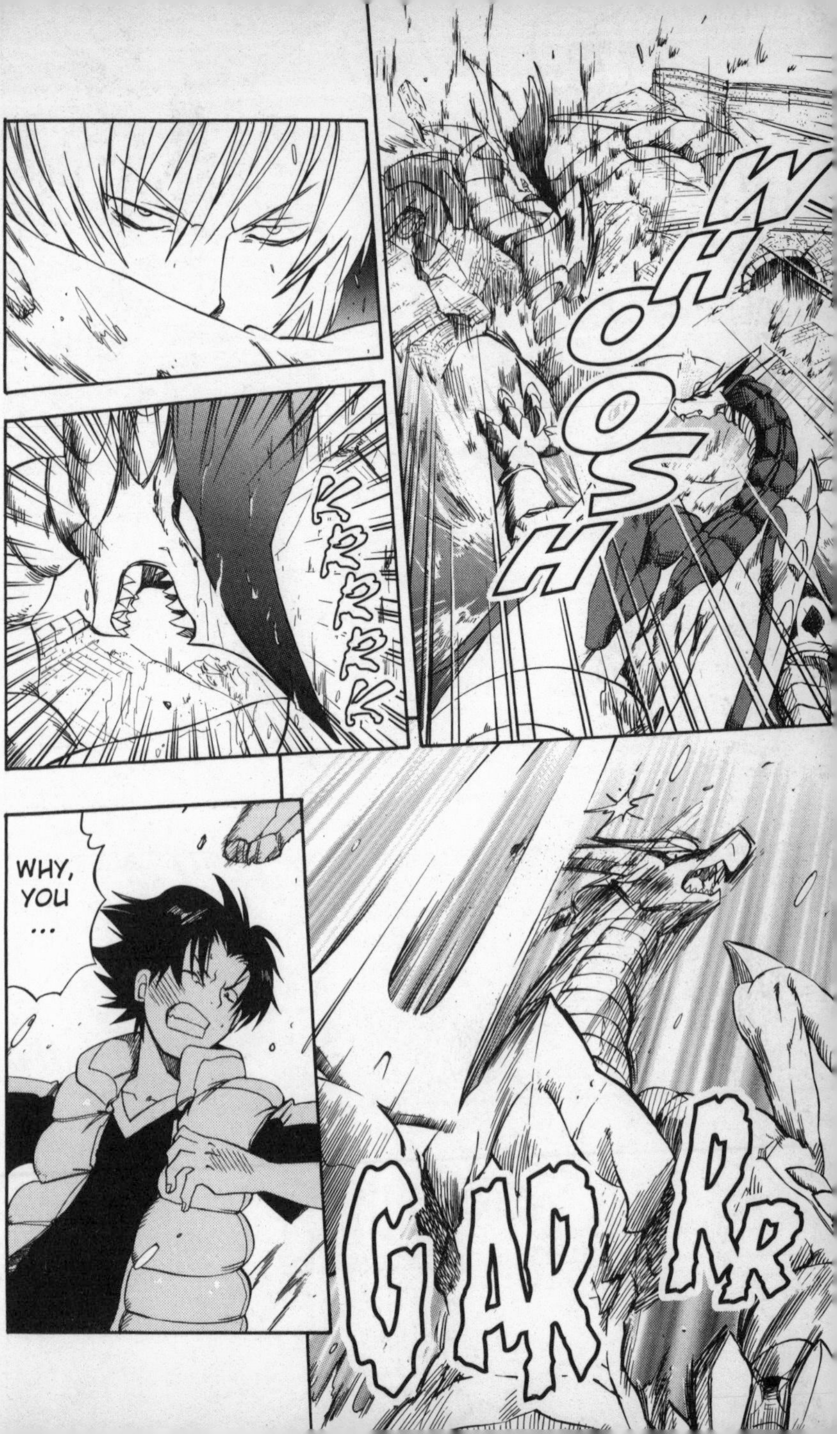
WHOOSH
KRRRRK
GARRR
WHY, YOU ...

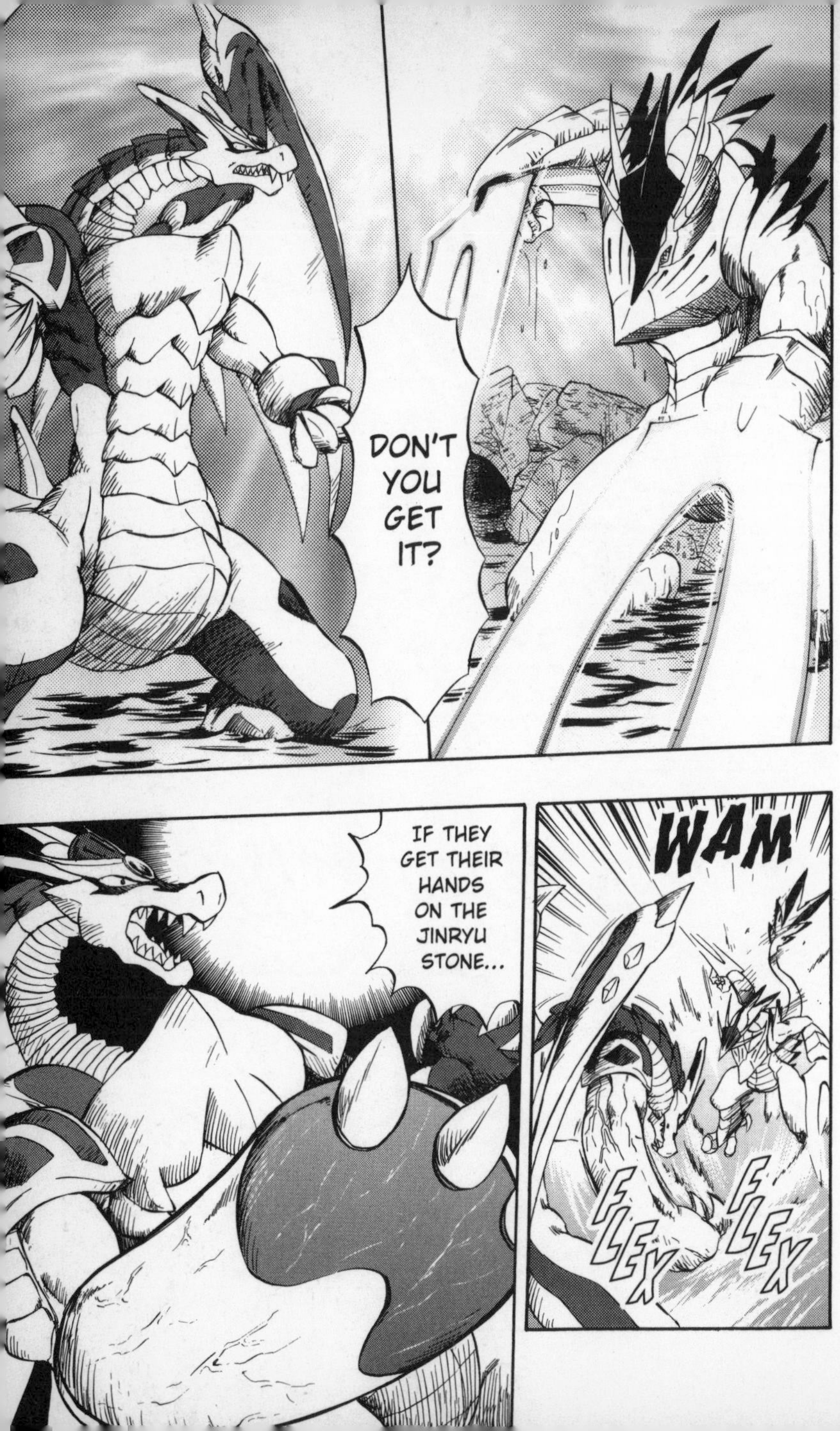
DON'T YOU GET IT?
WAM
FLEX
FLEX
IF THEY GET THEIR HANDS ON THE JINRYU STONE...

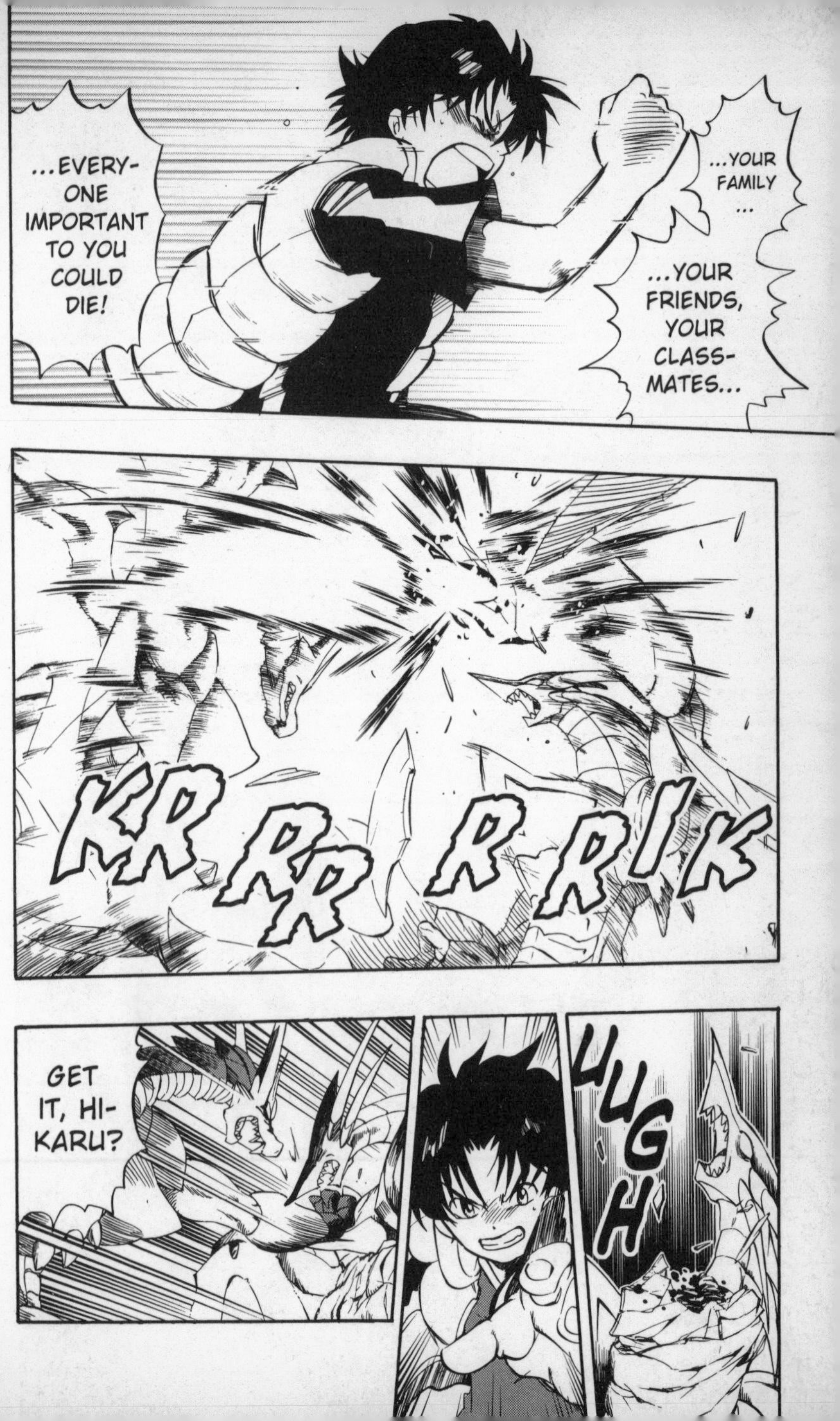
...YOUR FAMILY ...
...YOUR FRIENDS, YOUR CLASS-MATES...
...EVERY-ONE IMPORTANT TO YOU COULD DIE!
KRRRRRIK
UUGH
GET IT, HI-KARU?

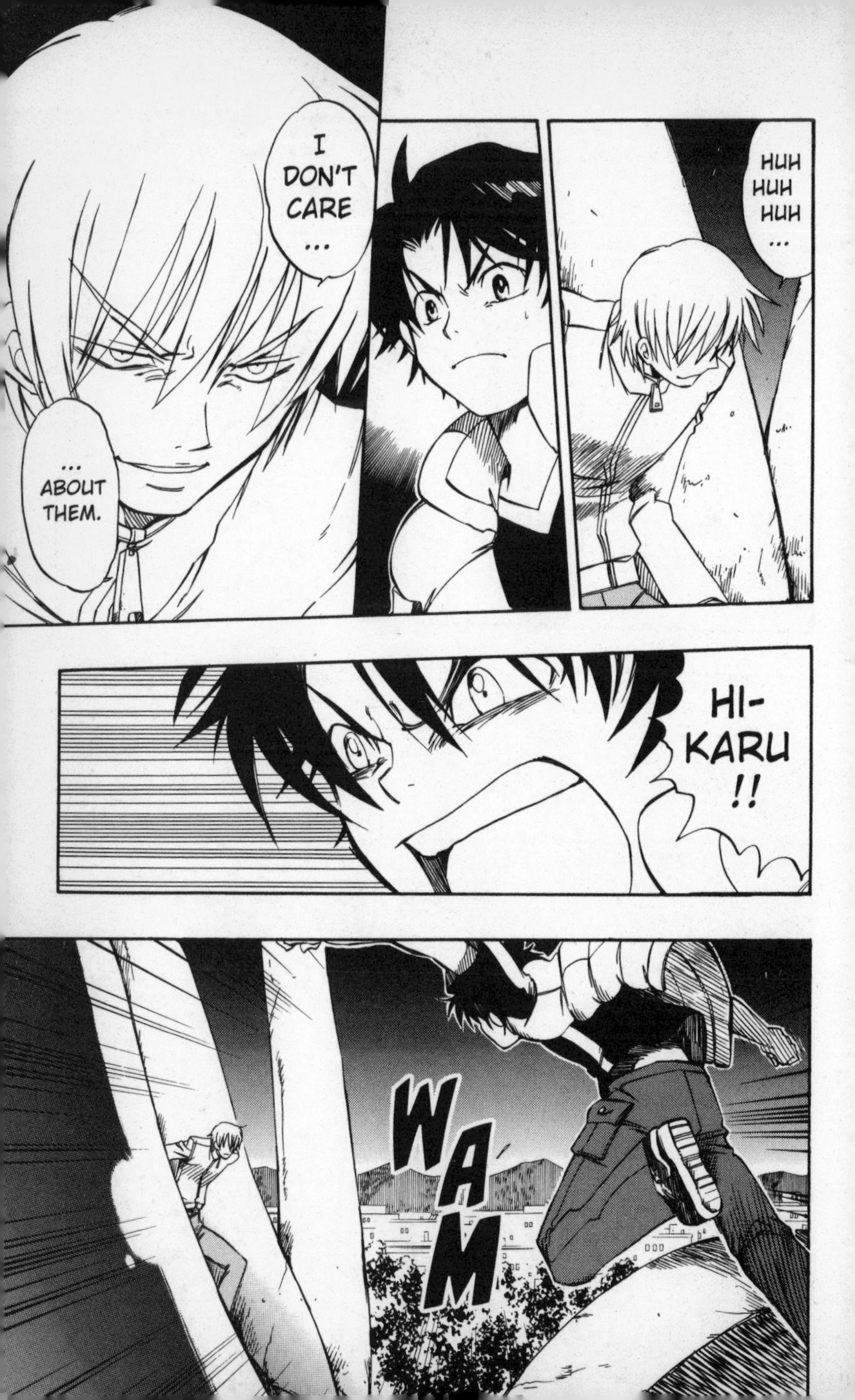
HUH HUH HUH ...
I DON'T CARE ...
... ABOUT THEM.
HI-KARU !!
WAM

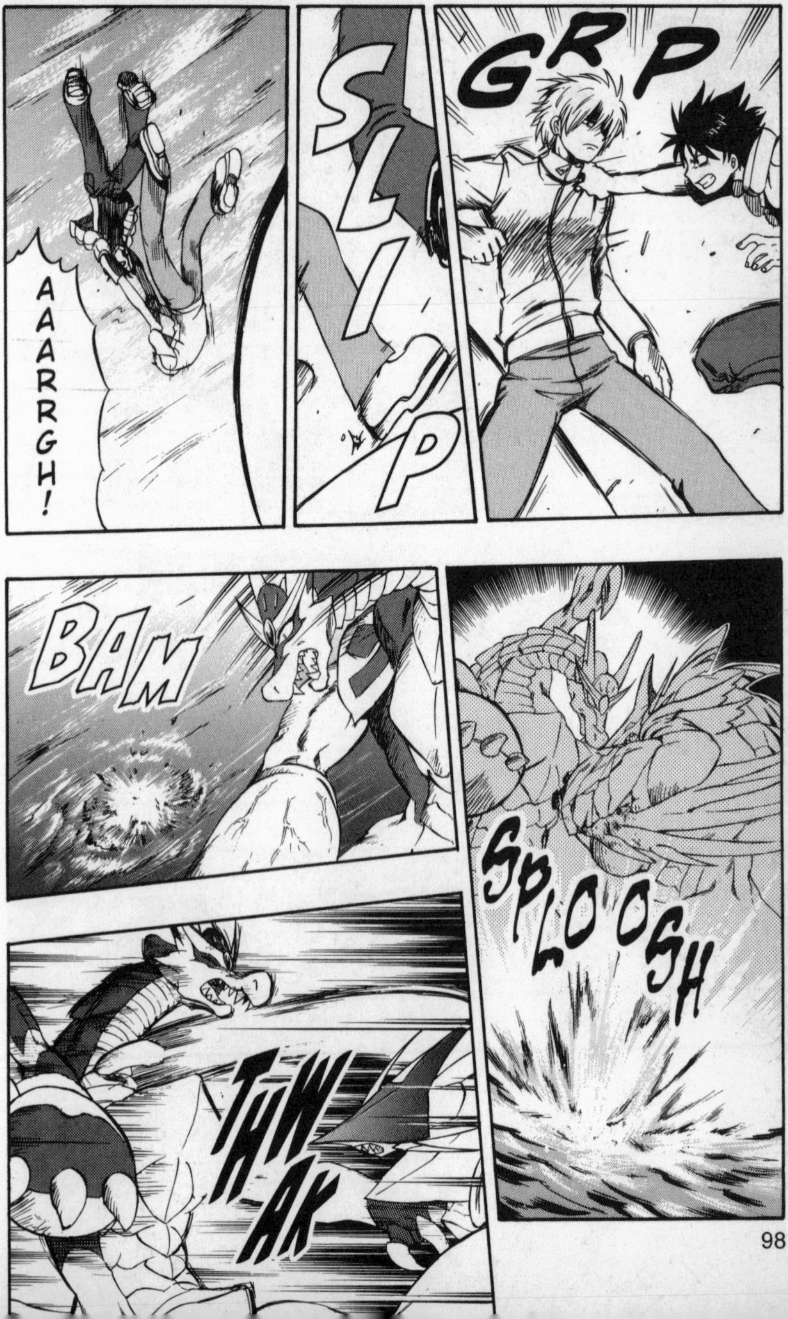
GRP
SLIP
AAAARRGH!
SPLOOSH
BAM
THWHAK

READ THIS WAY

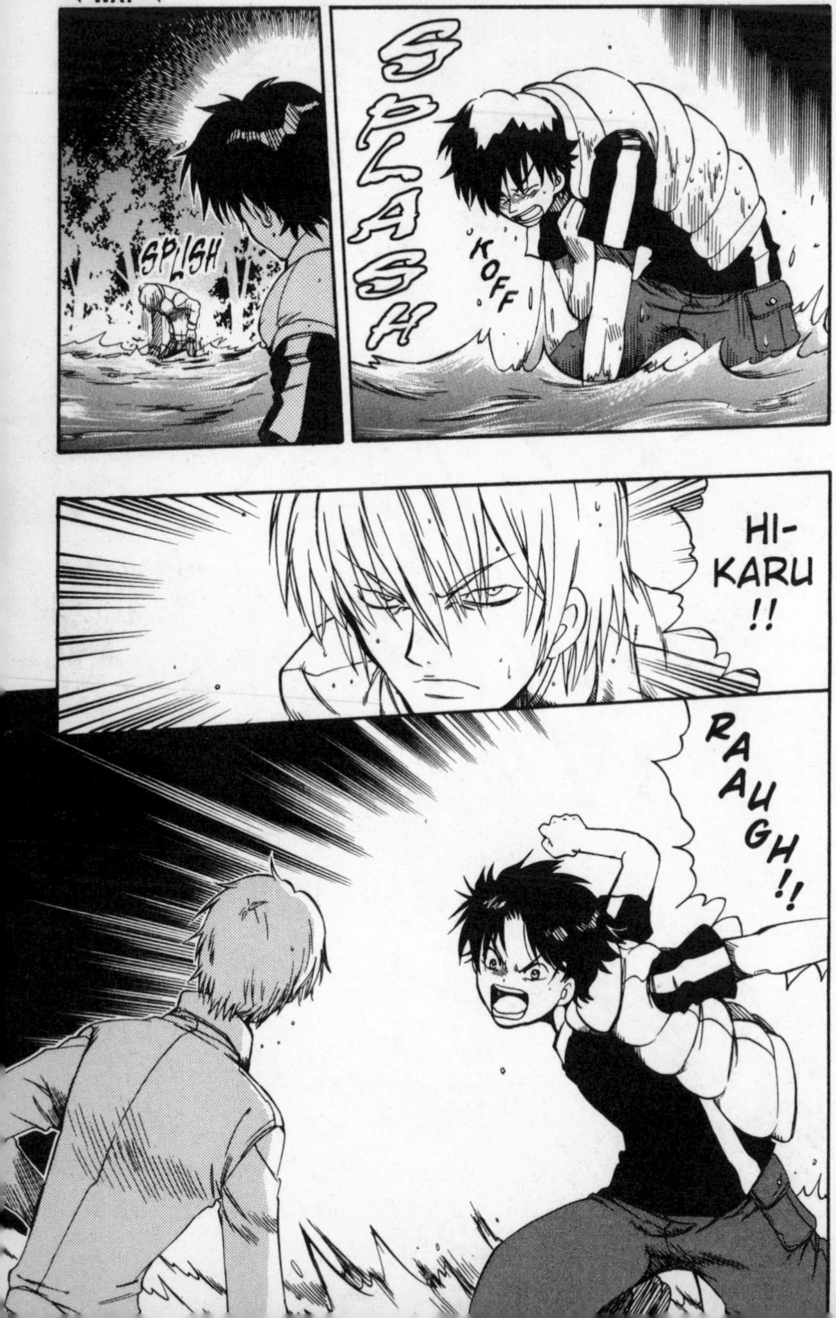
SPLASH
KOFF
SPLISH
HI-KARU!!
RAAUGH!!

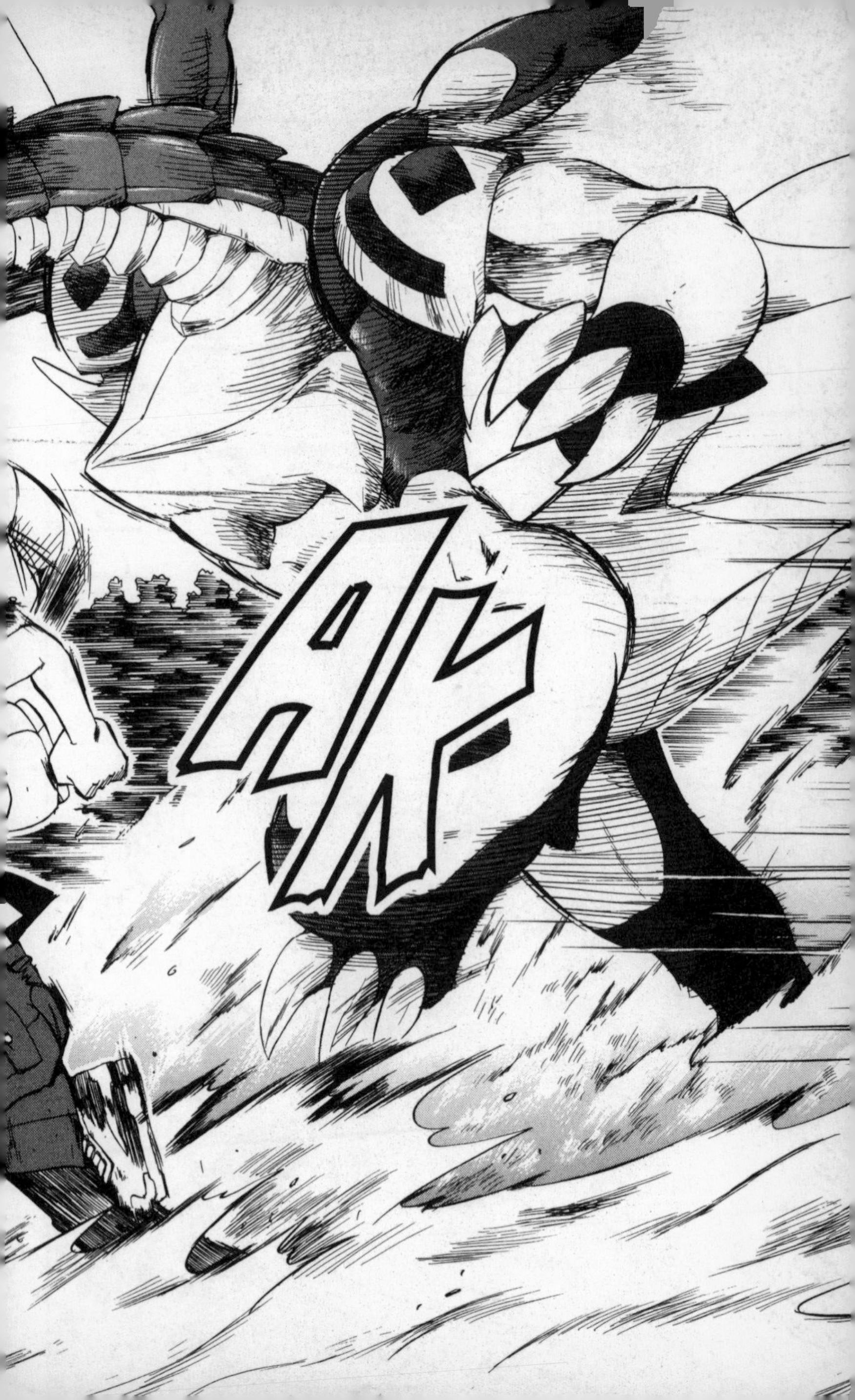

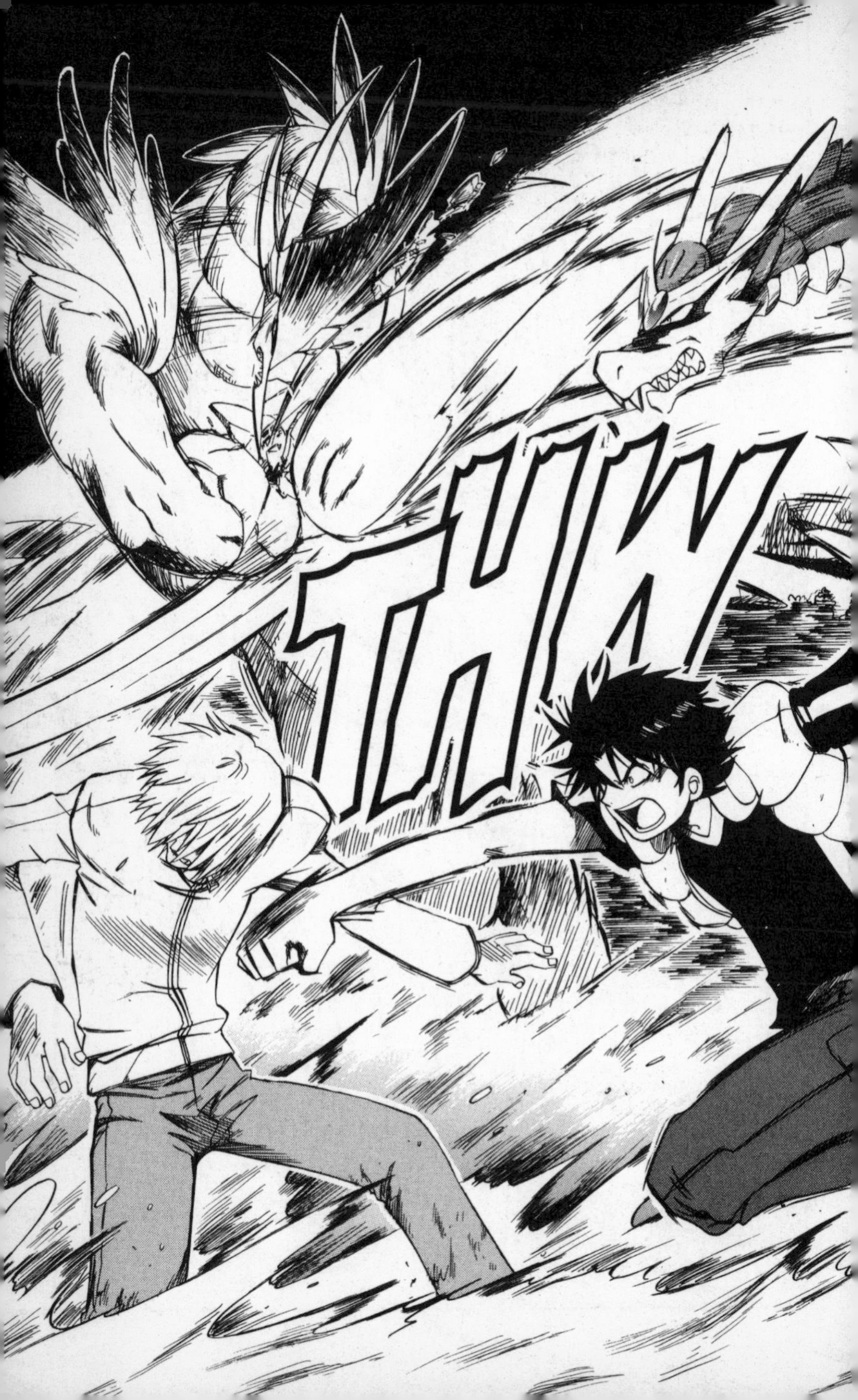
THK

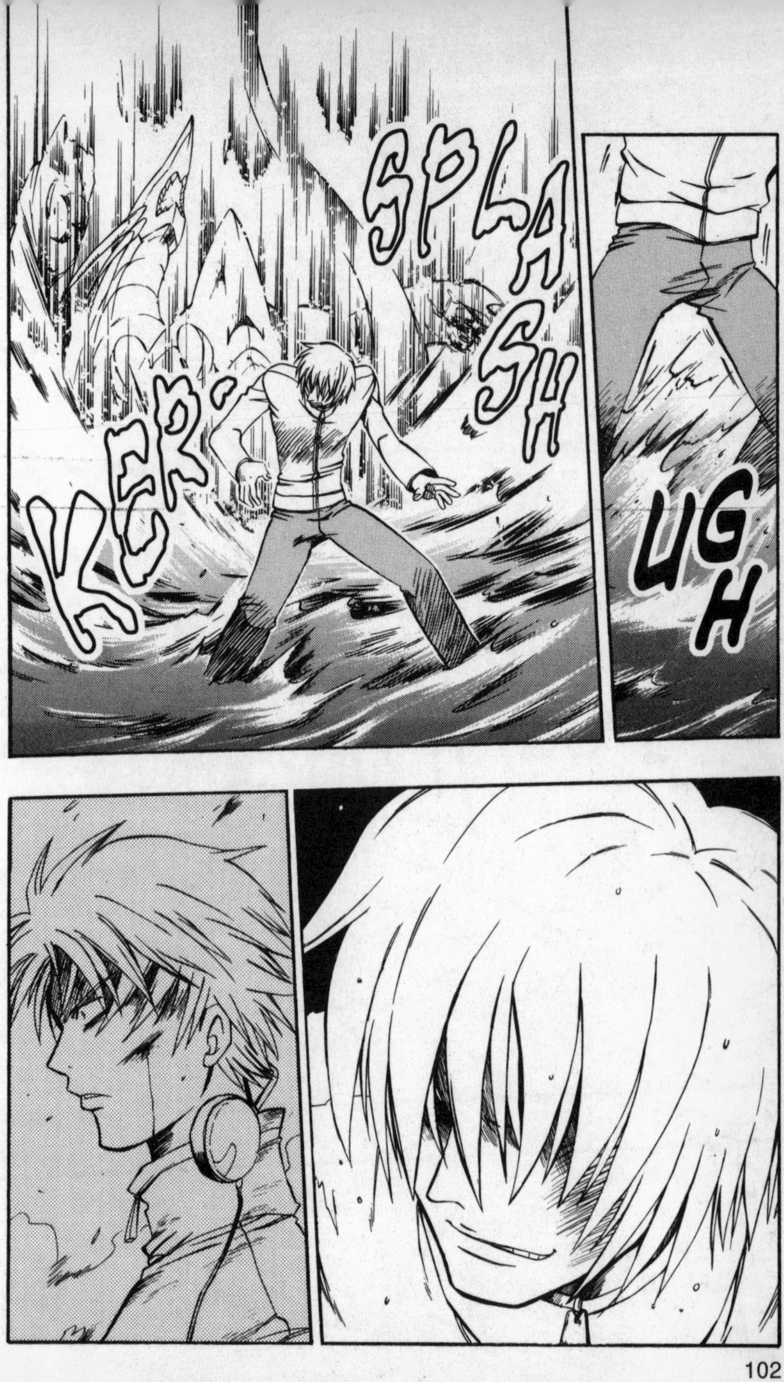
UGH
SPLASH
KER-

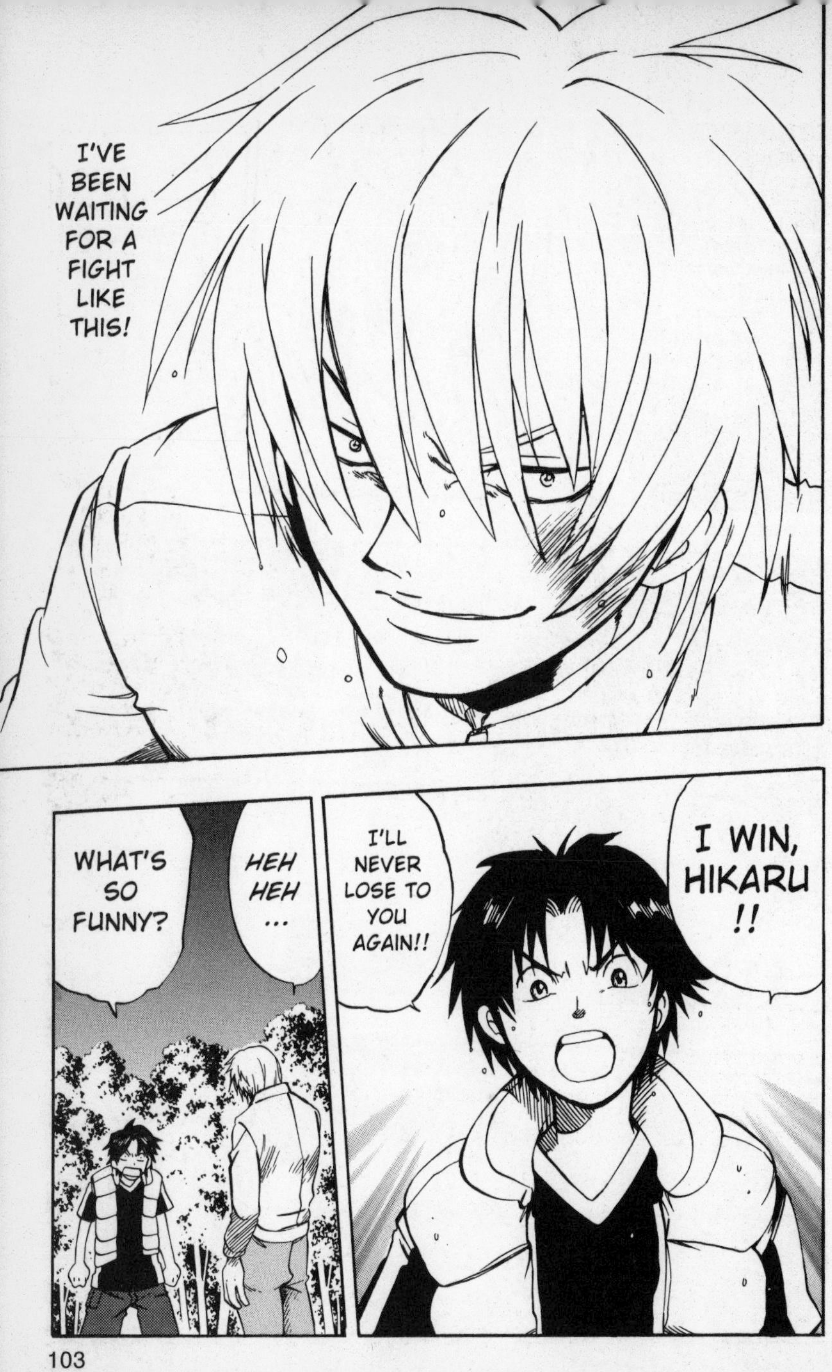
I'VE BEEN WAITING FOR A FIGHT LIKE THIS!
I WIN, HIKARU!!
I'LL NEVER LOSE TO YOU AGAIN!!
HEH HEH ...
WHAT'S SO FUNNY?

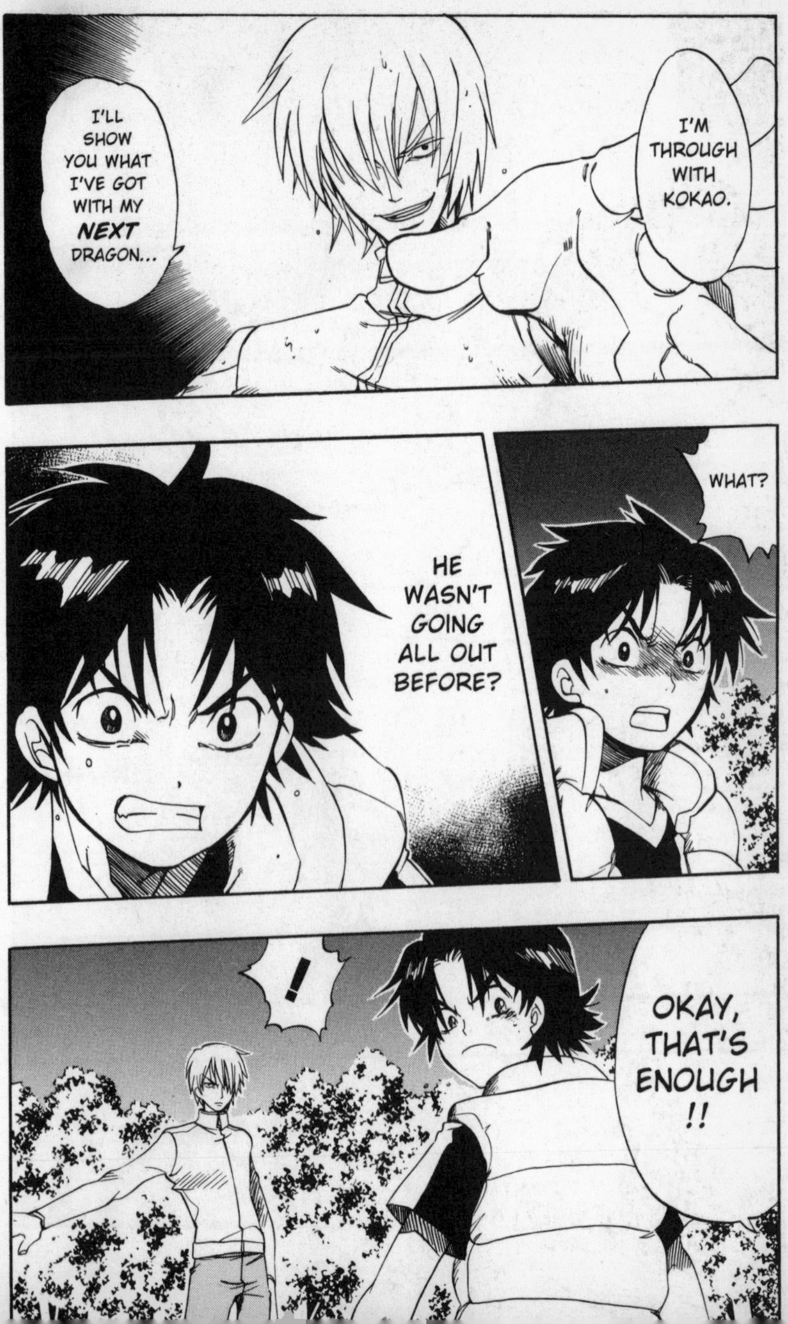
I'M THROUGH WITH KOKAO.
I'LL SHOW YOU WHAT I'VE GOT WITH MY ***NEXT*** DRAGON...
WHAT?
HE WASN'T GOING ALL OUT BEFORE?
OKAY, THAT'S ENOUGH!!
!

READ THIS WAY

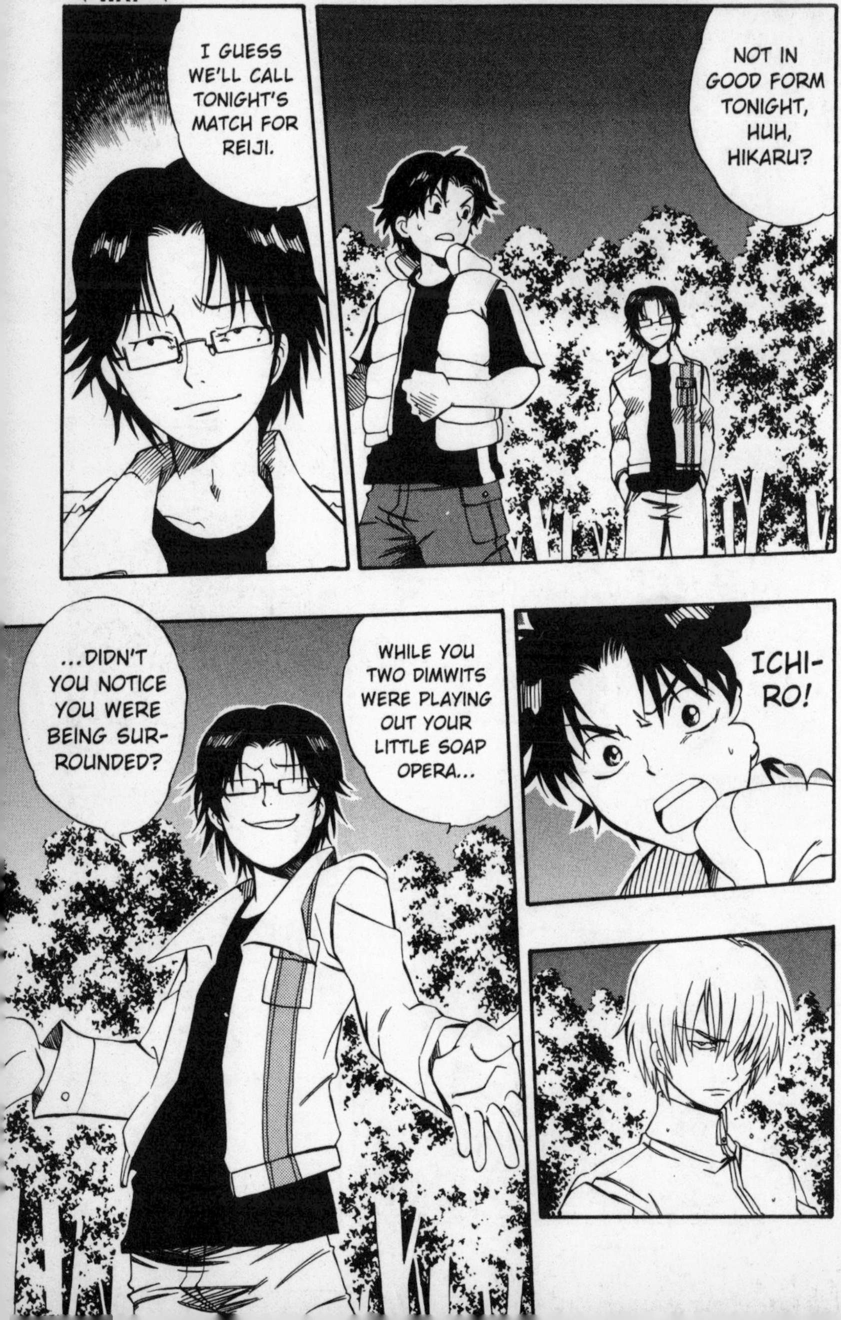
NOT IN GOOD FORM TONIGHT, HUH, HIKARU?
I GUESS WE'LL CALL TONIGHT'S MATCH FOR REIJI.
ICHI-RO!
WHILE YOU TWO DIMWITS WERE PLAYING OUT YOUR LITTLE SOAP OPERA...
...DIDN'T YOU NOTICE YOU WERE BEING SUR-ROUNDED?

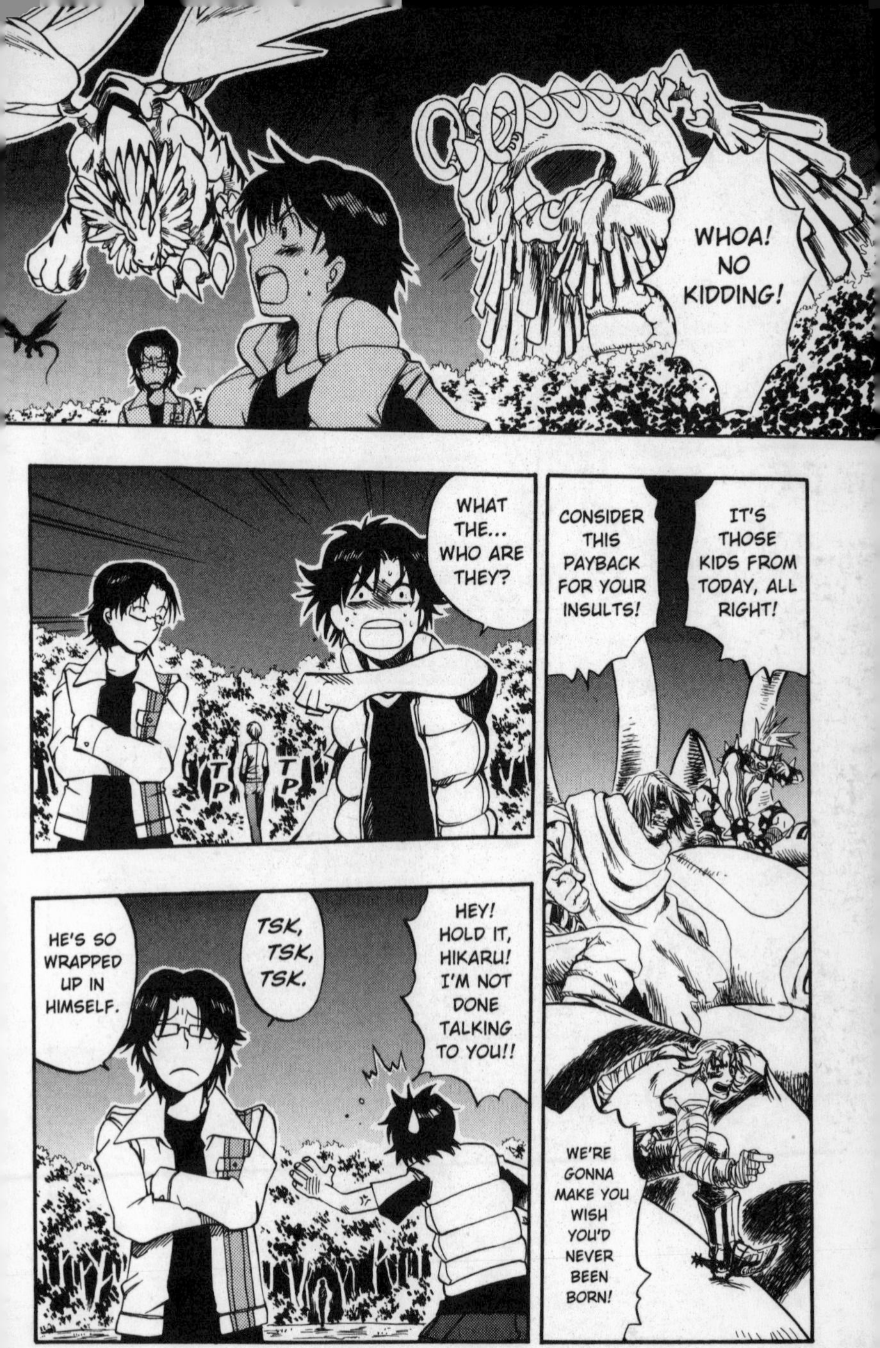
WHOA! NO KIDDING!
IT'S THOSE KIDS FROM TODAY, ALL RIGHT!
CONSIDER THIS PAYBACK FOR YOUR INSULTS!
WE'RE GONNA MAKE YOU WISH YOU'D NEVER BEEN BORN!
WHAT THE... WHO ARE THEY?
TP
TP
HEY! HOLD IT, HIKARU! I'M NOT DONE TALKING TO YOU!!
TSK, TSK, TSK.
HE'S SO WRAPPED UP IN HIMSELF.

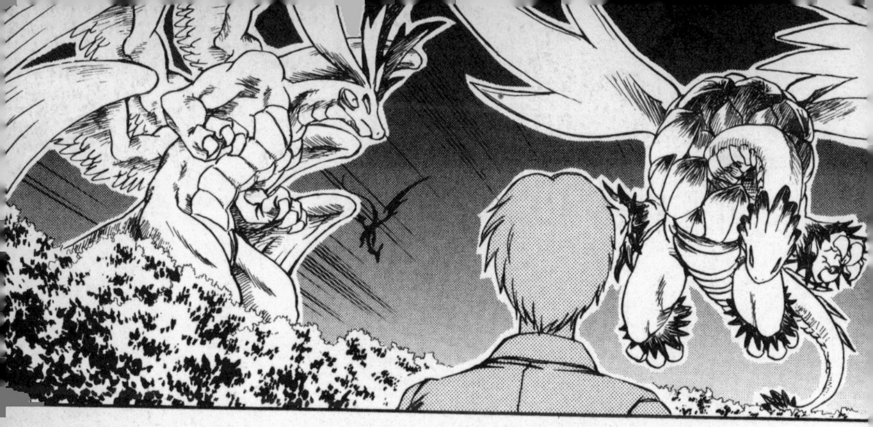

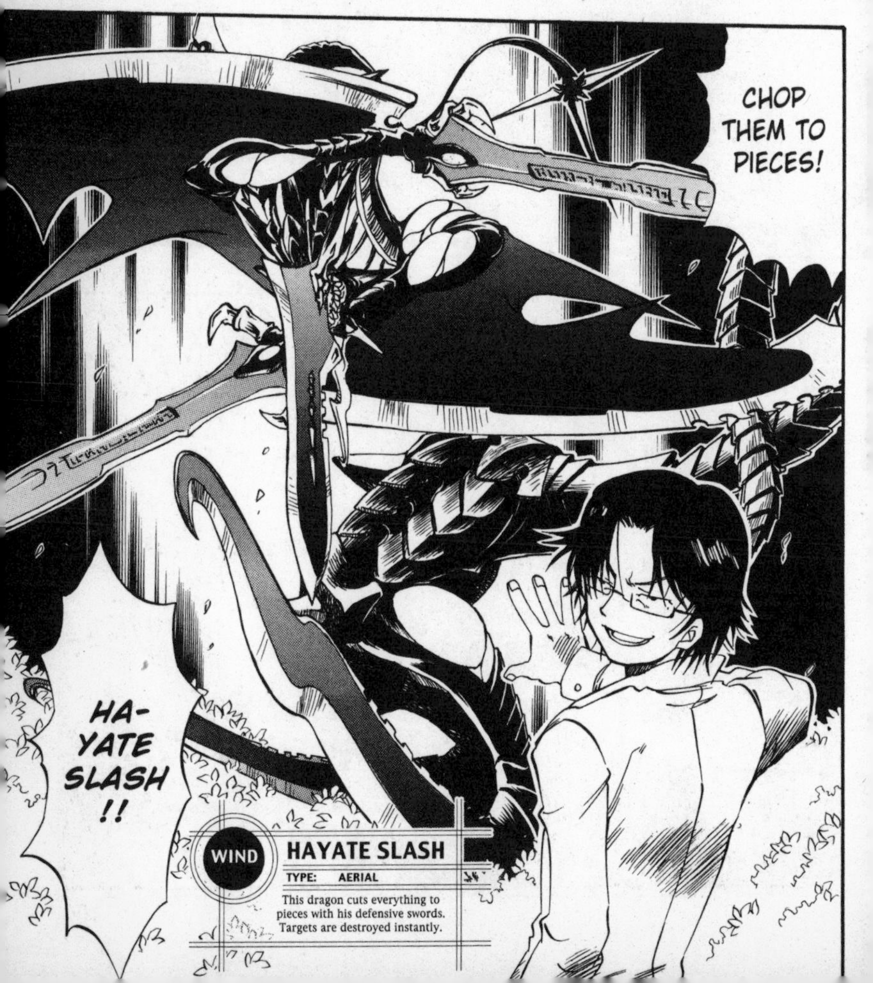
CHOP THEM TO PIECES!
HA-YATE SLASH!!
WIND
HAYATE SLASH
TYPE: AERIAL
This dragon cuts everything to pieces with his defensive swords. Targets are destroyed instantly.

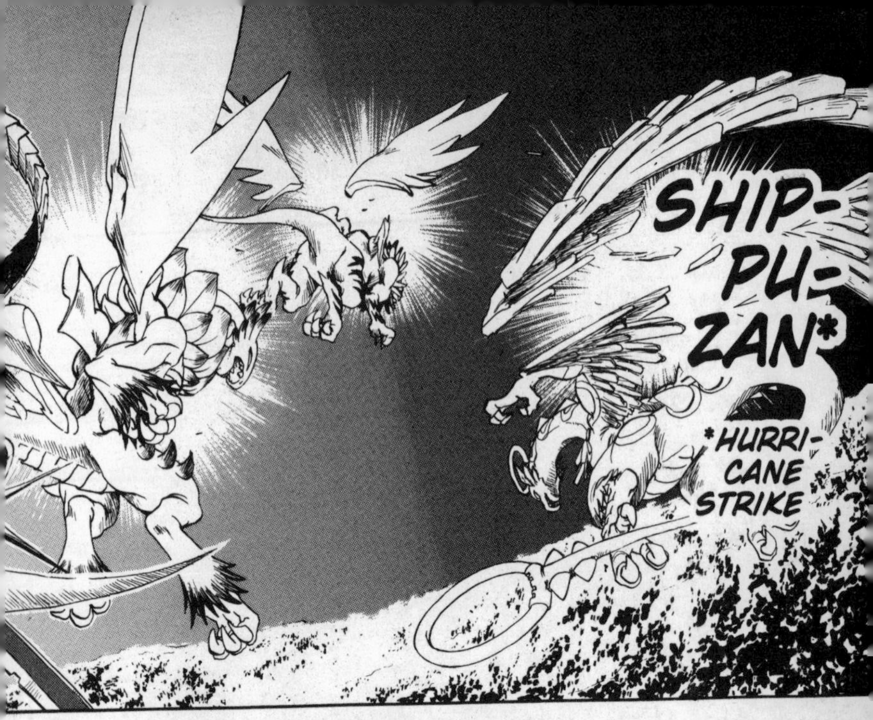
SHIP-PU-ZAN*
*HURRI-CANE STRIKE

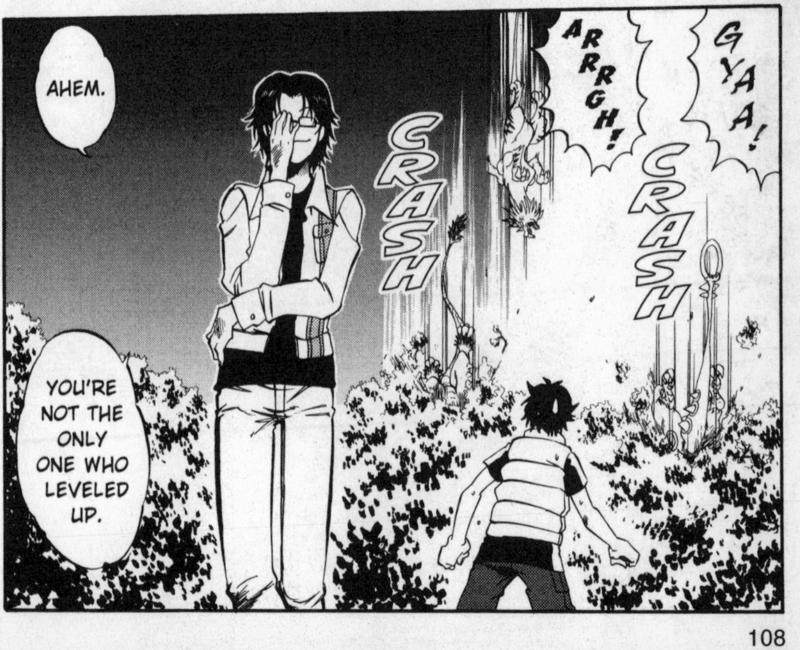
GYAA!
ARRGH!
CRASH
CRASH
AHEM.
YOU'RE NOT THE ONLY ONE WHO LEVELED UP.

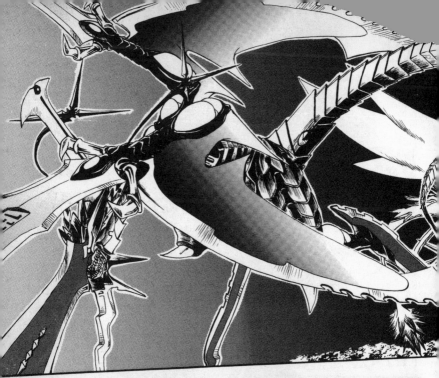

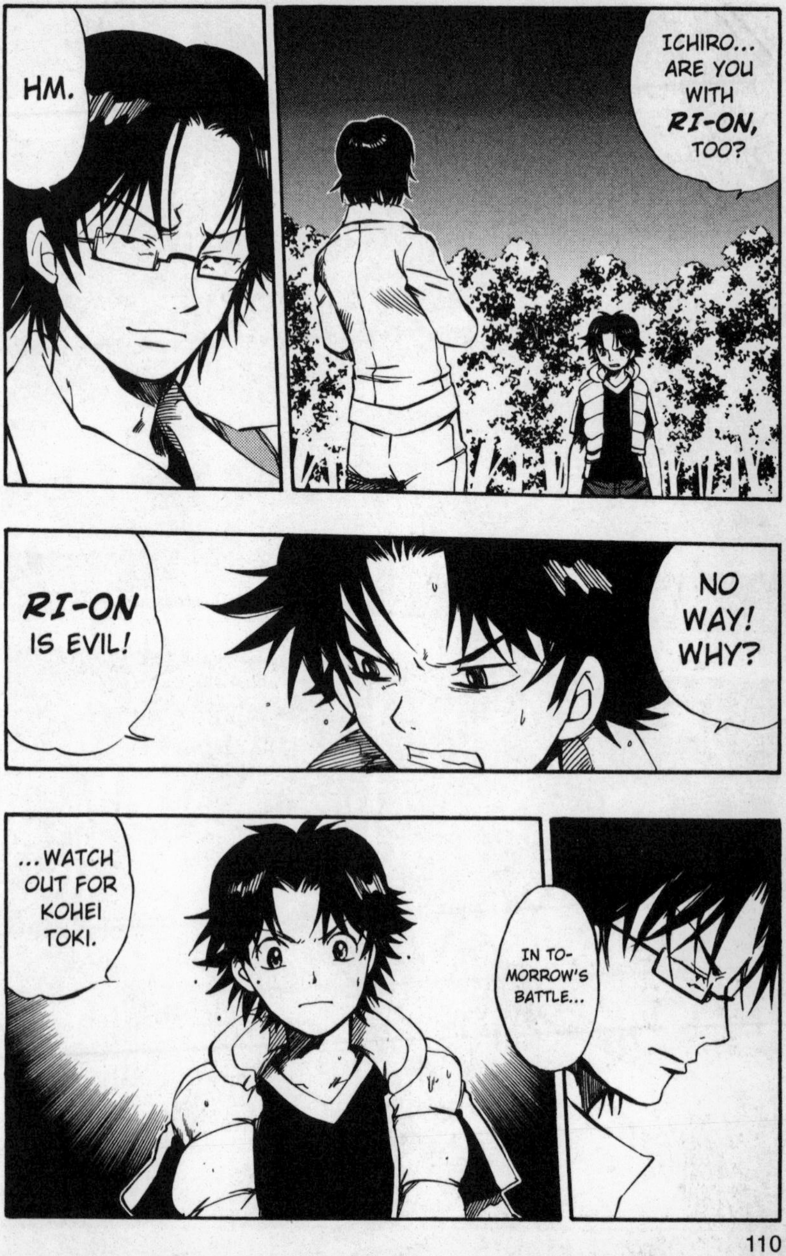
ICHIRO... ARE YOU WITH RI-ON, TOO?
HM.
NO WAY! WHY?
RI-ON IS EVIL!
IN TO-MORROW'S BATTLE...
...WATCH OUT FOR KOHEI TOKI.

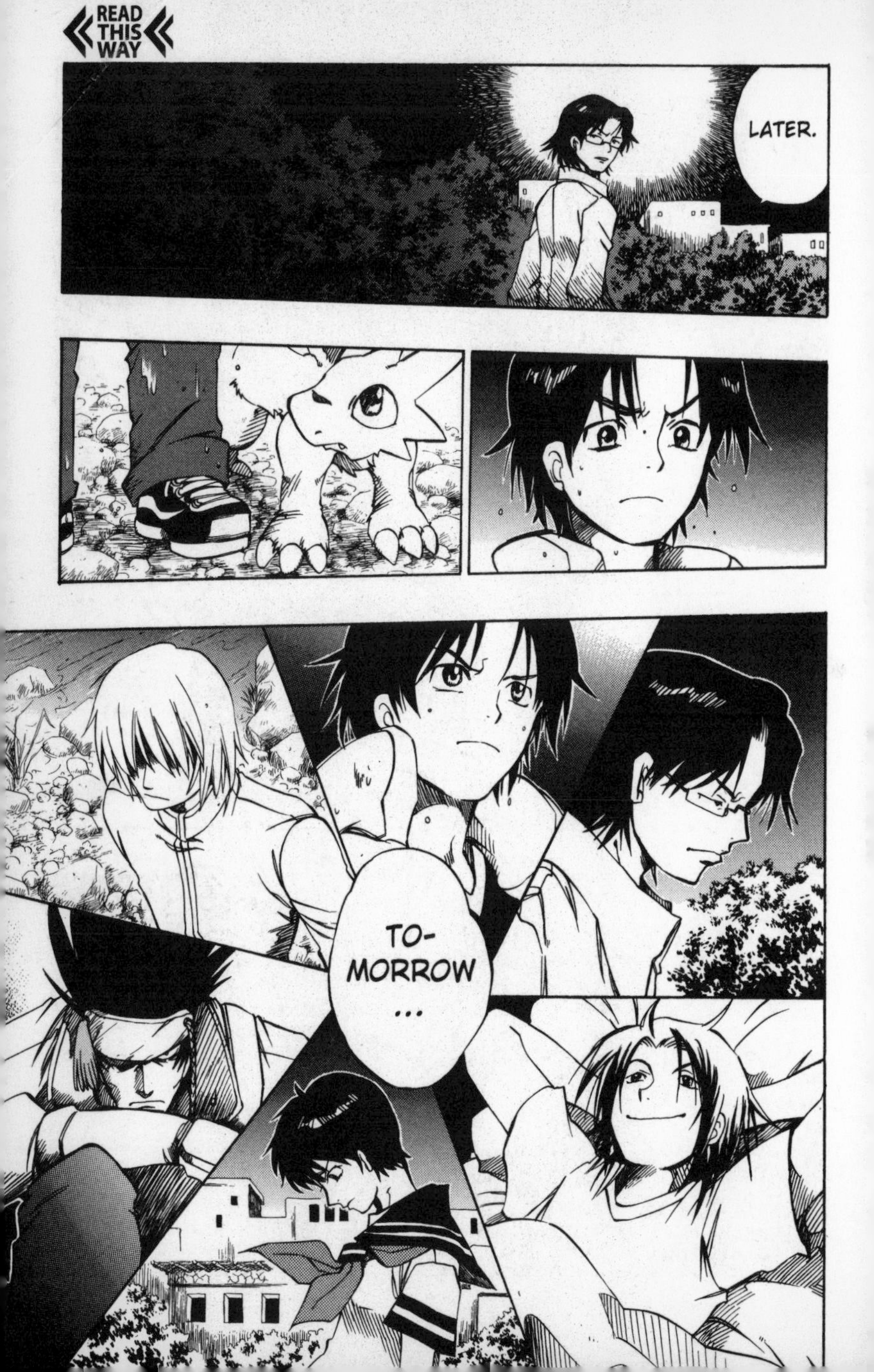
READ THIS WAY
LATER.
TO-MORROW
...

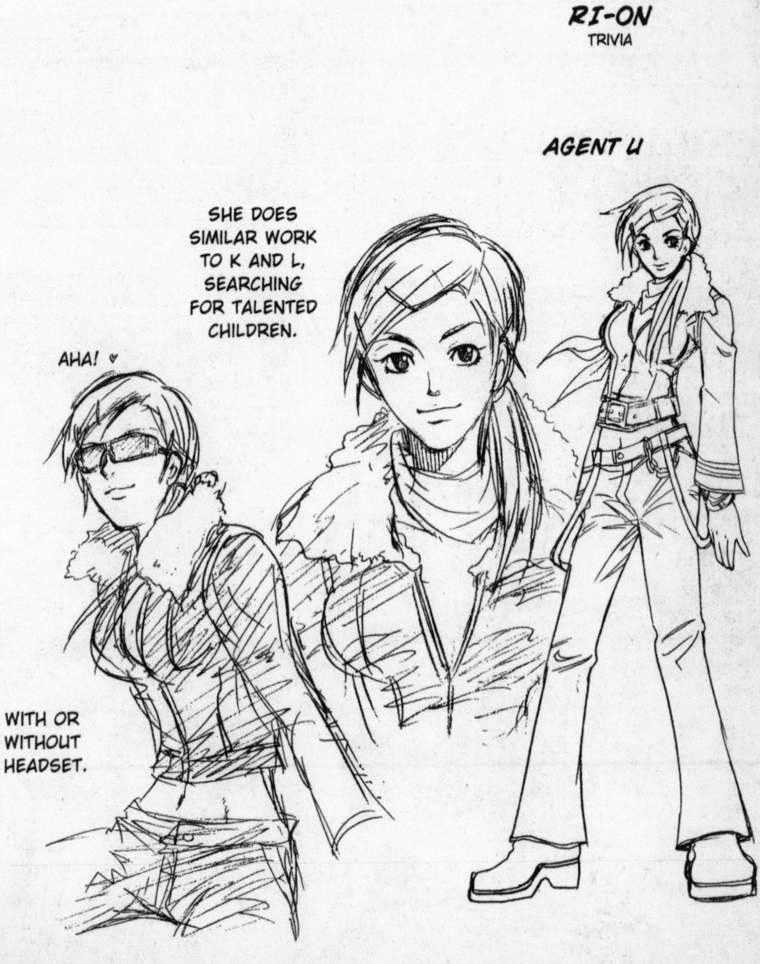
RI-ON
TRIVIA
AGENT U
SHE DOES SIMILAR WORK TO K AND L, SEARCHING FOR TALENTED CHILDREN.
AHA! ♡
WITH OR WITHOUT HEADSET.

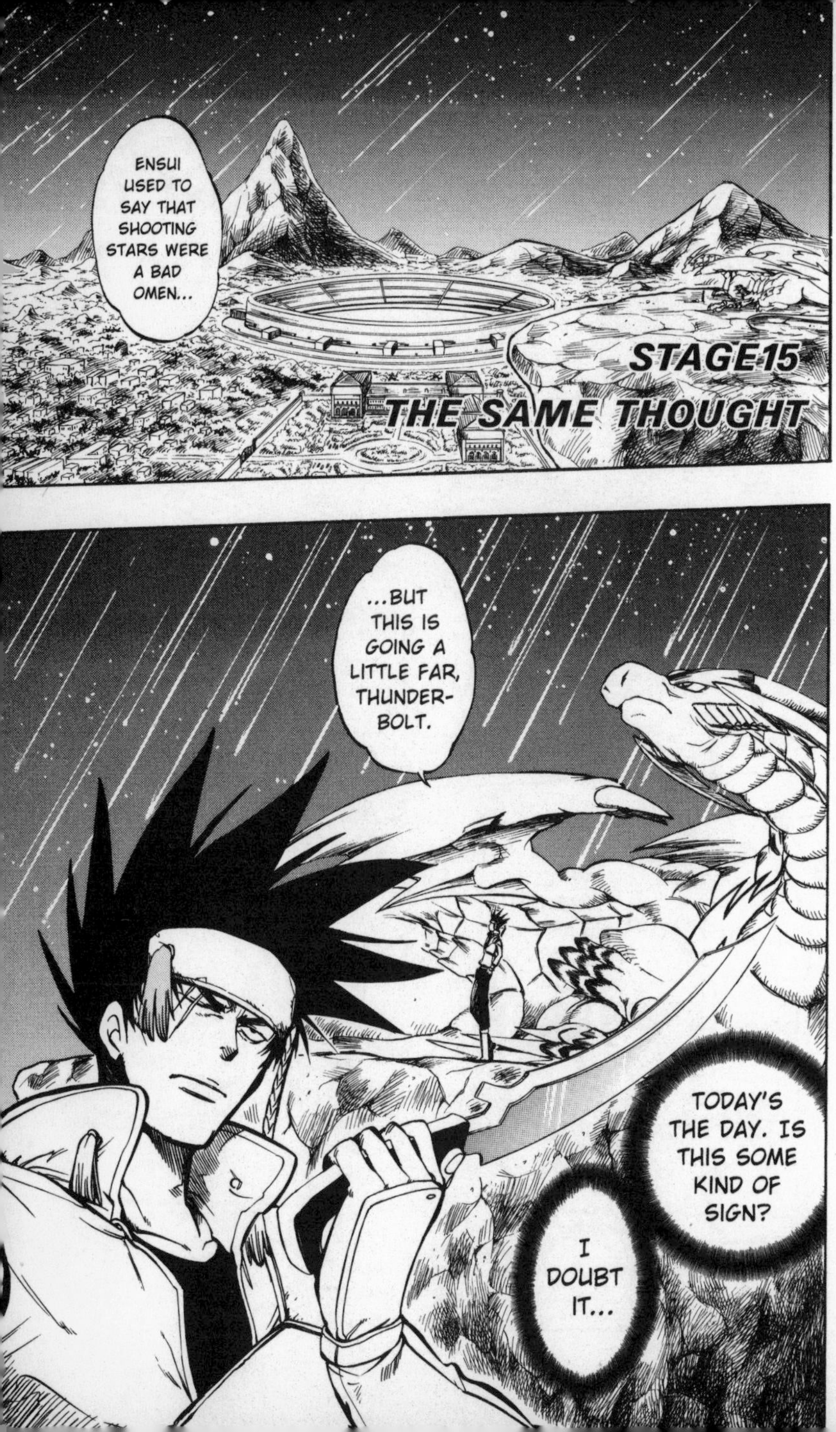
ENSUI USED TO SAY THAT SHOOTING STARS WERE A BAD OMEN...
STAGE 15
THE SAME THOUGHT
...BUT THIS IS GOING A LITTLE FAR, THUNDER-BOLT.
TODAY'S THE DAY. IS THIS SOME KIND OF SIGN?
I DOUBT IT...

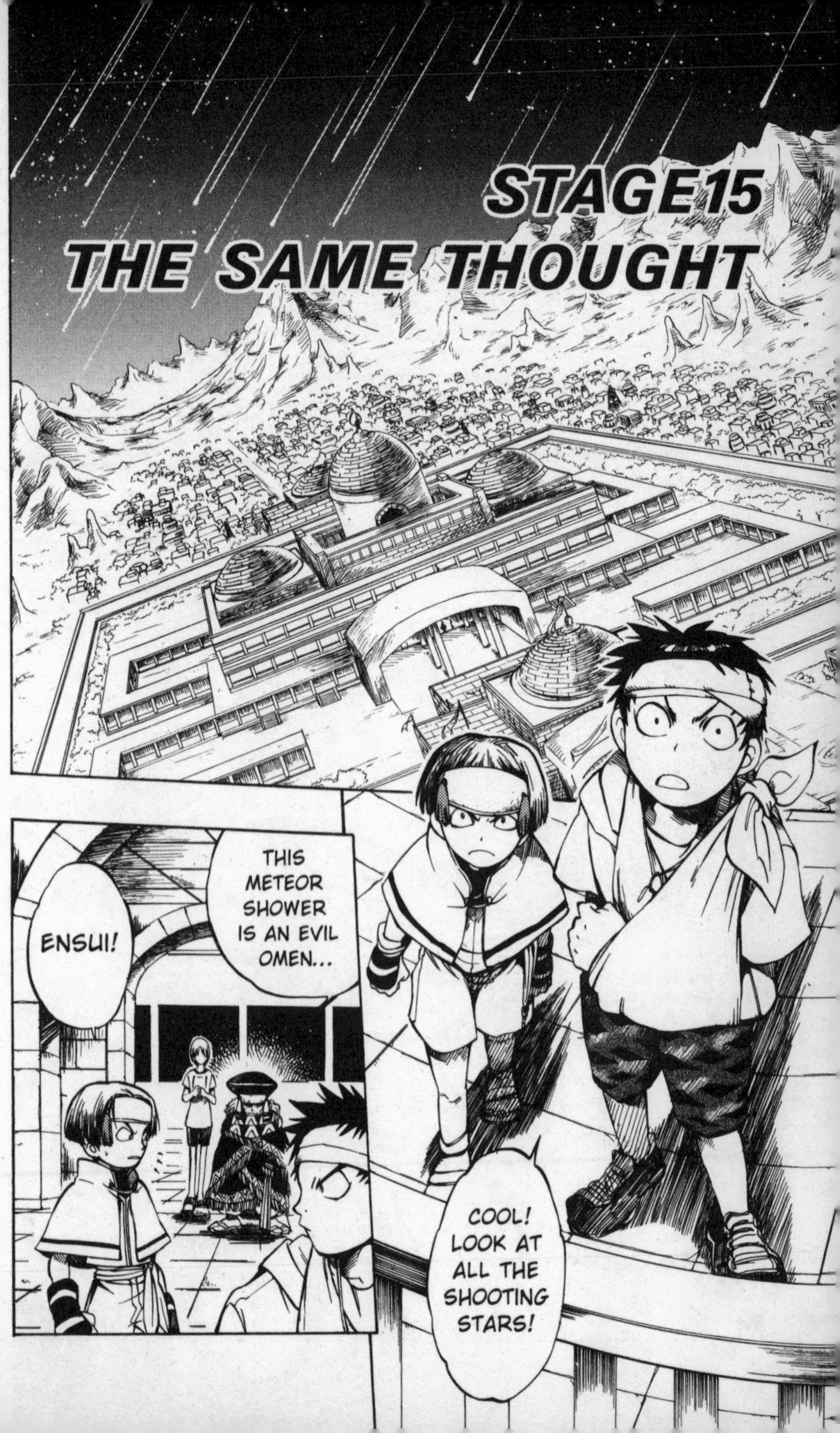
STAGE 15
THE SAME THOUGHT
COOL! LOOK AT ALL THE SHOOTING STARS!
THIS METEOR SHOWER IS AN EVIL OMEN...
ENSUI!

READ THIS WAY

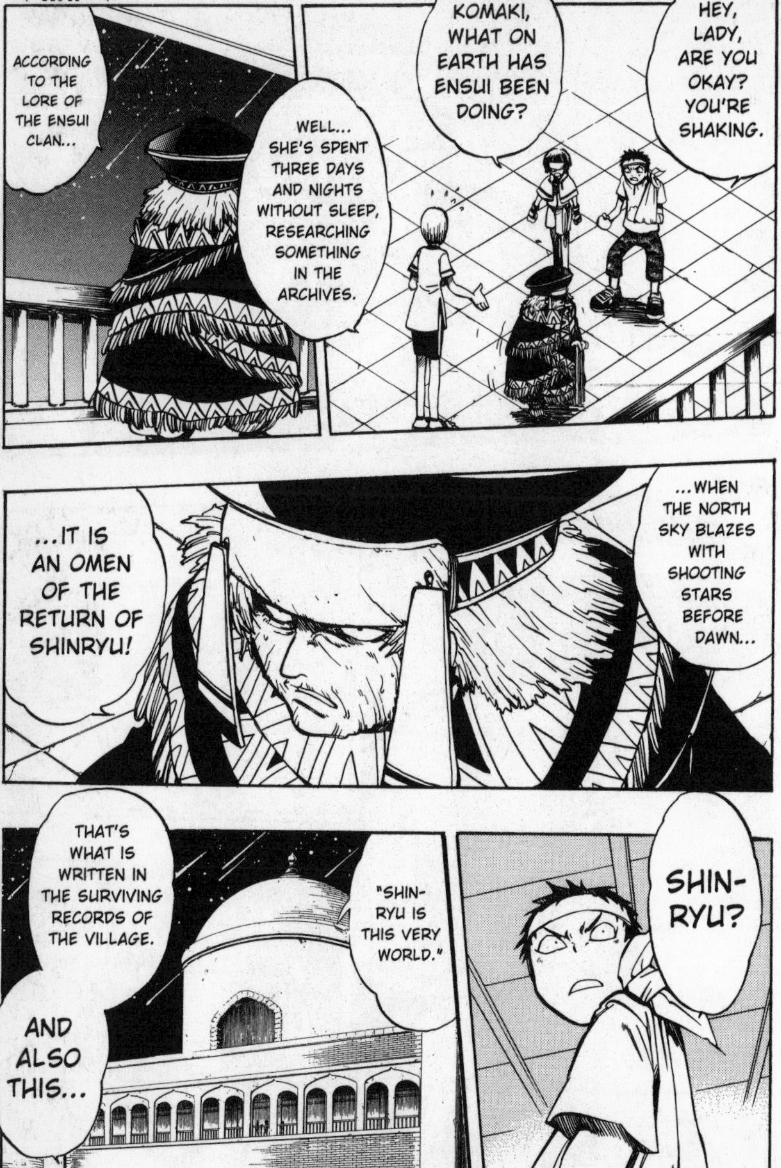

HEY, LADY, ARE YOU OKAY? YOU'RE SHAKING.
KOMAKI, WHAT ON EARTH HAS ENSUI BEEN DOING?
WELL... SHE'S SPENT THREE DAYS AND NIGHTS WITHOUT SLEEP, RESEARCHING SOMETHING IN THE ARCHIVES.
ACCORDING TO THE LORE OF THE ENSUI CLAN...
...WHEN THE NORTH SKY BLAZES WITH SHOOTING STARS BEFORE DAWN...
...IT IS AN OMEN OF THE RETURN OF SHINRYU!
SHIN-RYU?
"SHIN-RYU IS THIS VERY WORLD."
THAT'S WHAT IS WRITTEN IN THE SURVIVING RECORDS OF THE VILLAGE.
AND ALSO THIS...

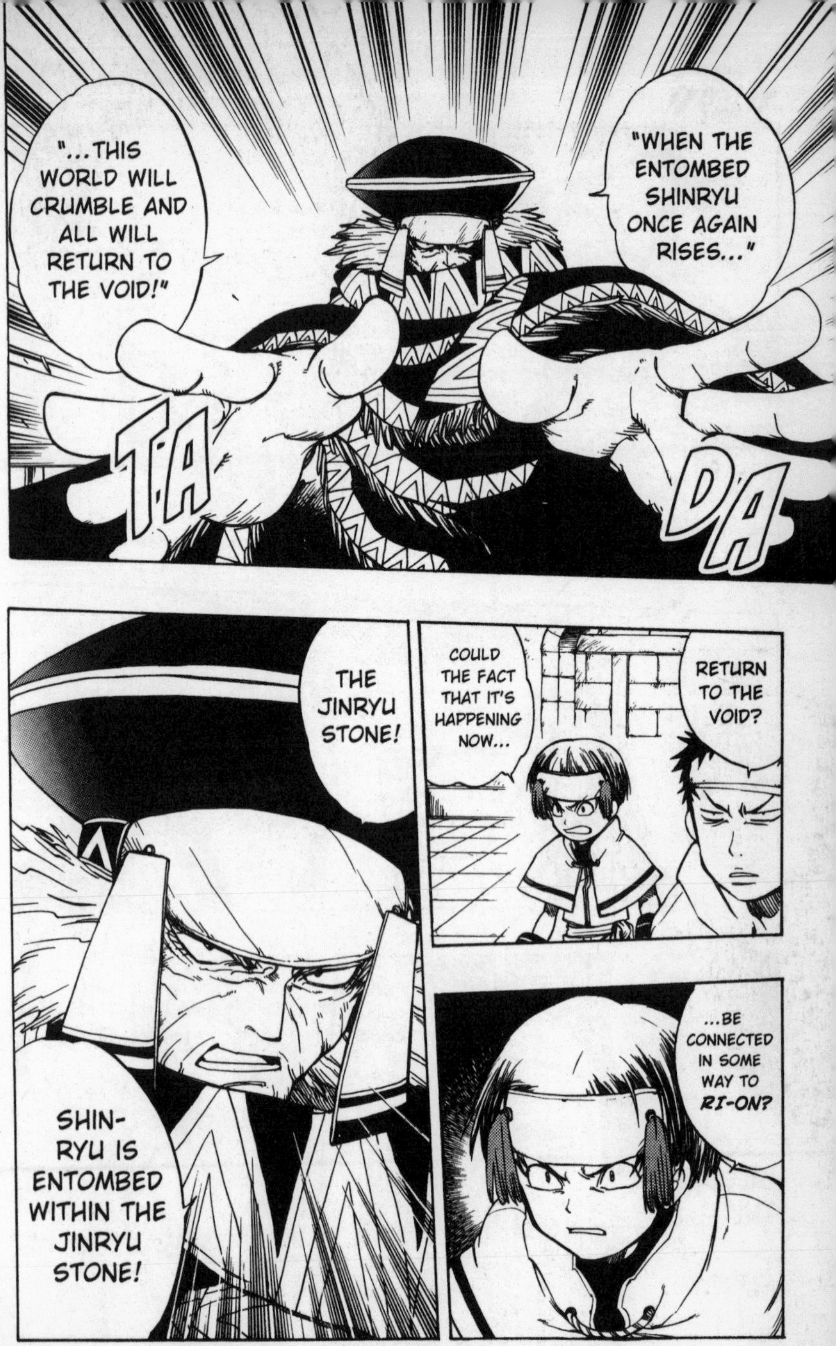
"WHEN THE ENTOMBED SHINRYU ONCE AGAIN RISES..."
"...THIS WORLD WILL CRUMBLE AND ALL WILL RETURN TO THE VOID!"
T-A
DA
RETURN TO THE VOID?
COULD THE FACT THAT IT'S HAPPENING NOW...
...BE CONNECTED IN SOME WAY TO *RI-ON*?
THE JINRYU STONE!
SHIN-RYU IS ENTOMBED WITHIN THE JINRYU STONE!

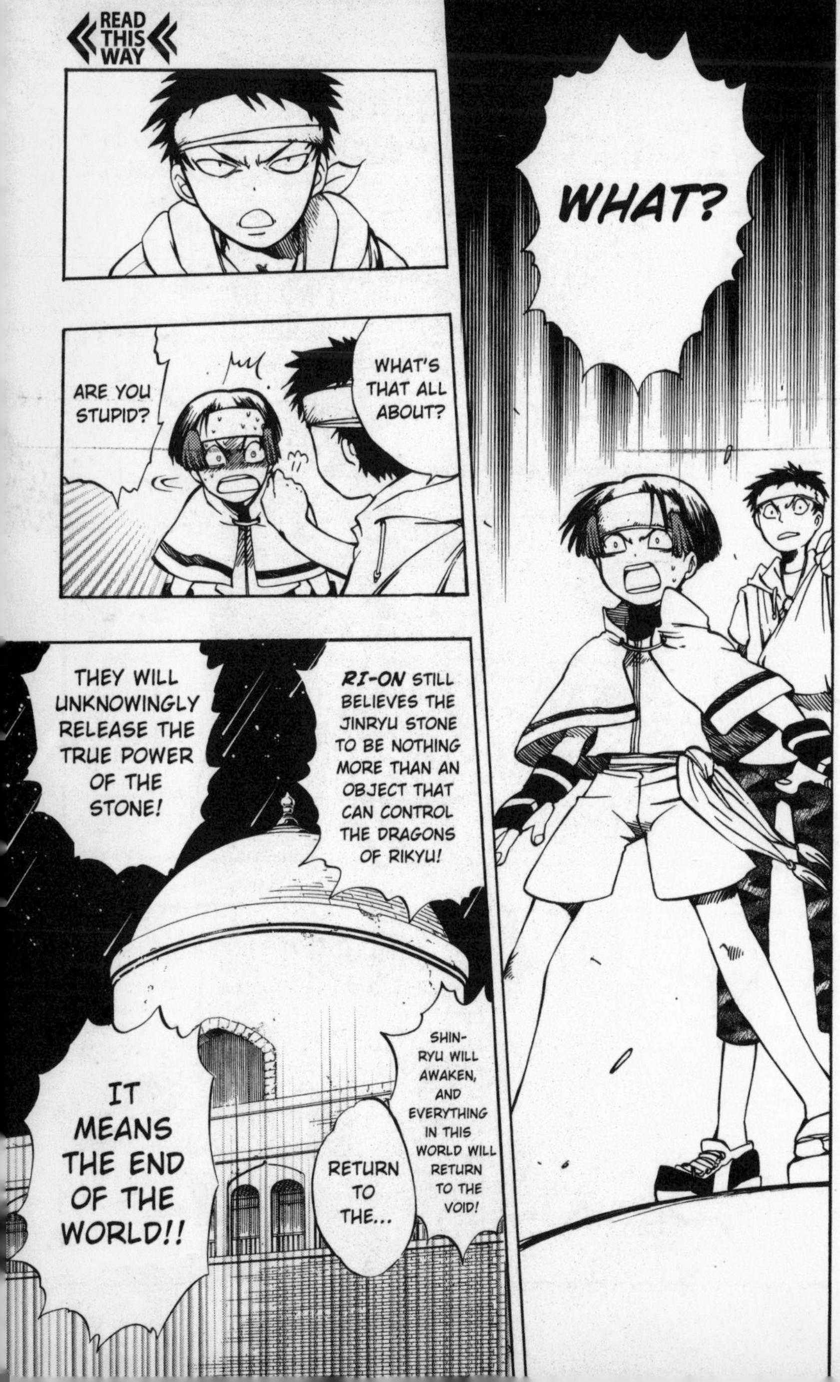
READ THIS WAY
WHAT?
WHAT'S THAT ALL ABOUT?
ARE YOU STUPID?
RI-ON STILL BELIEVES THE JINRYU STONE TO BE NOTHING MORE THAN AN OBJECT THAT CAN CONTROL THE DRAGONS OF RIKYU!
THEY WILL UNKNOWINGLY RELEASE THE TRUE POWER OF THE STONE!
SHIN-RYU WILL AWAKEN, AND EVERYTHING IN THIS WORLD WILL RETURN TO THE VOID!
RETURN TO THE...
IT MEANS THE END OF THE WORLD!!

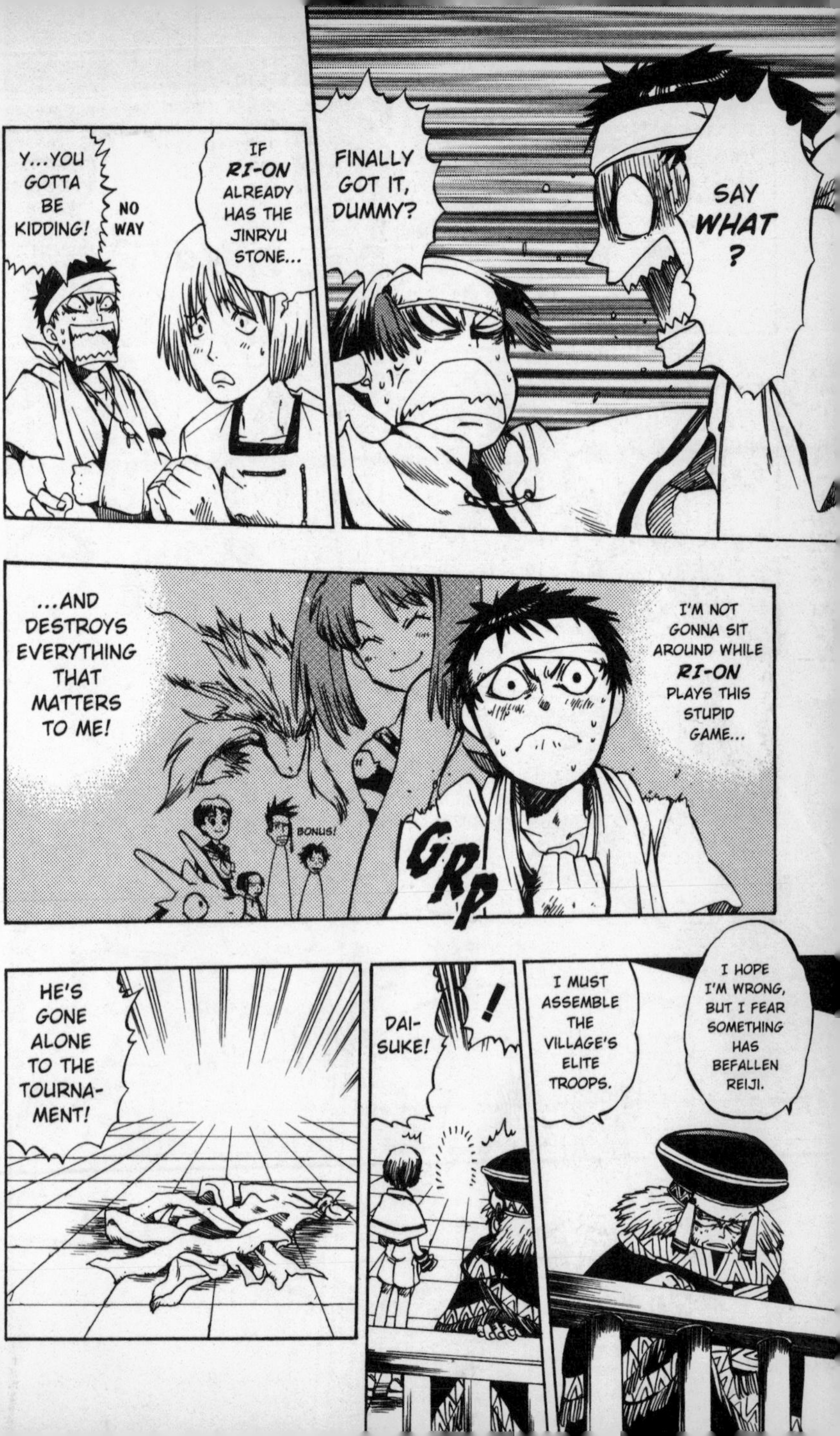

SAY WHAT?
FINALLY GOT IT, DUMMY?
IF RI-ON ALREADY HAS THE JINRYU STONE...
NO WAY
Y...YOU GOTTA BE KIDDING!
I'M NOT GONNA SIT AROUND WHILE RI-ON PLAYS THIS STUPID GAME...
...AND DESTROYS EVERYTHING THAT MATTERS TO ME!
BONUS!
GRP
I HOPE I'M WRONG, BUT I FEAR SOMETHING HAS BEFALLEN REIJI.
I MUST ASSEMBLE THE VILLAGE'S ELITE TROOPS.
!
DAI-SUKE!
HE'S GONE ALONE TO THE TOURNA-MENT!

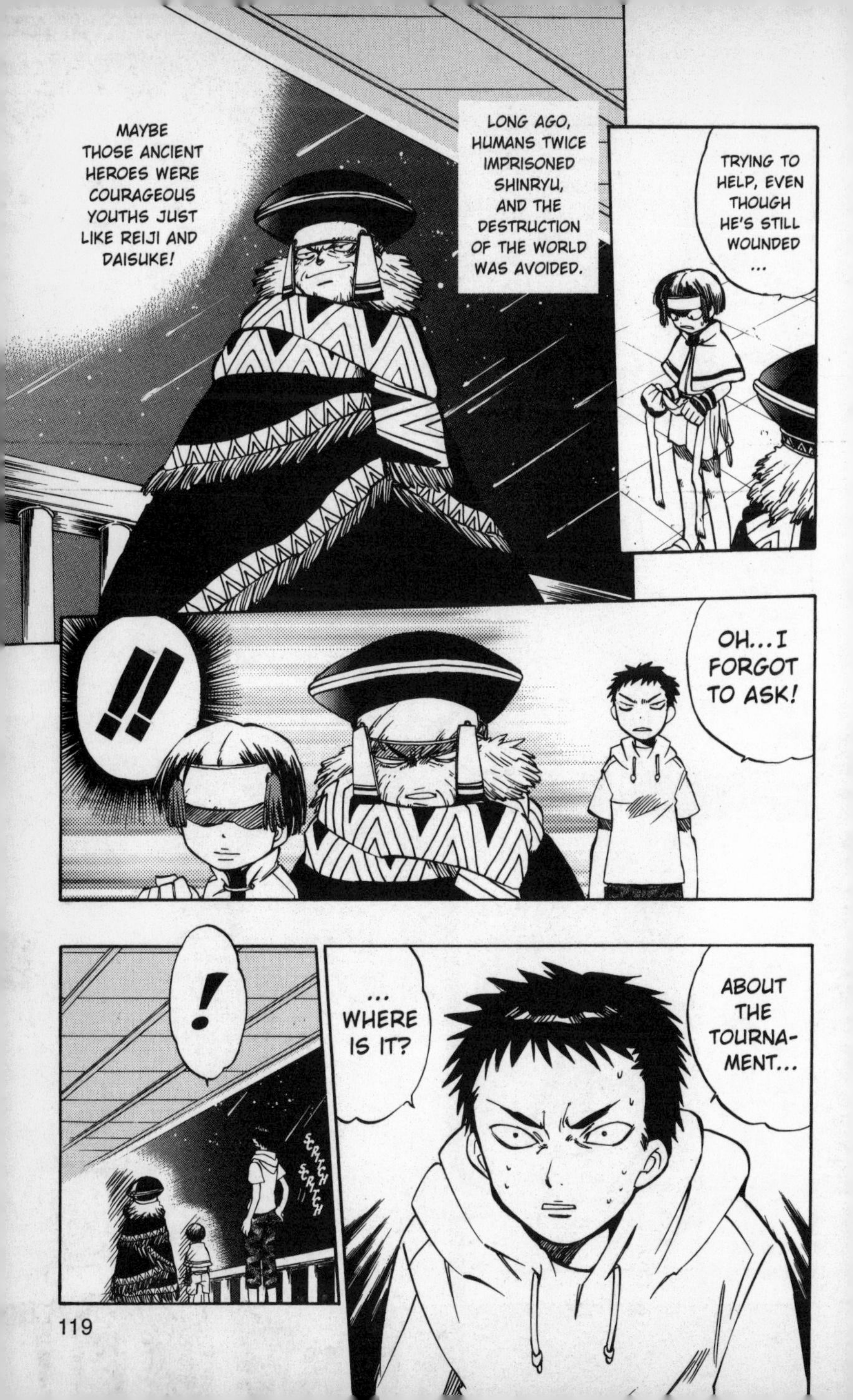
TRYING TO HELP, EVEN THOUGH HE'S STILL WOUNDED ...
LONG AGO, HUMANS TWICE IMPRISONED SHINRYU, AND THE DESTRUCTION OF THE WORLD WAS AVOIDED.
MAYBE THOSE ANCIENT HEROES WERE COURAGEOUS YOUTHS JUST LIKE REIJI AND DAISUKE!
OH... I FORGOT TO ASK!
!!
ABOUT THE TOURNA-MENT...
... WHERE IS IT?
!
SCRITCH SCRITCH

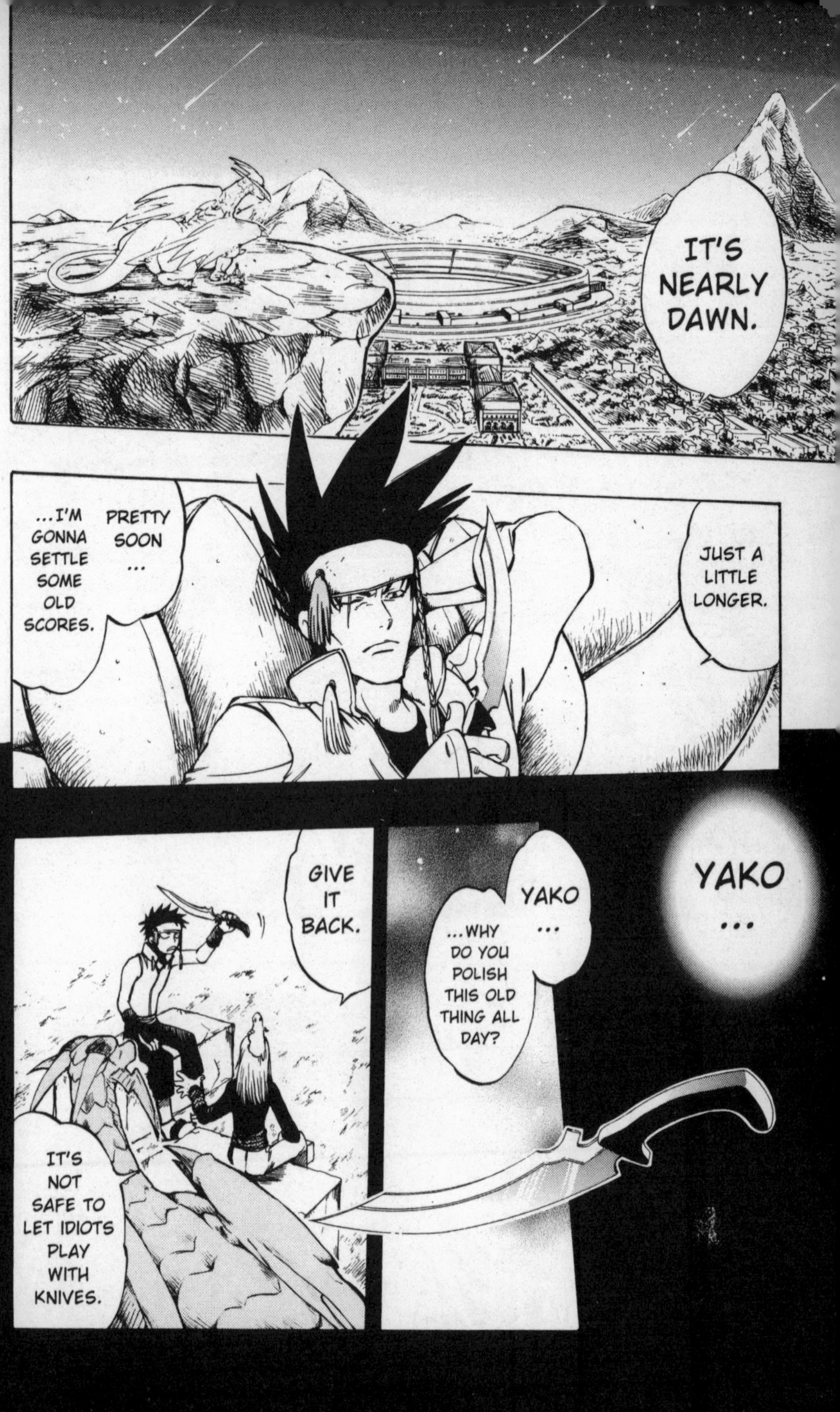
IT'S NEARLY DAWN.
JUST A LITTLE LONGER.
PRETTY SOON ...
...I'M GONNA SETTLE SOME OLD SCORES.
YAKO ...
YAKO ...
...WHY DO YOU POLISH THIS OLD THING ALL DAY?
GIVE IT BACK.
IT'S NOT SAFE TO LET IDIOTS PLAY WITH KNIVES.

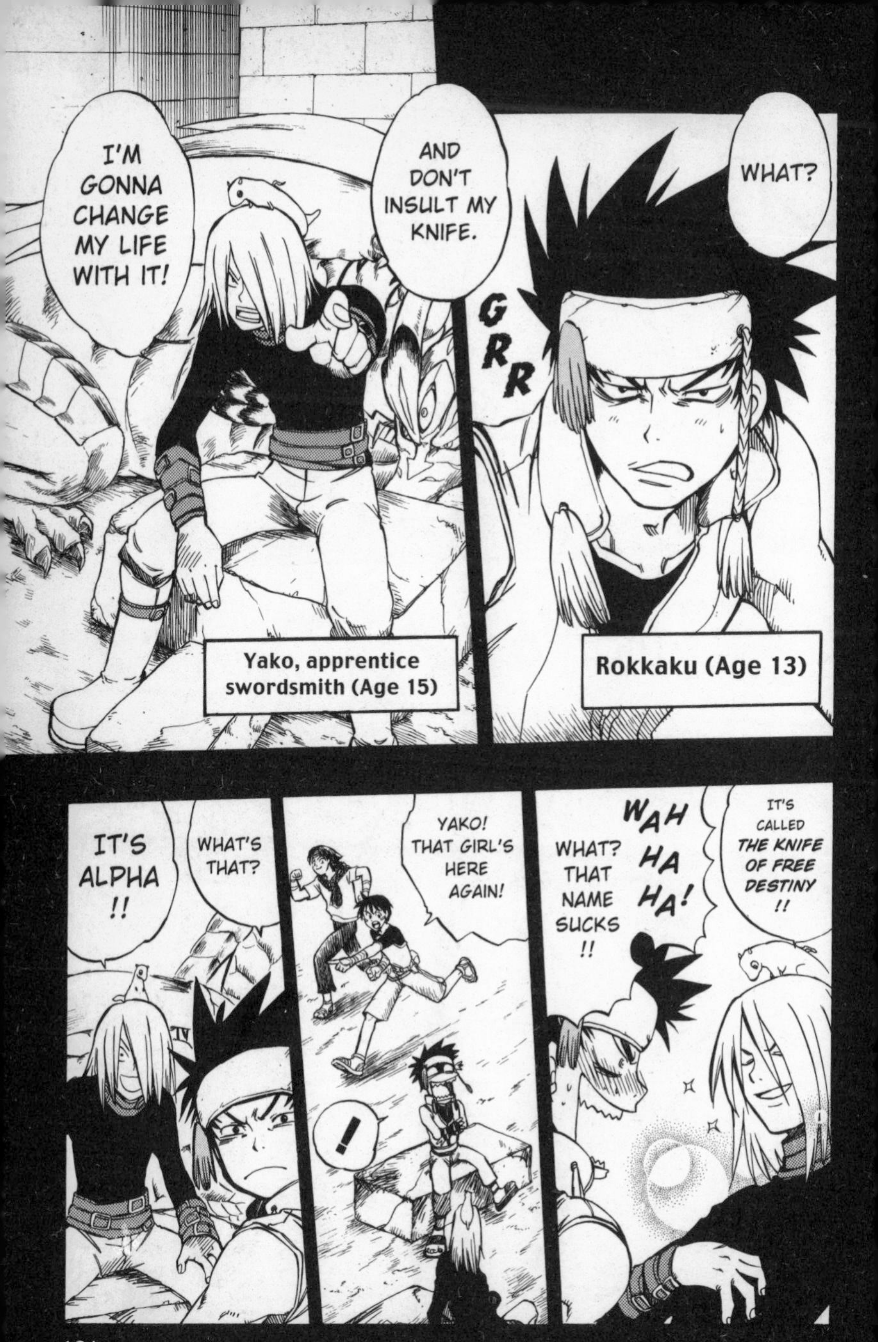
WHAT?
GRR
Rokkaku (Age 13)
AND DON'T INSULT MY KNIFE.
I'M GONNA CHANGE MY LIFE WITH IT!
Yako, apprentice swordsmith (Age 15)
IT'S CALLED THE KNIFE OF FREE DESTINY !!
WAH HA HA!
WHAT? THAT NAME SUCKS !!
YAKO! THAT GIRL'S HERE AGAIN!
!
WHAT'S THAT?
IT'S ALPHA !!

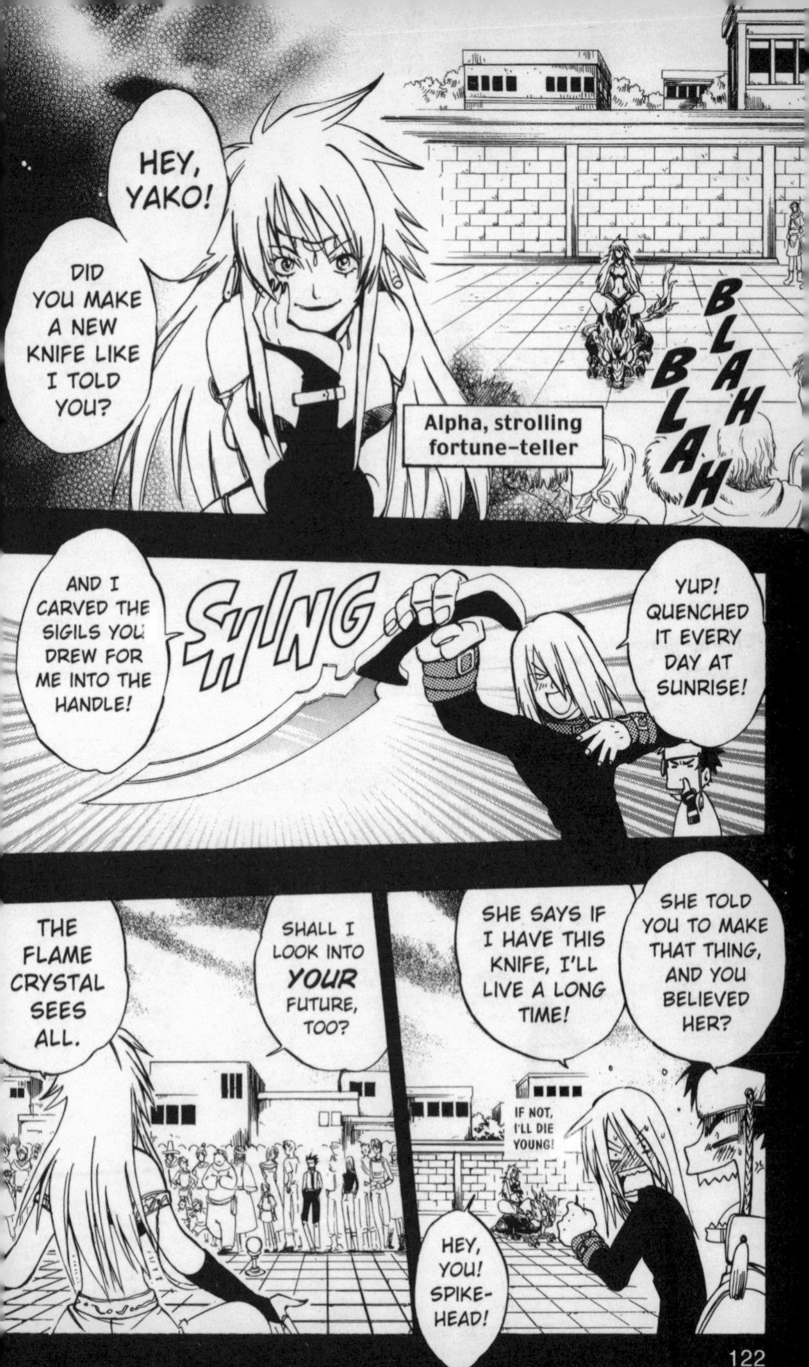
HEY, YAKO!
DID YOU MAKE A NEW KNIFE LIKE I TOLD YOU?
Alpha, strolling fortune-teller
BLAH BLAH
YUP! QUENCHED IT EVERY DAY AT SUNRISE!
SHING
AND I CARVED THE SIGILS YOU DREW FOR ME INTO THE HANDLE!
SHE TOLD YOU TO MAKE THAT THING, AND YOU BELIEVED HER?
SHE SAYS IF I HAVE THIS KNIFE, I'LL LIVE A LONG TIME!
IF NOT, I'LL DIE YOUNG!
HEY, YOU! SPIKE-HEAD!
SHALL I LOOK INTO YOUR FUTURE, TOO?
THE FLAME CRYSTAL SEES ALL.

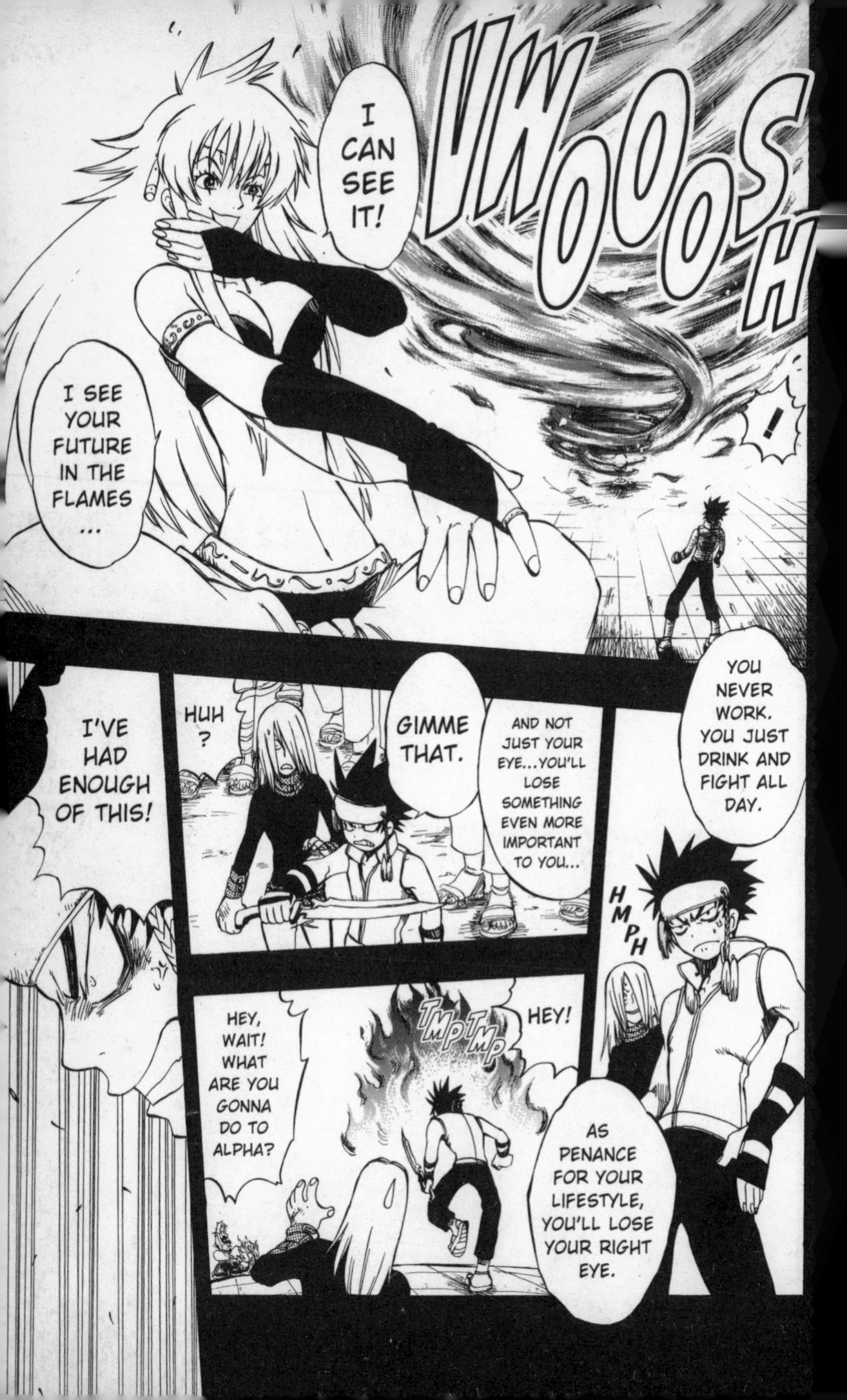
WHOOOOSH
I CAN SEE IT!
!
I SEE YOUR FUTURE IN THE FLAMES ...
YOU NEVER WORK. YOU JUST DRINK AND FIGHT ALL DAY.
HMPH
AS PENANCE FOR YOUR LIFESTYLE, YOU'LL LOSE YOUR RIGHT EYE.
AND NOT JUST YOUR EYE...YOU'LL LOSE SOMETHING EVEN MORE IMPORTANT TO YOU...
GIMME THAT.
HUH ?
HEY!
TMP TMP
HEY, WAIT! WHAT ARE YOU GONNA DO TO ALPHA?
I'VE HAD ENOUGH OF THIS!

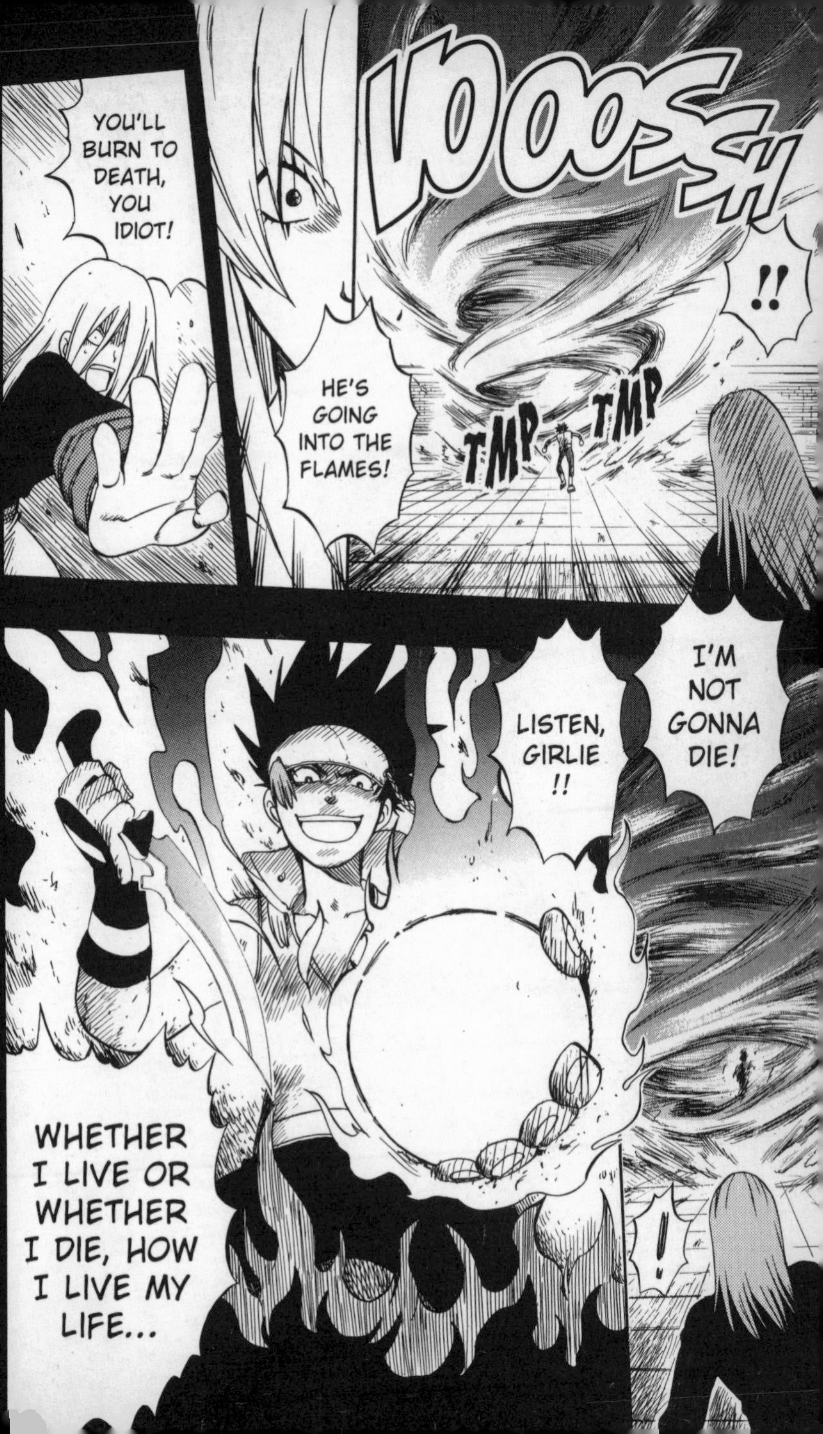
VOOOSH
!!
HE'S GOING INTO THE FLAMES!
TMP TMP
YOU'LL BURN TO DEATH, YOU IDIOT!
I'M NOT GONNA DIE!
LISTEN, GIRLIE!!
!
WHETHER I LIVE OR WHETHER I DIE, HOW I LIVE MY LIFE...

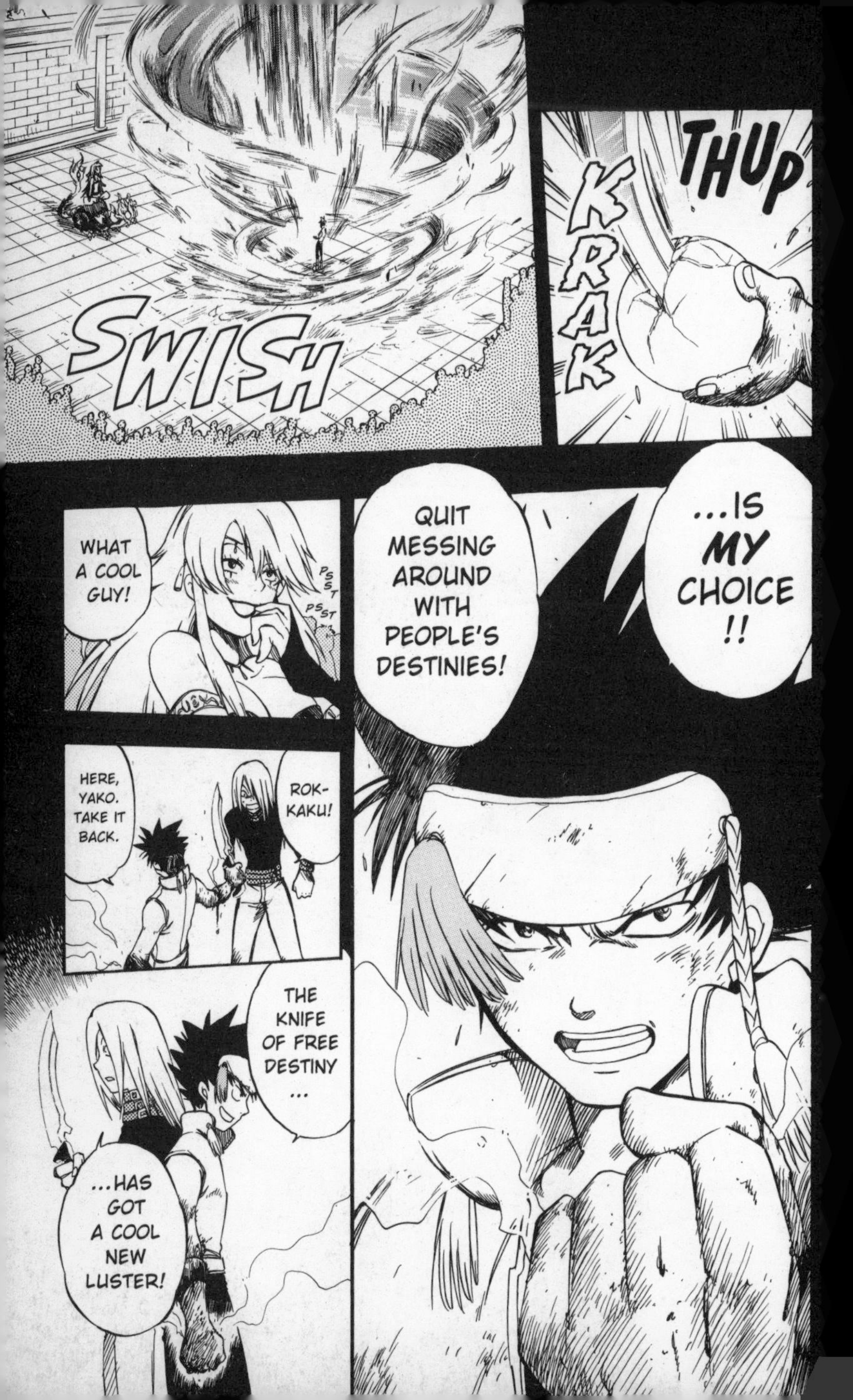
THUP
KRAK
SWISH
...IS MY CHOICE!!
QUIT MESSING AROUND WITH PEOPLE'S DESTINIES!
WHAT A COOL GUY!
PSST PSST
ROK-KAKU!
HERE, YAKO. TAKE IT BACK.
THE KNIFE OF FREE DESTINY ...
...HAS GOT A COOL NEW LUSTER!

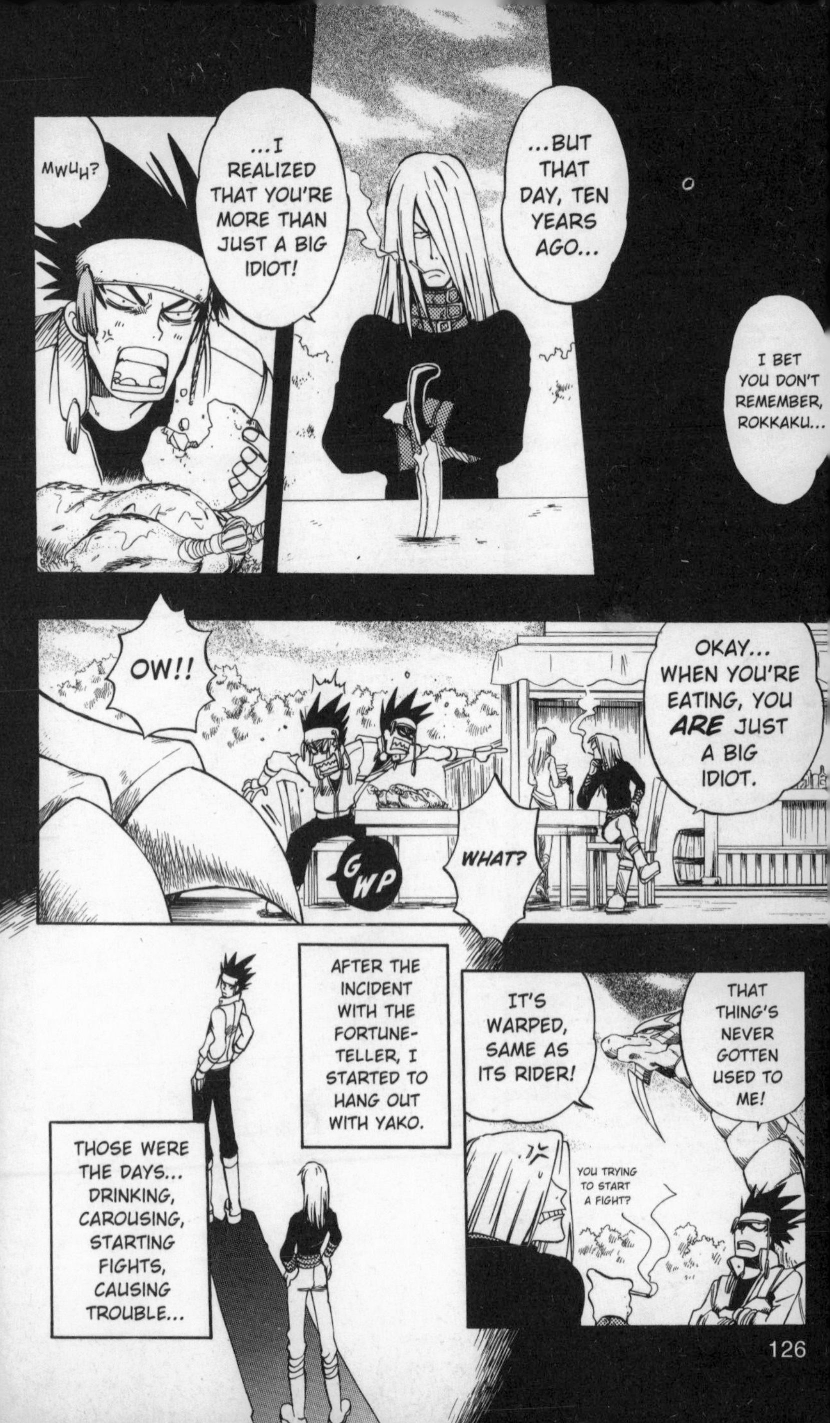
I BET YOU DON'T REMEMBER, ROKKAKU...
...BUT THAT DAY, TEN YEARS AGO...
...I REALIZED THAT YOU'RE MORE THAN JUST A BIG IDIOT!
MWUH?
OKAY... WHEN YOU'RE EATING, YOU **ARE** JUST A BIG IDIOT.
WHAT?
GWP
OW!!
THAT THING'S NEVER GOTTEN USED TO ME!
IT'S WARPED, SAME AS ITS RIDER!
YOU TRYING TO START A FIGHT?
AFTER THE INCIDENT WITH THE FORTUNE-TELLER, I STARTED TO HANG OUT WITH YAKO.
THOSE WERE THE DAYS... DRINKING, CAROUSING, STARTING FIGHTS, CAUSING TROUBLE...

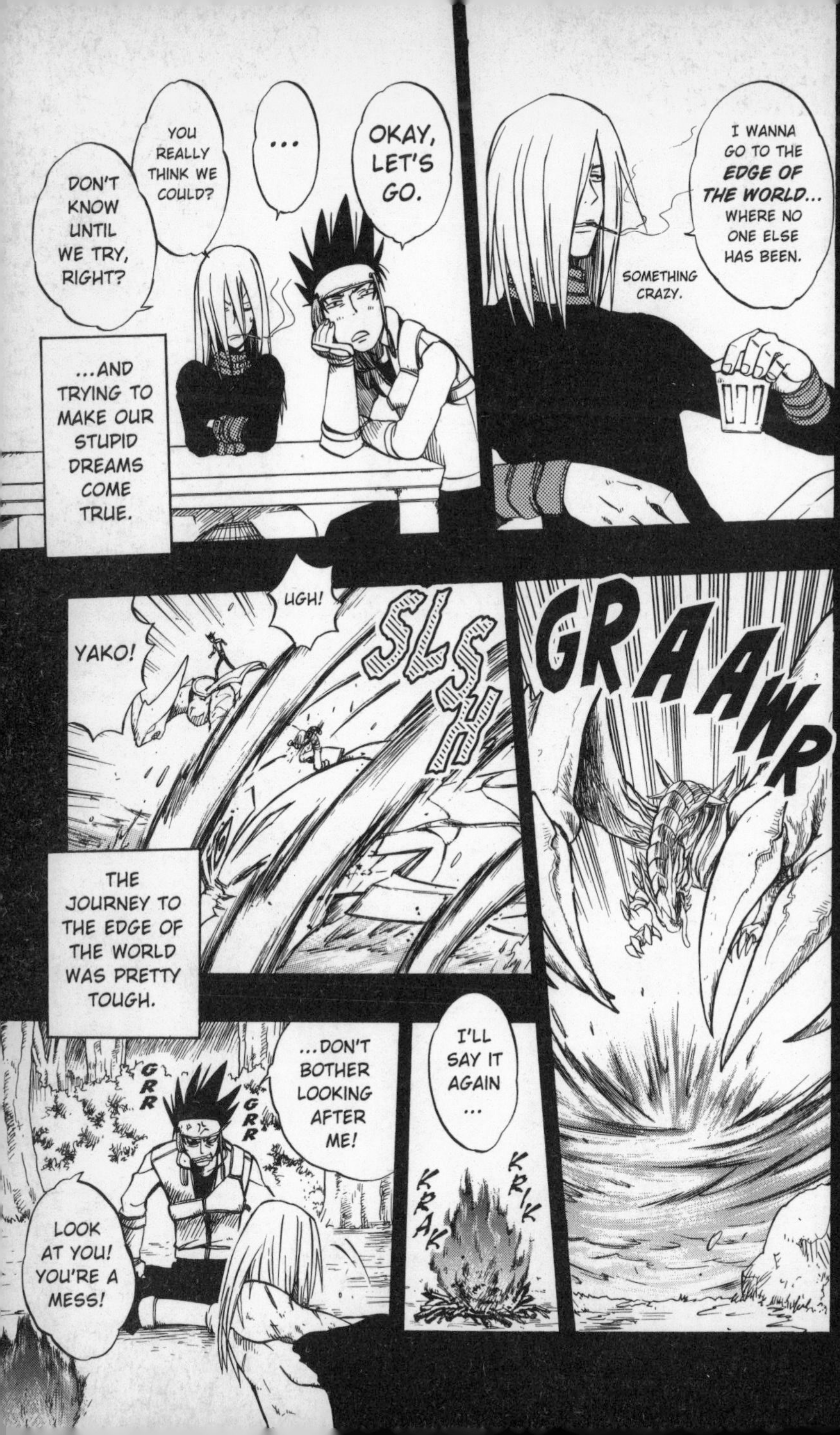
I WANNA GO TO THE **EDGE OF THE WORLD...** WHERE NO ONE ELSE HAS BEEN.
SOMETHING CRAZY.
OKAY, LET'S GO.
...
YOU REALLY THINK WE COULD?
DON'T KNOW UNTIL WE TRY, RIGHT?
...AND TRYING TO MAKE OUR STUPID DREAMS COME TRUE.
GRAAWR
SLSH
UGH!
YAKO!
THE JOURNEY TO THE EDGE OF THE WORLD WAS PRETTY TOUGH.
I'LL SAY IT AGAIN ...
KRIK
KRAK
...DON'T BOTHER LOOKING AFTER ME!
GRR
GRR
LOOK AT YOU! YOU'RE A MESS!

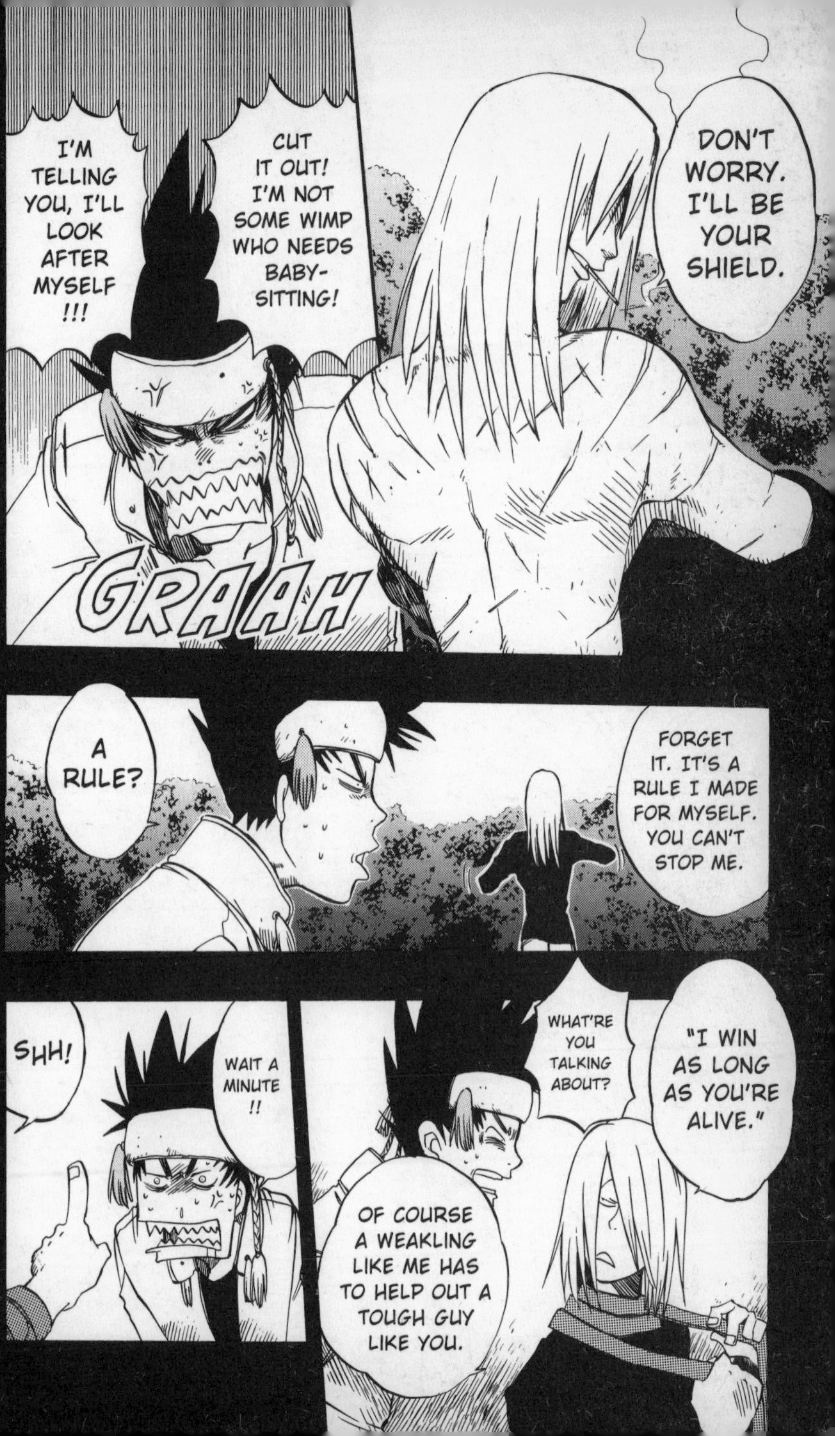
DON'T WORRY. I'LL BE YOUR SHIELD.
CUT IT OUT! I'M NOT SOME WIMP WHO NEEDS BABY-SITTING!
I'M TELLING YOU, I'LL LOOK AFTER MYSELF!!!
GRAAH
FORGET IT. IT'S A RULE I MADE FOR MYSELF. YOU CAN'T STOP ME.
A RULE?
"I WIN AS LONG AS YOU'RE ALIVE."
WHAT'RE YOU TALKING ABOUT?
OF COURSE A WEAKLING LIKE ME HAS TO HELP OUT A TOUGH GUY LIKE YOU.
WAIT A MINUTE !!
SHH!

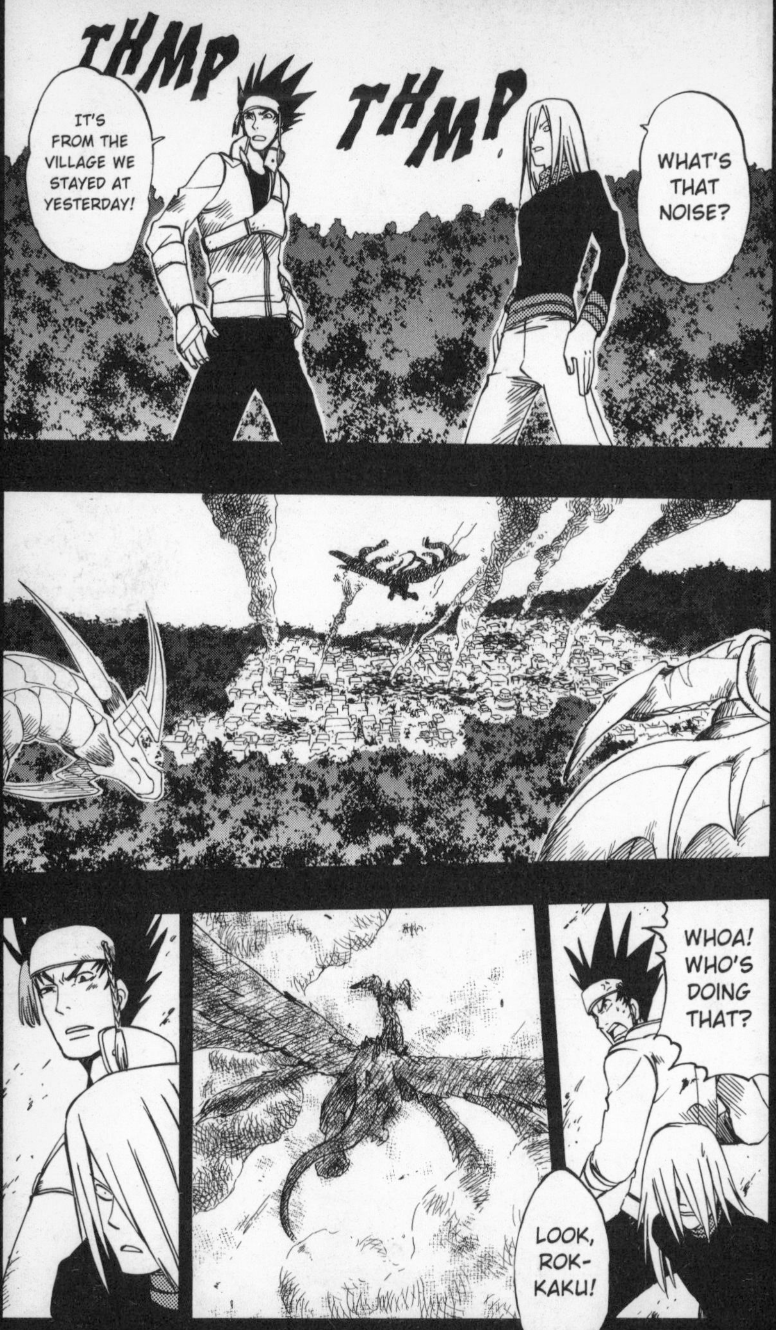
THMP THMP
WHAT'S THAT NOISE?
IT'S FROM THE VILLAGE WE STAYED AT YESTERDAY!
WHOA! WHO'S DOING THAT?
LOOK, ROK-KAKU!

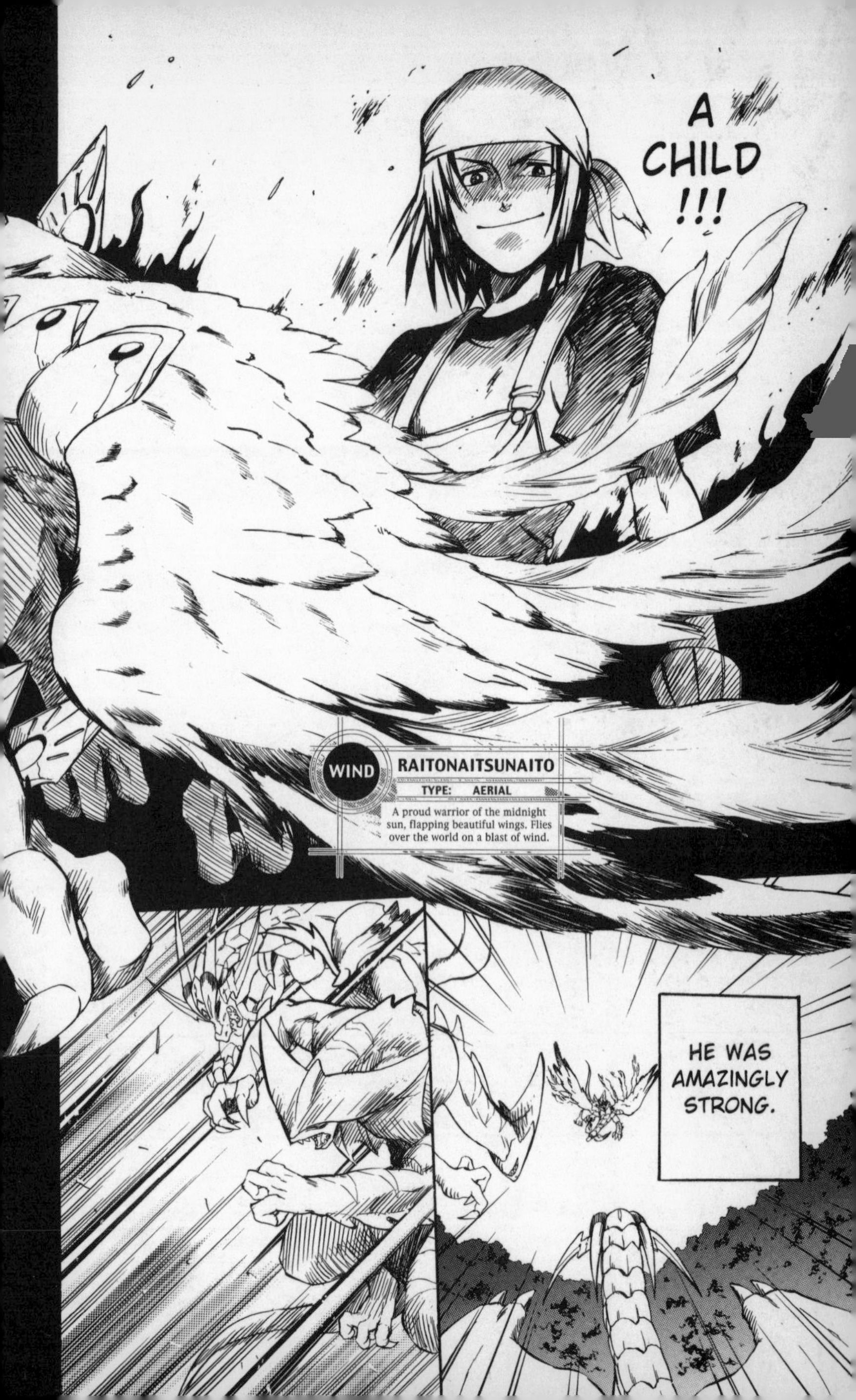
A CHILD !!!
WIND
RAITONAITSUNAITO
TYPE: AERIAL
A proud warrior of the midnight sun, flapping beautiful wings. Flies over the world on a blast of wind.
HE WAS AMAZINGLY STRONG.

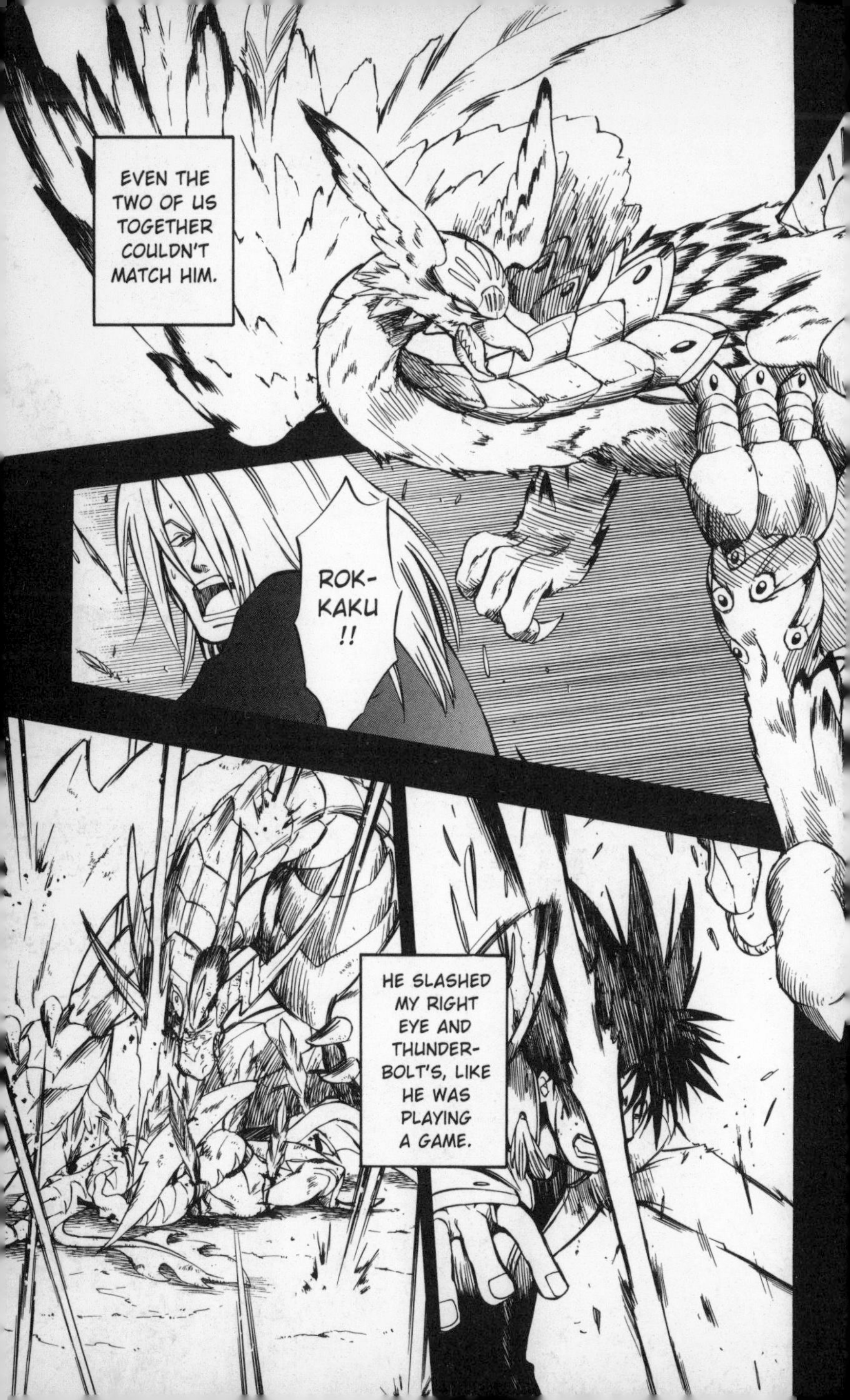
EVEN THE TWO OF US TOGETHER COULDN'T MATCH HIM.
ROK-KAKU !!
HE SLASHED MY RIGHT EYE AND THUNDER-BOLT'S, LIKE HE WAS PLAYING A GAME.

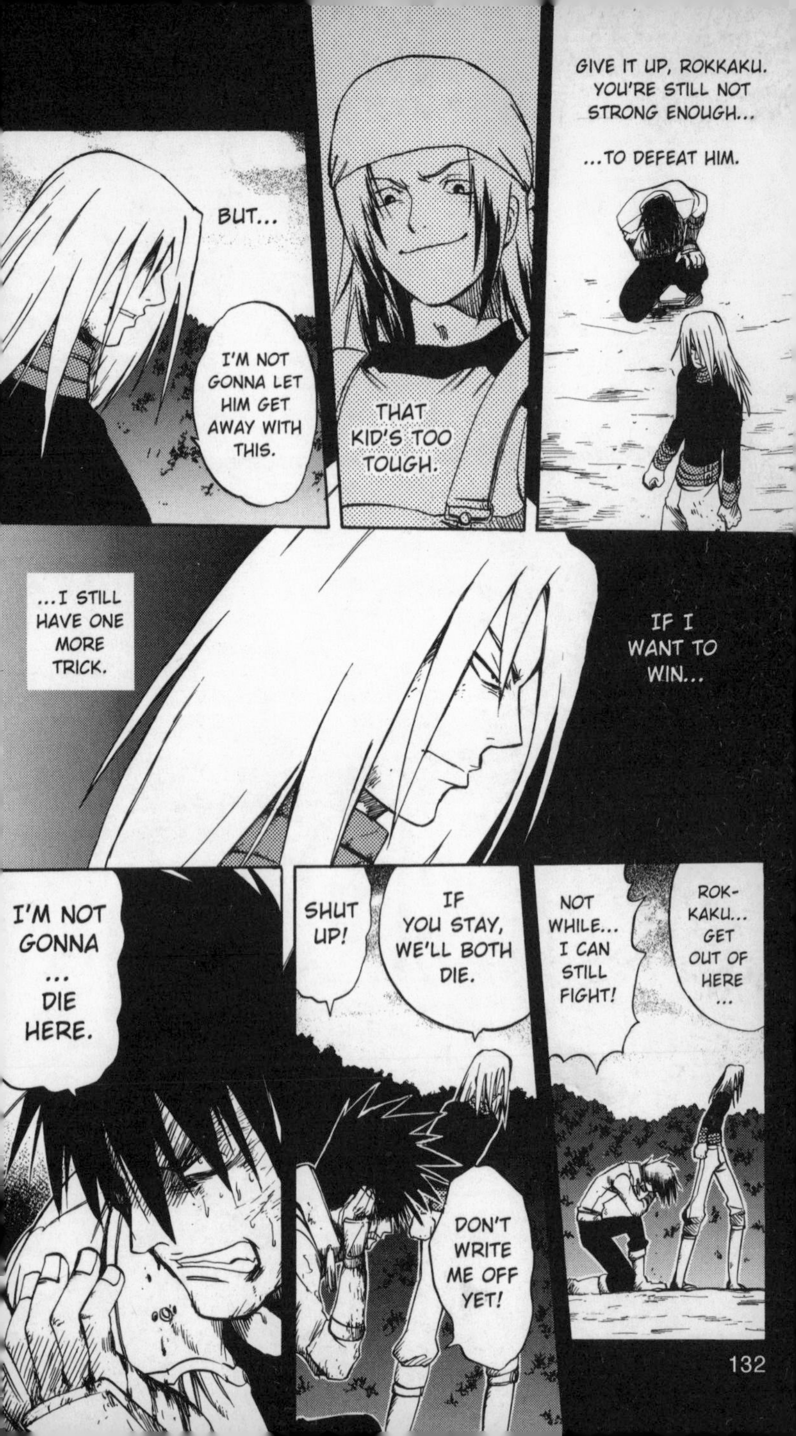
GIVE IT UP, ROKKAKU. YOU'RE STILL NOT STRONG ENOUGH...
...TO DEFEAT HIM.
THAT KID'S TOO TOUGH.
BUT...
I'M NOT GONNA LET HIM GET AWAY WITH THIS.
IF I WANT TO WIN...
...I STILL HAVE ONE MORE TRICK.
ROK-KAKU... GET OUT OF HERE ...
NOT WHILE... I CAN STILL FIGHT!
IF YOU STAY, WE'LL BOTH DIE.
SHUT UP!
DON'T WRITE ME OFF YET!
I'M NOT GONNA ... DIE HERE.

READ THIS WAY

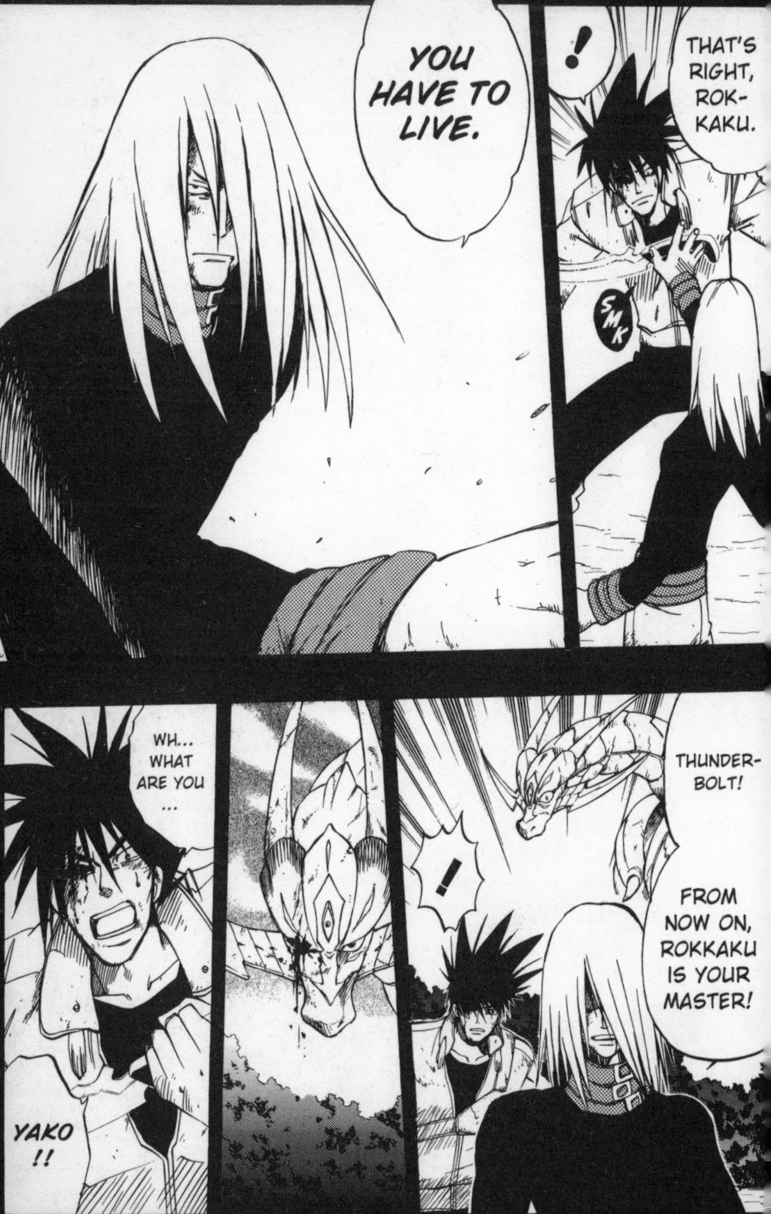
!
THAT'S RIGHT, ROK-KAKU.
SMK
YOU HAVE TO LIVE.
THUNDER-BOLT!
!
FROM NOW ON, ROKKAKU IS YOUR MASTER!
WH... WHAT ARE YOU ...
YAKO !!

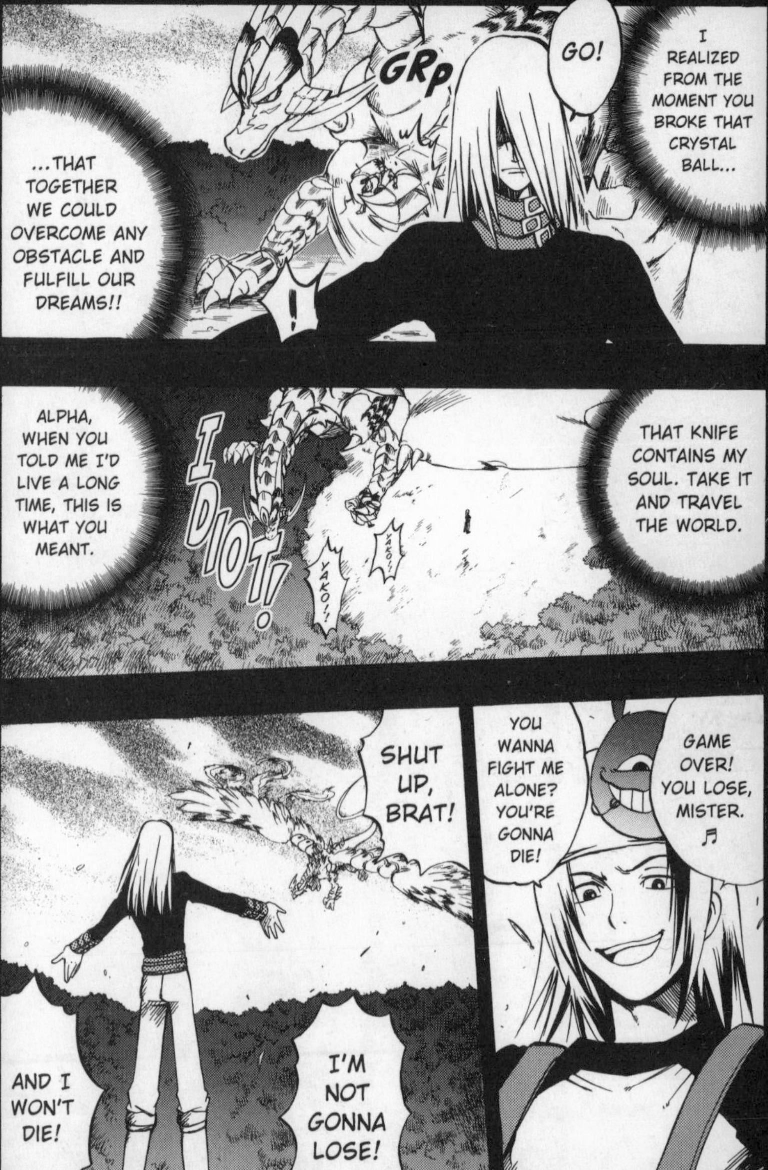
I REALIZED FROM THE MOMENT YOU BROKE THAT CRYSTAL BALL...
GO!
GRP
...THAT TOGETHER WE COULD OVERCOME ANY OBSTACLE AND FULFILL OUR DREAMS!!
!
THAT KNIFE CONTAINS MY SOUL. TAKE IT AND TRAVEL THE WORLD.
YAKO!!
YAKO!!
IDIOT!!
ALPHA, WHEN YOU TOLD ME I'D LIVE A LONG TIME, THIS IS WHAT YOU MEANT.
GAME OVER! YOU LOSE, MISTER. ♪
YOU WANNA FIGHT ME ALONE? YOU'RE GONNA DIE!
SHUT UP, BRAT!
I'M NOT GONNA LOSE!
AND I WON'T DIE!

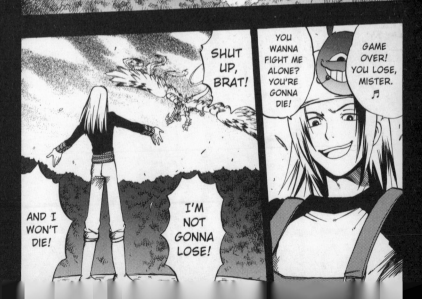

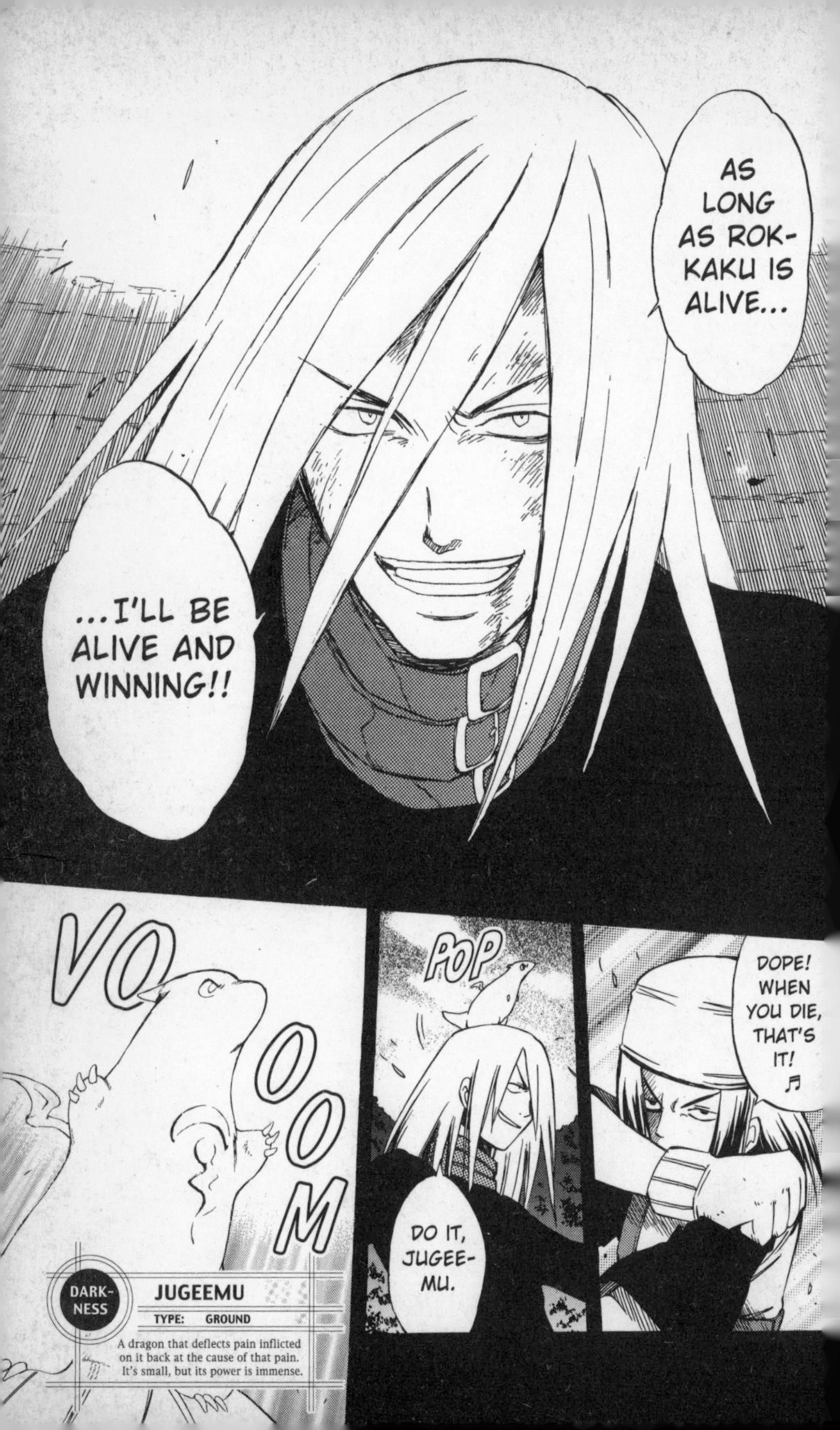
AS LONG AS ROK-KAKU IS ALIVE...
...I'LL BE ALIVE AND WINNING!!
DOPE! WHEN YOU DIE, THAT'S IT! ♬
POP
DO IT, JUGEE-MU.
VOOOOM
DARK-NESS
JUGEEMU
TYPE: GROUND
A dragon that deflects pain inflicted on it back at the cause of that pain. It's small, but its power is immense.

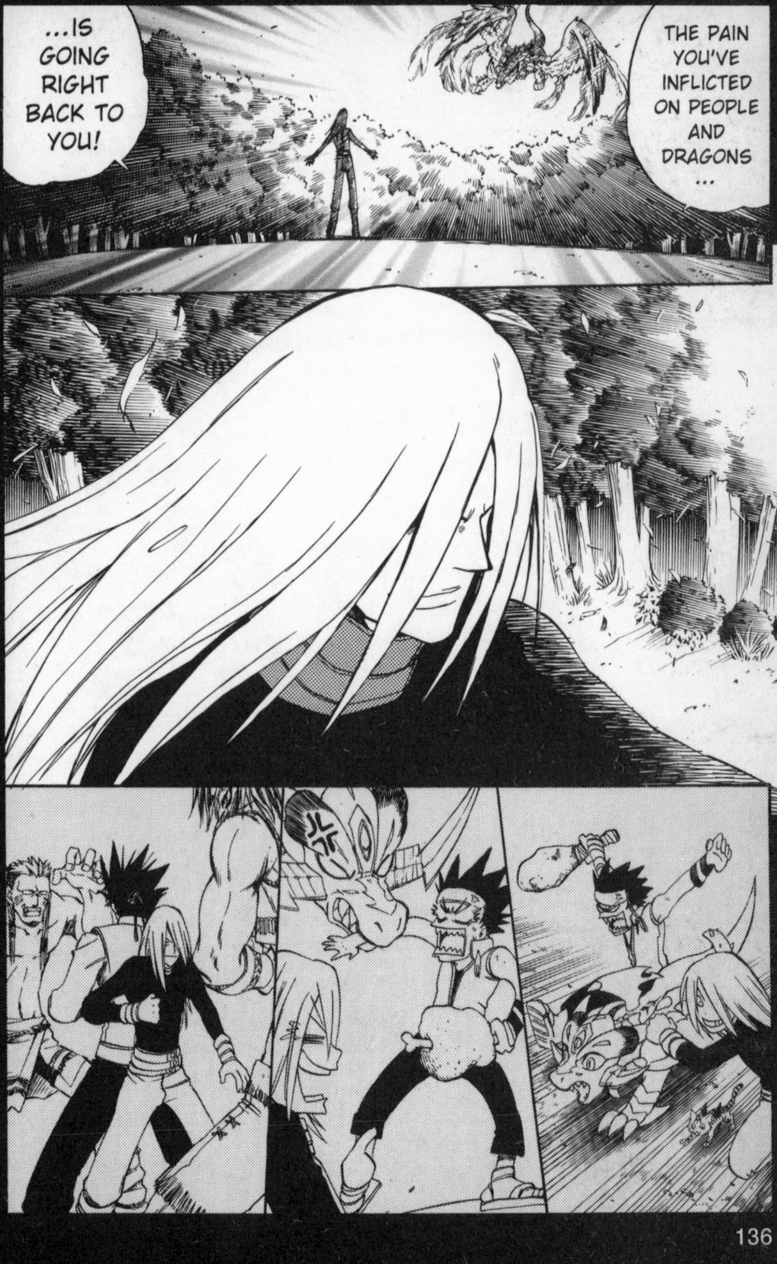
THE PAIN YOU'VE INFLICTED ON PEOPLE AND DRAGONS ...
...IS GOING RIGHT BACK TO YOU!

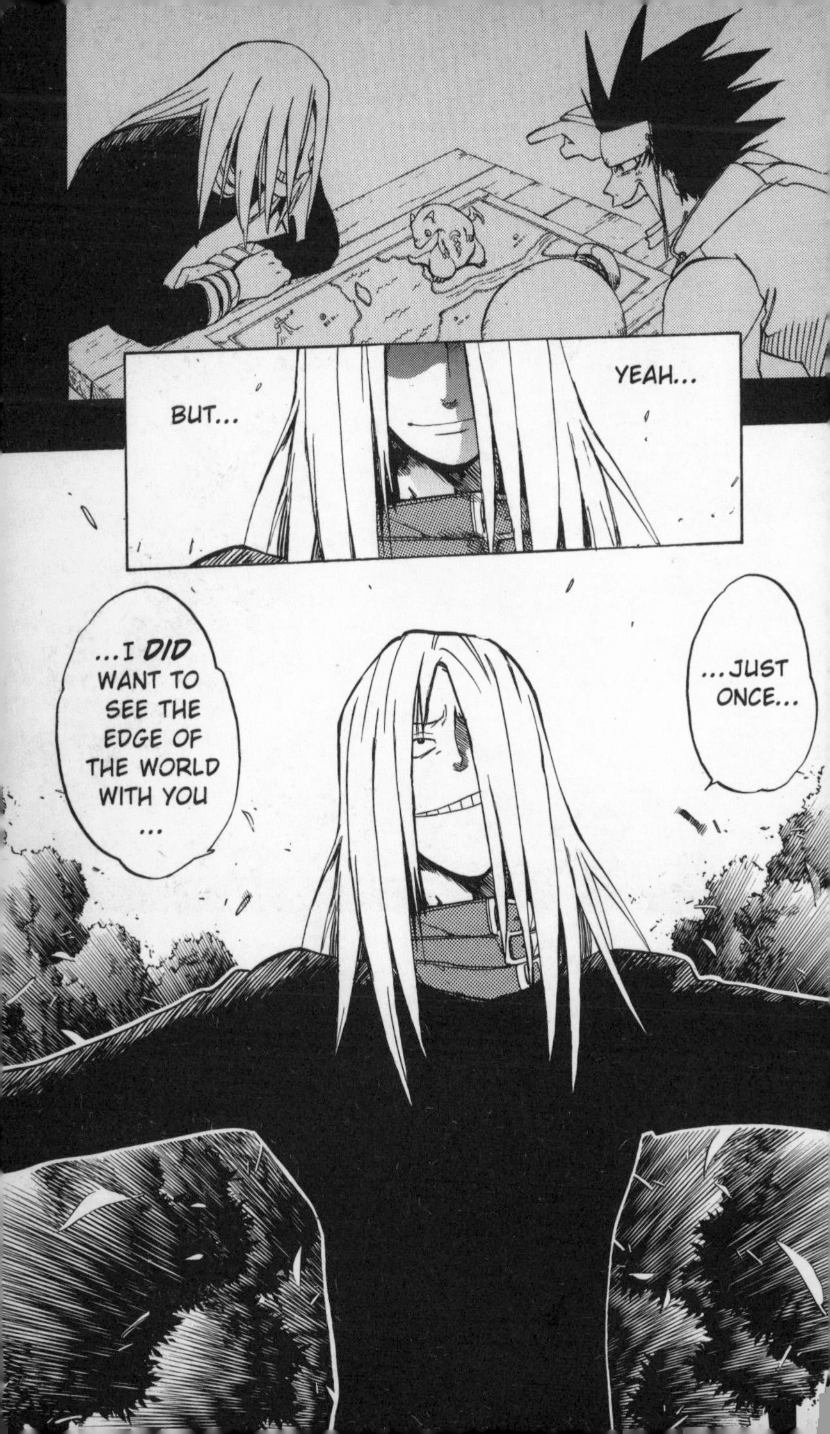
YEAH...
BUT...
...JUST ONCE...
...I DID WANT TO SEE THE EDGE OF THE WORLD WITH YOU ...

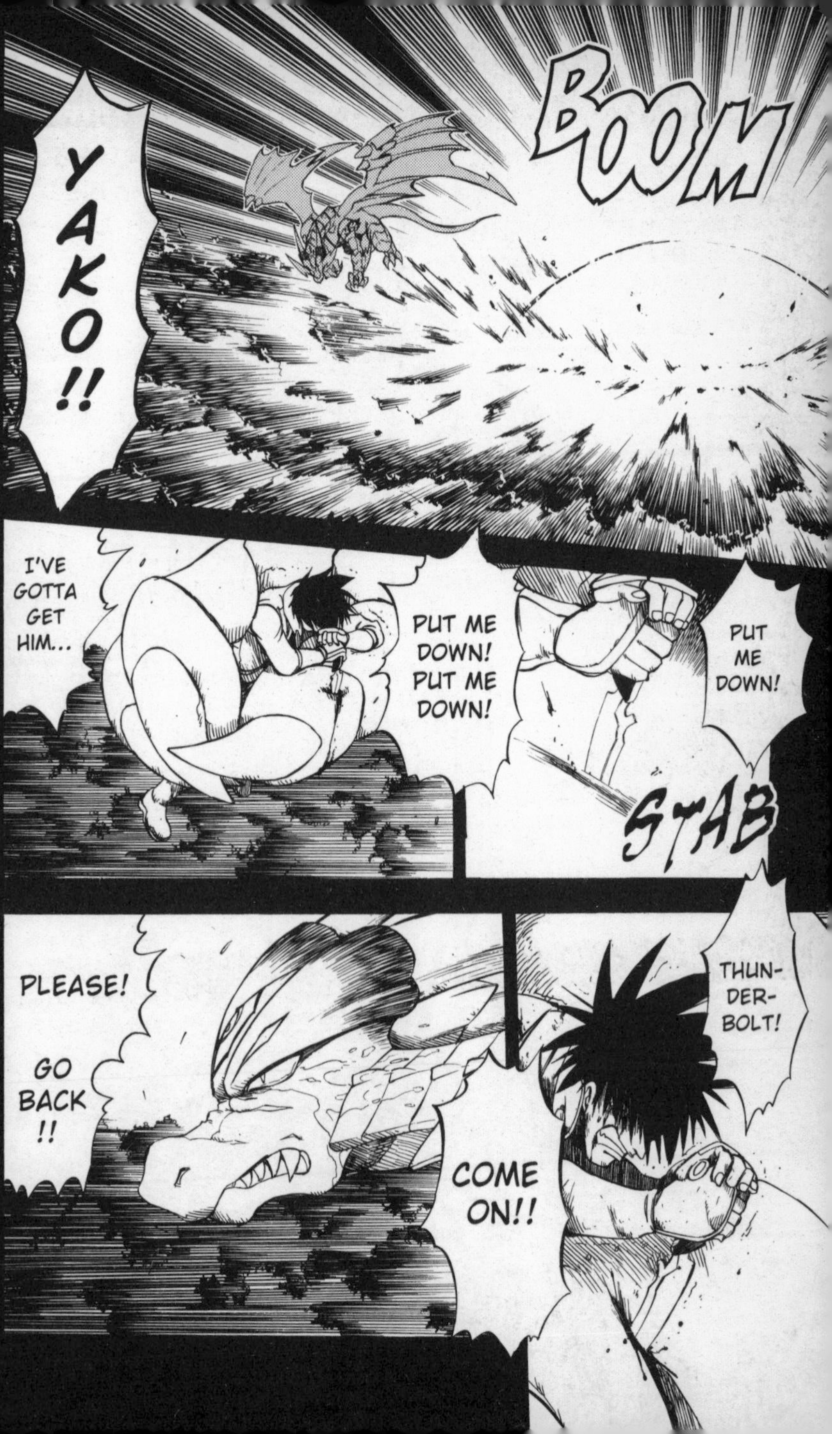
BOOM
YAKO!!
PUT ME DOWN!
STAB
PUT ME DOWN! PUT ME DOWN!
I'VE GOTTA GET HIM...
THUNDER-BOLT!
COME ON!!
PLEASE!
GO BACK!!

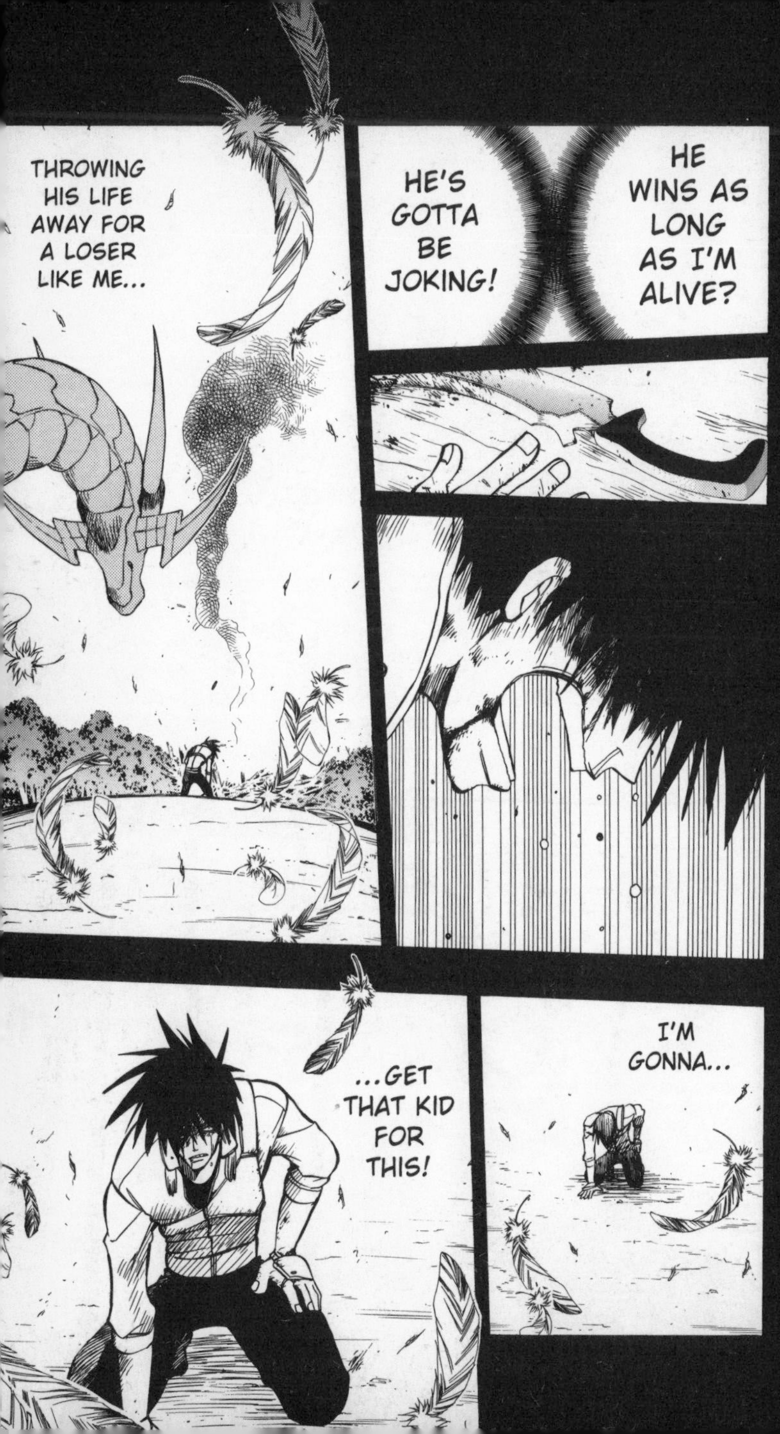
HE WINS AS LONG AS I'M ALIVE?
HE'S GOTTA BE JOKING!
THROWING HIS LIFE AWAY FOR A LOSER LIKE ME...
I'M GONNA...
...GET THAT KID FOR THIS!

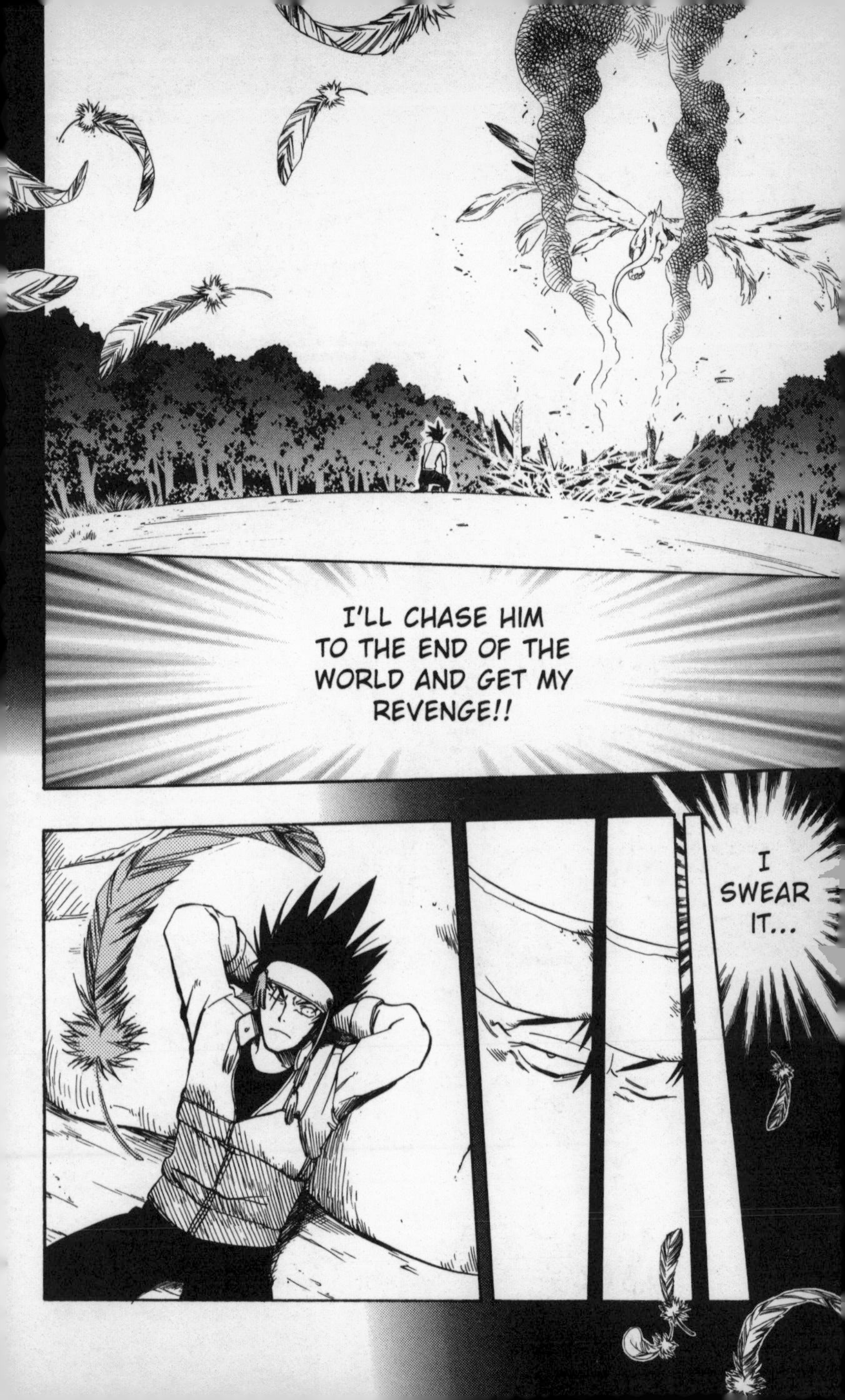
I'LL CHASE HIM TO THE END OF THE WORLD AND GET MY REVENGE!!
I SWEAR IT...

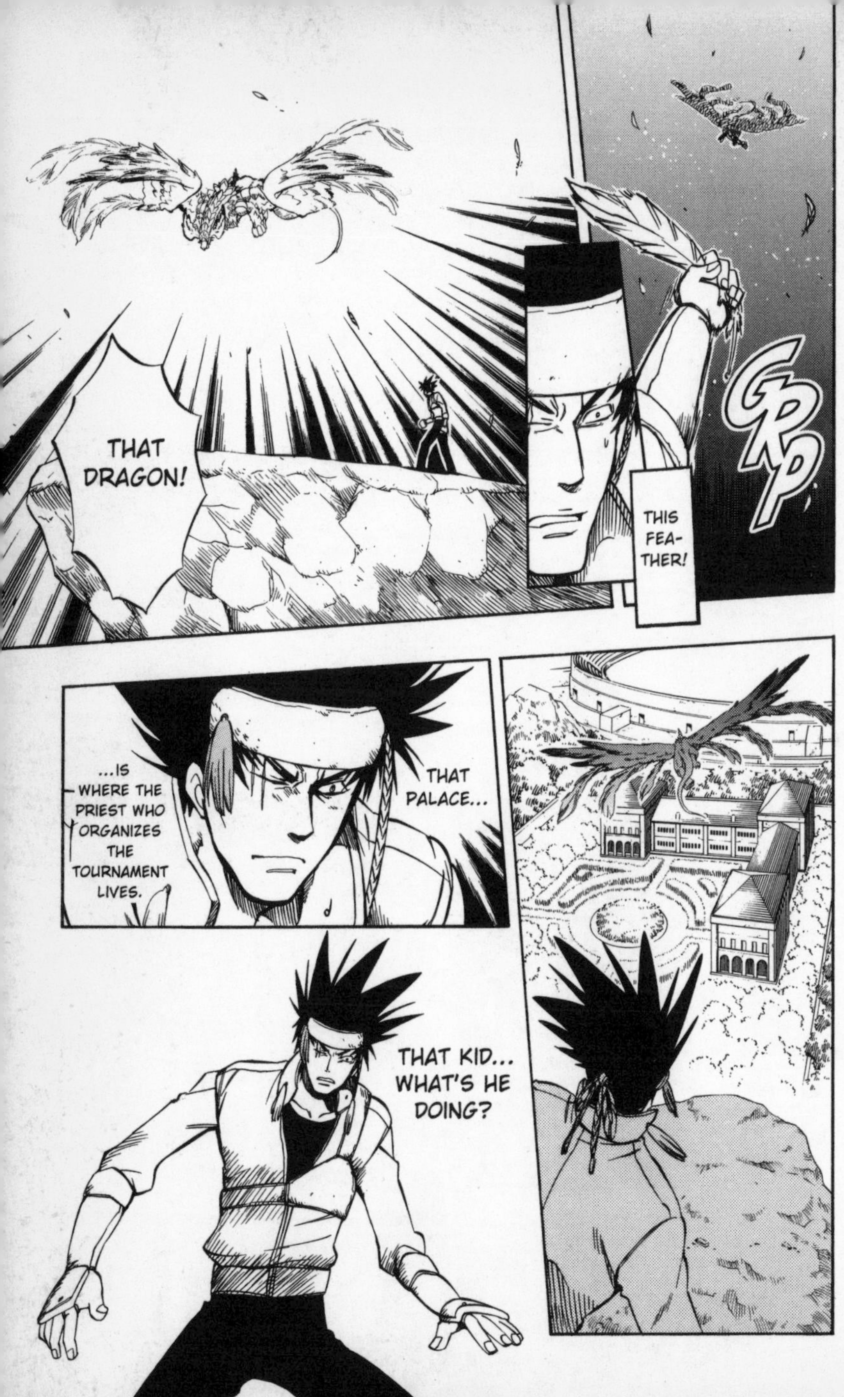
GRP
THIS FEA-THER!
THAT DRAGON!
THAT PALACE...
...IS WHERE THE PRIEST WHO ORGANIZES THE TOURNAMENT LIVES.
THAT KID... WHAT'S HE DOING?

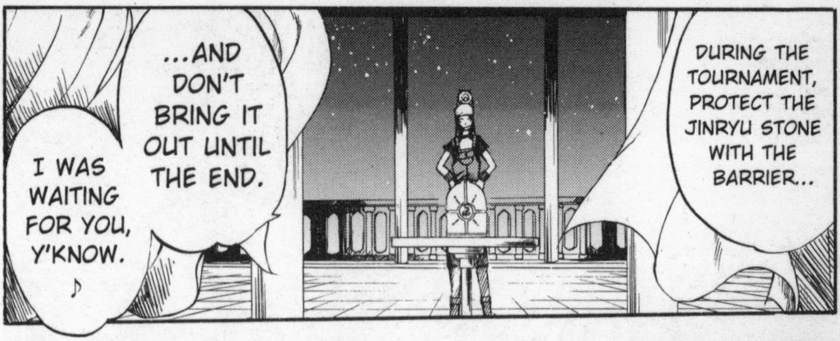
DURING THE TOURNAMENT, PROTECT THE JINRYU STONE WITH THE BARRIER...
...AND DON'T BRING IT OUT UNTIL THE END.
I WAS WAITING FOR YOU, Y'KNOW. ♪

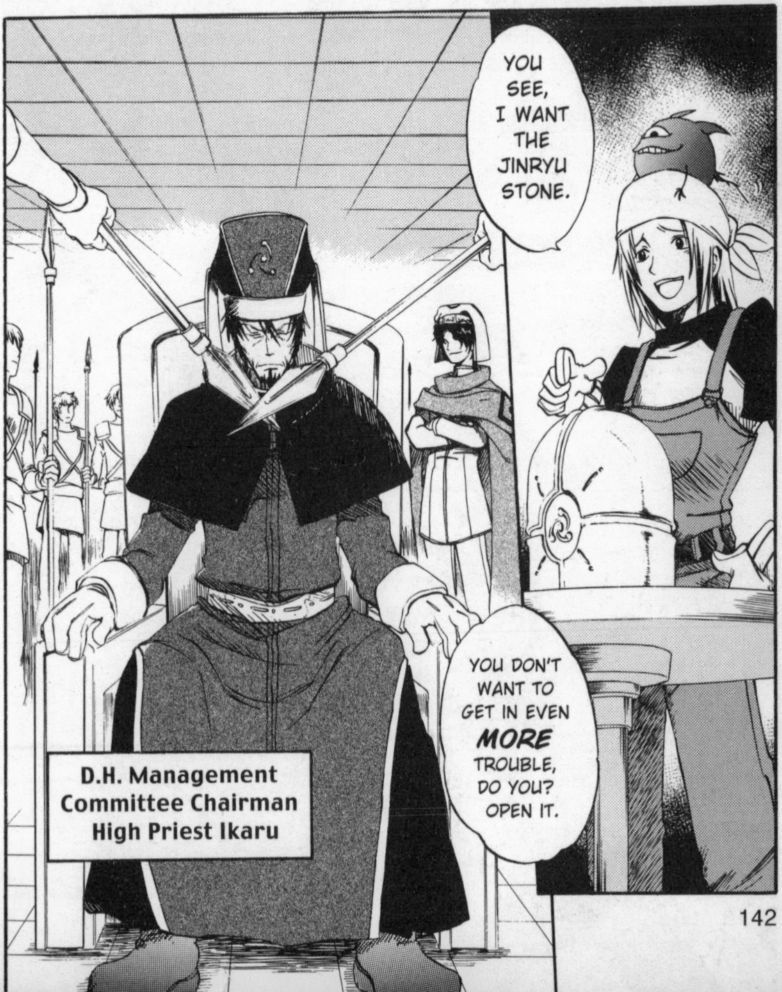
YOU SEE, I WANT THE JINRYU STONE.
YOU DON'T WANT TO GET IN EVEN MORE TROUBLE, DO YOU? OPEN IT.
D.H. Management Committee Chairman High Priest Ikaru

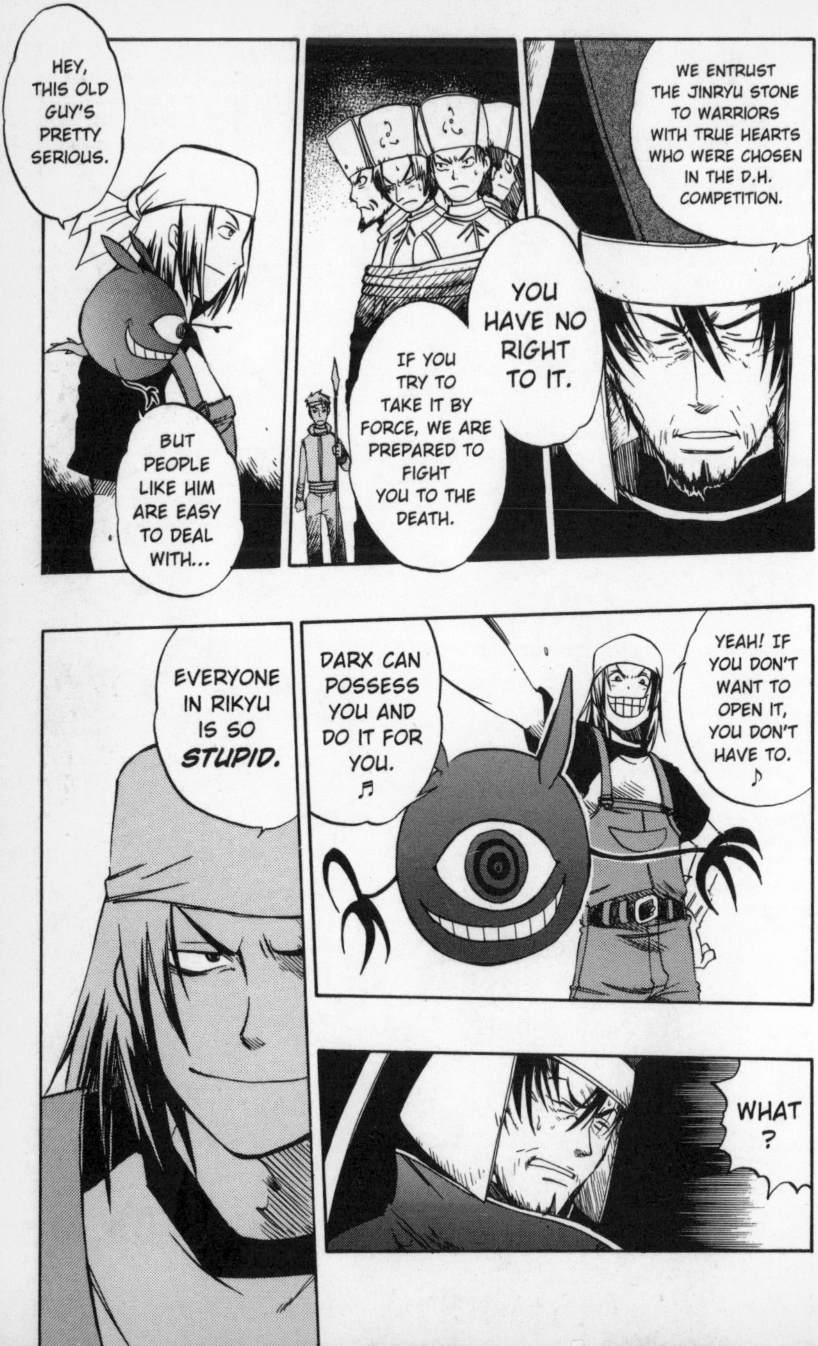
WE ENTRUST THE JINRYU STONE TO WARRIORS WITH TRUE HEARTS WHO WERE CHOSEN IN THE D.H. COMPETITION.
YOU HAVE NO RIGHT TO IT.
IF YOU TRY TO TAKE IT BY FORCE, WE ARE PREPARED TO FIGHT YOU TO THE DEATH.
HEY, THIS OLD GUY'S PRETTY SERIOUS.
BUT PEOPLE LIKE HIM ARE EASY TO DEAL WITH...
YEAH! IF YOU DON'T WANT TO OPEN IT, YOU DON'T HAVE TO. ♪
DARX CAN POSSESS YOU AND DO IT FOR YOU. ♬
WHAT?
EVERYONE IN RIKYU IS SO ***STUPID.***

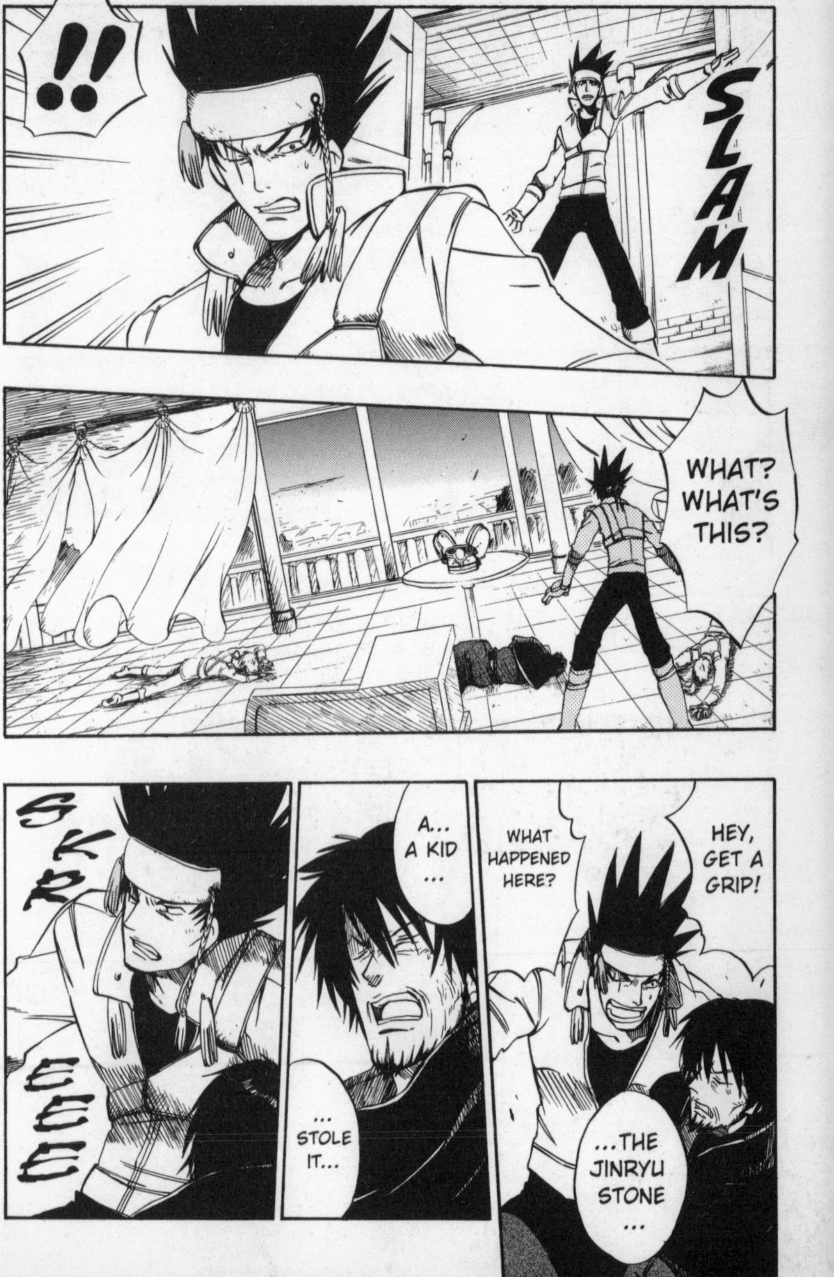
SLAM
!!
WHAT? WHAT'S THIS?
HEY, GET A GRIP!
WHAT HAPPENED HERE?
...THE JINRYU STONE ...
A... A KID ...
... STOLE IT...
SKREEE

READ THIS WAY

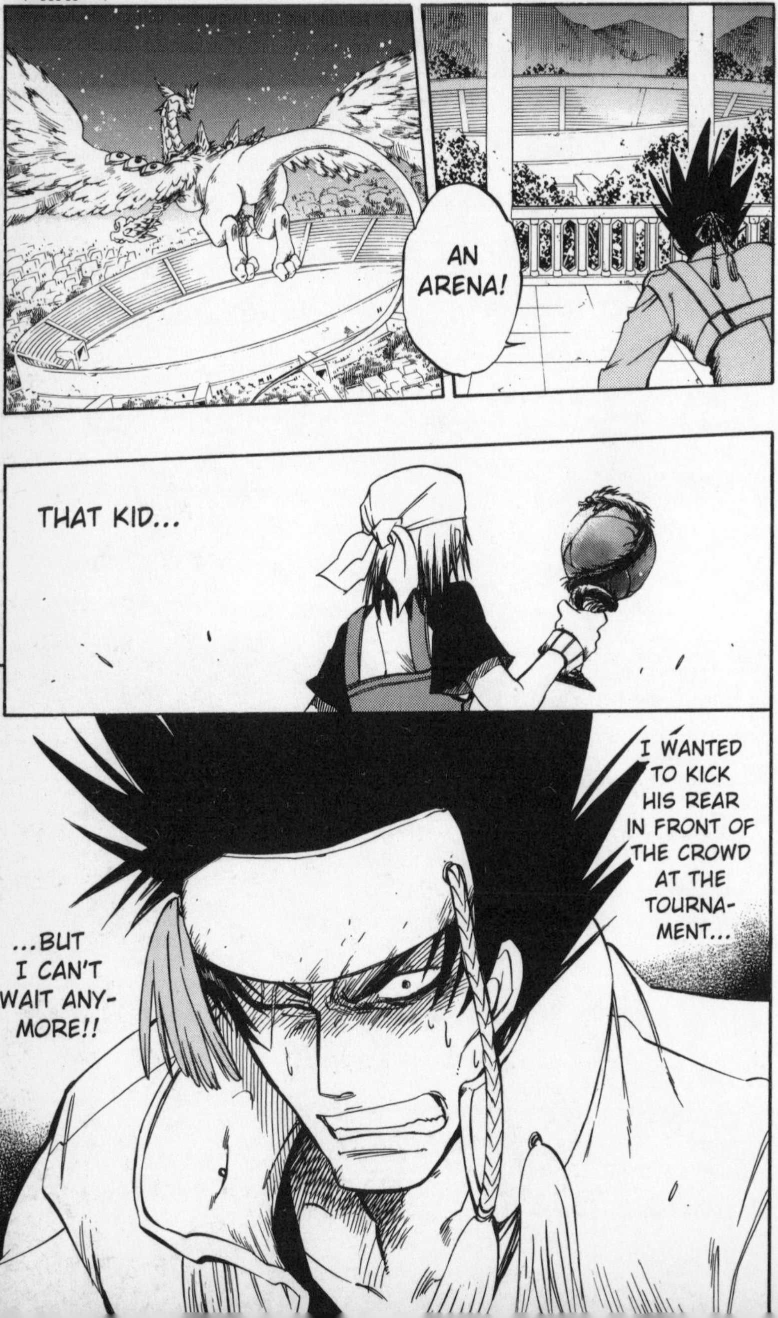
AN ARENA!
THAT KID...
I WANTED TO KICK HIS REAR IN FRONT OF THE CROWD AT THE TOURNAMENT...
...BUT I CAN'T WAIT ANYMORE!!

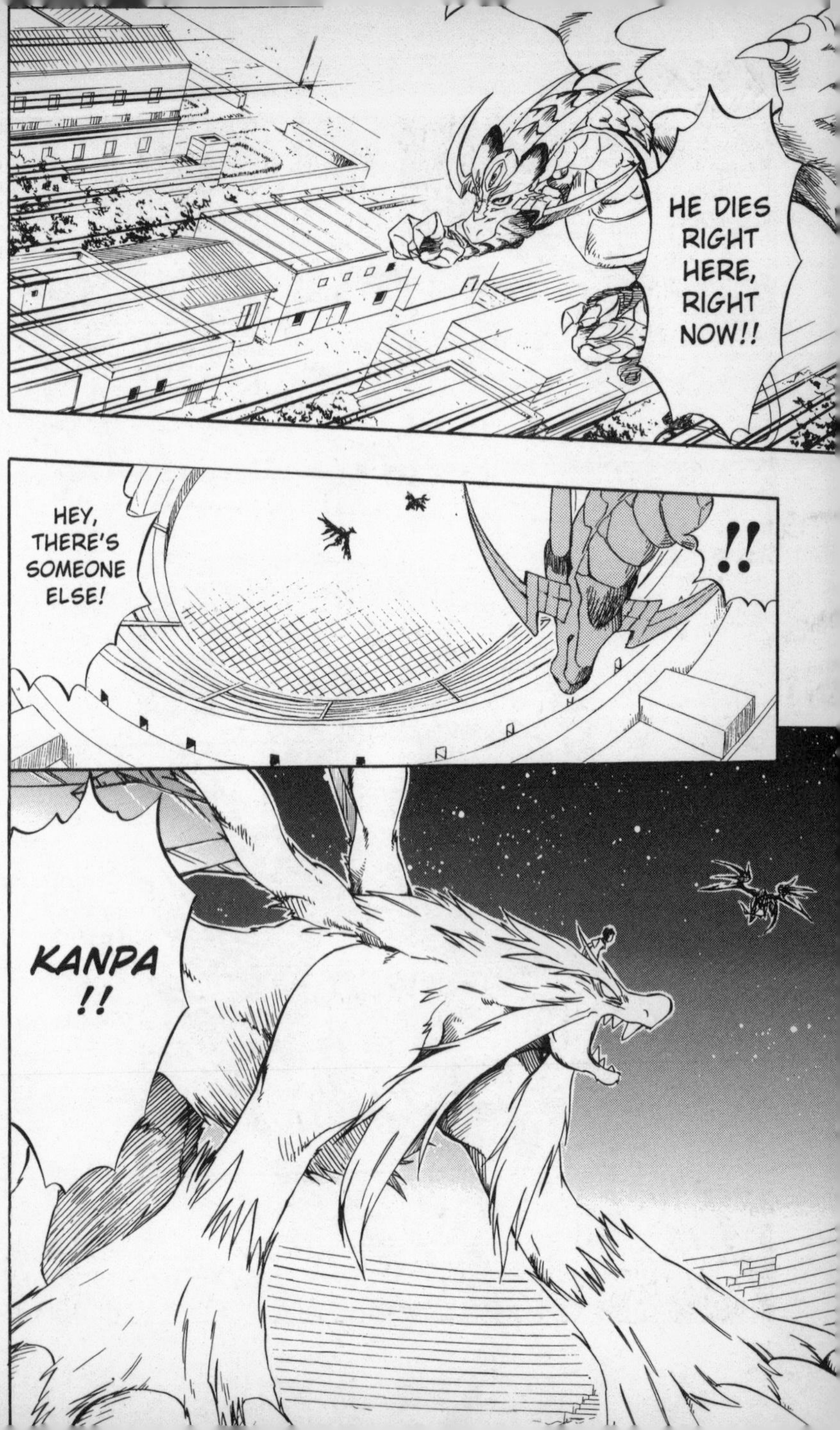
HE DIES RIGHT HERE, RIGHT NOW!!
!!
HEY, THERE'S SOMEONE ELSE!
KANPA !!

READ THIS WAY

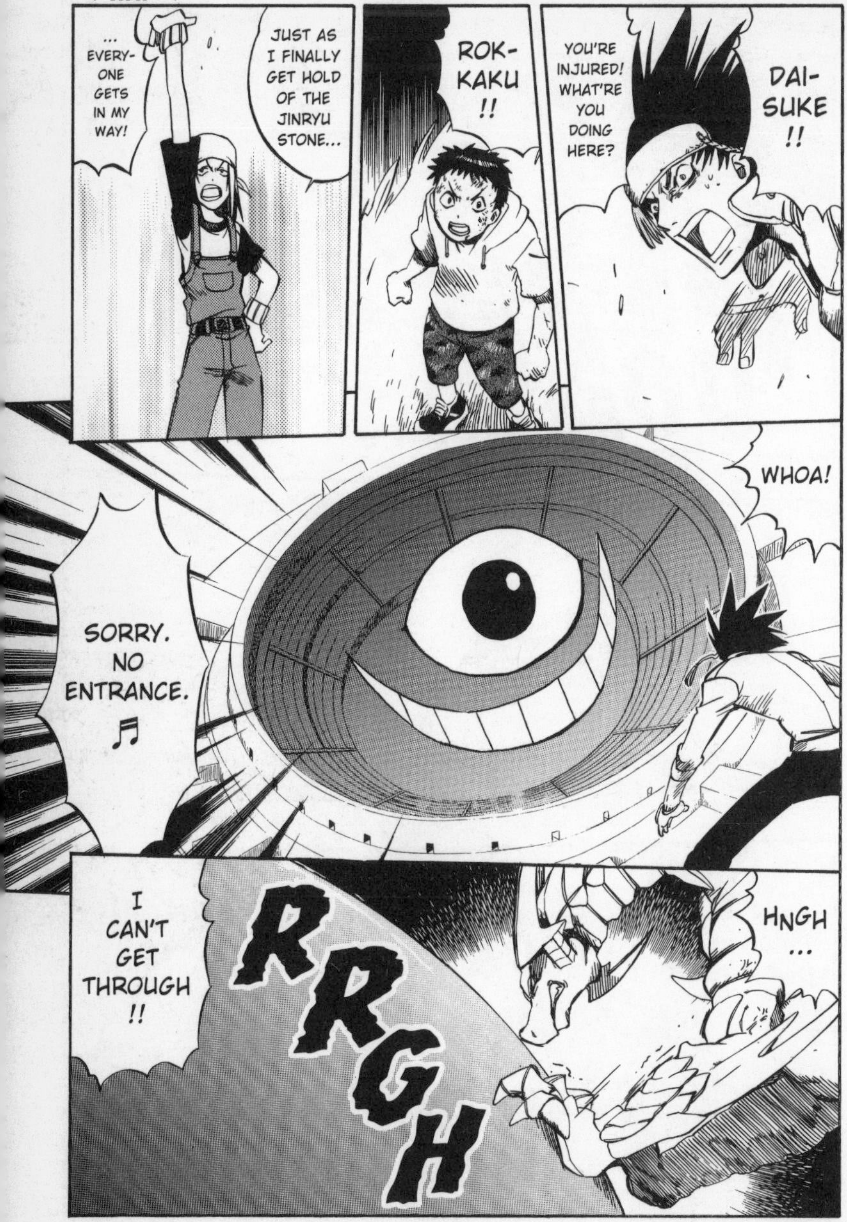
DAI-SUKE!!
YOU'RE INJURED! WHAT'RE YOU DOING HERE?
ROK-KAKU!!
JUST AS I FINALLY GET HOLD OF THE JINRYU STONE...
...EVERY-ONE GETS IN MY WAY!
WHOA!
SORRY. NO ENTRANCE. ♬
HNGH...
RRGH
I CAN'T GET THROUGH!!

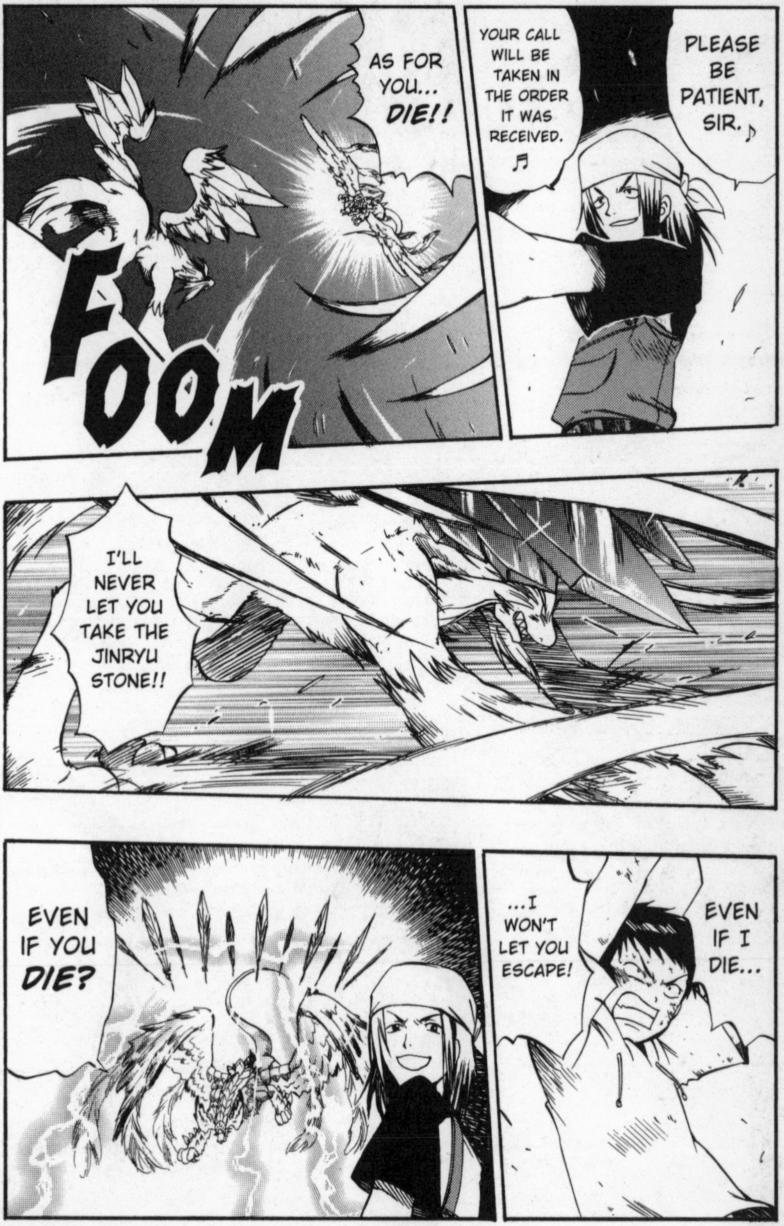
PLEASE BE PATIENT, SIR. ♪
YOUR CALL WILL BE TAKEN IN THE ORDER IT WAS RECEIVED. ♬
AS FOR YOU... DIE!!
FOOM
I'LL NEVER LET YOU TAKE THE JINRYU STONE!!
EVEN IF I DIE...
...I WON'T LET YOU ESCAPE!
EVEN IF YOU DIE?

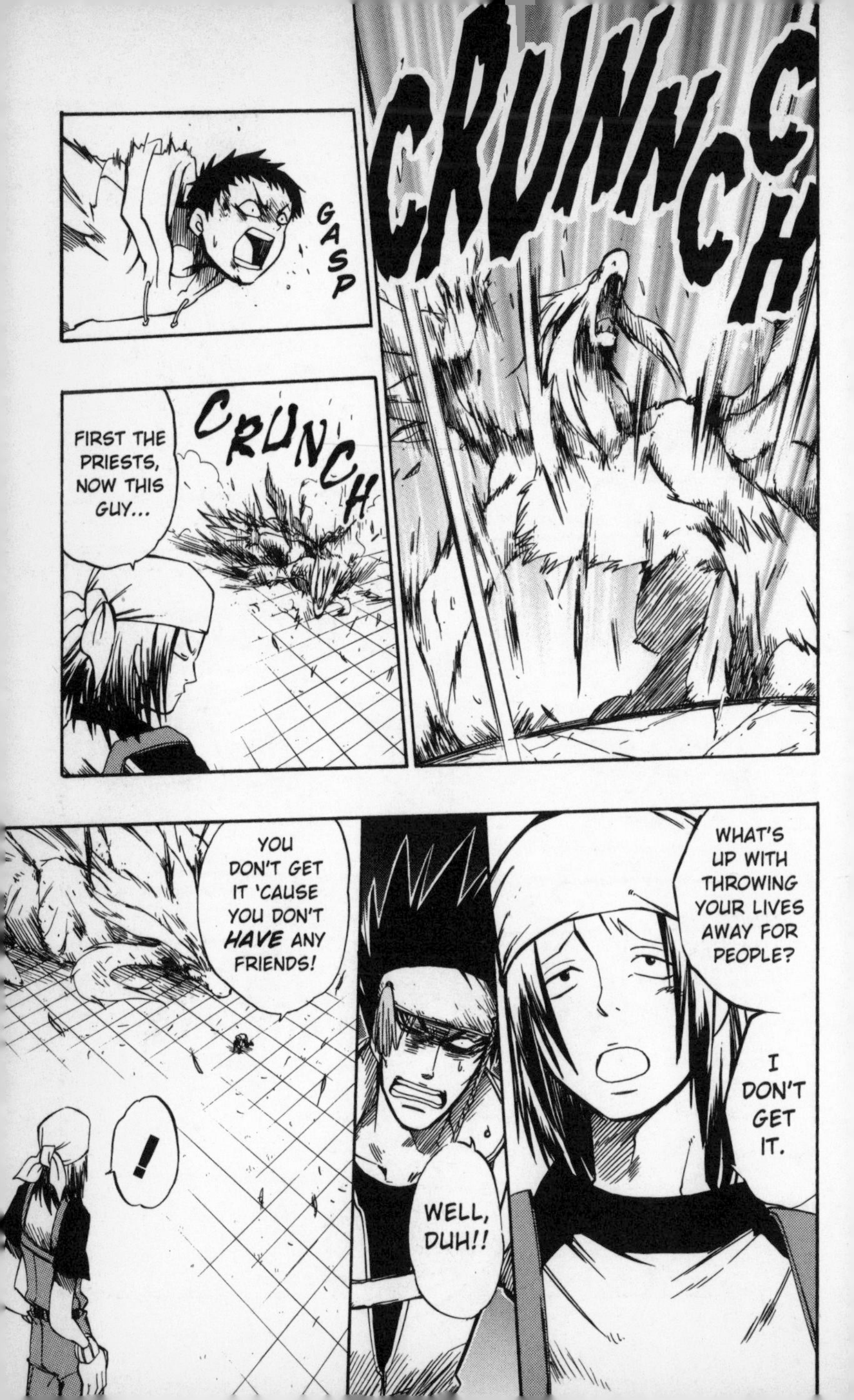
CRUNCH
GASP
CRUNCH
FIRST THE PRIESTS, NOW THIS GUY...
WHAT'S UP WITH THROWING YOUR LIVES AWAY FOR PEOPLE?
I DON'T GET IT.
WELL, DUH!!
YOU DON'T GET IT 'CAUSE YOU DON'T *HAVE* ANY FRIENDS!
!

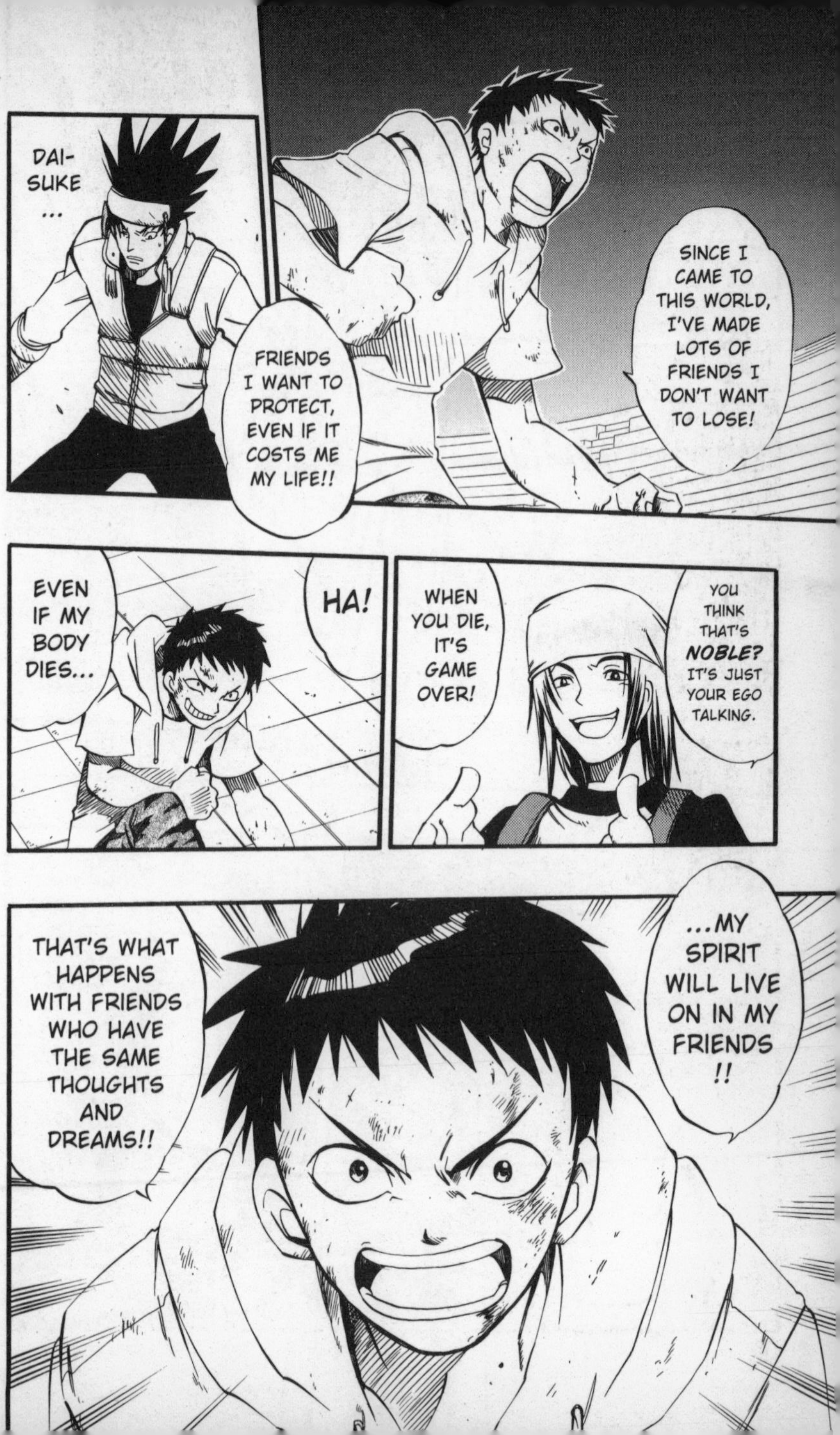
SINCE I CAME TO THIS WORLD, I'VE MADE LOTS OF FRIENDS I DON'T WANT TO LOSE!
FRIENDS I WANT TO PROTECT, EVEN IF IT COSTS ME MY LIFE!!
DAI-SUKE ...
YOU THINK THAT'S ***NOBLE?*** IT'S JUST YOUR EGO TALKING.
WHEN YOU DIE, IT'S GAME OVER!
HA!
EVEN IF MY BODY DIES...
...MY SPIRIT WILL LIVE ON IN MY FRIENDS !!
THAT'S WHAT HAPPENS WITH FRIENDS WHO HAVE THE SAME THOUGHTS AND DREAMS!!

READ THIS WAY

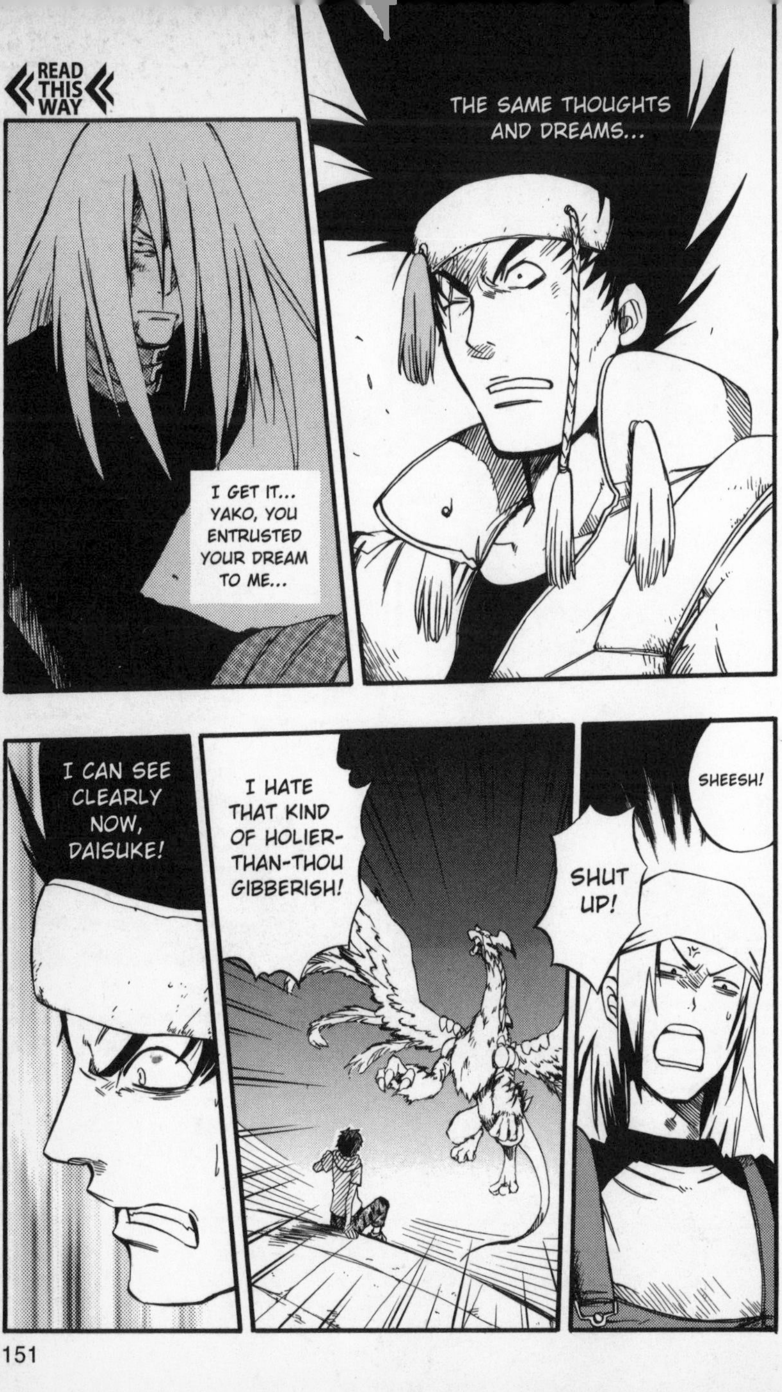

THE SAME THOUGHTS AND DREAMS...
I GET IT... YAKO, YOU ENTRUSTED YOUR DREAM TO ME...
SHEESH!
SHUT UP!
I HATE THAT KIND OF HOLIER-THAN-THOU GIBBERISH!
I CAN SEE CLEARLY NOW, DAISUKE!

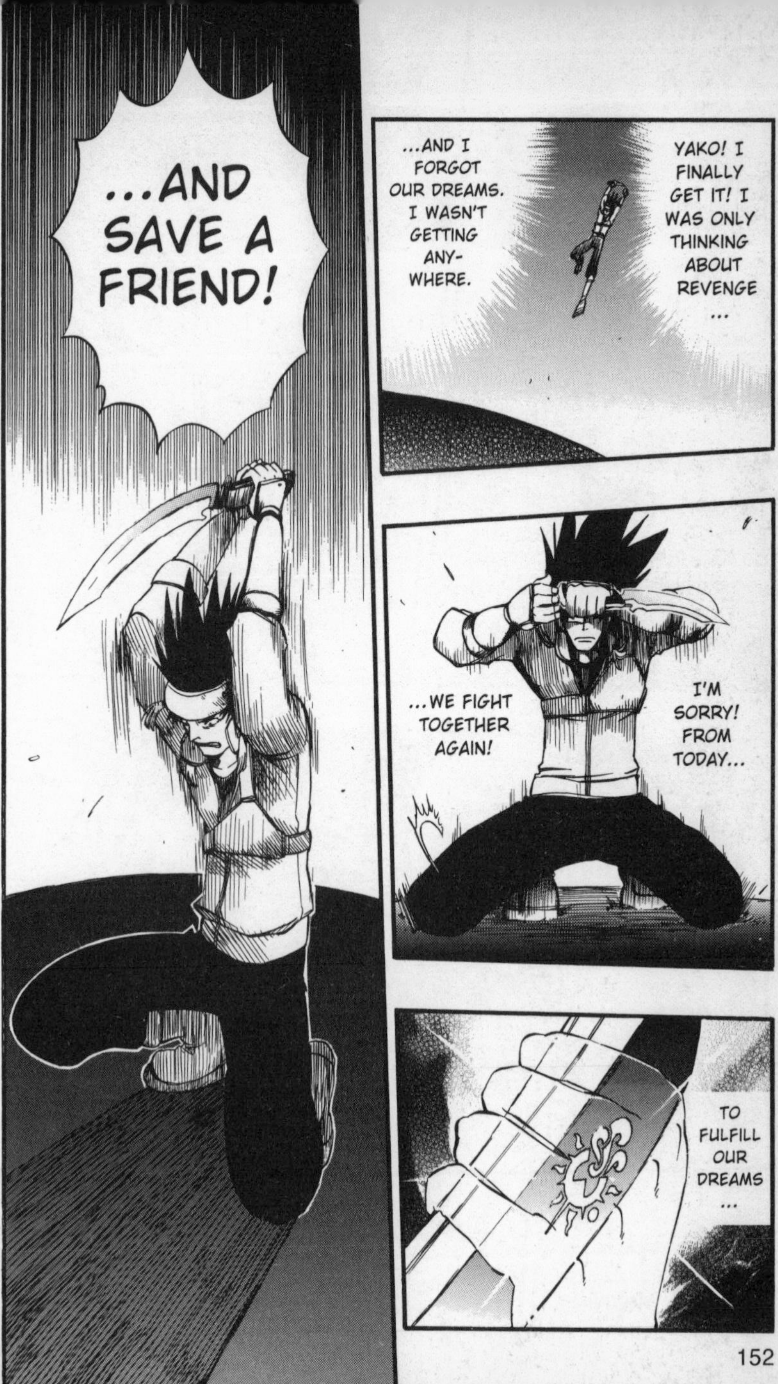
YAKO! I FINALLY GET IT! I WAS ONLY THINKING ABOUT REVENGE ...
...AND I FORGOT OUR DREAMS. I WASN'T GETTING ANY-WHERE.
I'M SORRY! FROM TODAY...
...WE FIGHT TOGETHER AGAIN!
TO FULFILL OUR DREAMS ...
...AND SAVE A FRIEND!

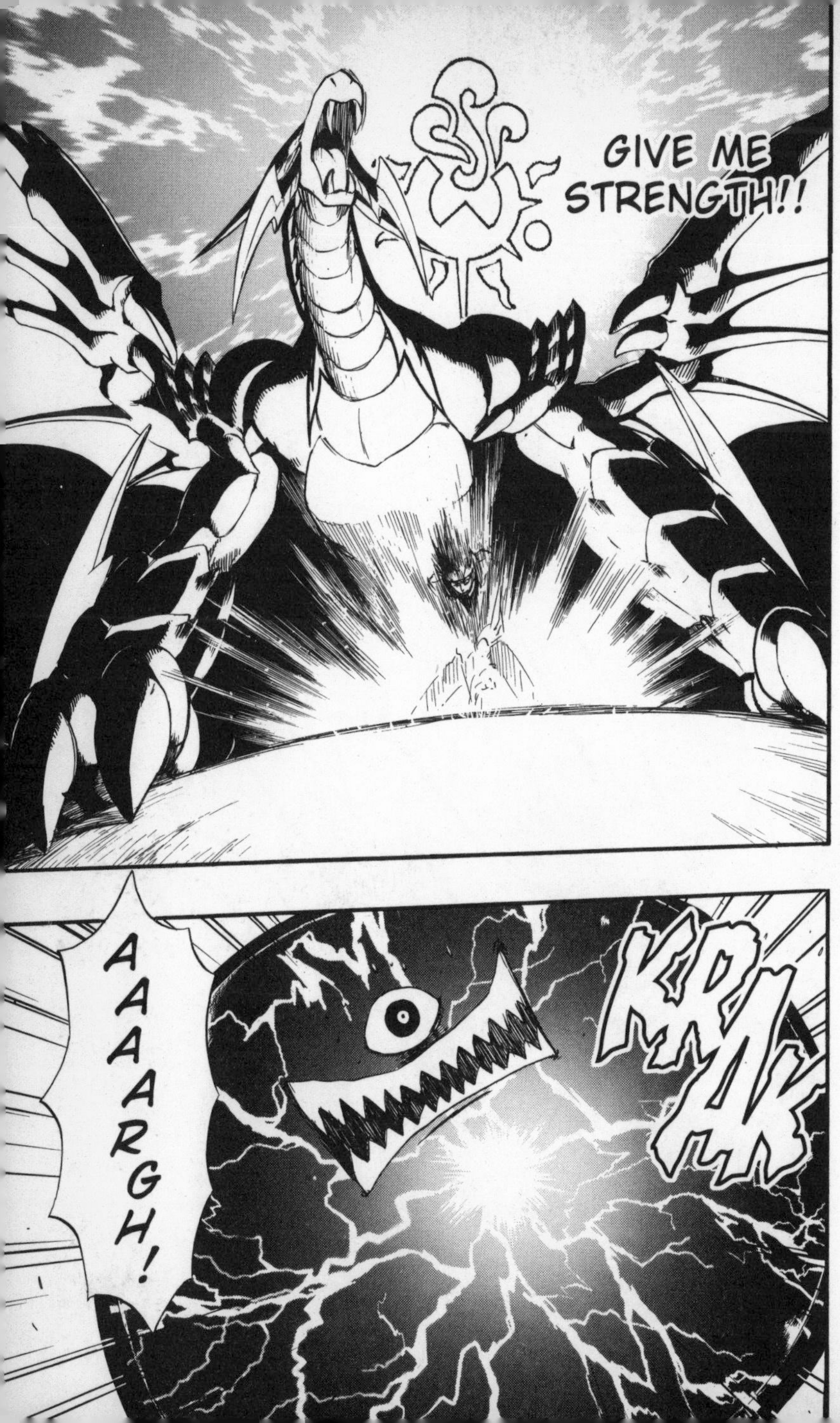
GIVE ME STRENGTH!!
KRAK
AAAARGH!

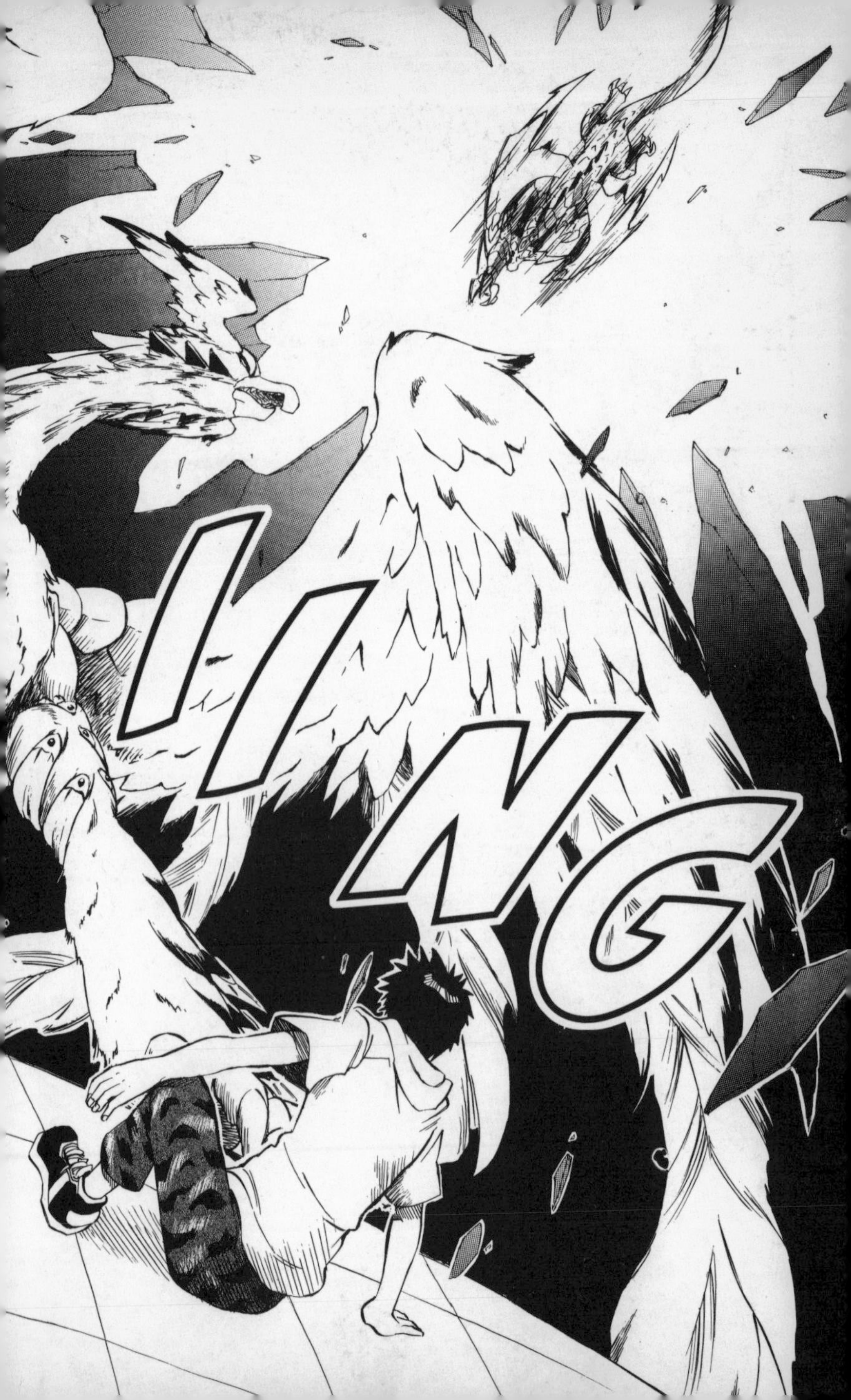
VING

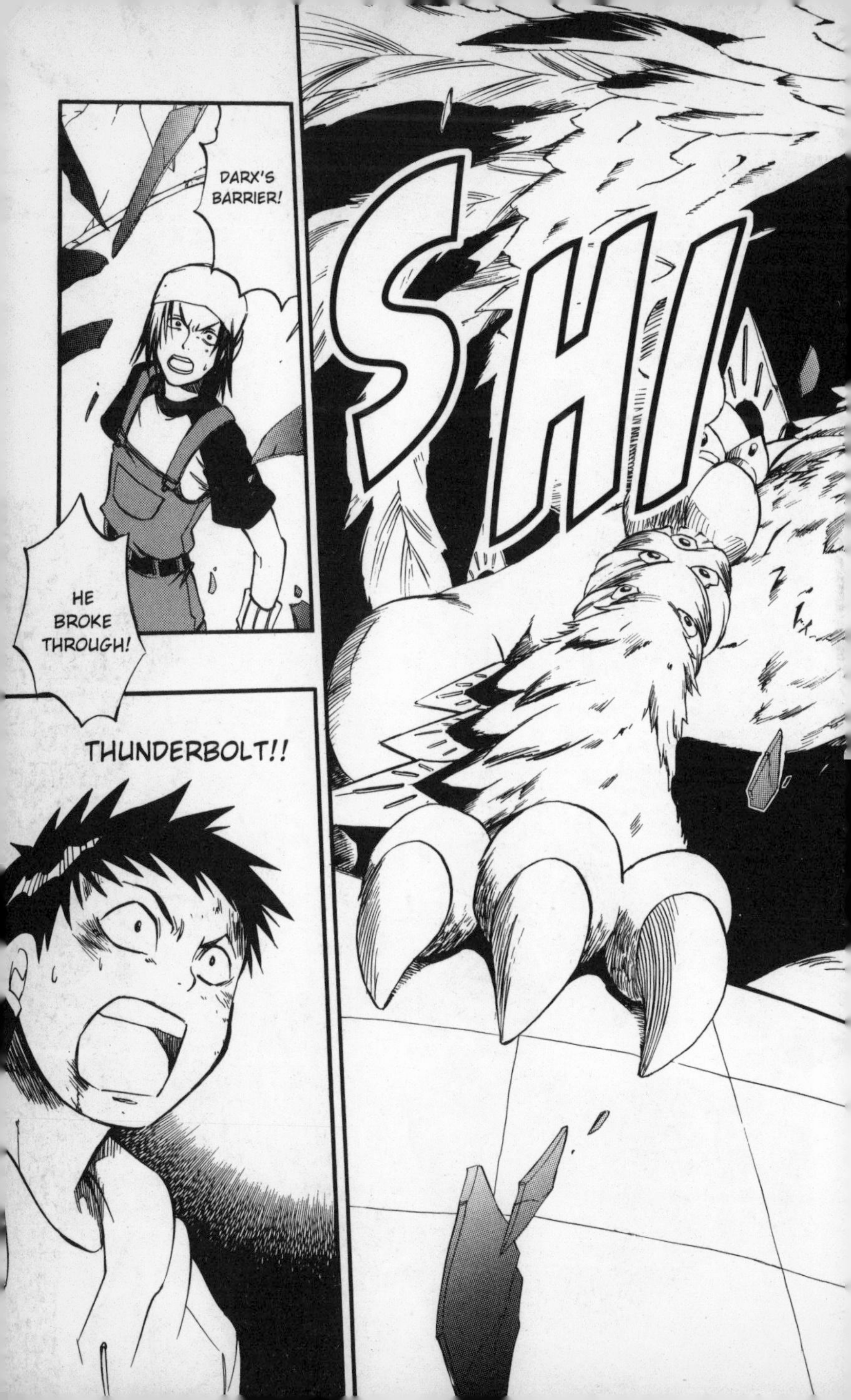
SHI
DARX'S BARRIER!
HE BROKE THROUGH!
THUNDERBOLT!!

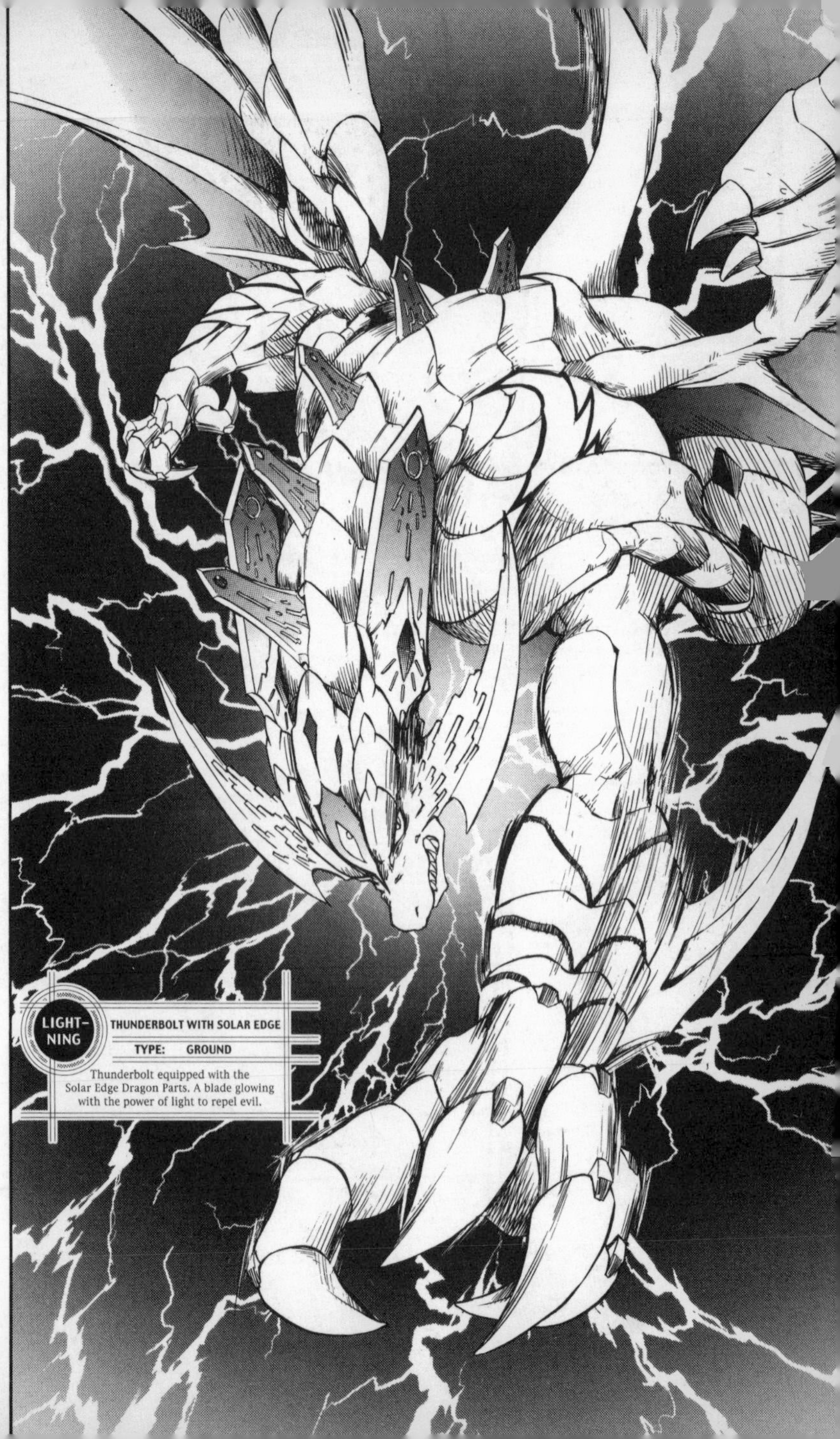
LIGHT-NING
THUNDERBOLT WITH SOLAR EDGE
TYPE: GROUND
Thunderbolt equipped with the Solar Edge Dragon Parts. A blade glowing with the power of light to repel evil.

READ THIS WAY

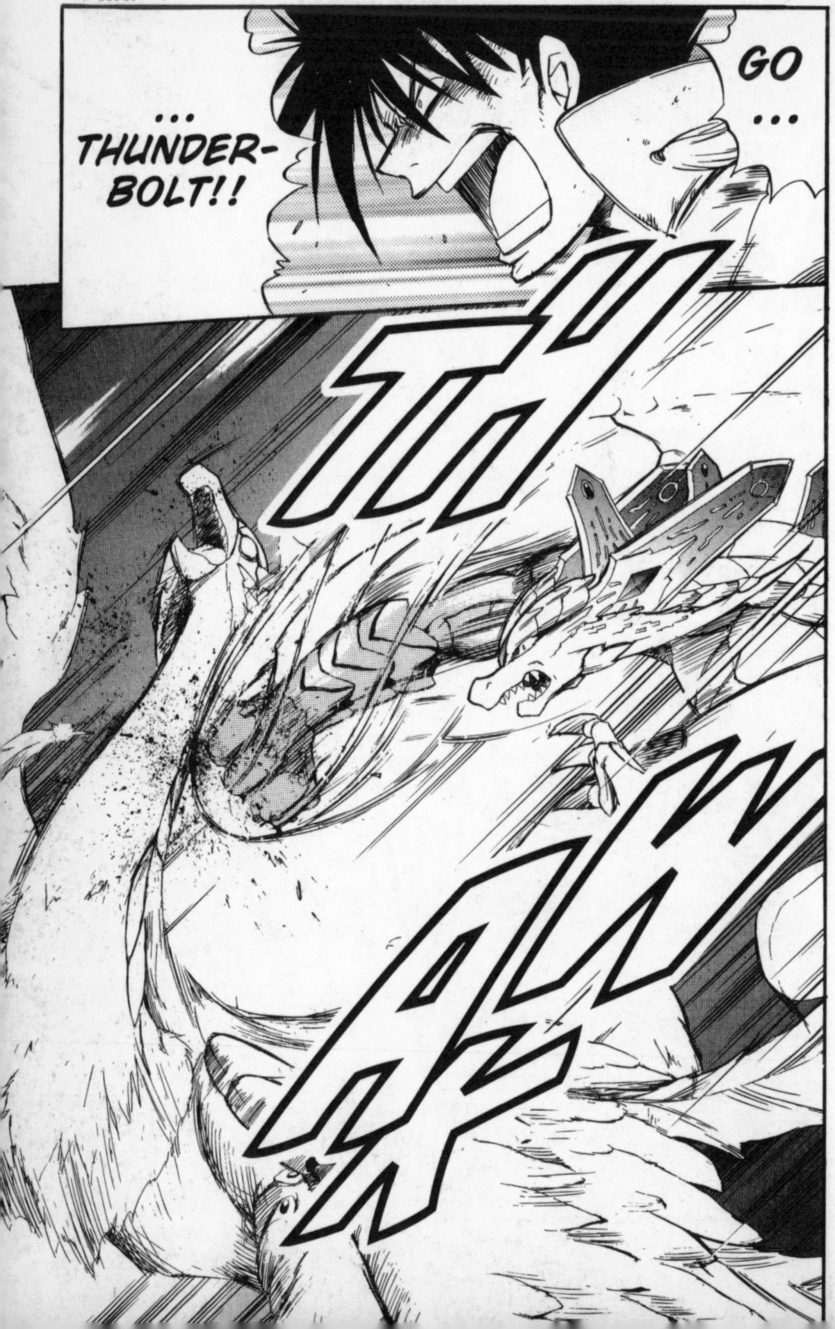
GO ...
... THUNDER-BOLT!!

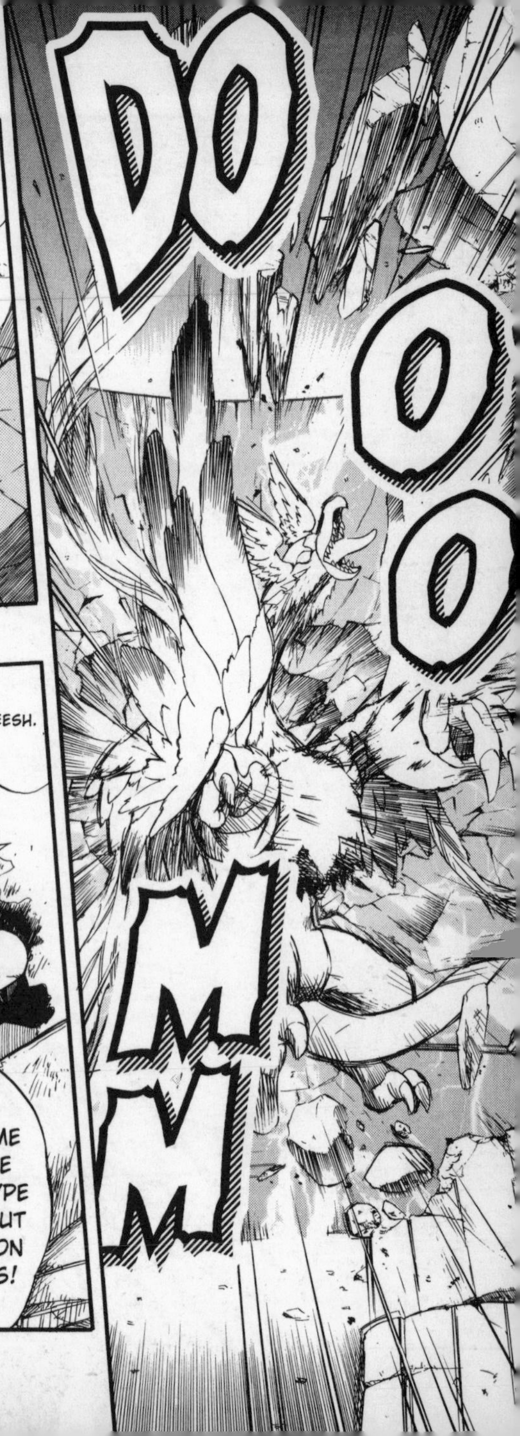
DOOOMMM
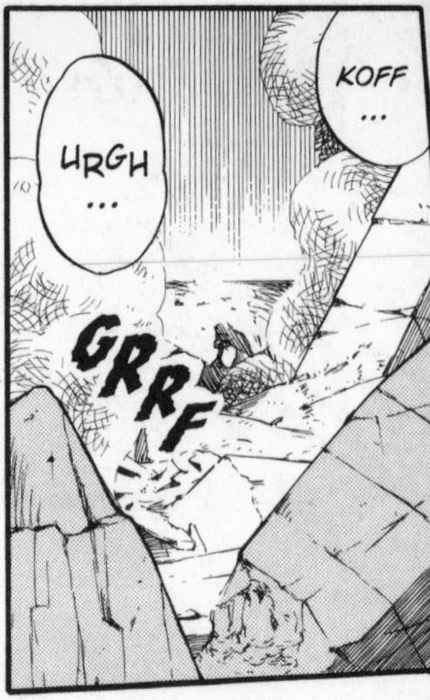
KOFF ...
URGH ...
GRRRF
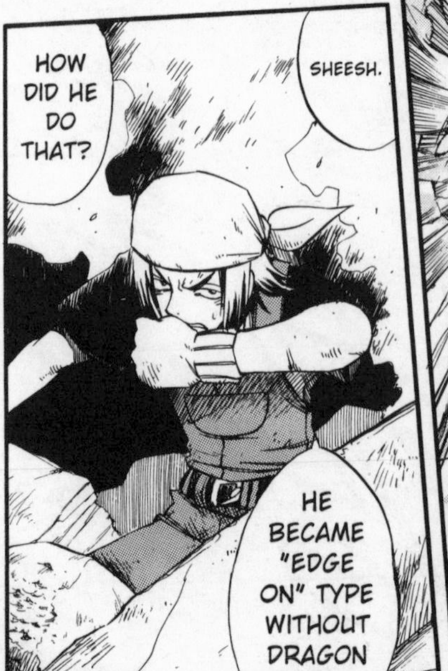
SHEESH.
HOW DID HE DO THAT?
HE BECAME "EDGE ON" TYPE WITHOUT DRAGON PARTS!

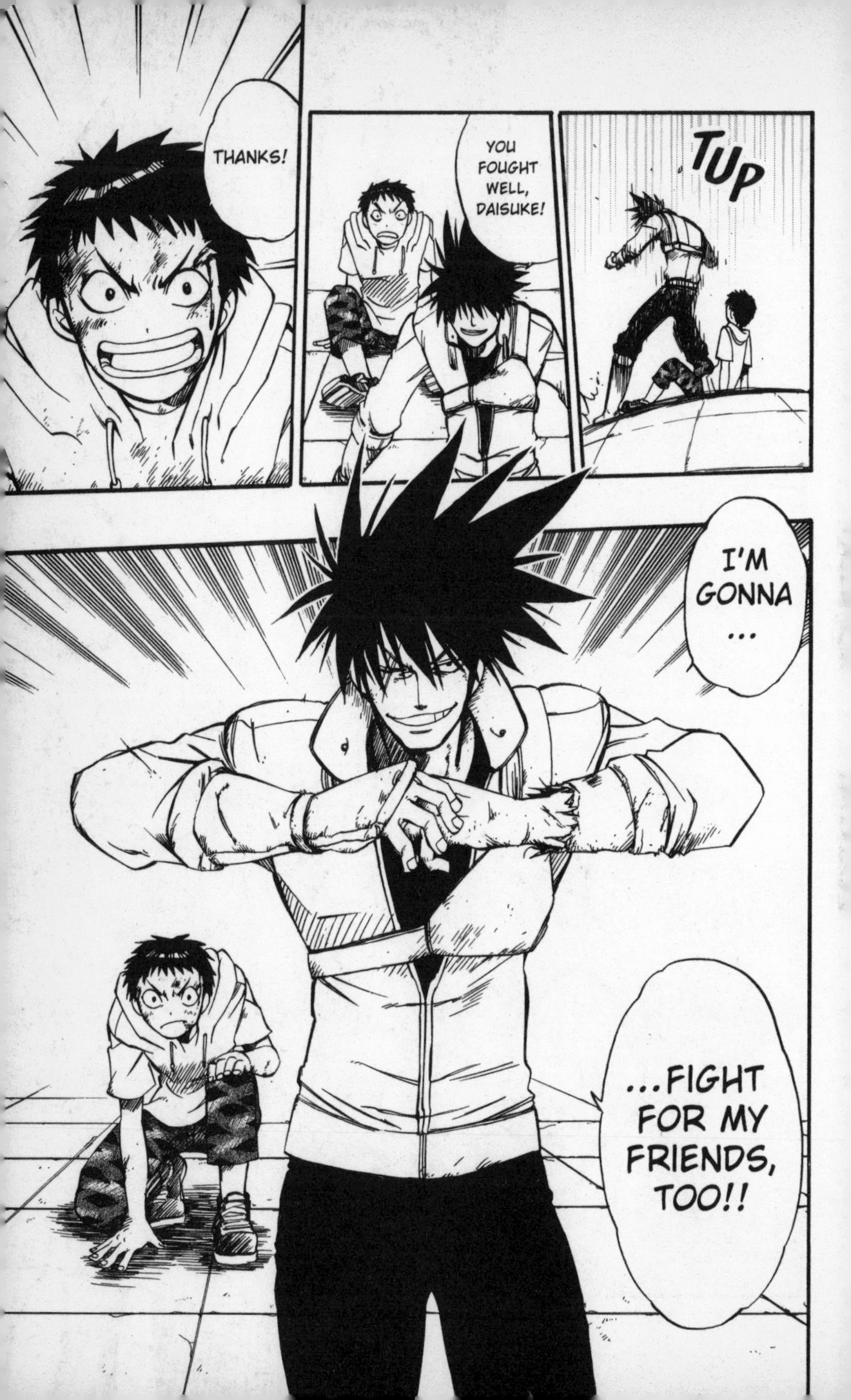
TUP
YOU FOUGHT WELL, DAISUKE!
THANKS!
I'M GONNA ...
...FIGHT FOR MY FRIENDS, TOO!!

STAGE16 GATE

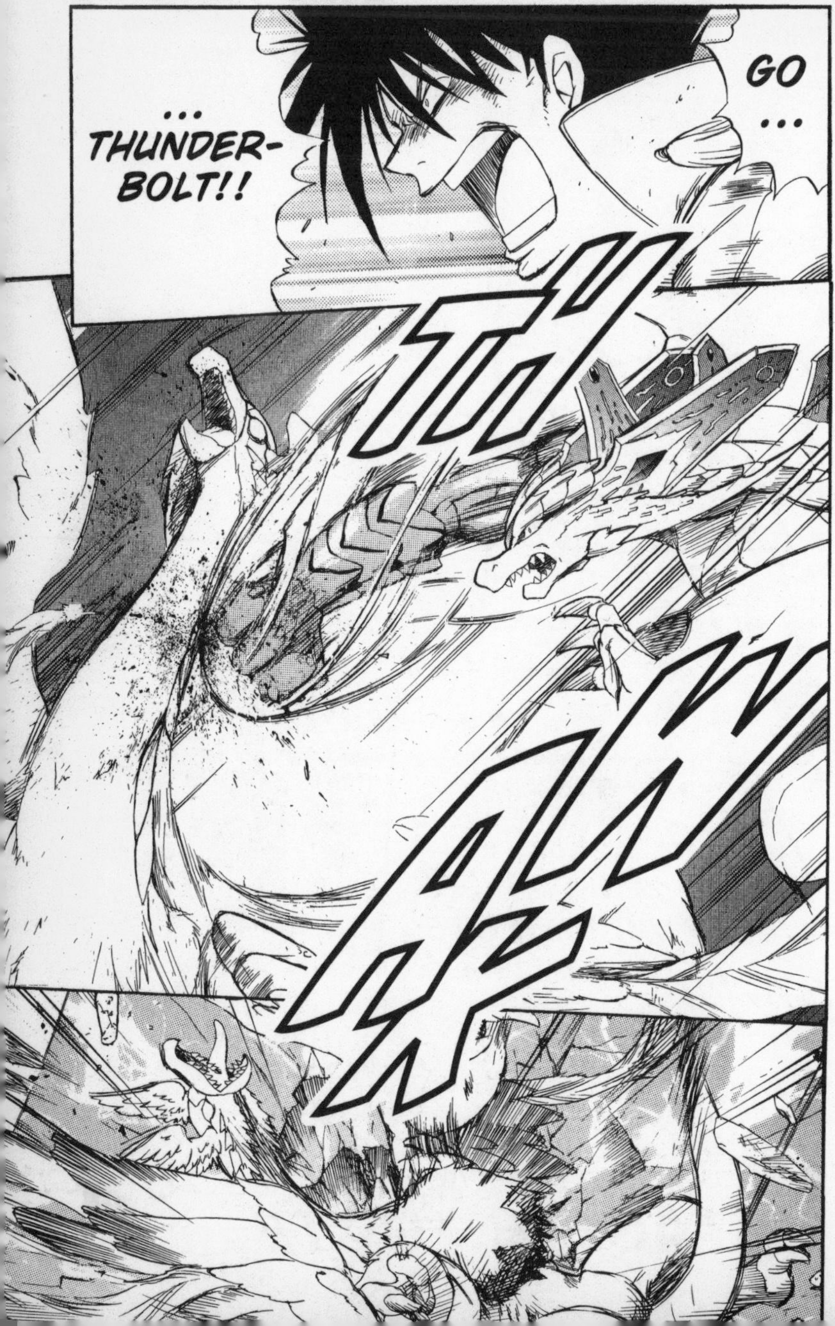
GO ...
... THUNDER-BOLT!!

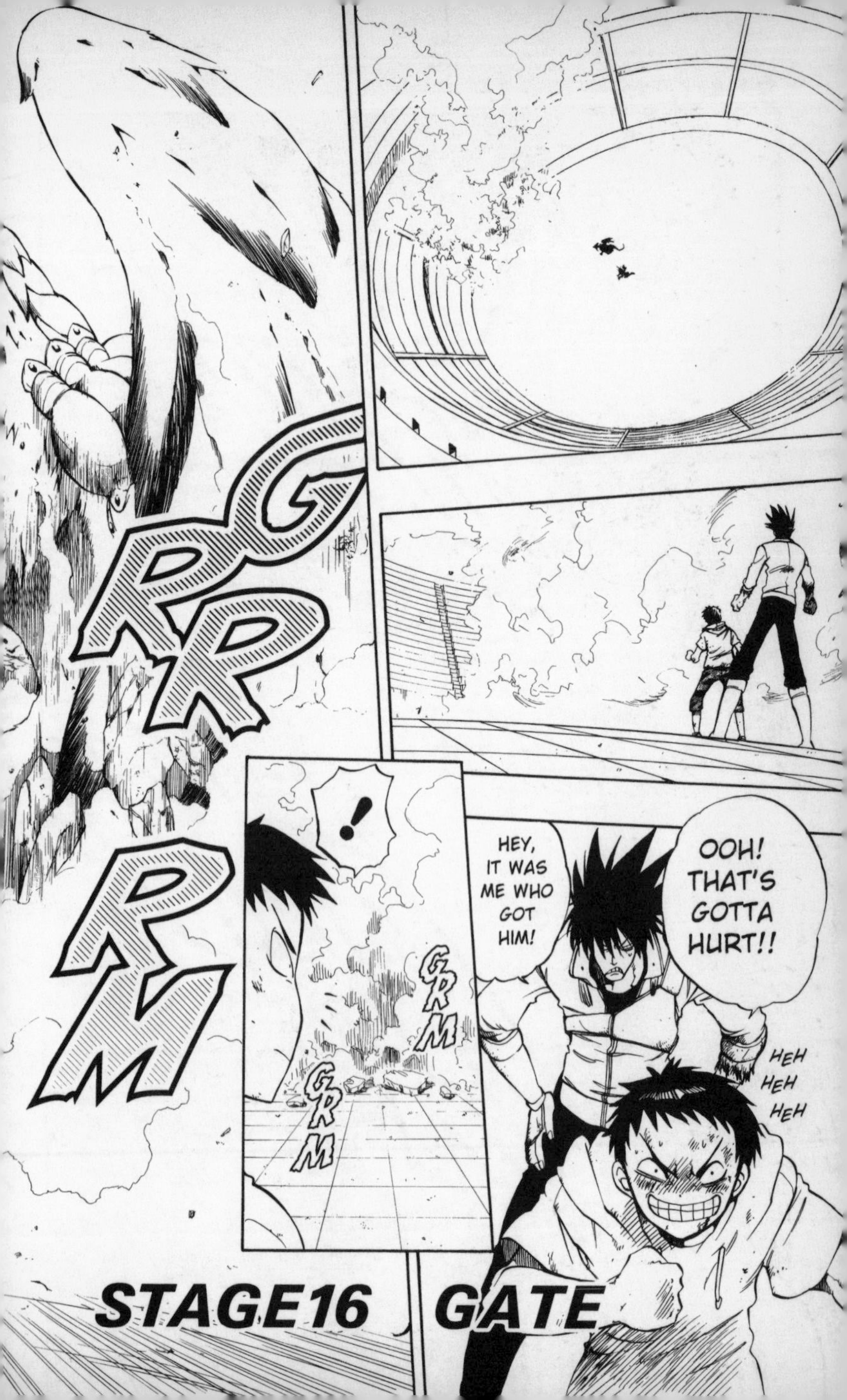
OOH! THAT'S GOTTA HURT!!
HEY, IT WAS ME WHO GOT HIM!
HEH HEH HEH
!
GRM
GRM
GRRRM
STAGE 16 GATE

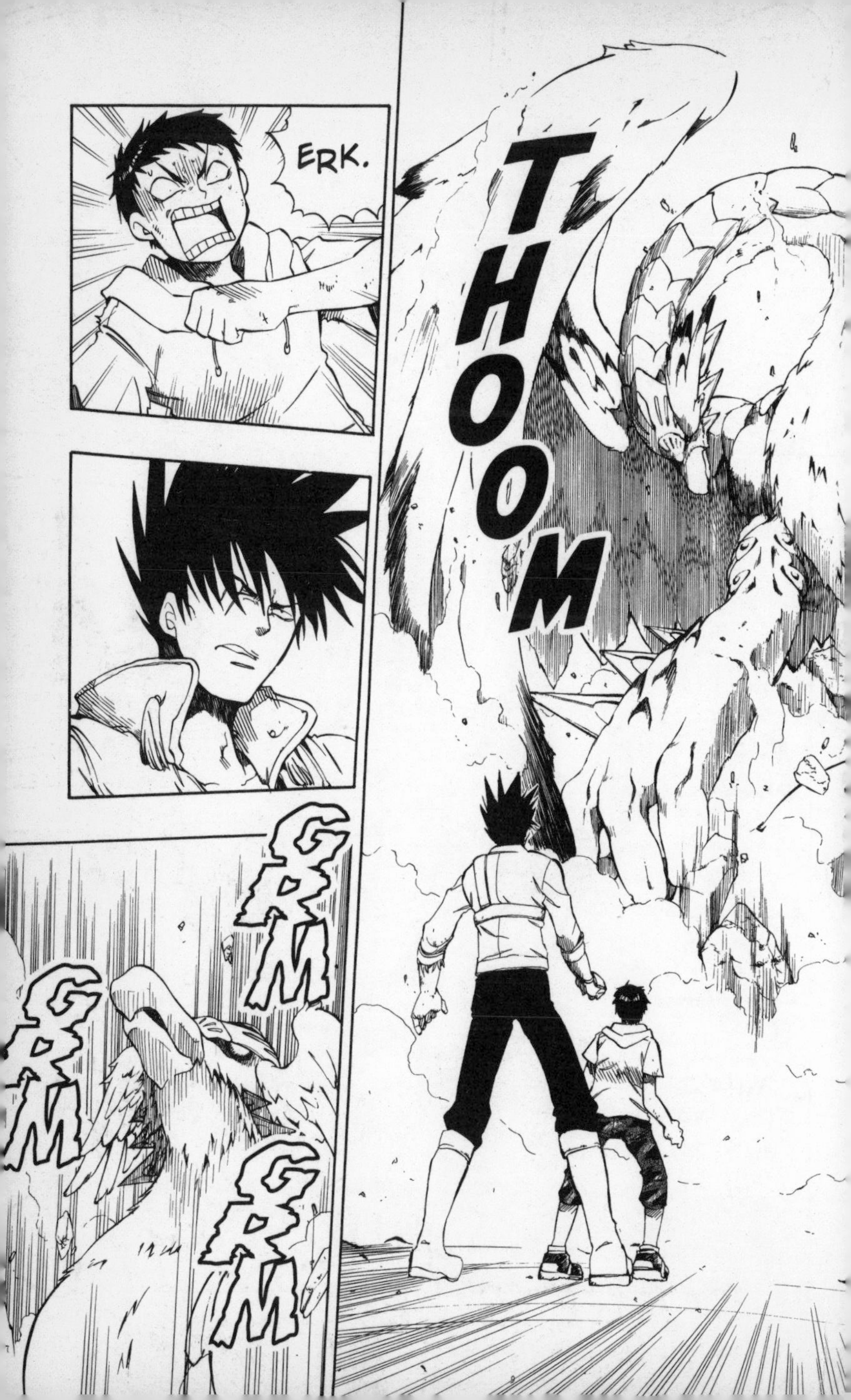
THOOM
ERK.
GRM
GRM
GRM

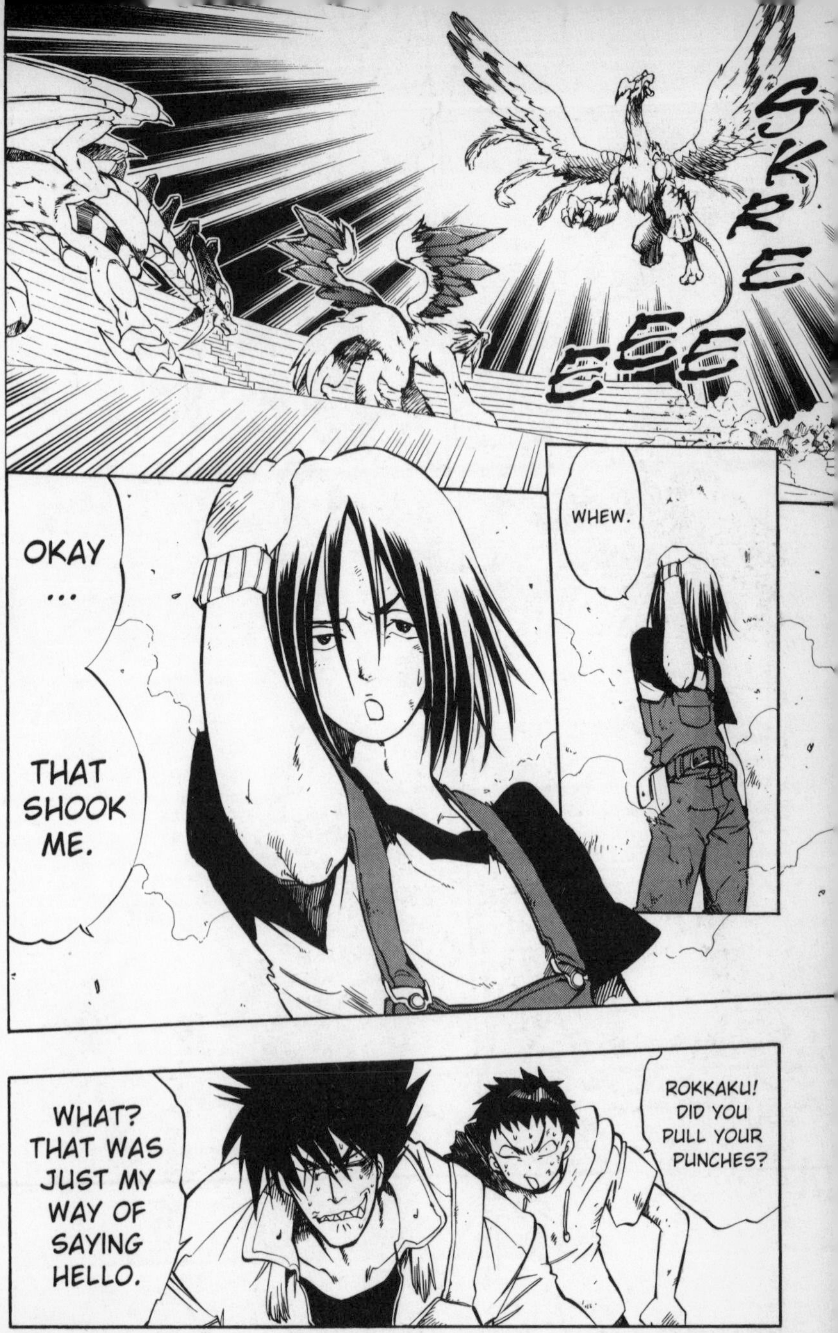
SKREEEEE
WHEW.
OKAY ...
THAT SHOOK ME.
ROKKAKU! DID YOU PULL YOUR PUNCHES?
WHAT? THAT WAS JUST MY WAY OF SAYING HELLO.

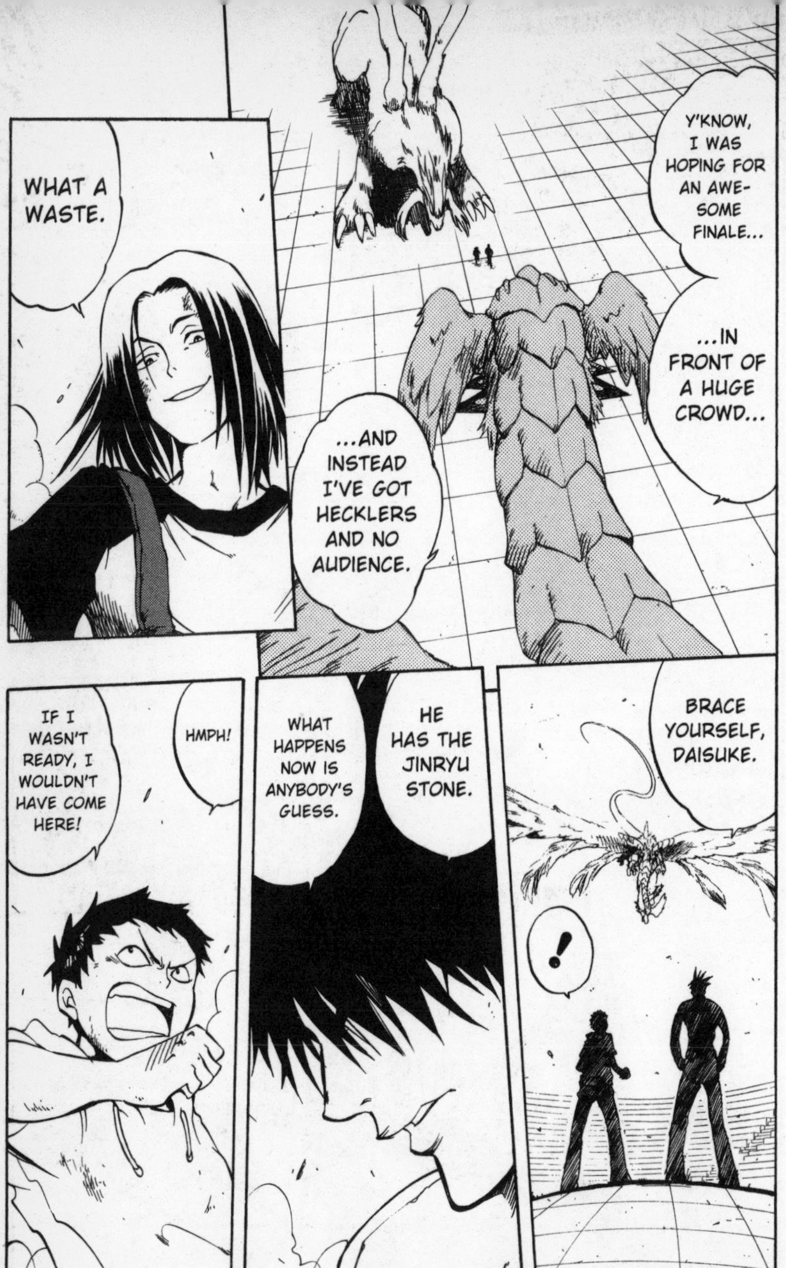
Y'KNOW, I WAS HOPING FOR AN AWE-SOME FINALE...
...IN FRONT OF A HUGE CROWD...
...AND INSTEAD I'VE GOT HECKLERS AND NO AUDIENCE.
WHAT A WASTE.
BRACE YOURSELF, DAISUKE.
!
HE HAS THE JINRYU STONE.
WHAT HAPPENS NOW IS ANYBODY'S GUESS.
HMPH!
IF I WASN'T READY, I WOULDN'T HAVE COME HERE!

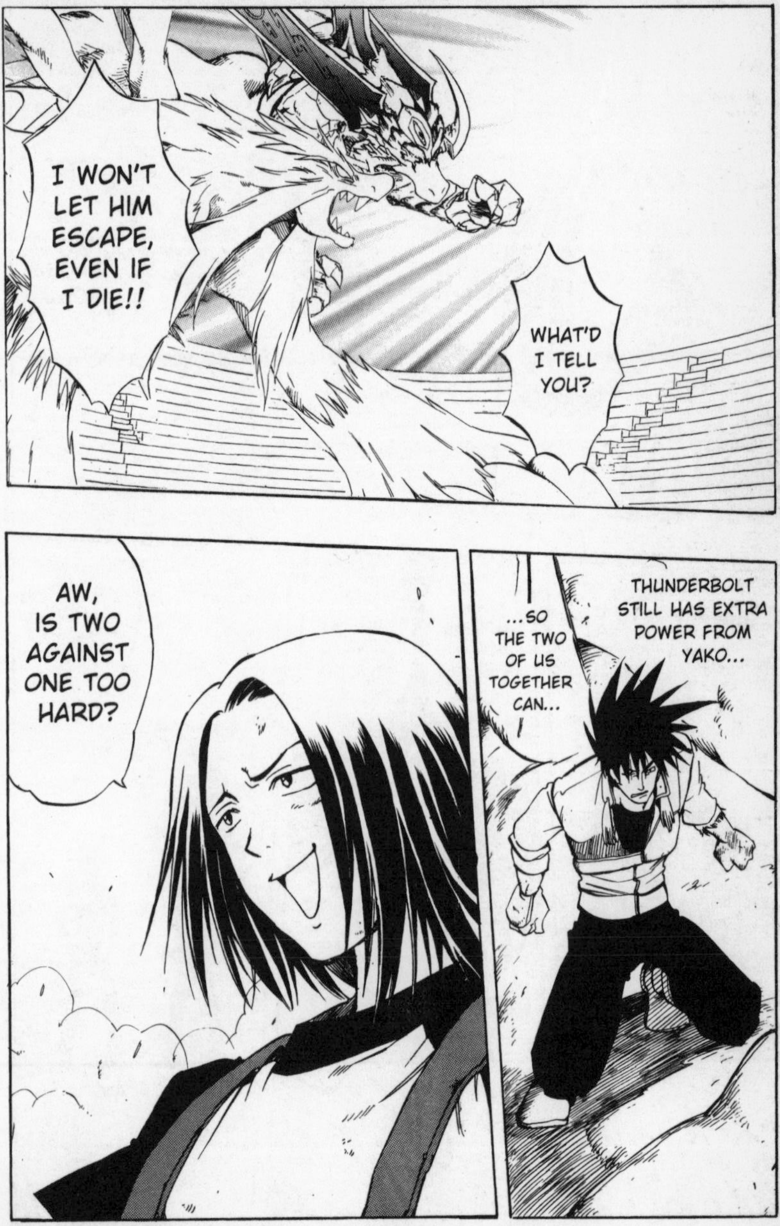
WHAT'D I TELL YOU?
I WON'T LET HIM ESCAPE, EVEN IF I DIE!!
THUNDERBOLT STILL HAS EXTRA POWER FROM YAKO...
...SO THE TWO OF US TOGETHER CAN...
AW, IS TWO AGAINST ONE TOO HARD?

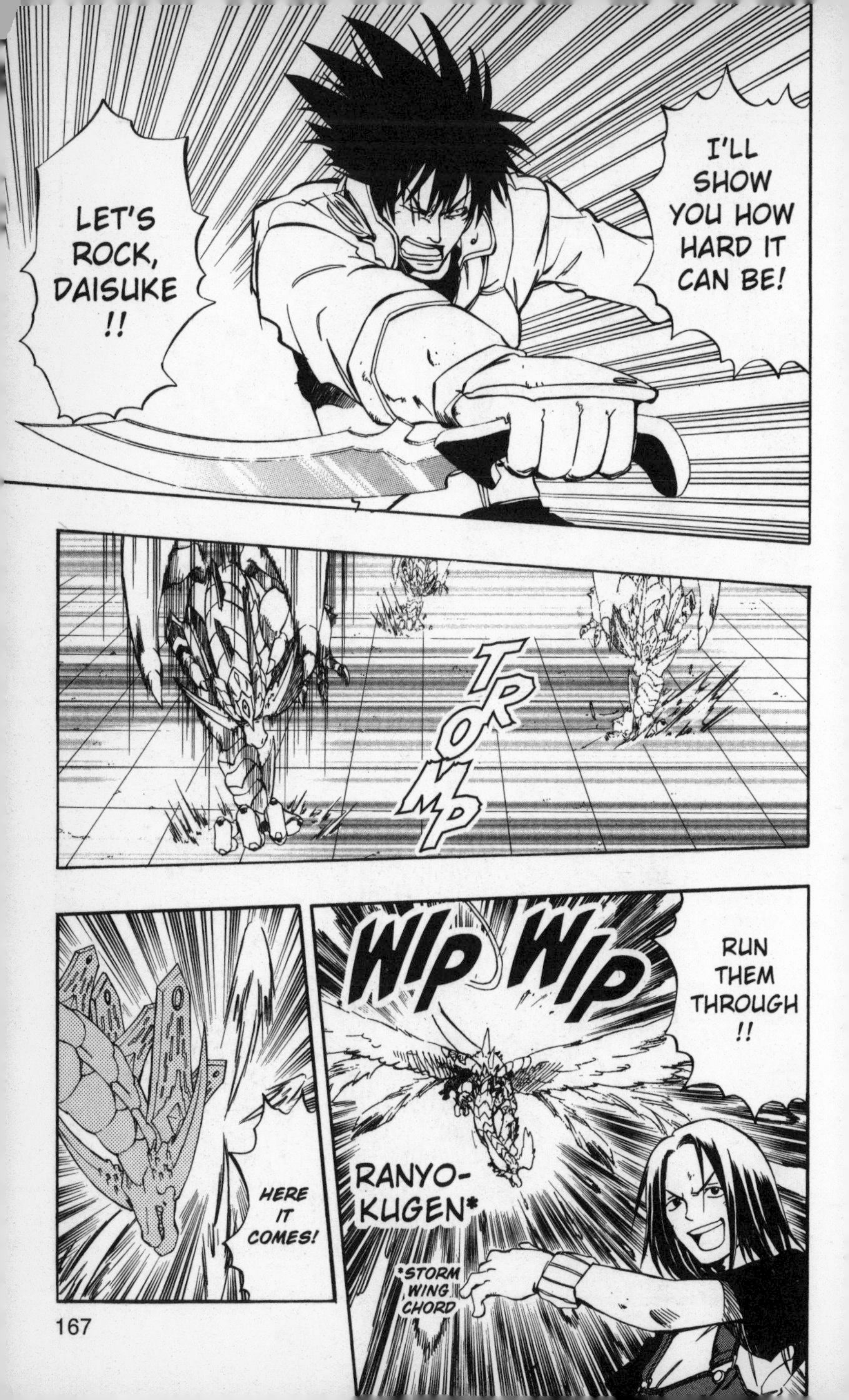
I'LL SHOW YOU HOW HARD IT CAN BE!
LET'S ROCK, DAISUKE!!
TROMP
RUN THEM THROUGH!!
WIP WIP
RANYO-KUGEN*
*STORM WING CHORD
HERE IT COMES!

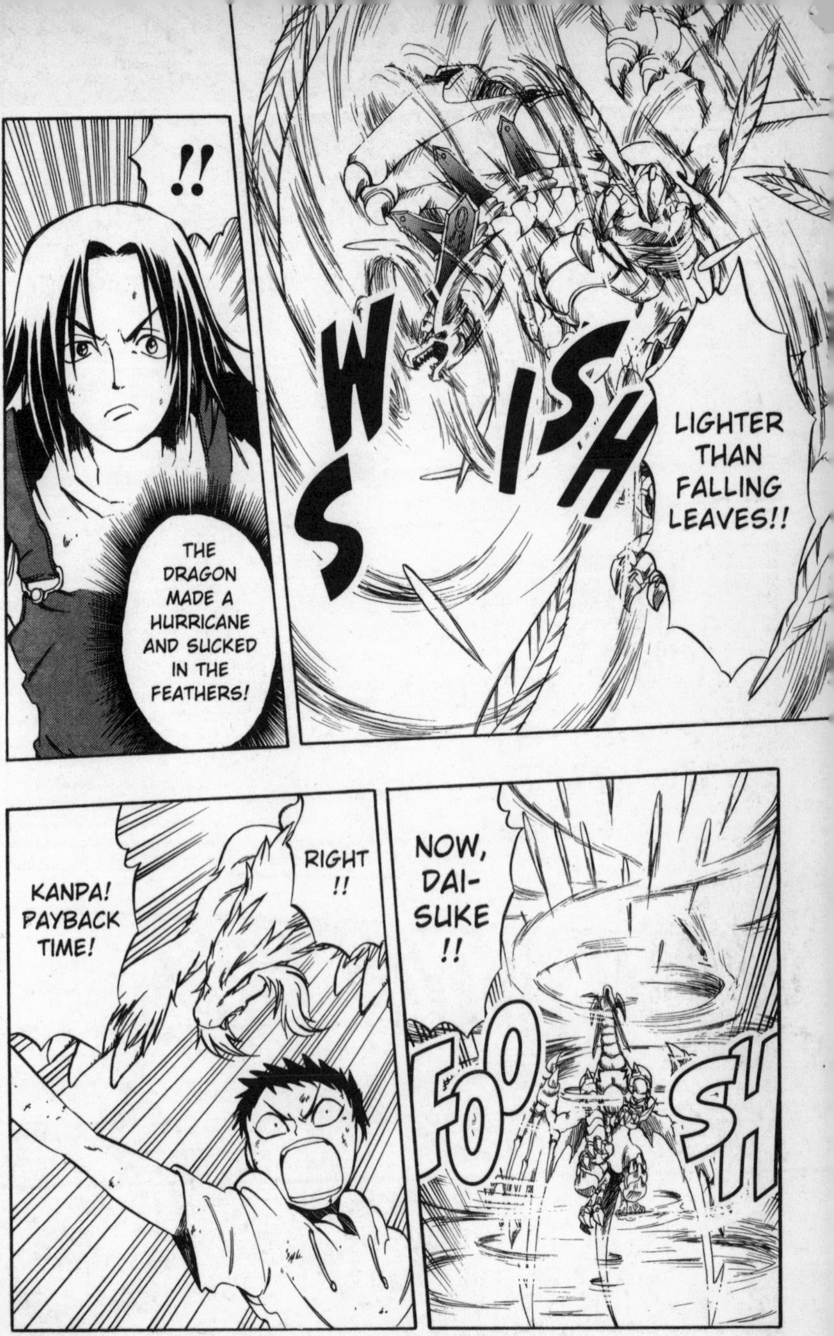
SWISH
LIGHTER THAN FALLING LEAVES!!
!!
THE DRAGON MADE A HURRICANE AND SUCKED IN THE FEATHERS!
NOW, DAI-SUKE!!
FOOOSH
RIGHT!!
KANPA! PAYBACK TIME!

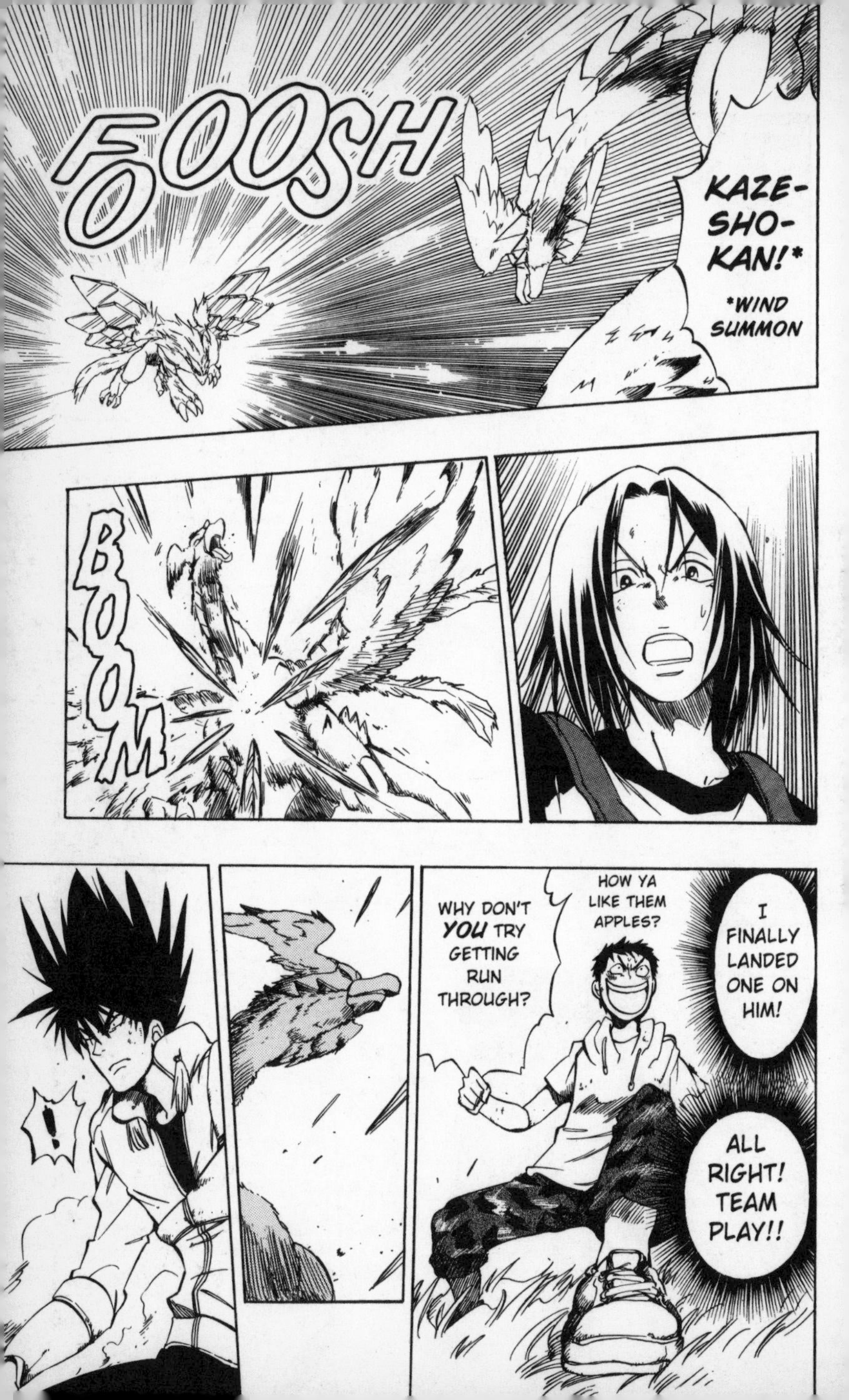
KAZE-SHO-KAN!*
*WIND SUMMON
FOOOSH
BOOOM
I FINALLY LANDED ONE ON HIM!
ALL RIGHT! TEAM PLAY!!
HOW YA LIKE THEM APPLES?
WHY DON'T YOU TRY GETTING RUN THROUGH?
!

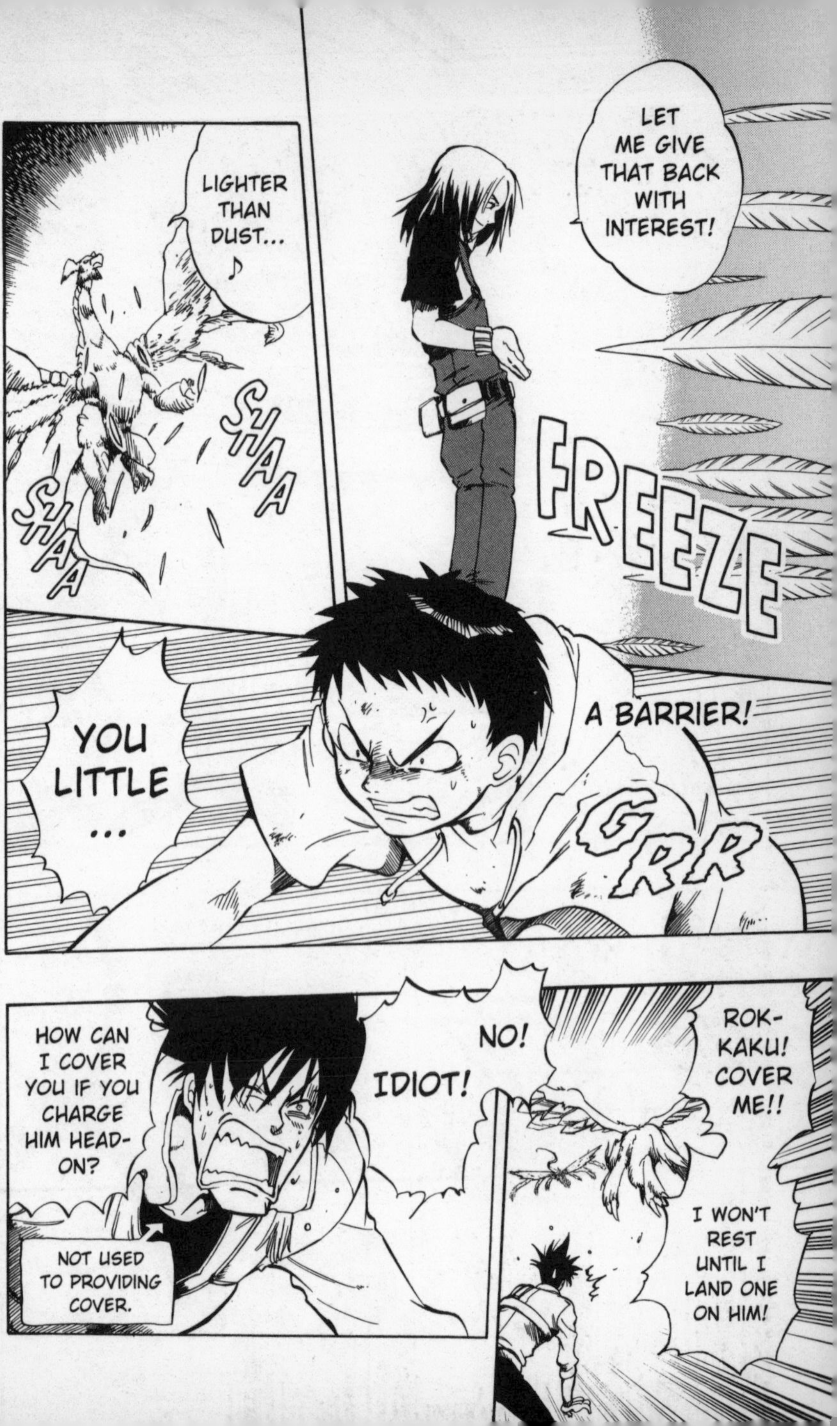

LET ME GIVE THAT BACK WITH INTEREST!
FREEZE
LIGHTER THAN DUST... ♪
SHAA
SHAA
A BARRIER!
GRR
YOU LITTLE ...
ROK-KAKU! COVER ME!!
I WON'T REST UNTIL I LAND ONE ON HIM!
NO!
IDIOT!
HOW CAN I COVER YOU IF YOU CHARGE HIM HEAD-ON?
NOT USED TO PROVIDING COVER.

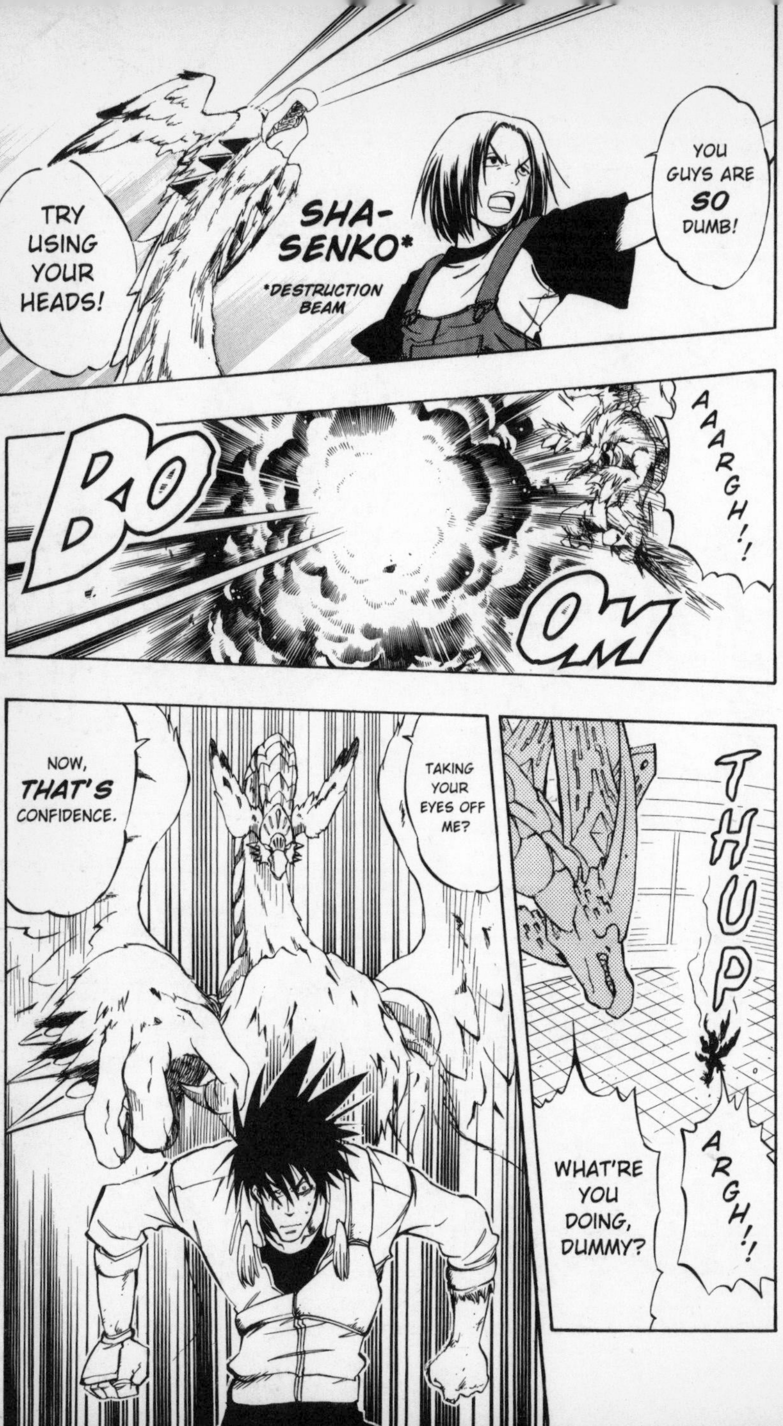
YOU GUYS ARE SO DUMB!
SHA-SENKO*
*DESTRUCTION BEAM
TRY USING YOUR HEADS!
AAARGH!!
BOOM
THUP
ARGH!!
WHAT'RE YOU DOING, DUMMY?
TAKING YOUR EYES OFF ME?
NOW, THAT'S CONFIDENCE.

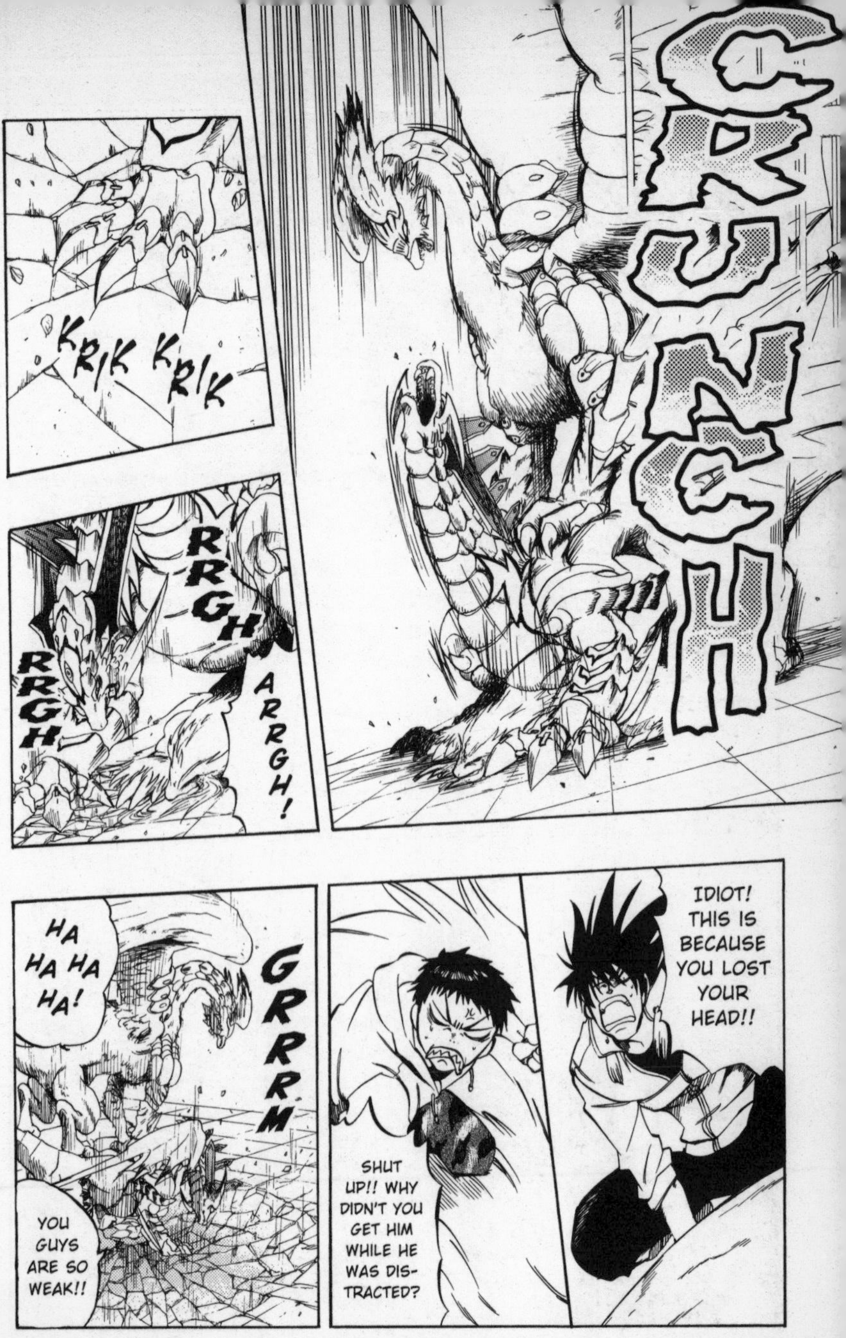
CRUNCH
KRIK KRIK
RRGH
RRGH
ARRGH!
IDIOT! THIS IS BECAUSE YOU LOST YOUR HEAD!!
SHUT UP!! WHY DIDN'T YOU GET HIM WHILE HE WAS DIS-TRACTED?
HA HA HA HA!
GRRRM
YOU GUYS ARE SO WEAK!!

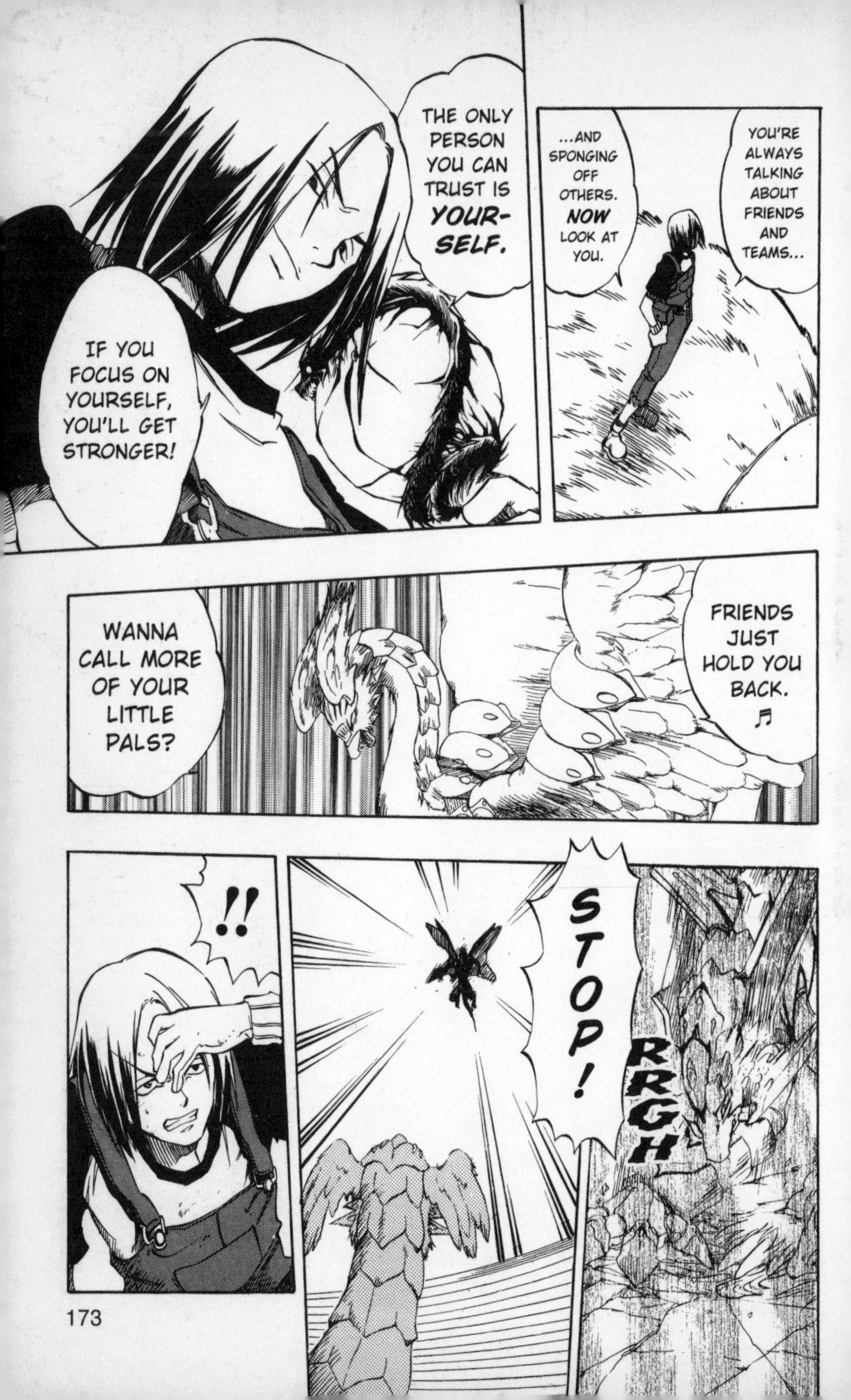
YOU'RE ALWAYS TALKING ABOUT FRIENDS AND TEAMS...
...AND SPONGING OFF OTHERS. NOW LOOK AT YOU.
THE ONLY PERSON YOU CAN TRUST IS YOURSELF.
IF YOU FOCUS ON YOURSELF, YOU'LL GET STRONGER!
FRIENDS JUST HOLD YOU BACK. ♬
WANNA CALL MORE OF YOUR LITTLE PALS?
STOP!
RRGH
!!

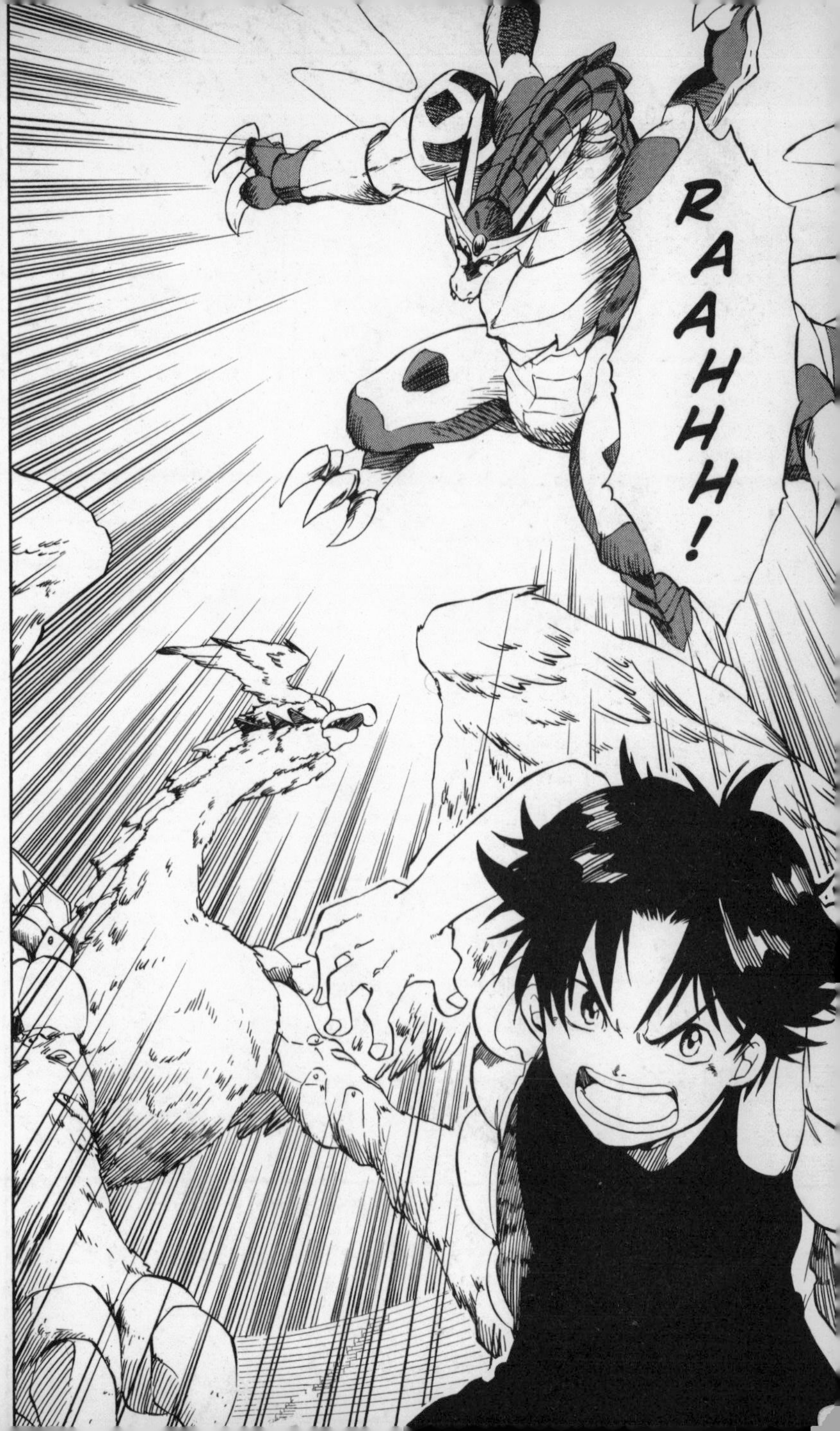
RAHHH!

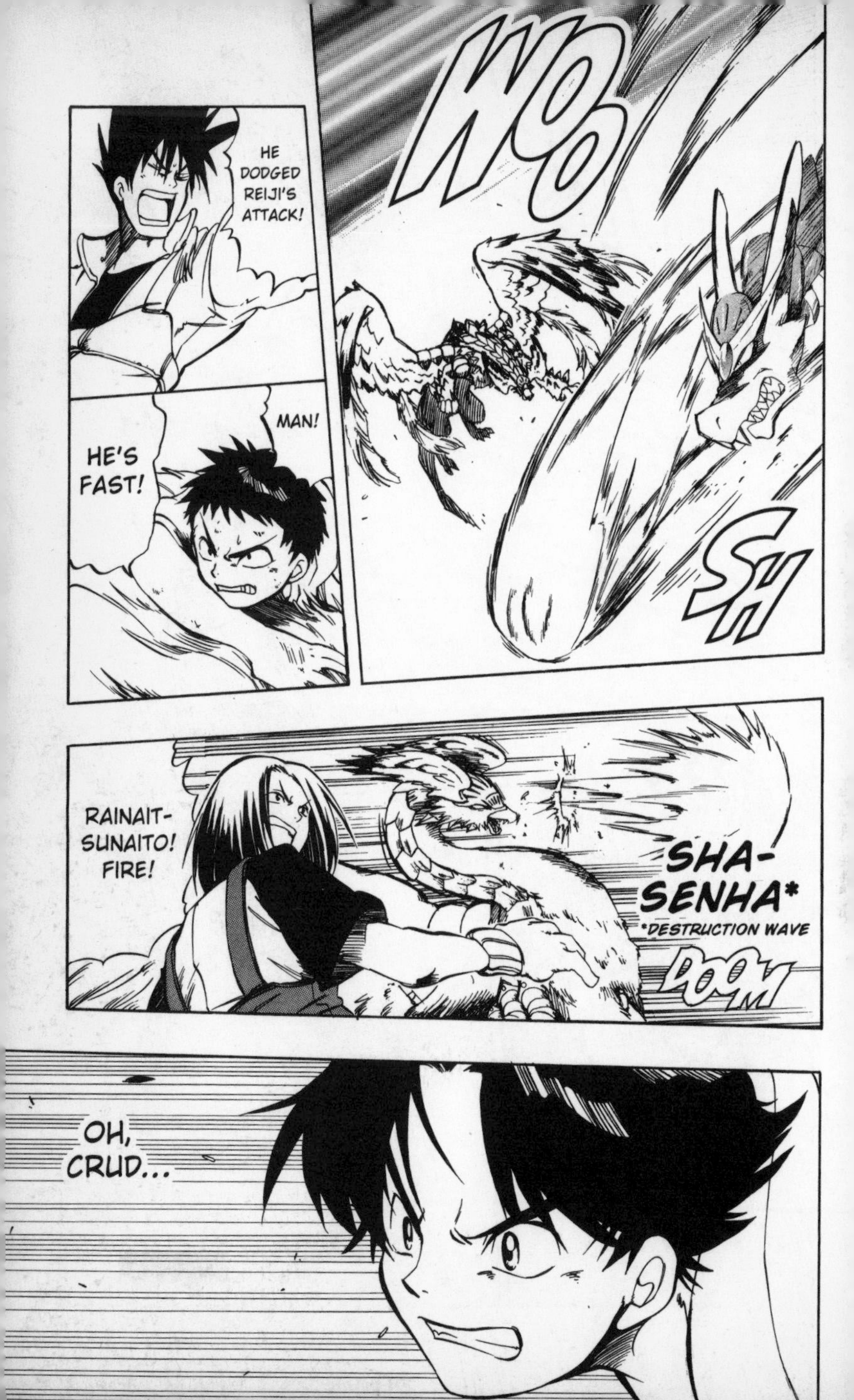
NO
SH
HE DODGED REIJI'S ATTACK!
MAN!
HE'S FAST!
SHA-SENHA*
*DESTRUCTION WAVE
DOOM
RAINAIT-SUNAITO! FIRE!
OH, CRUD...

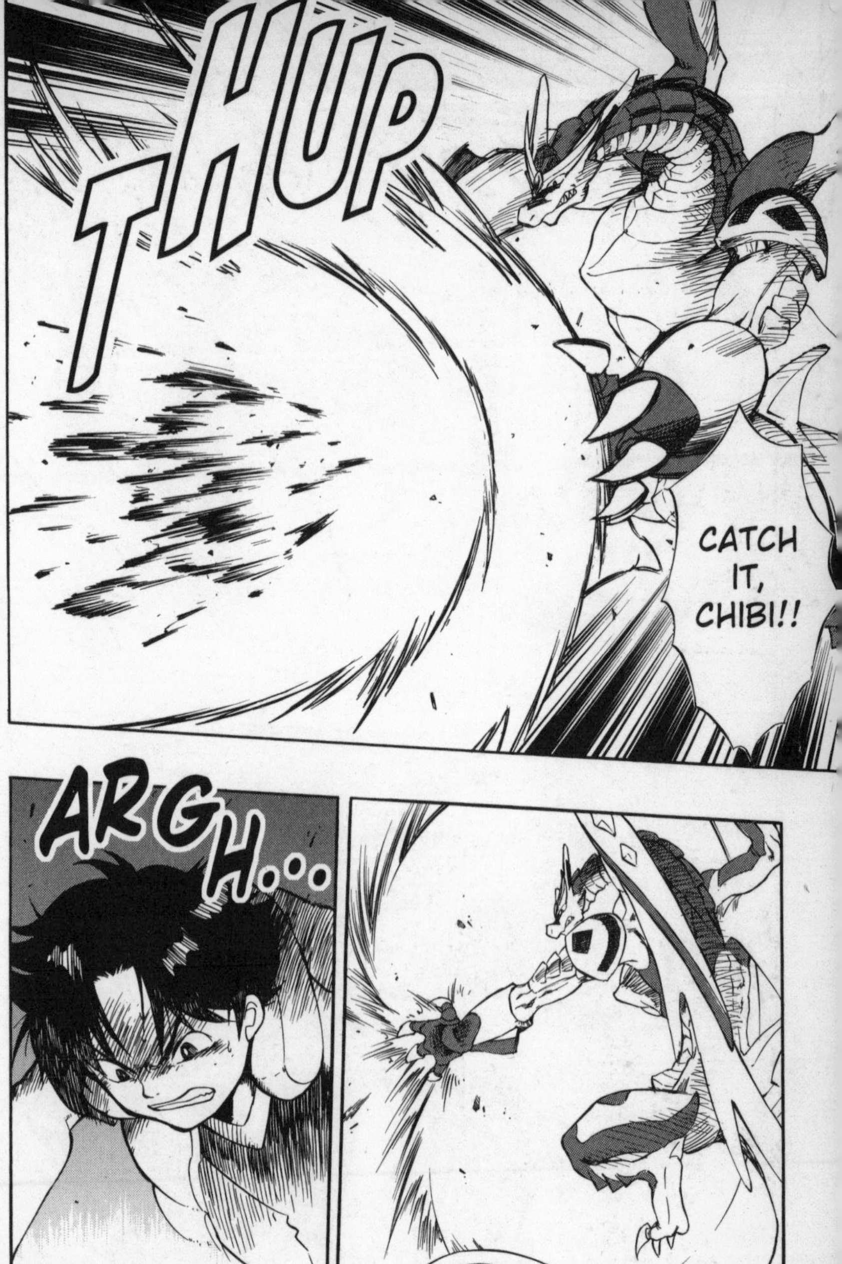
THUP
CATCH IT, CHIBI!!
ARGH...

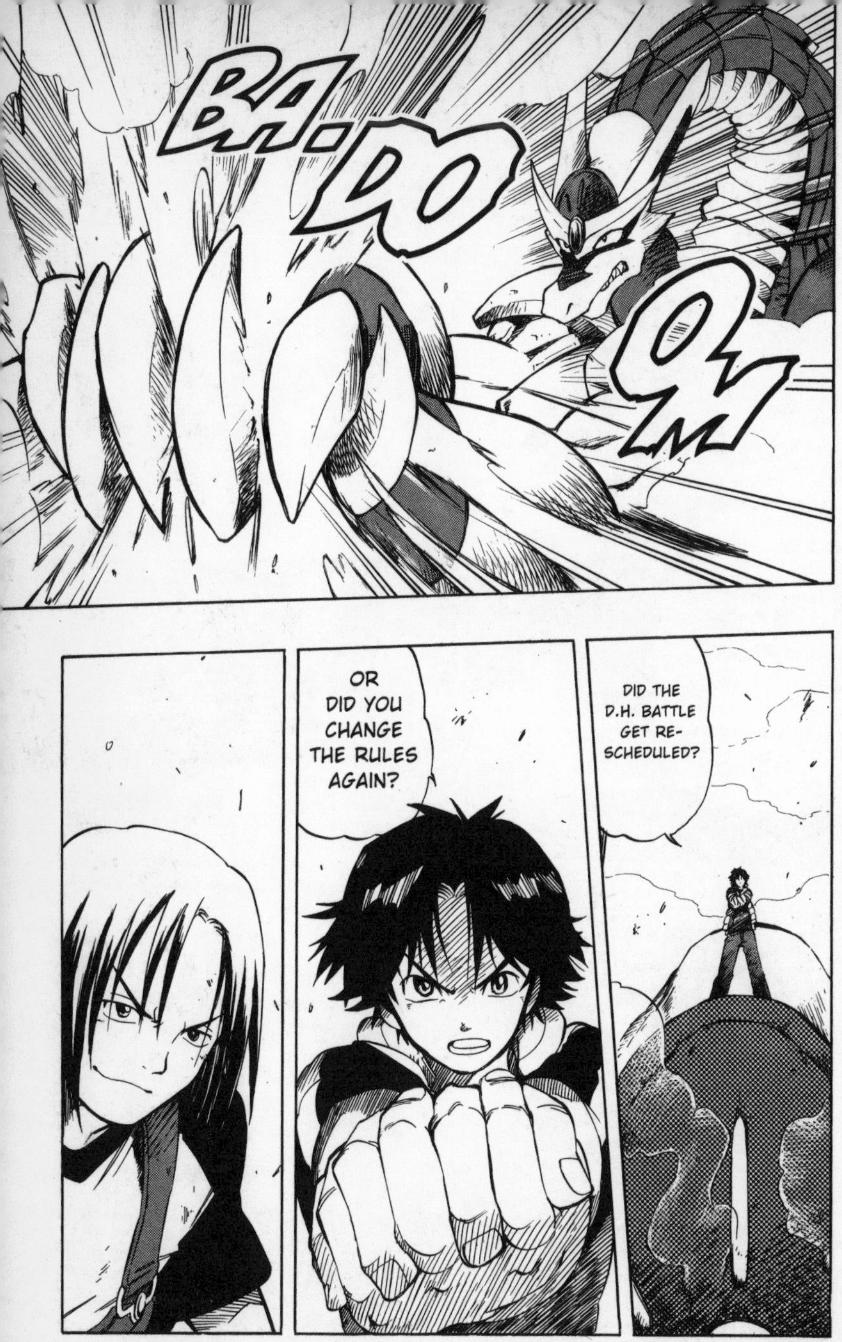
BA-DO
DID THE D.H. BATTLE GET RE-SCHEDULED?
OR DID YOU CHANGE THE RULES AGAIN?

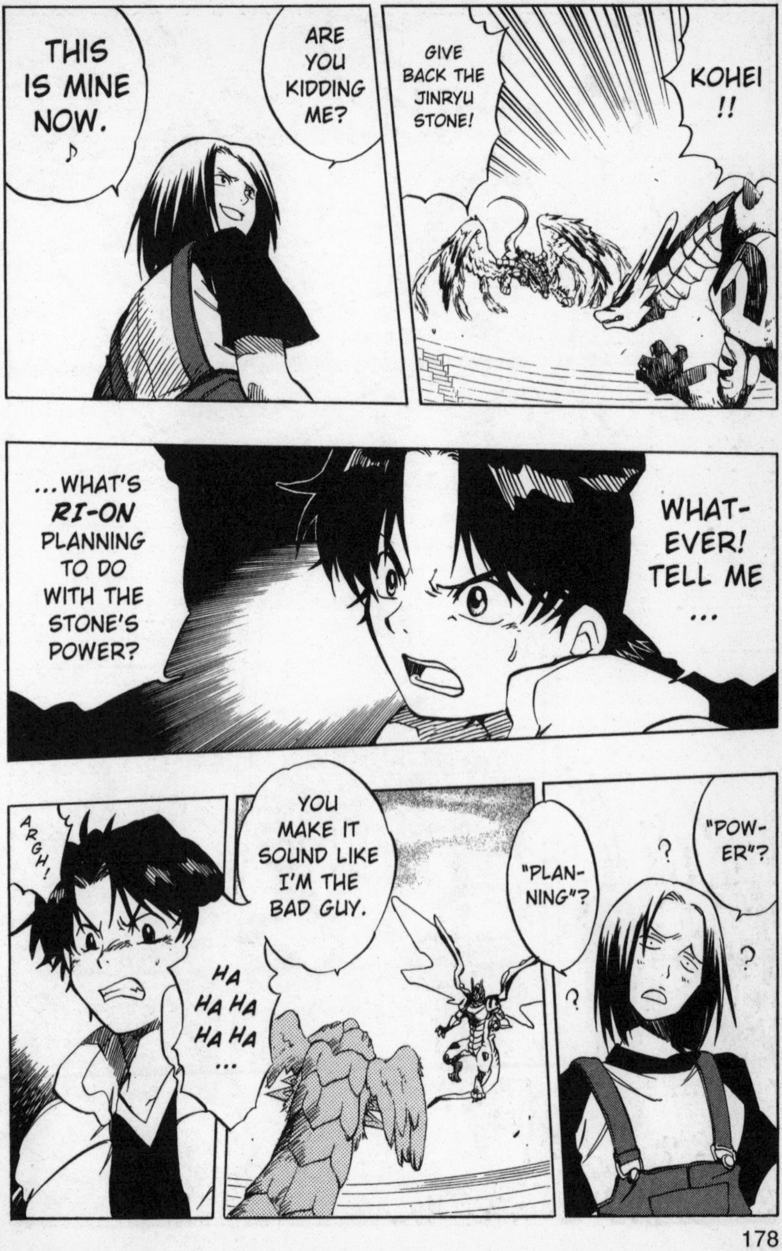
KOHEI !!
GIVE BACK THE JINRYU STONE!
ARE YOU KIDDING ME?
THIS IS MINE NOW. ♪
WHATEVER! TELL ME ...
...WHAT'S *RI-ON* PLANNING TO DO WITH THE STONE'S POWER?
"POWER"?
"PLANNING"?
YOU MAKE IT SOUND LIKE I'M THE BAD GUY.
HA HA HA HA HA ...
ARGH!

READ THIS WAY

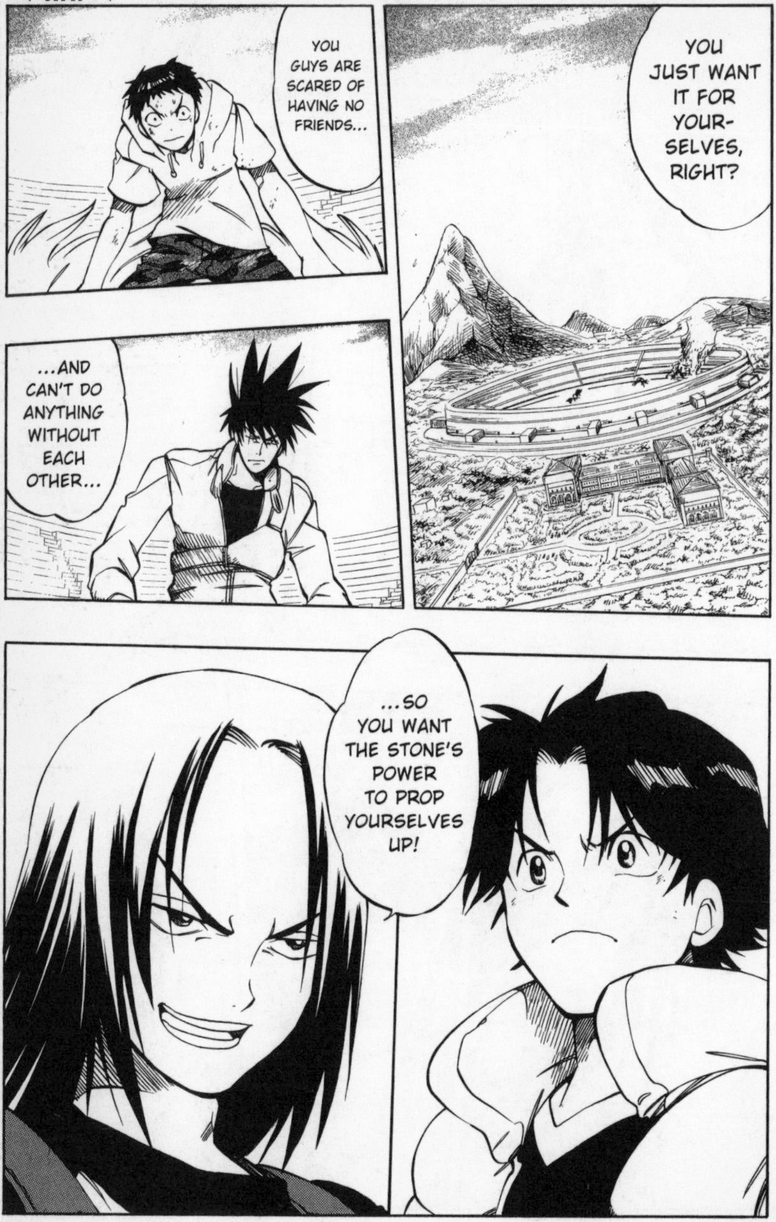
YOU JUST WANT IT FOR YOUR-SELVES, RIGHT?
YOU GUYS ARE SCARED OF HAVING NO FRIENDS...
...AND CAN'T DO ANYTHING WITHOUT EACH OTHER...
...SO YOU WANT THE STONE'S POWER TO PROP YOURSELVES UP!

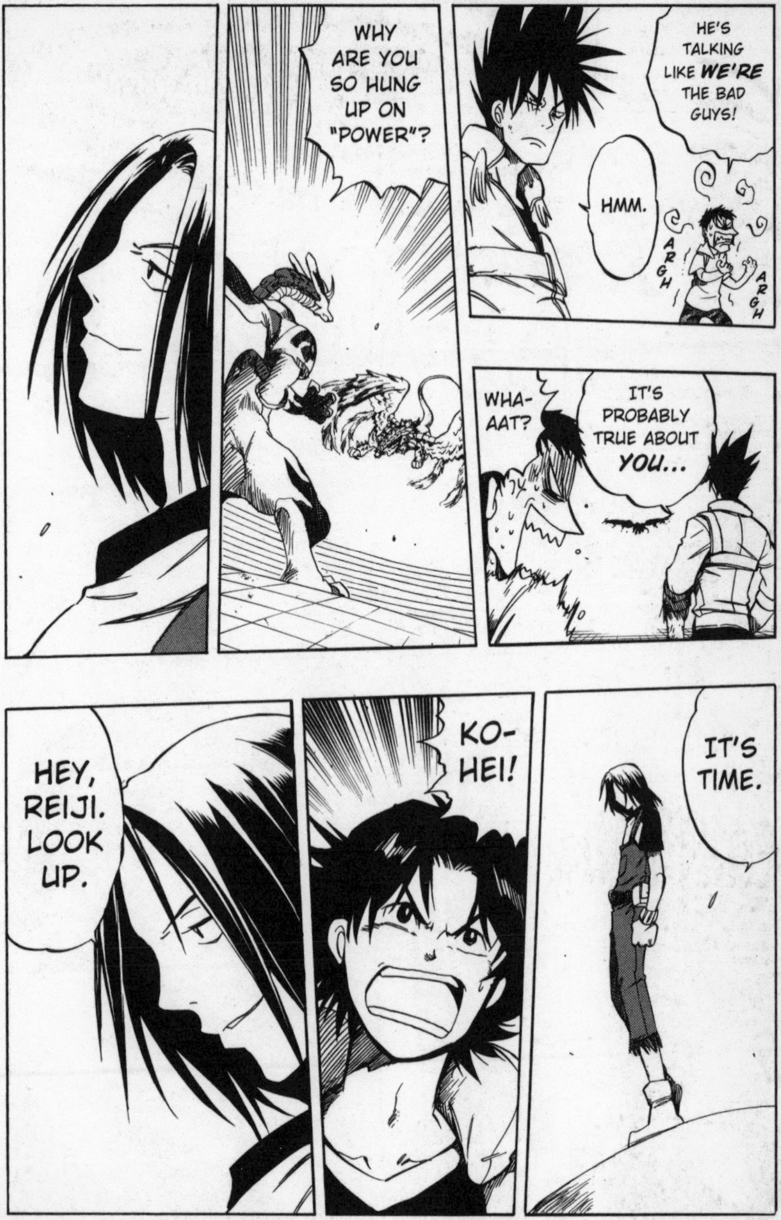
HE'S TALKING LIKE WE'RE THE BAD GUYS!
HMM.
ARGH
ARGH
IT'S PROBABLY TRUE ABOUT YOU...
WHA-AAT?
WHY ARE YOU SO HUNG UP ON "POWER"?
IT'S TIME.
KO-HEI!
HEY, REIJI. LOOK UP.

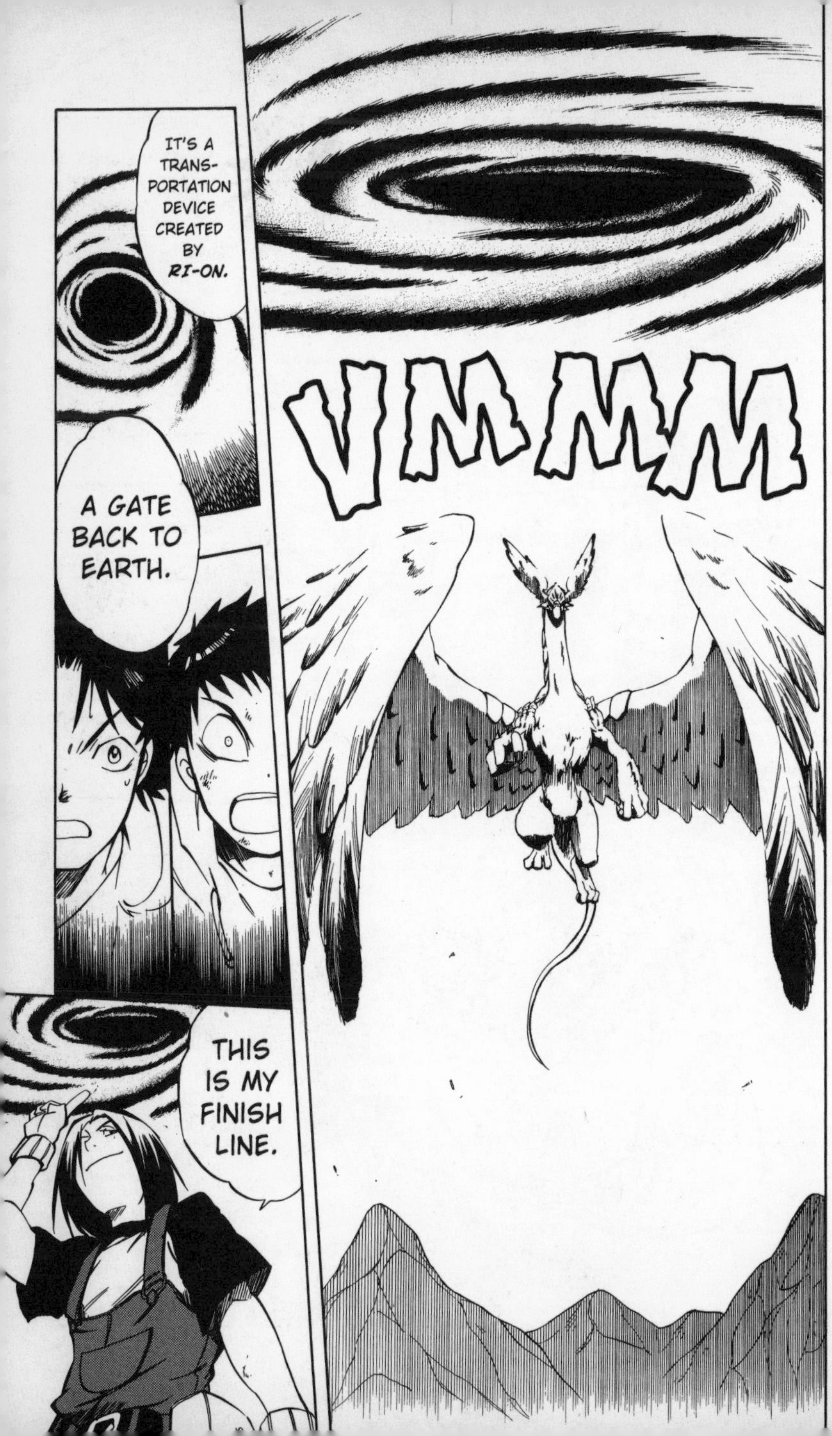
VMMM
IT'S A TRANS-PORTATION DEVICE CREATED BY *RI-ON*.
A GATE BACK TO EARTH.
THIS IS MY FINISH LINE.

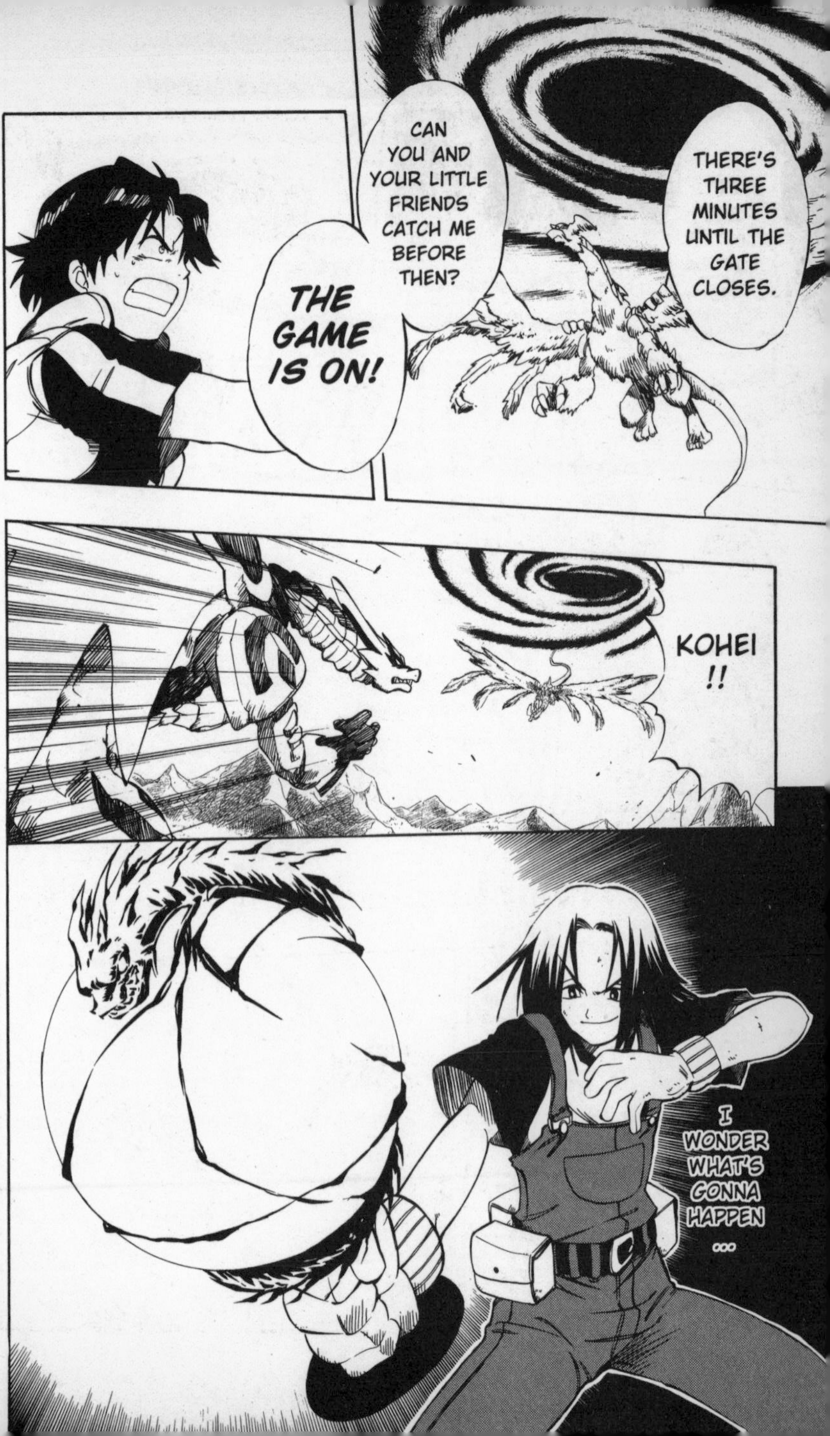
THERE'S THREE MINUTES UNTIL THE GATE CLOSES.
CAN YOU AND YOUR LITTLE FRIENDS CATCH ME BEFORE THEN?
THE GAME IS ON!
KOHEI !!
I WONDER WHAT'S GONNA HAPPEN ...

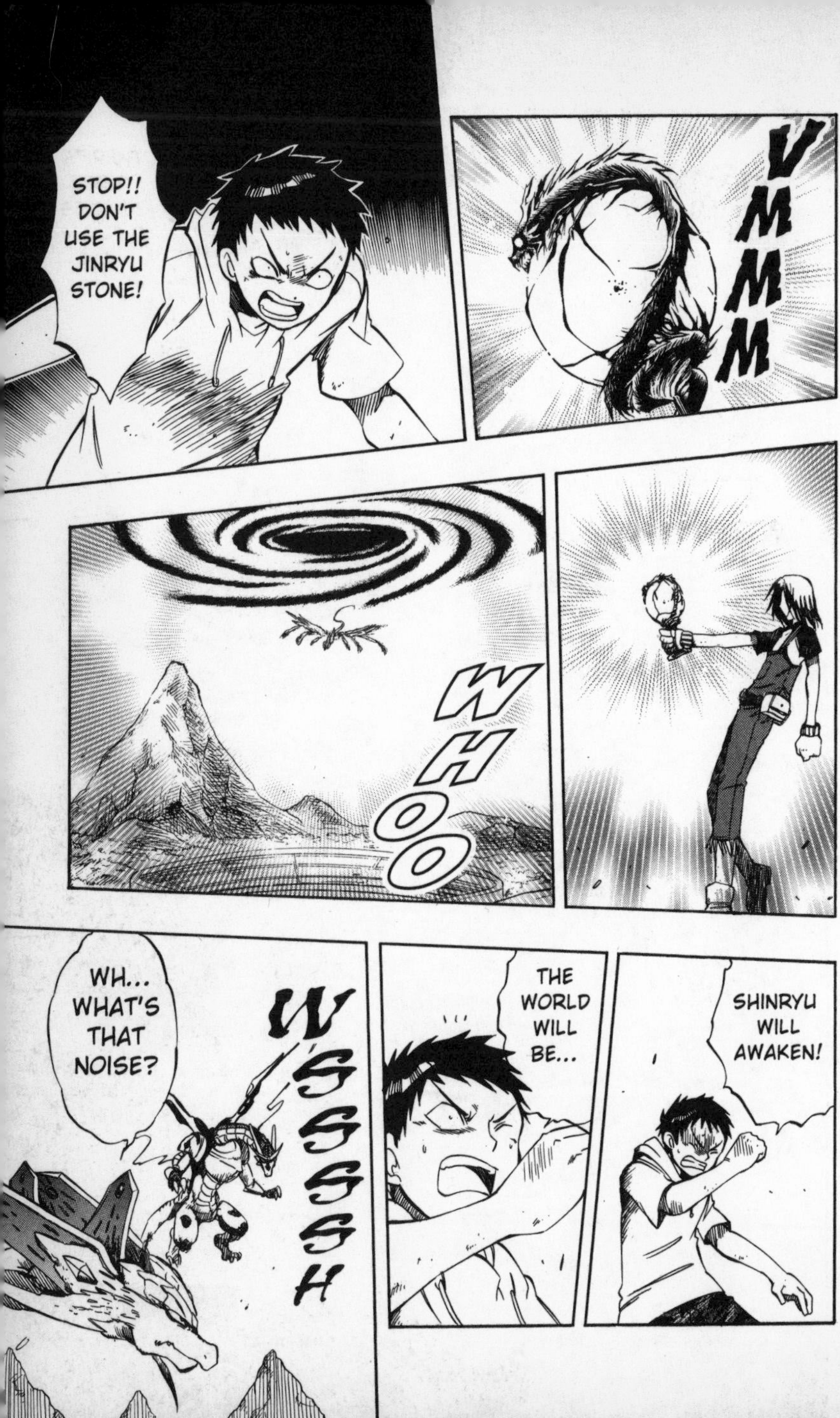
VMMM
STOP!! DON'T USE THE JINRYU STONE!
WHOOO
SHINRYU WILL AWAKEN!
THE WORLD WILL BE...
WH... WHAT'S THAT NOISE?
WSSSSH

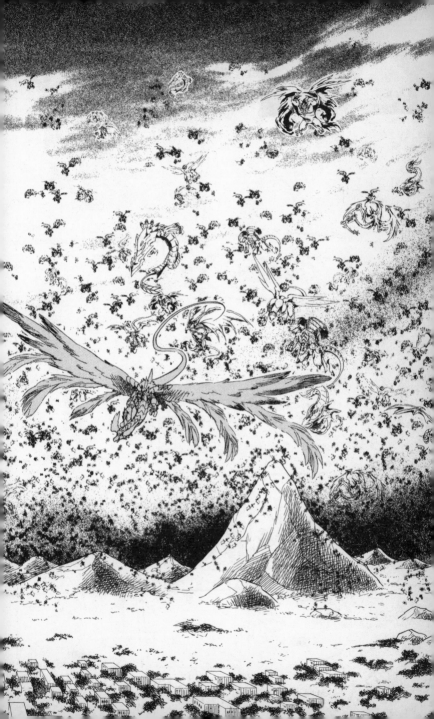

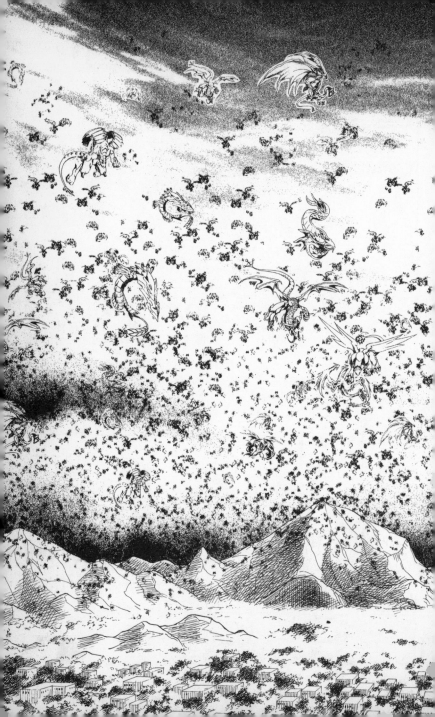

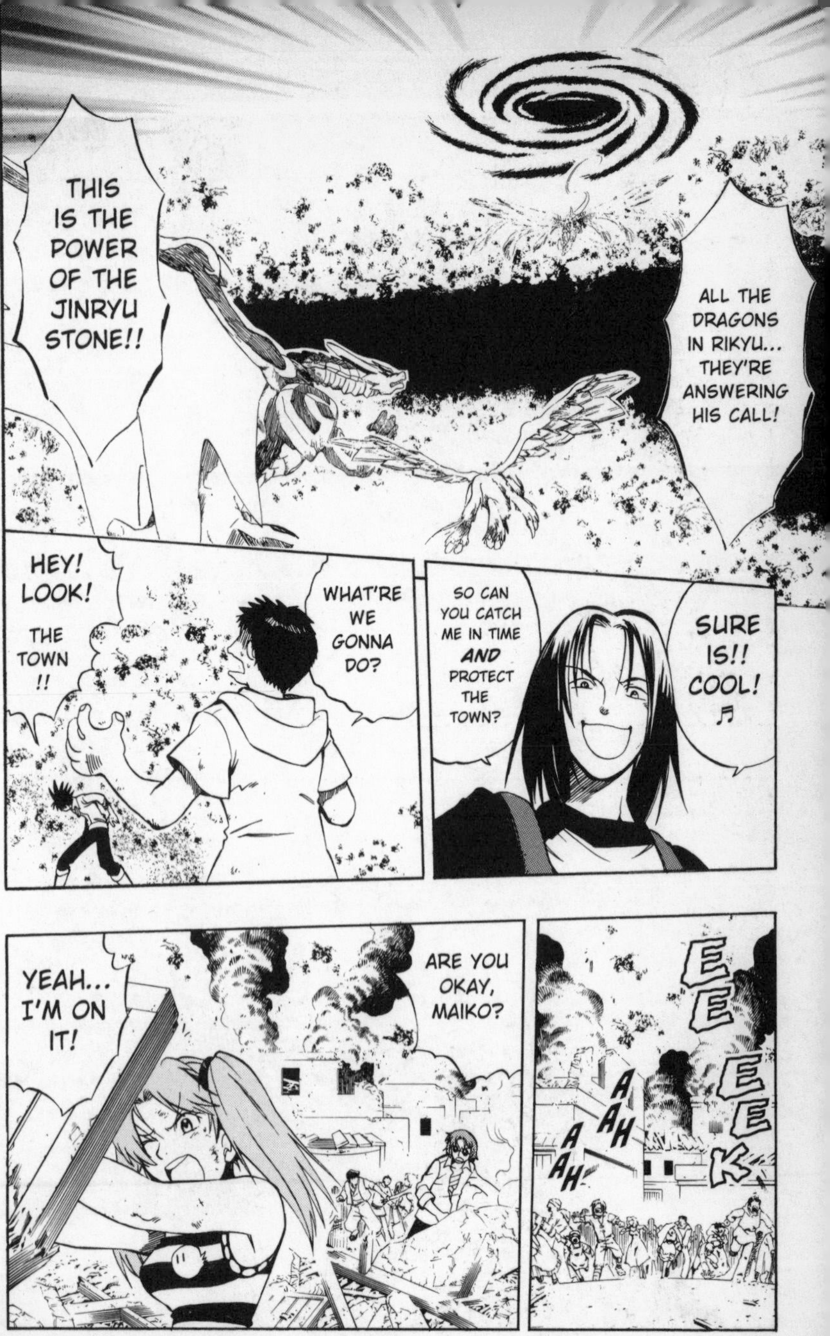
ALL THE DRAGONS IN RIKYU... THEY'RE ANSWERING HIS CALL!
THIS IS THE POWER OF THE JINRYU STONE!!
SURE IS!! COOL! ♬
SO CAN YOU CATCH ME IN TIME *AND* PROTECT THE TOWN?
WHAT'RE WE GONNA DO?
HEY! LOOK!
THE TOWN !!
EEEEEK
AAAH
AAAH
ARE YOU OKAY, MAIKO?
YEAH... I'M ON IT!

READ THIS WAY

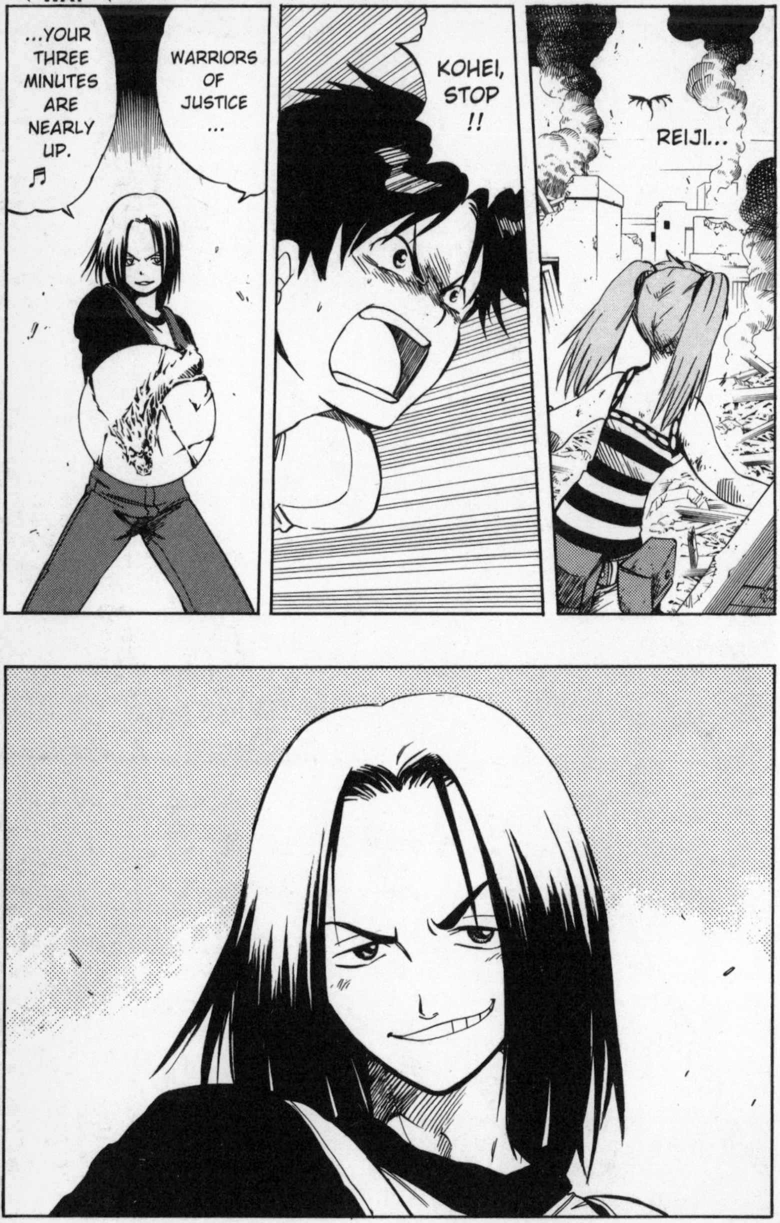
REIJI...
KOHEI, STOP !!
WARRIORS OF JUSTICE ...
...YOUR THREE MINUTES ARE NEARLY UP. ♬

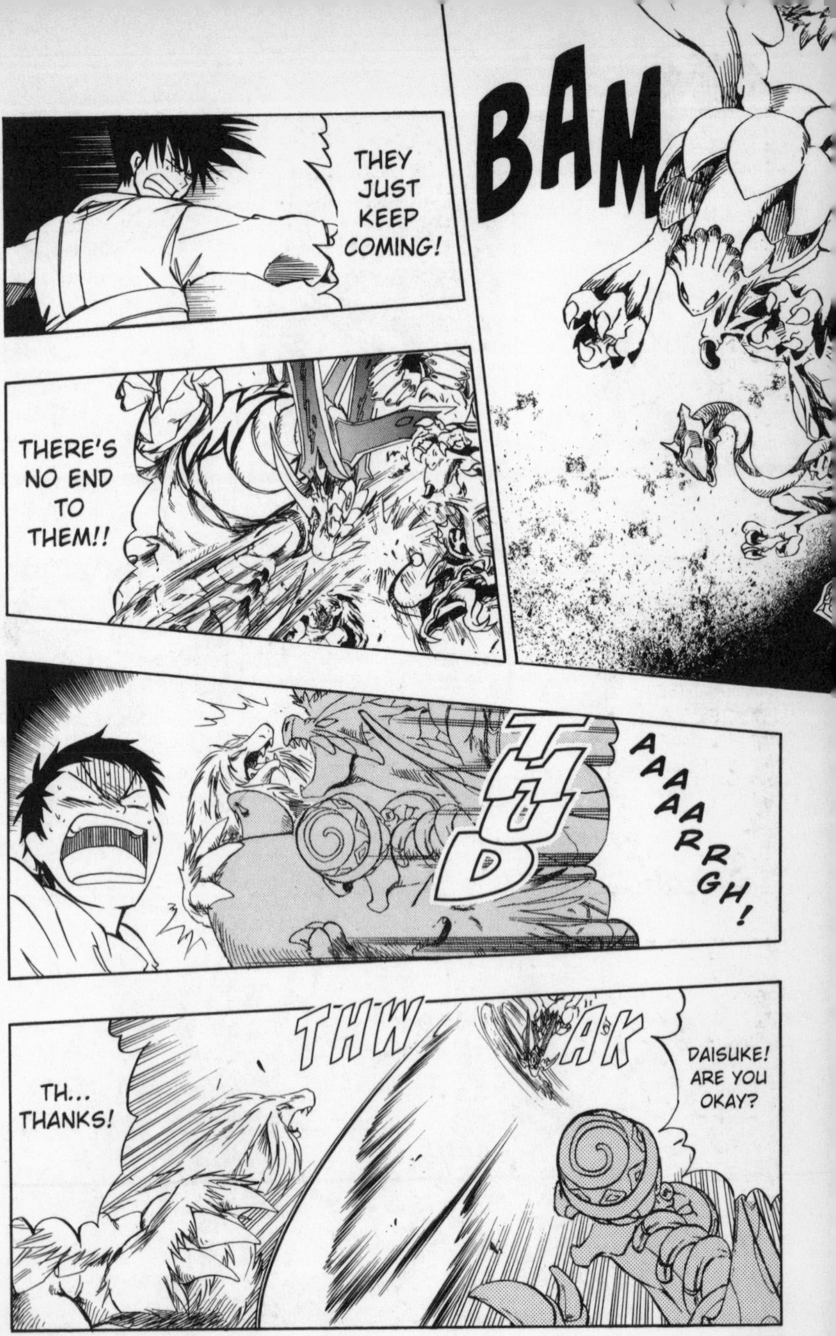
BAM
THEY JUST KEEP COMING!
THERE'S NO END TO THEM!!
AAAARRGH!
THUD
DAISUKE! ARE YOU OKAY?
THWAK
TH... THANKS!

READ THIS WAY

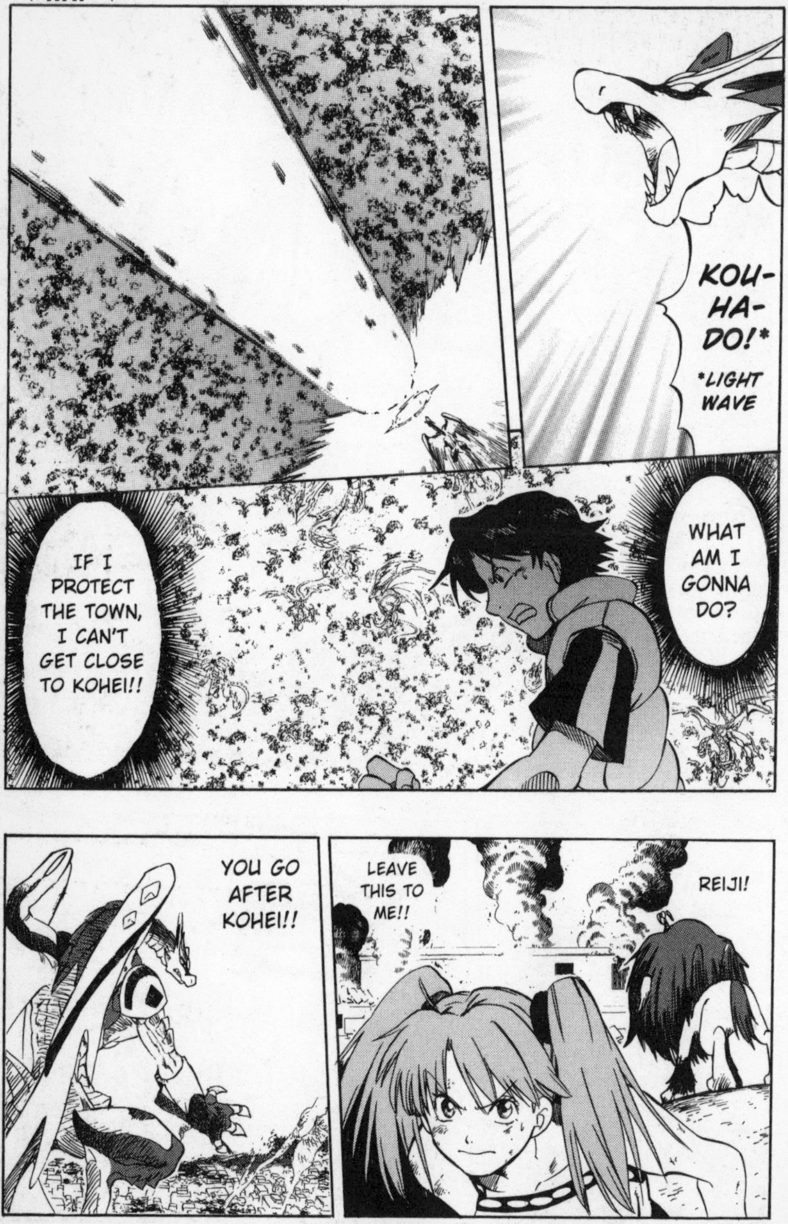
KOU-HA-DO!*
*LIGHT WAVE
WHAT AM I GONNA DO?
IF I PROTECT THE TOWN, I CAN'T GET CLOSE TO KOHEI!!
REIJI!
LEAVE THIS TO ME!!
YOU GO AFTER KOHEI!!

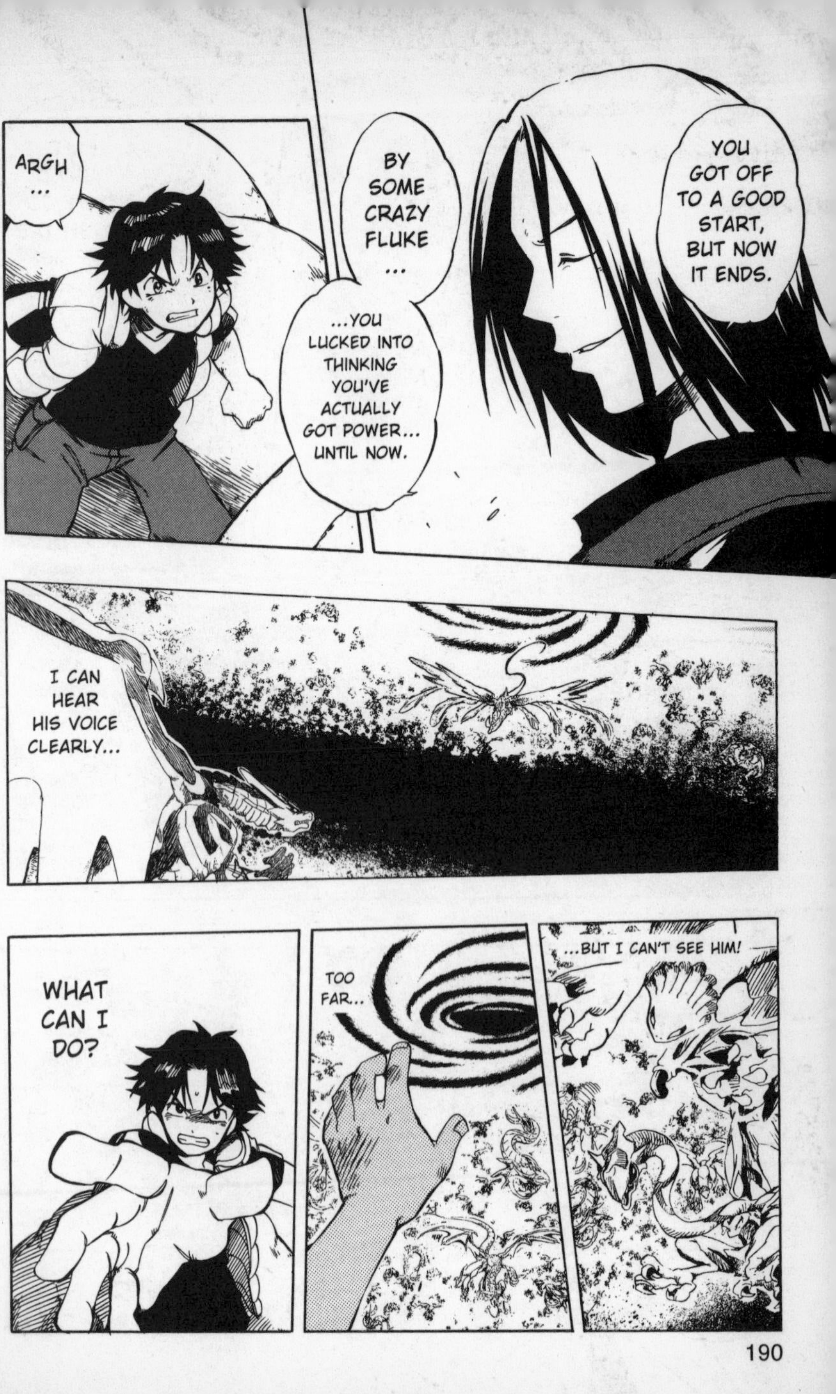
YOU GOT OFF TO A GOOD START, BUT NOW IT ENDS.
BY SOME CRAZY FLUKE...
...YOU LUCKED INTO THINKING YOU'VE ACTUALLY GOT POWER... UNTIL NOW.
ARGH...
I CAN HEAR HIS VOICE CLEARLY...
...BUT I CAN'T SEE HIM!
TOO FAR...
WHAT CAN I DO?

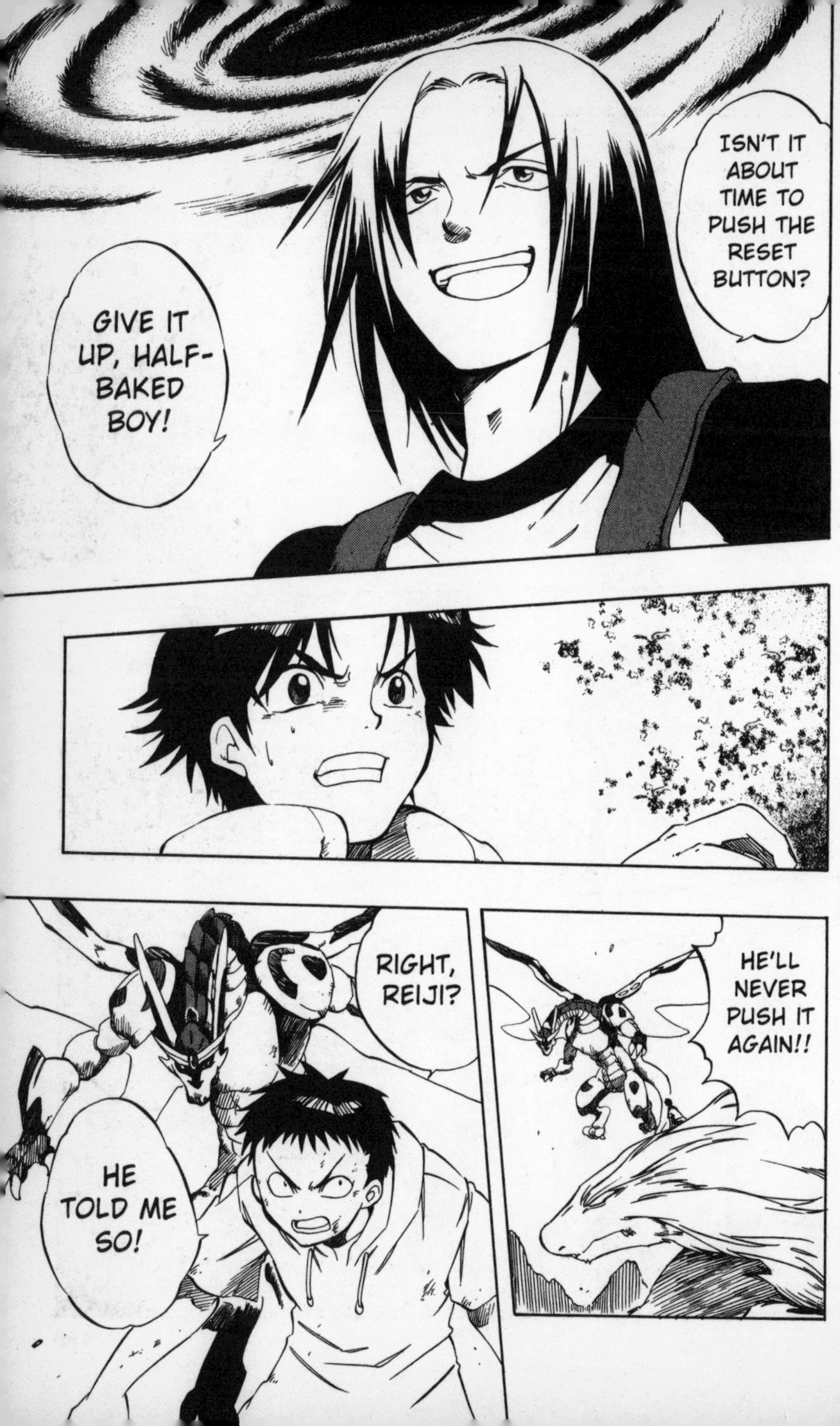
ISN'T IT ABOUT TIME TO PUSH THE RESET BUTTON?
GIVE IT UP, HALF-BAKED BOY!
HE'LL NEVER PUSH IT AGAIN!!
RIGHT, REIJI?
HE TOLD ME SO!

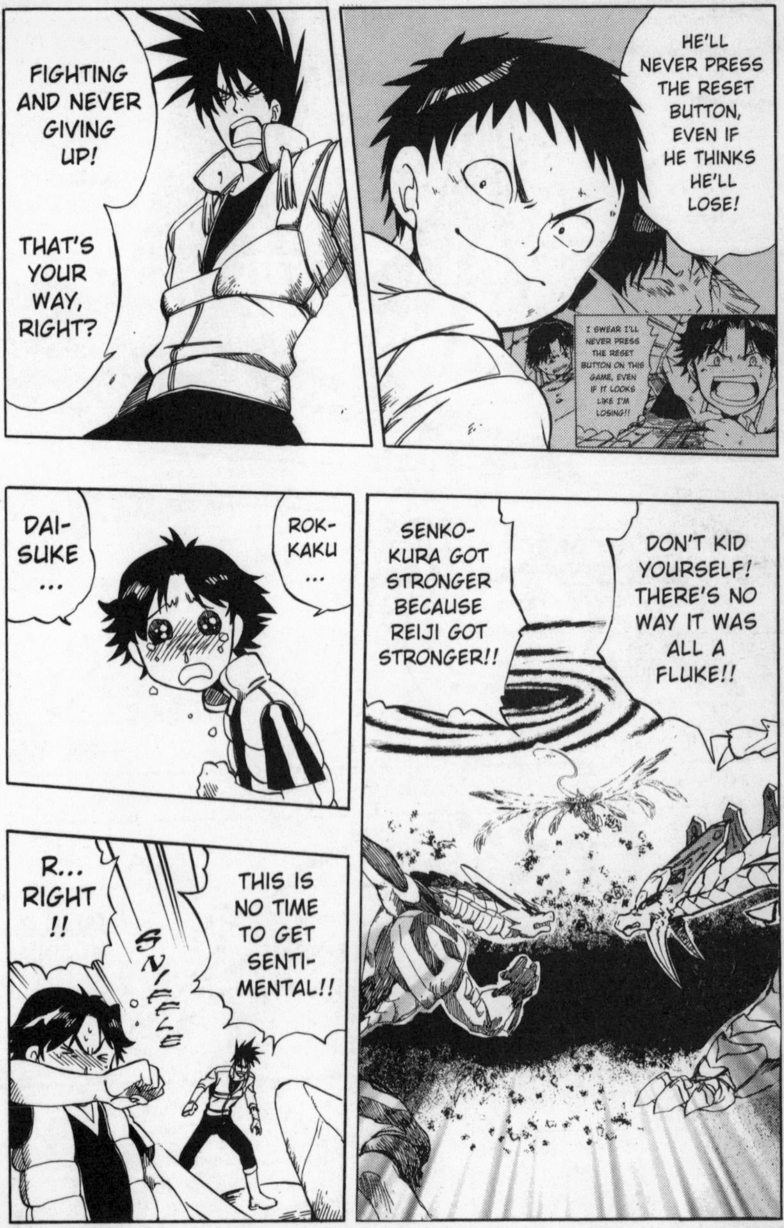
HE'LL NEVER PRESS THE RESET BUTTON, EVEN IF HE THINKS HE'LL LOSE!
I SWEAR I'LL NEVER PRESS THE RESET BUTTON ON THIS GAME, EVEN IF IT LOOKS LIKE I'M LOSING!!
FIGHTING AND NEVER GIVING UP!
THAT'S YOUR WAY, RIGHT?
DON'T KID YOURSELF! THERE'S NO WAY IT WAS ALL A FLUKE!!
SENKO-KURA GOT STRONGER BECAUSE REIJI GOT STRONGER!!
ROK-KAKU...
DAI-SUKE...
THIS IS NO TIME TO GET SENTI-MENTAL!!
SNIFFLE
R... RIGHT!!

READ THIS WAY

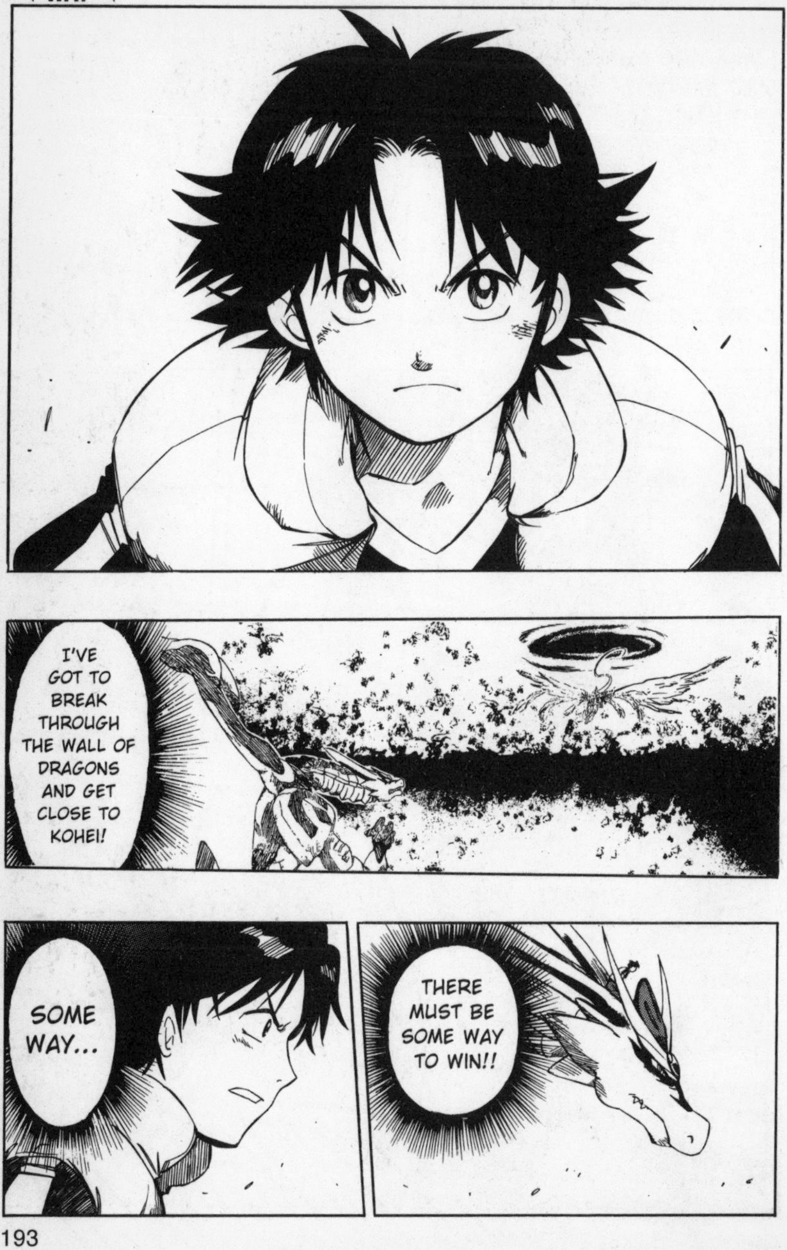
I'VE GOT TO BREAK THROUGH THE WALL OF DRAGONS AND GET CLOSE TO KOHEI!
THERE MUST BE SOME WAY TO WIN!!
SOME WAY...

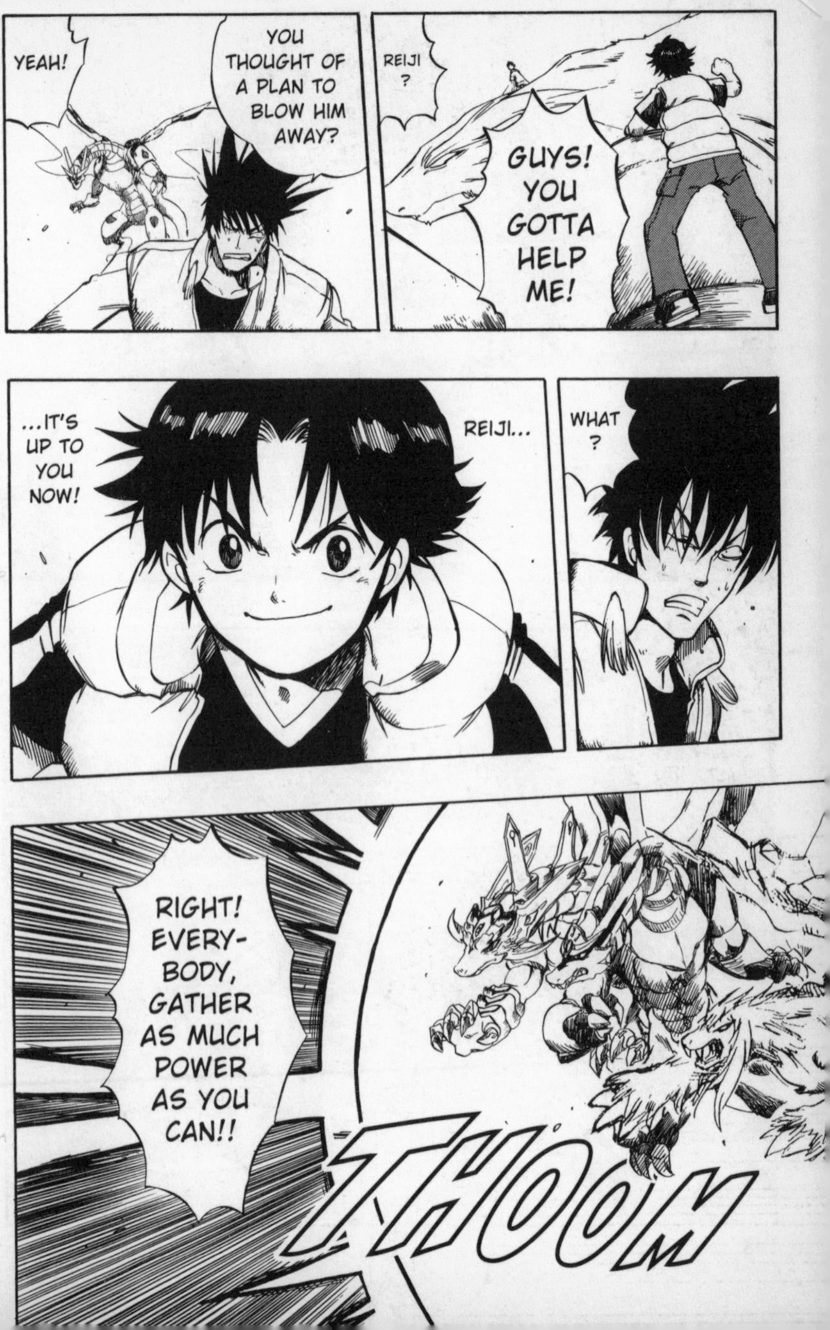
REIJI ?
GUYS! YOU GOTTA HELP ME!
YOU THOUGHT OF A PLAN TO BLOW HIM AWAY?
YEAH!
WHAT ?
REIJI...
...IT'S UP TO YOU NOW!
RIGHT! EVERY-BODY, GATHER AS MUCH POWER AS YOU CAN!!
THOOM

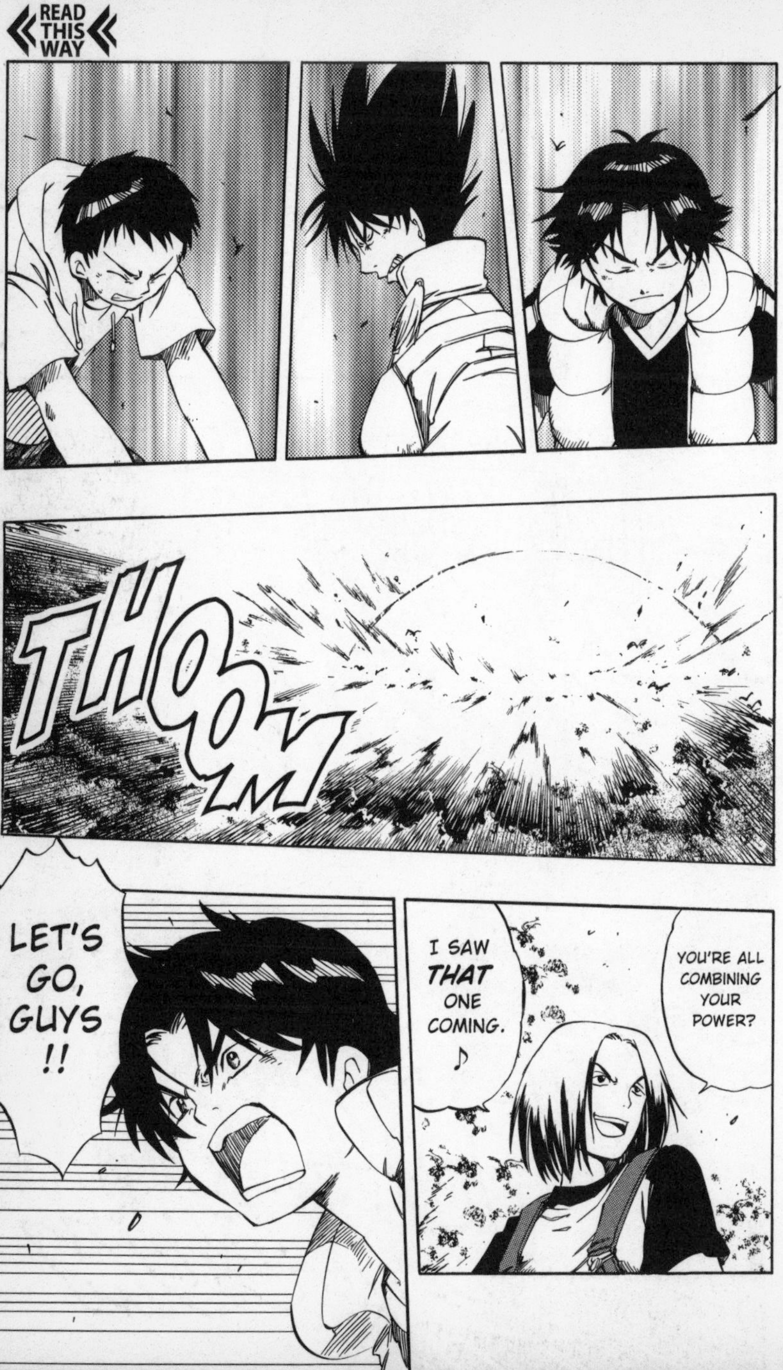
READ THIS WAY
THOOOM
YOU'RE ALL COMBINING YOUR POWER?
I SAW THAT ONE COMING. ♪
LET'S GO, GUYS !!

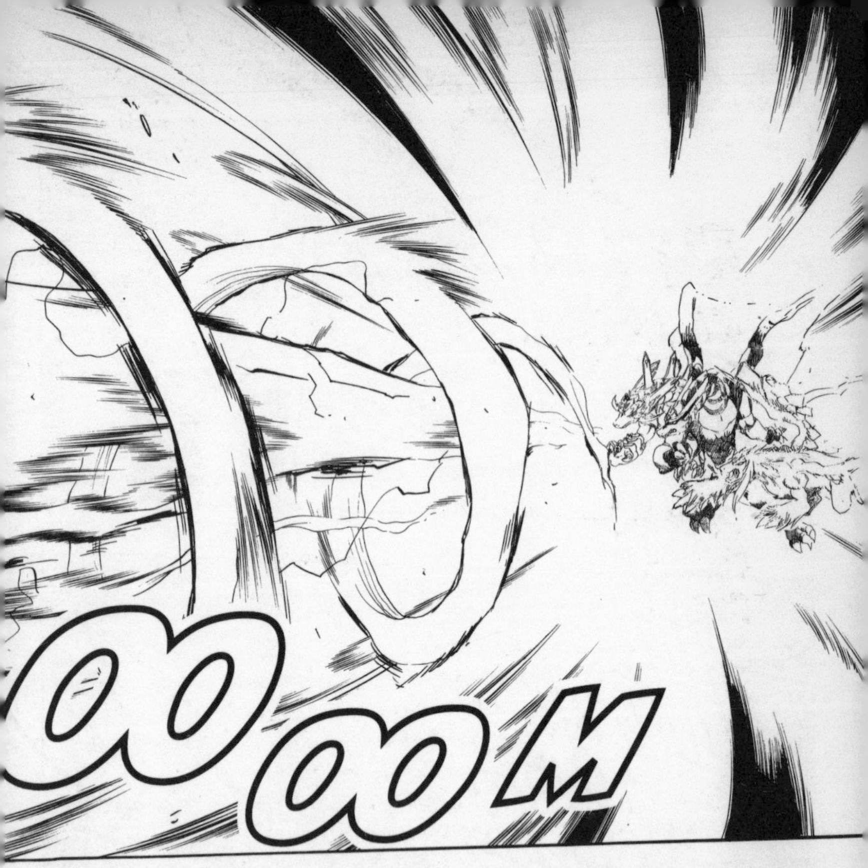
OOOOM

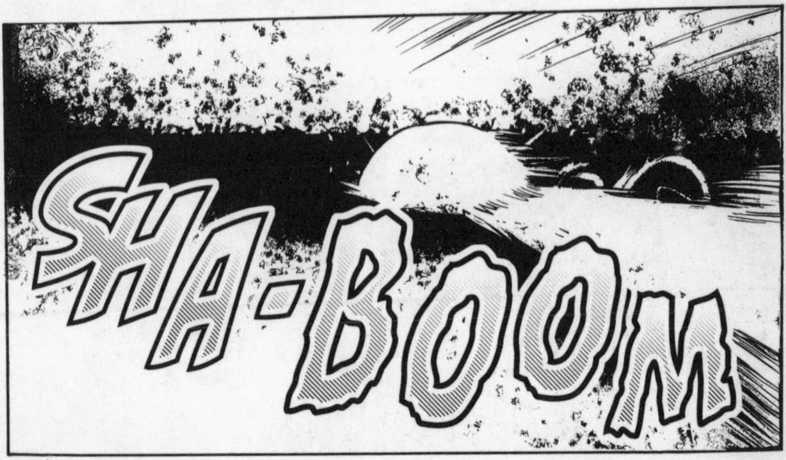
SHA-BOOM

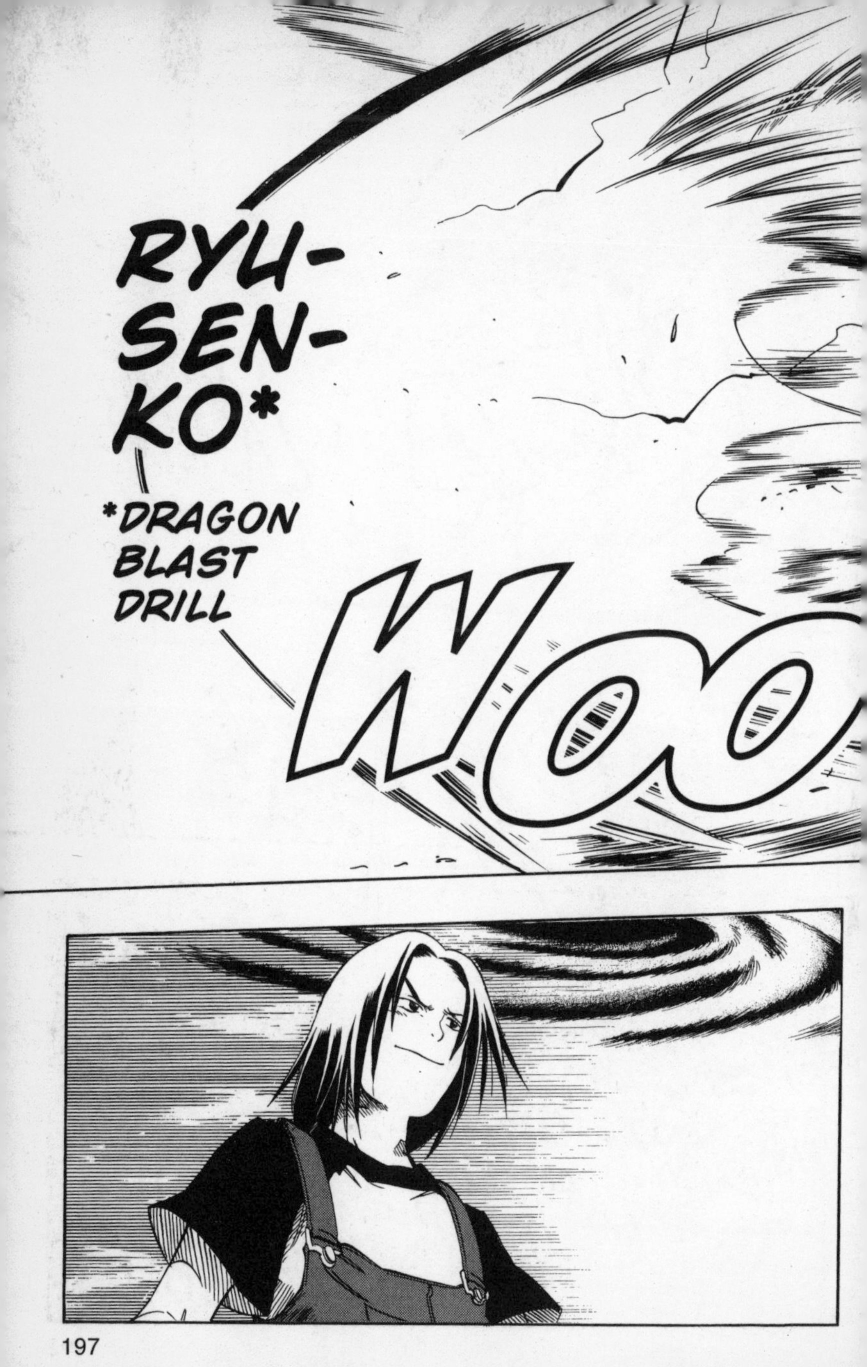
RYU-
SEN-
KO*
*DRAGON
BLAST
DRILL
WOO

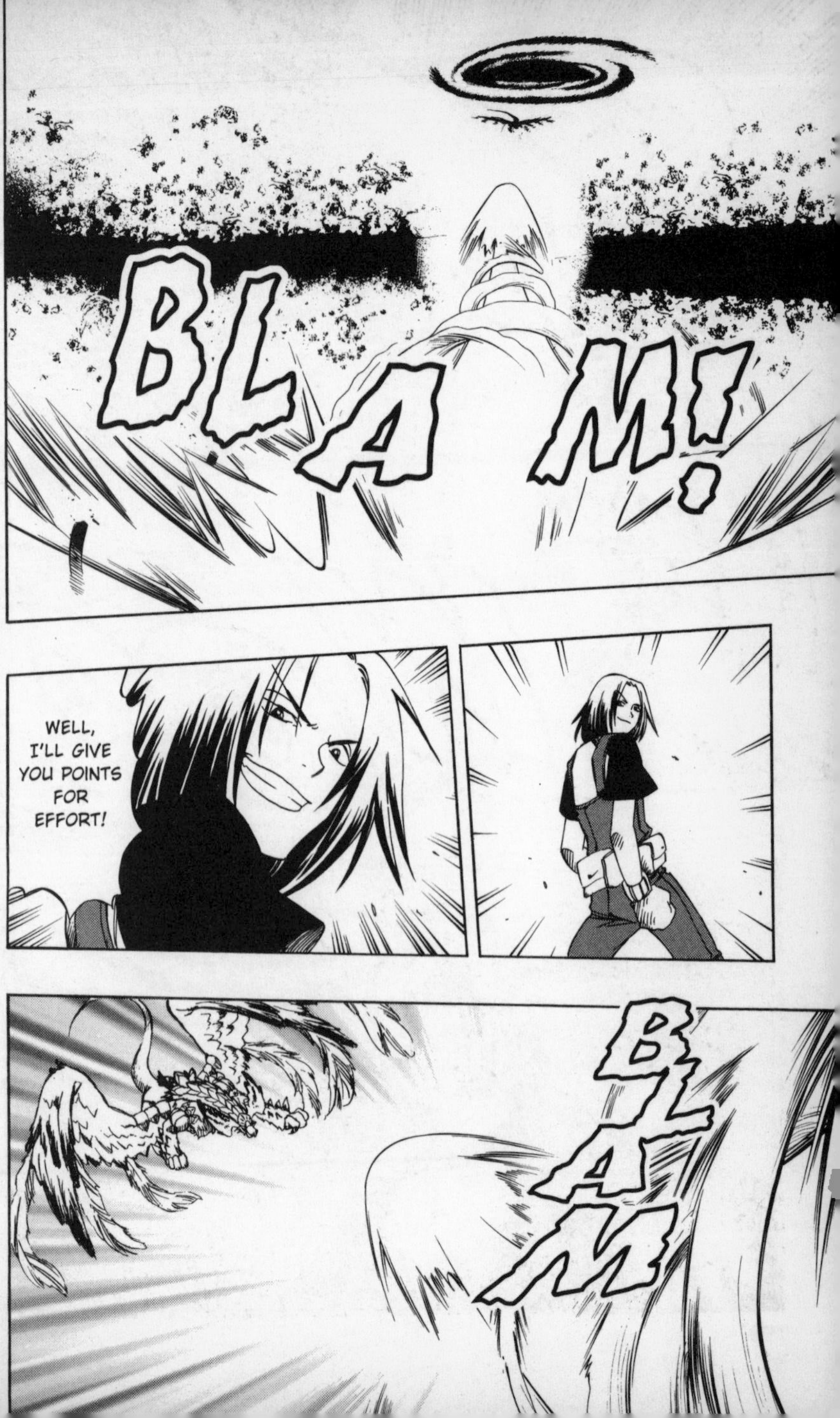
BLAM!
WELL, I'LL GIVE YOU POINTS FOR EFFORT!
BLAM

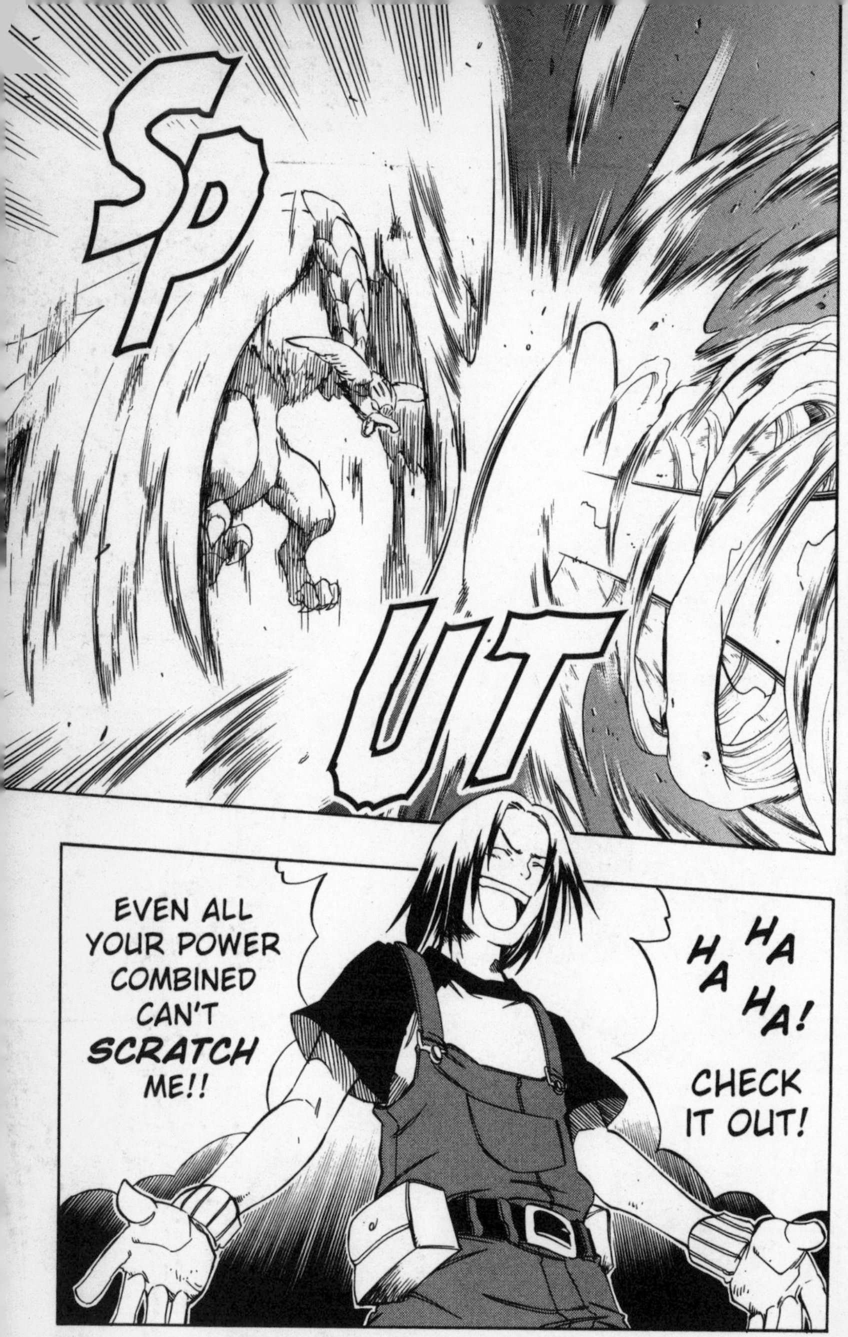
SPUT
HA HA HA HA!
CHECK IT OUT!
EVEN ALL YOUR POWER COMBINED CAN'T SCRATCH ME!!

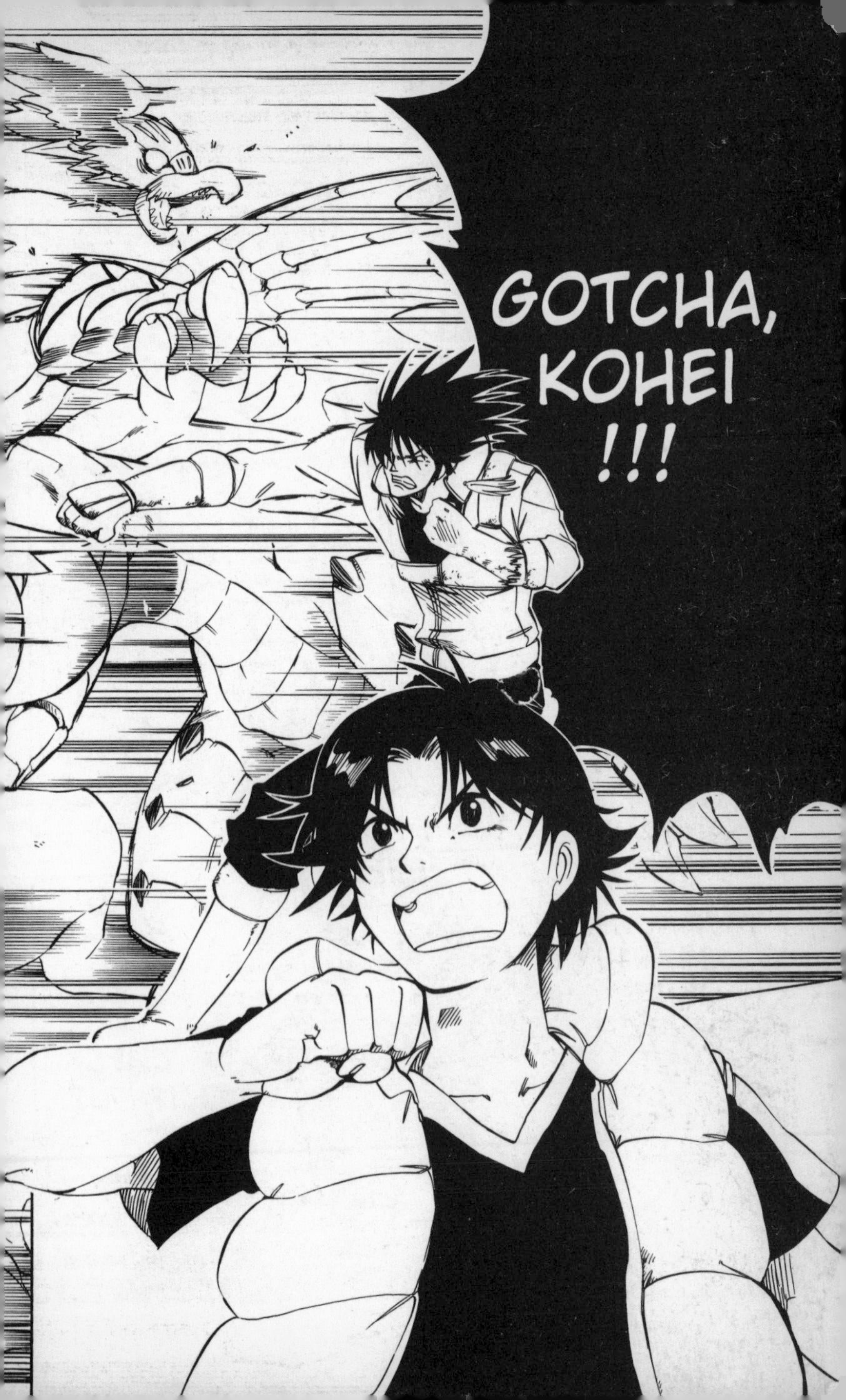
GOTCHA, KOHEI !!!

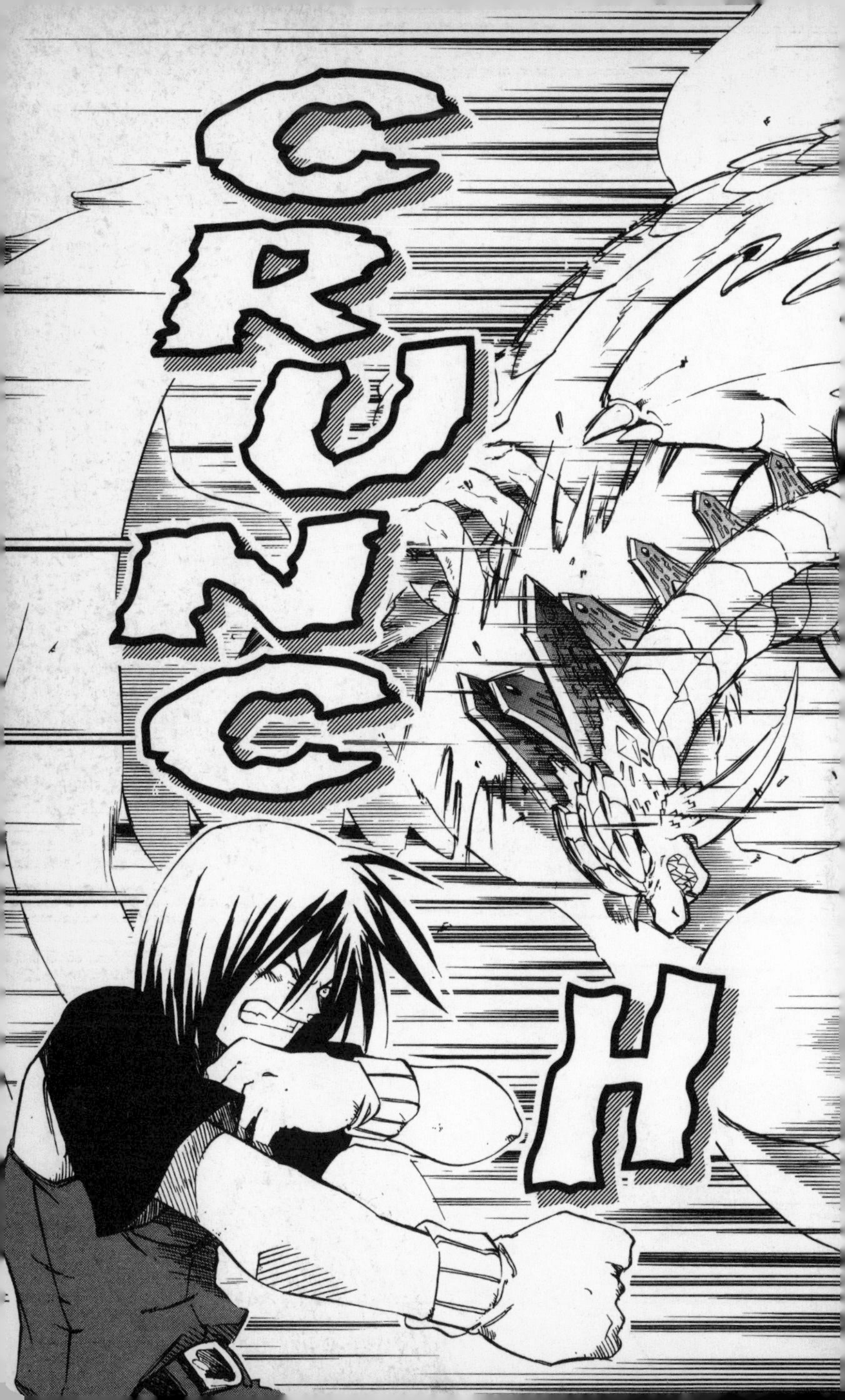
CRUNCH

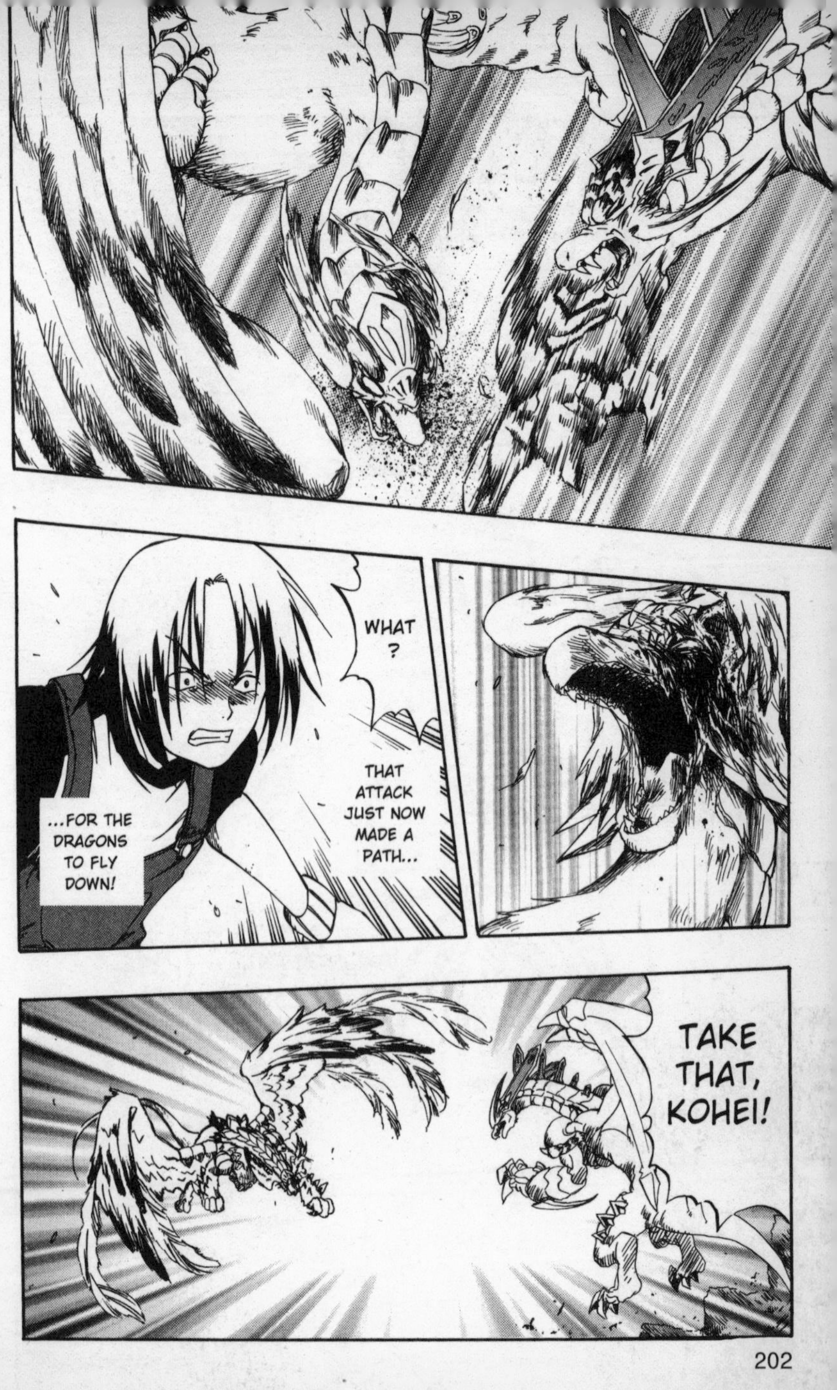
WHAT ?
THAT ATTACK JUST NOW MADE A PATH...
...FOR THE DRAGONS TO FLY DOWN!
TAKE THAT, KOHEI!

READ THIS WAY

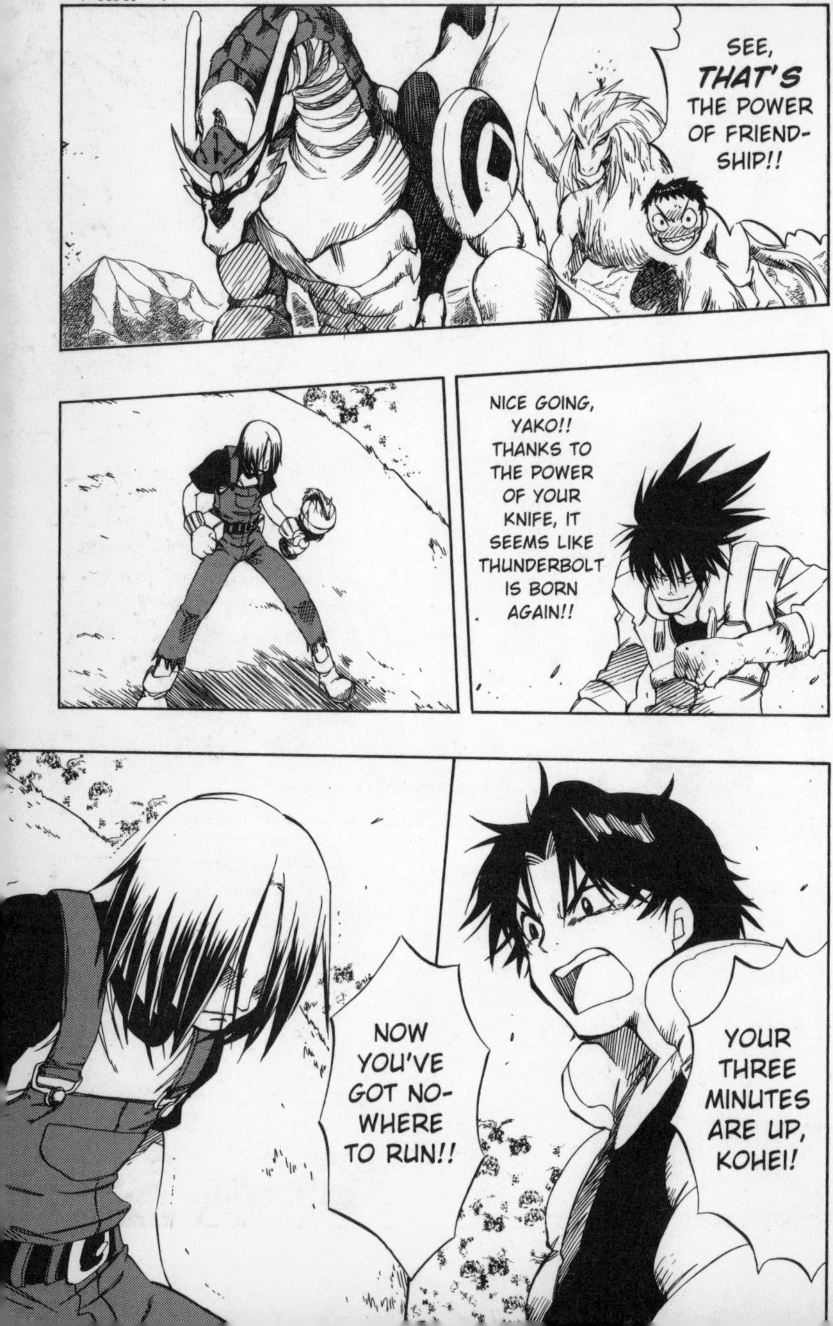

SEE, *THAT'S* THE POWER OF FRIEND-SHIP!!
NICE GOING, YAKO!! THANKS TO THE POWER OF YOUR KNIFE, IT SEEMS LIKE THUNDERBOLT IS BORN AGAIN!!
YOUR THREE MINUTES ARE UP, KOHEI!
NOW YOU'VE GOT NO-WHERE TO RUN!!

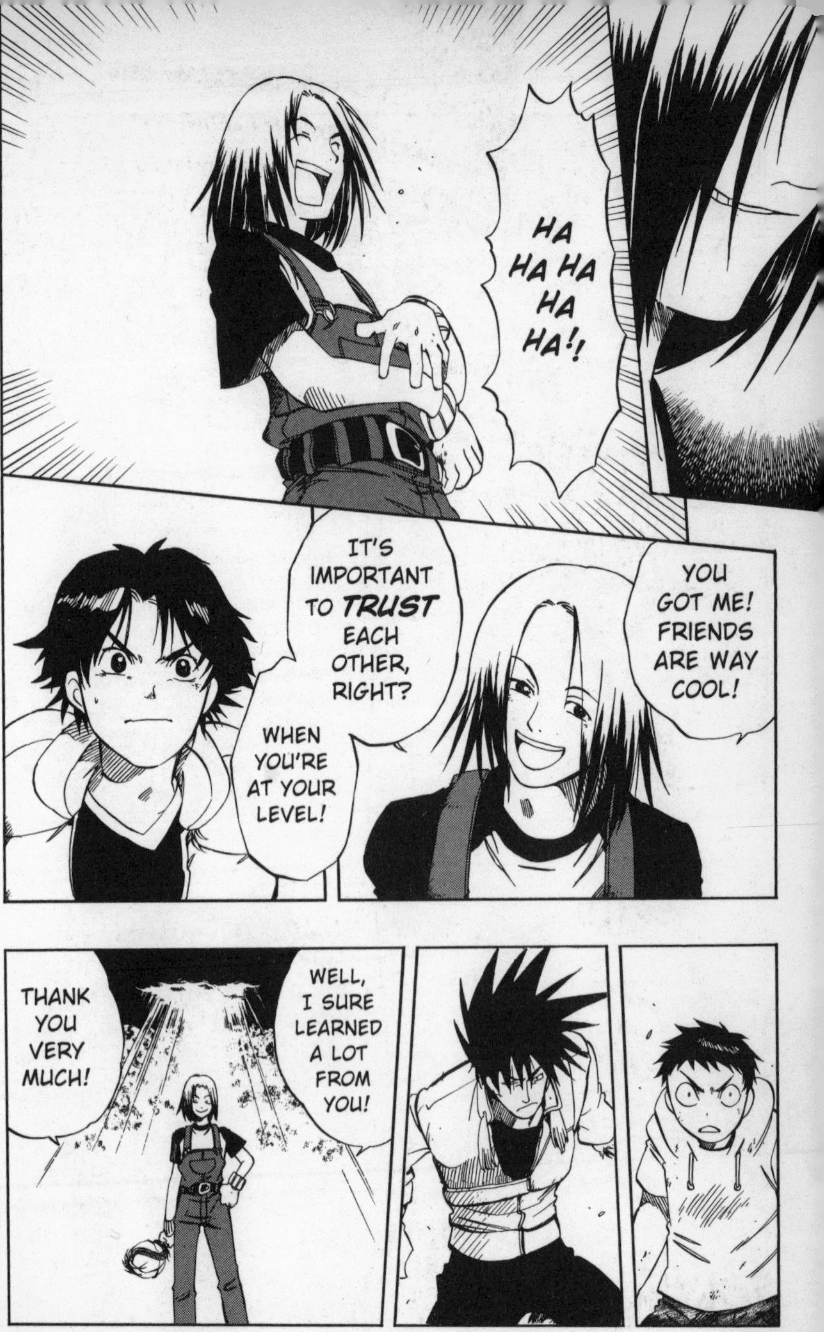
HA HA HA HA HA!!
YOU GOT ME! FRIENDS ARE WAY COOL!
IT'S IMPORTANT TO TRUST EACH OTHER, RIGHT?
WHEN YOU'RE AT YOUR LEVEL!
WELL, I SURE LEARNED A LOT FROM YOU!
THANK YOU VERY MUCH!

READ THIS WAY

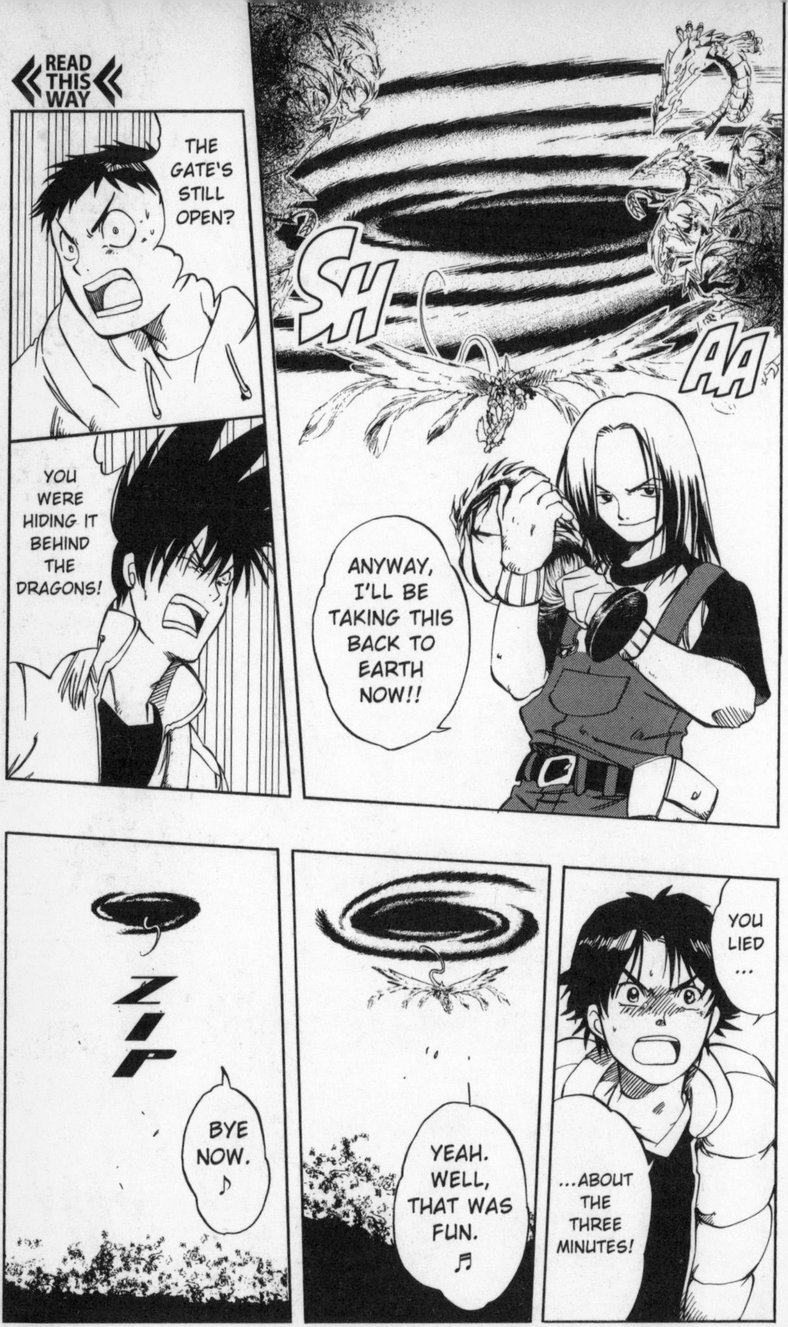
SH
AA
ANYWAY, I'LL BE TAKING THIS BACK TO EARTH NOW!!
THE GATE'S STILL OPEN?
YOU WERE HIDING IT BEHIND THE DRAGONS!
YOU LIED...
...ABOUT THE THREE MINUTES!
YEAH. WELL, THAT WAS FUN. ♬
ZIP
BYE NOW. ♪

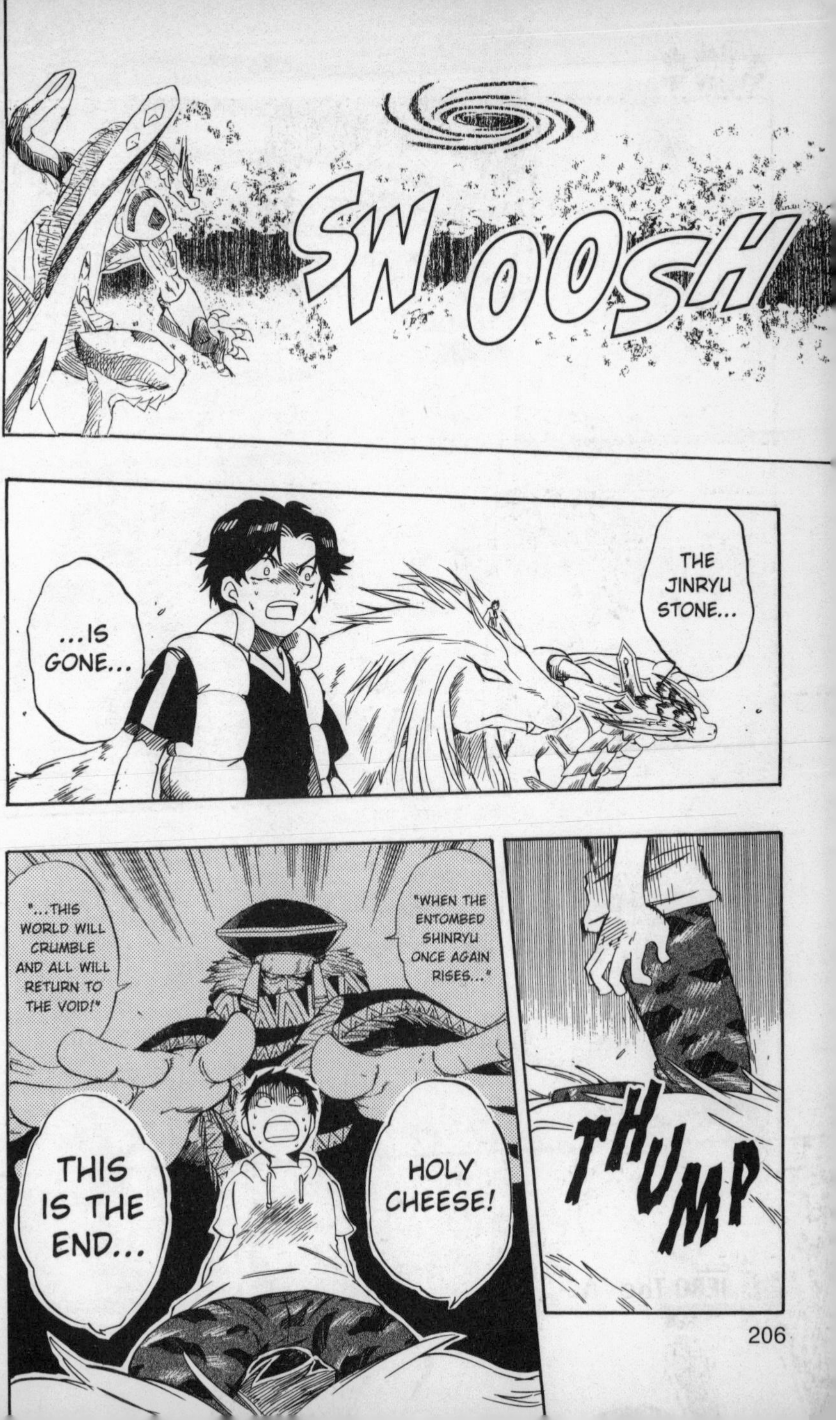
SWOOSH
THE JINRYU STONE...
...IS GONE...
THUMP
"WHEN THE ENTOMBED SHINRYU ONCE AGAIN RISES..."
"...THIS WORLD WILL CRUMBLE AND ALL WILL RETURN TO THE VOID!"
HOLY CHEESE!
THIS IS THE END...

READ THIS WAY

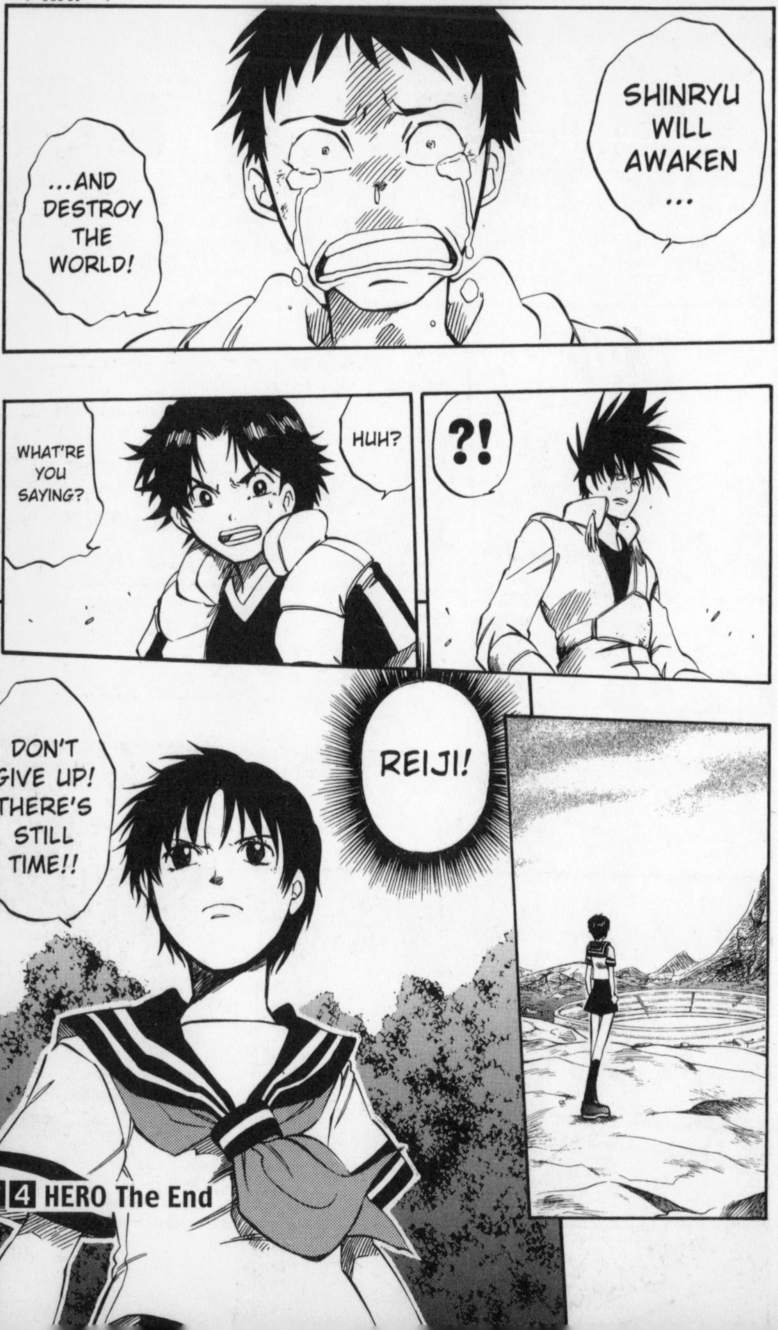
SHINRYU WILL AWAKEN ...
...AND DESTROY THE WORLD!
?!
HUH?
WHAT'RE YOU SAYING?
REIJI!
DON'T GIVE UP! THERE'S STILL TIME!!
4 HERO The End

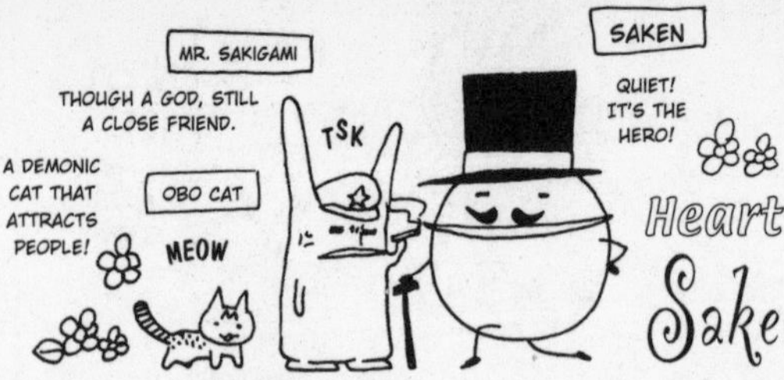
SAKEN
QUIET! IT'S THE HERO!
MR. SAKIGAMI
THOUGH A GOD, STILL A CLOSE FRIEND.
TSK
OBO CAT
A DEMONIC CAT THAT ATTRACTS PEOPLE!
MEOW

Heartwarming Saken Theater

BY KEN-ICHI SAKURA

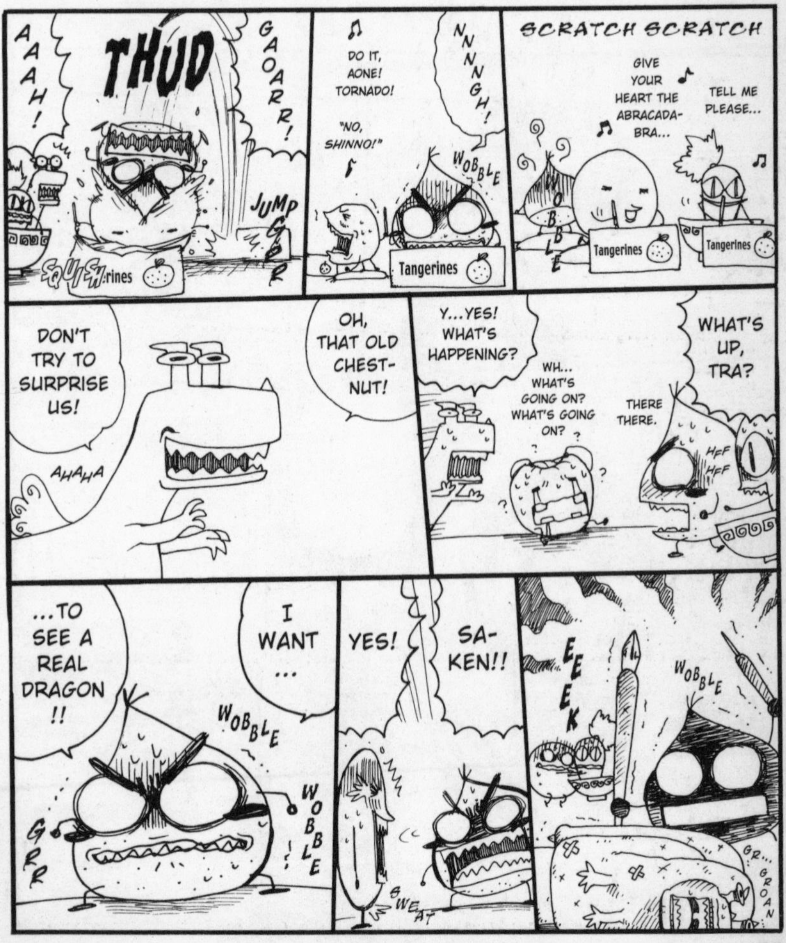
SCRATCH SCRATCH
TELL ME PLEASE...
GIVE YOUR HEART THE ABRACADABRA...
WOBBLE
Tangerines
Tangerines
NNNNGH!
DO IT, AONE! TORNADO!
"NO, SHINNO!"
WOBBLE
Tangerines
GAOARR!
THUD
AAAAH!
JUMP
SQUISH
rines
WHAT'S UP, TRA?
HFF HFF
THERE THERE.
WH... WHAT'S GOING ON? WHAT'S GOING ON?
Y...YES! WHAT'S HAPPENING?
OH, THAT OLD CHESTNUT!
DON'T TRY TO SURPRISE US!
AHAHA
WOBBLE
EEEK
GR... GROAN
SA-KEN!!
YES!
SWEAT
I WANT...
...TO SEE A REAL DRAGON!!
WOBBLE
WOBBLE
GRR

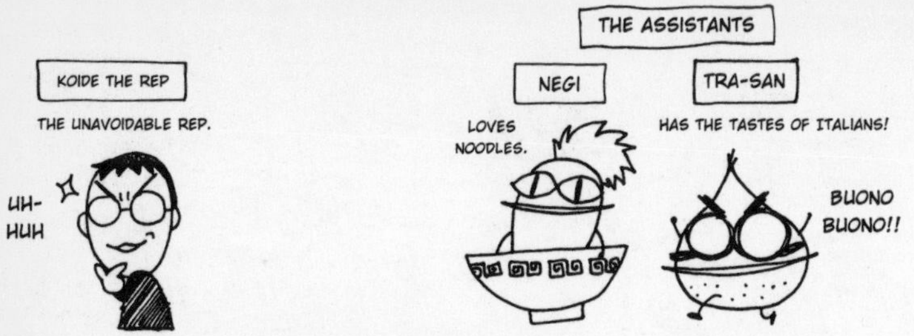
THE ASSISTANTS
TRA-SAN
HAS THE TASTES OF ITALIANS!
BUONO BUONO!!
NEGI
LOVES NOODLES.
KOIDE THE REP
THE UNAVOIDABLE REP.
UH-HUH

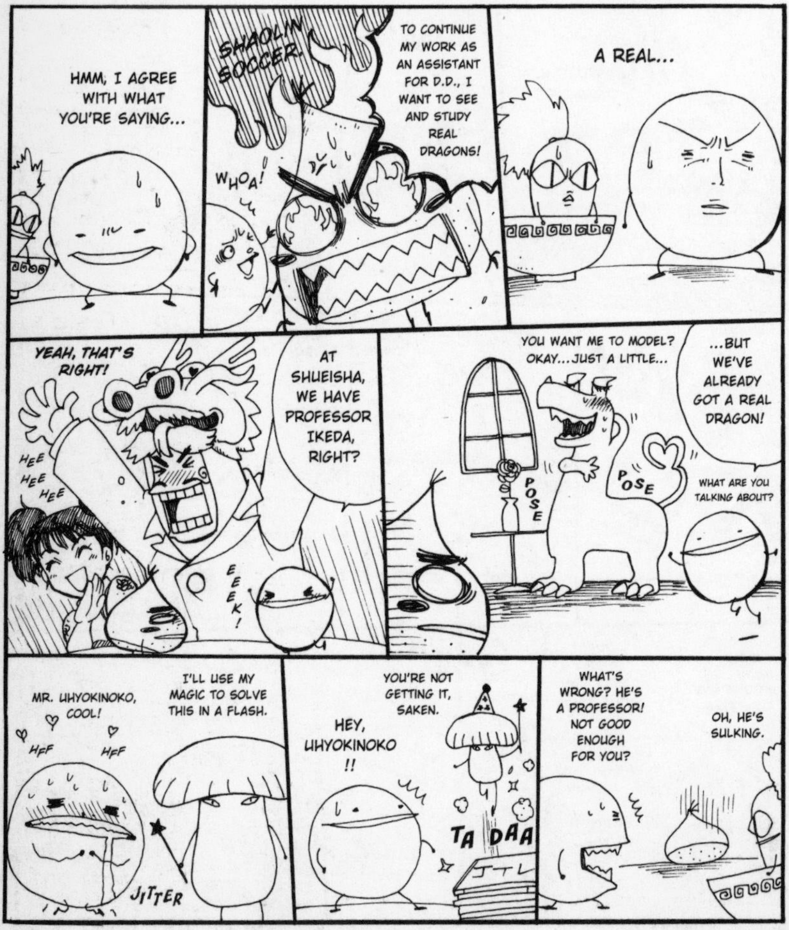
A REAL...
TO CONTINUE MY WORK AS AN ASSISTANT FOR D.D., I WANT TO SEE AND STUDY REAL DRAGONS!
SHAOLIN SOCCER
WHOA!
HMM, I AGREE WITH WHAT YOU'RE SAYING...
...BUT WE'VE ALREADY GOT A REAL DRAGON!
YOU WANT ME TO MODEL? OKAY... JUST A LITTLE...
POSE
POSE
WHAT ARE YOU TALKING ABOUT?
AT SHUEISHA, WE HAVE PROFESSOR IKEDA, RIGHT?
YEAH, THAT'S RIGHT!
HEE HEE HEE
EEEK!
OH, HE'S SULKING.
WHAT'S WRONG? HE'S A PROFESSOR! NOT GOOD ENOUGH FOR YOU?
YOU'RE NOT GETTING IT, SAKEN.
HEY, UHYOKINOKO!!
TA DAA
I'LL USE MY MAGIC TO SOLVE THIS IN A FLASH.
MR. UHYOKINOKO, COOL!
HFF
HFF
JITTER

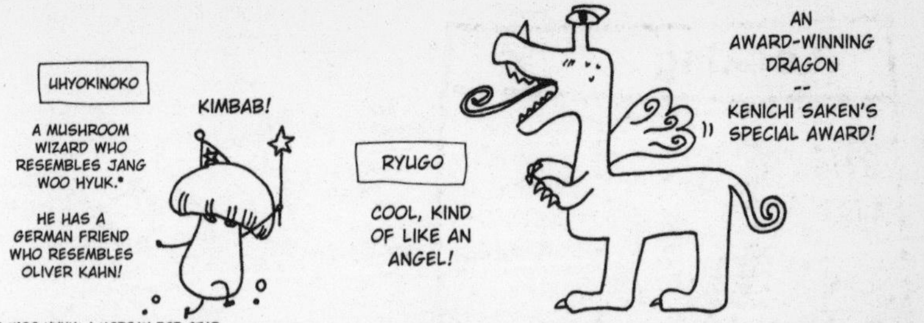
AN AWARD-WINNING DRAGON -- KENICHI SAKEN'S SPECIAL AWARD!
RYUGO
COOL, KIND OF LIKE AN ANGEL!
UHYOKINOKO
KIMBAB!
A MUSHROOM WIZARD WHO RESEMBLES JANG WOO HYUK.*
HE HAS A GERMAN FRIEND WHO RESEMBLES OLIVER KAHN!

*JANG WOO HYUK: A KOREAN POP STAR

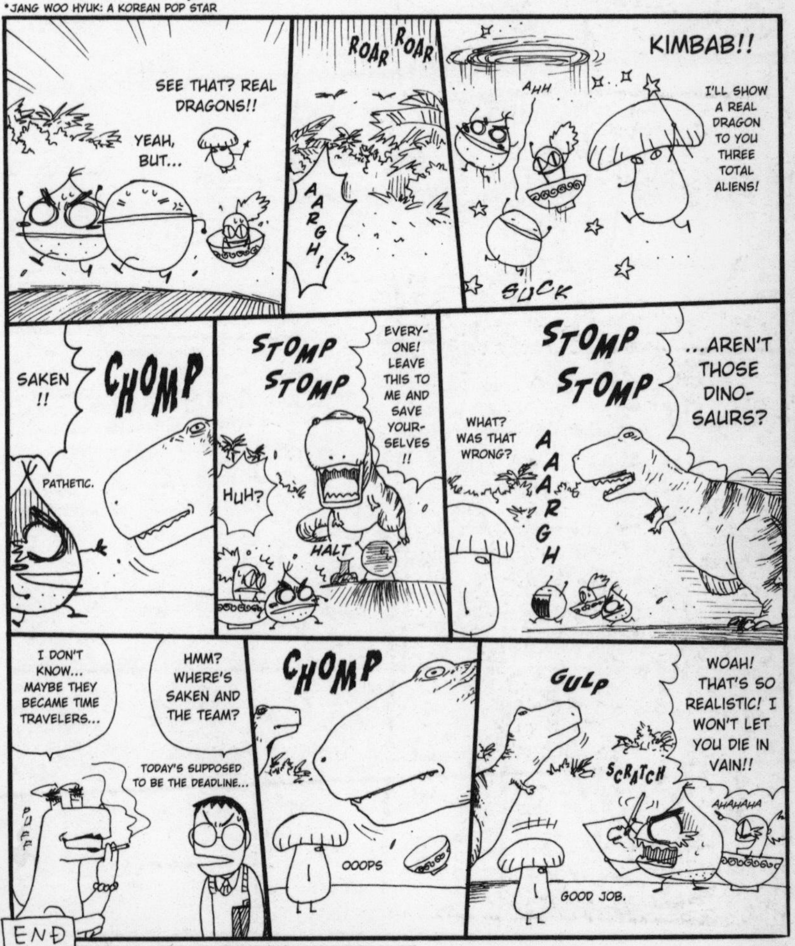
KIMBAB!!
I'LL SHOW A REAL DRAGON TO YOU THREE TOTAL ALIENS!
AHH
SUCK
ROAR ROAR
AARGH!
SEE THAT? REAL DRAGONS!!
YEAH, BUT...
...AREN'T THOSE DINOSAURS?
STOMP STOMP
WHAT? WAS THAT WRONG?
AAAARGH
EVERYONE! LEAVE THIS TO ME AND SAVE YOURSELVES!!
STOMP STOMP
HUH?
HALT
SAKEN!!
CHOMP
PATHETIC.
WOAH! THAT'S SO REALISTIC! I WON'T LET YOU DIE IN VAIN!!
GULP
SCRATCH
AHAHAHA
GOOD JOB.
CHOMP
OOOPS
HMM? WHERE'S SAKEN AND THE TEAM?
I DON'T KNOW... MAYBE THEY BECAME TIME TRAVELERS...
TODAY'S SUPPOSED TO BE THE DEADLINE...
PUFF
END

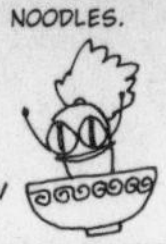
NOODLES.

Bonus 4-frame Strip

SCRIPT, ART: NAGI

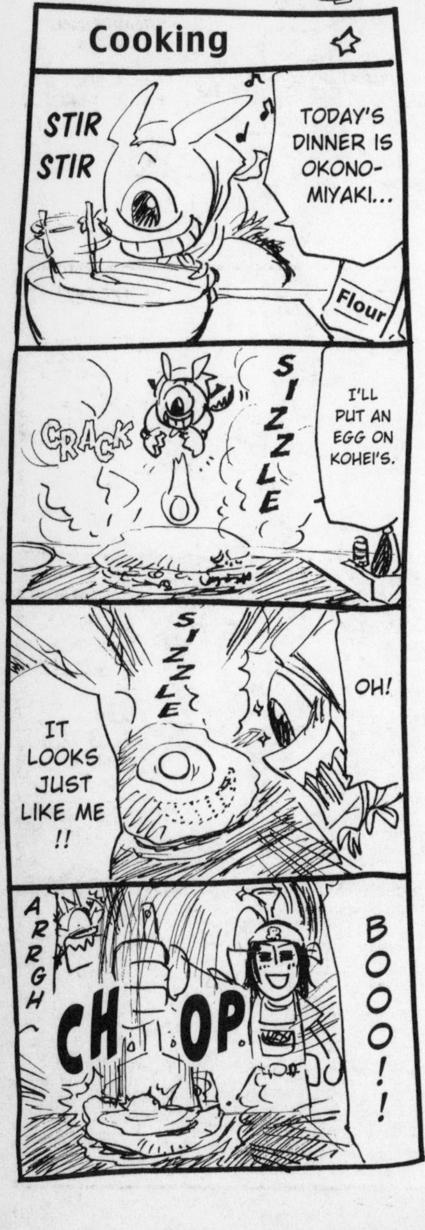
Cooking
TODAY'S DINNER IS OKONOMIYAKI...
STIR STIR
Flour
I'LL PUT AN EGG ON KOHEI'S.
SIZZLE
CRACK
OH!
SIZZLE
IT LOOKS JUST LIKE ME!!
BOOOO!!
CHOP
ARRGH

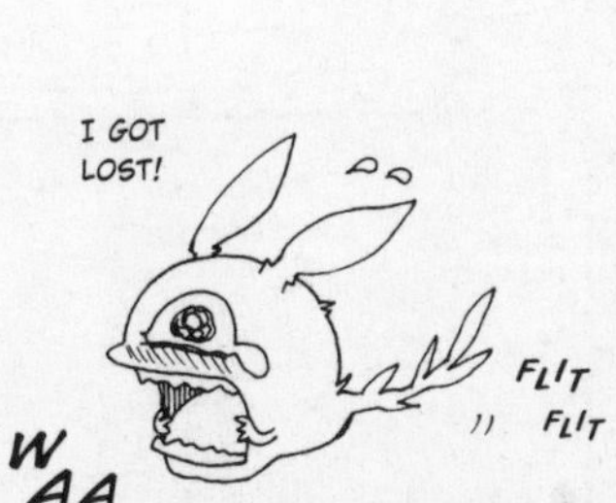
I GOT LOST!
FLIT FLIT
WAAH

COMING NEXT VOLUME...

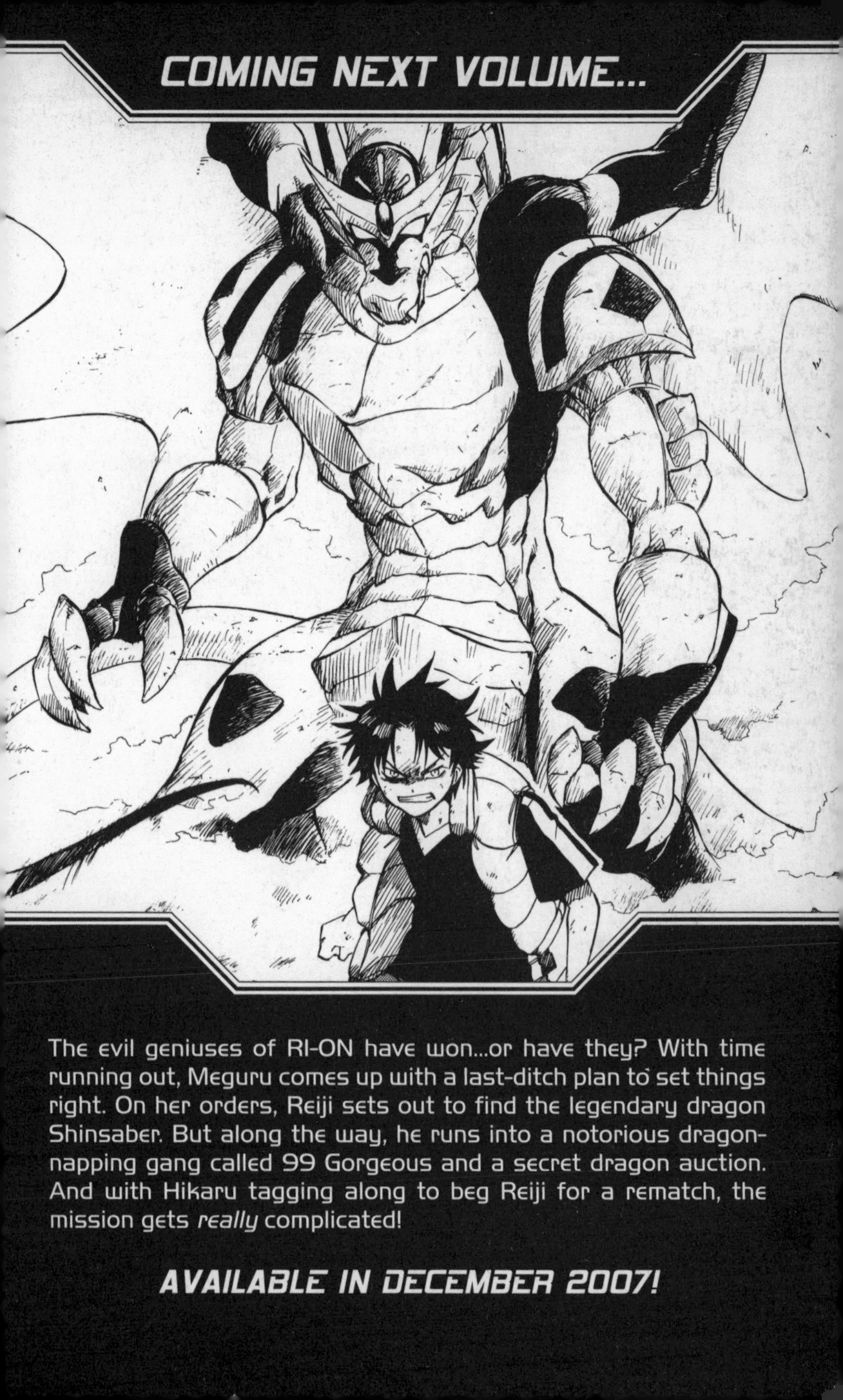

The evil geniuses of RI-ON have won...or have they? With time running out, Meguru comes up with a last-ditch plan to set things right. On her orders, Reiji sets out to find the legendary dragon Shinsaber. But along the way, he runs into a notorious dragon-napping gang called 99 Gorgeous and a secret dragon auction. And with Hikaru tagging along to beg Reiji for a rematch, the mission gets *really* complicated!

AVAILABLE IN DECEMBER 2007!

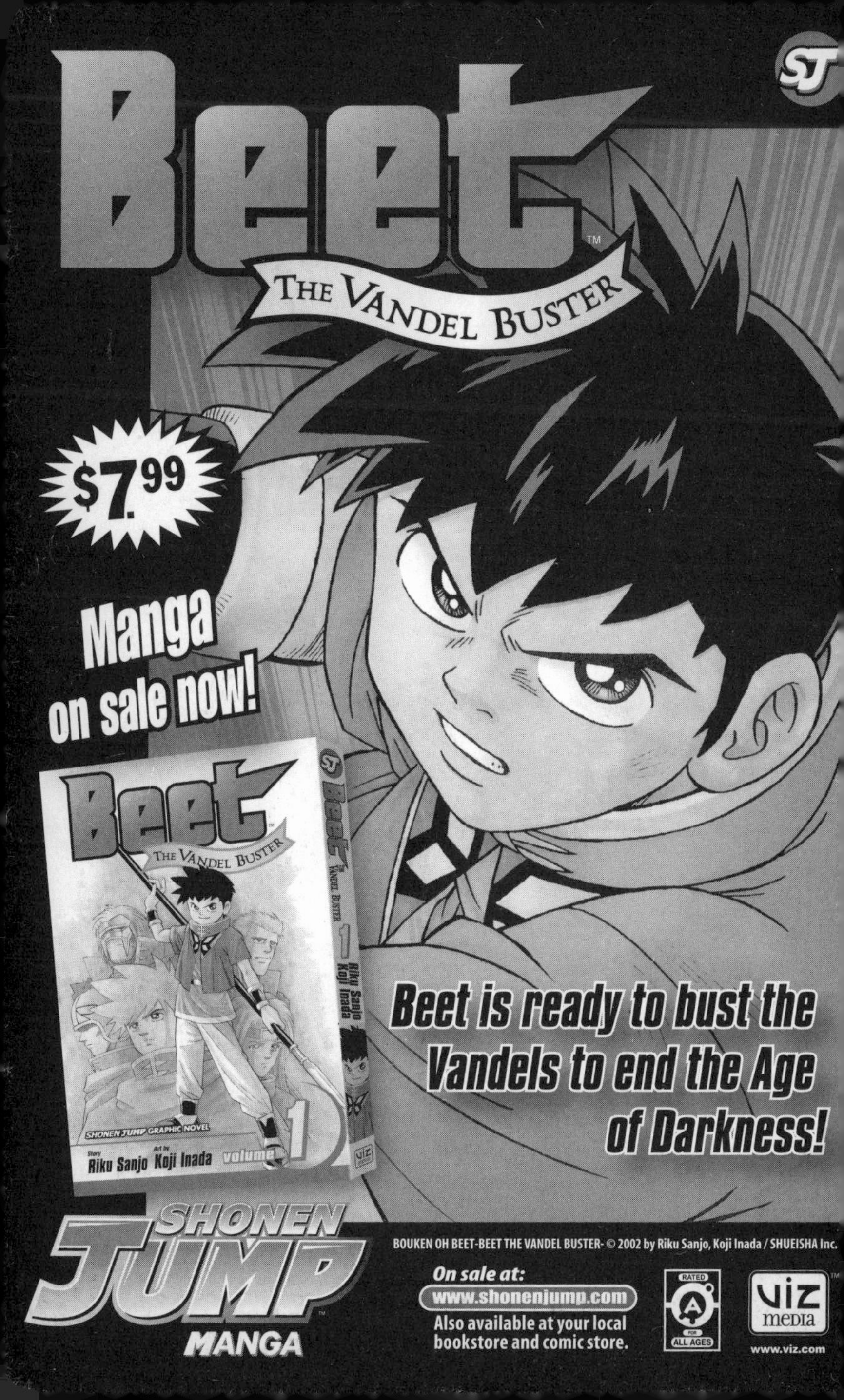

SJ
Beet™
THE VANDEL BUSTER
$7.99
Manga on sale now!
Beet
THE VANDEL BUSTER
SHONEN JUMP GRAPHIC NOVEL
Story Riku Sanjo Art by Koji Inada volume 1
Beet is ready to bust the Vandels to end the Age of Darkness!
SHONEN JUMP MANGA
BOUKEN OH BEET-BEET THE VANDEL BUSTER- © 2002 by Riku Sanjo, Koji Inada / SHUEISHA Inc.
On sale at:
www.shonenjump.com
Also available at your local bookstore and comic store.
RATED A FOR ALL AGES
VIZ media
www.viz.com

Tell us what you think about SHONEN JUMP manga!

Our survey is now available online.
Go to: www.SHONENJUMP.com/mangasurvey

Help us make our product offering better!

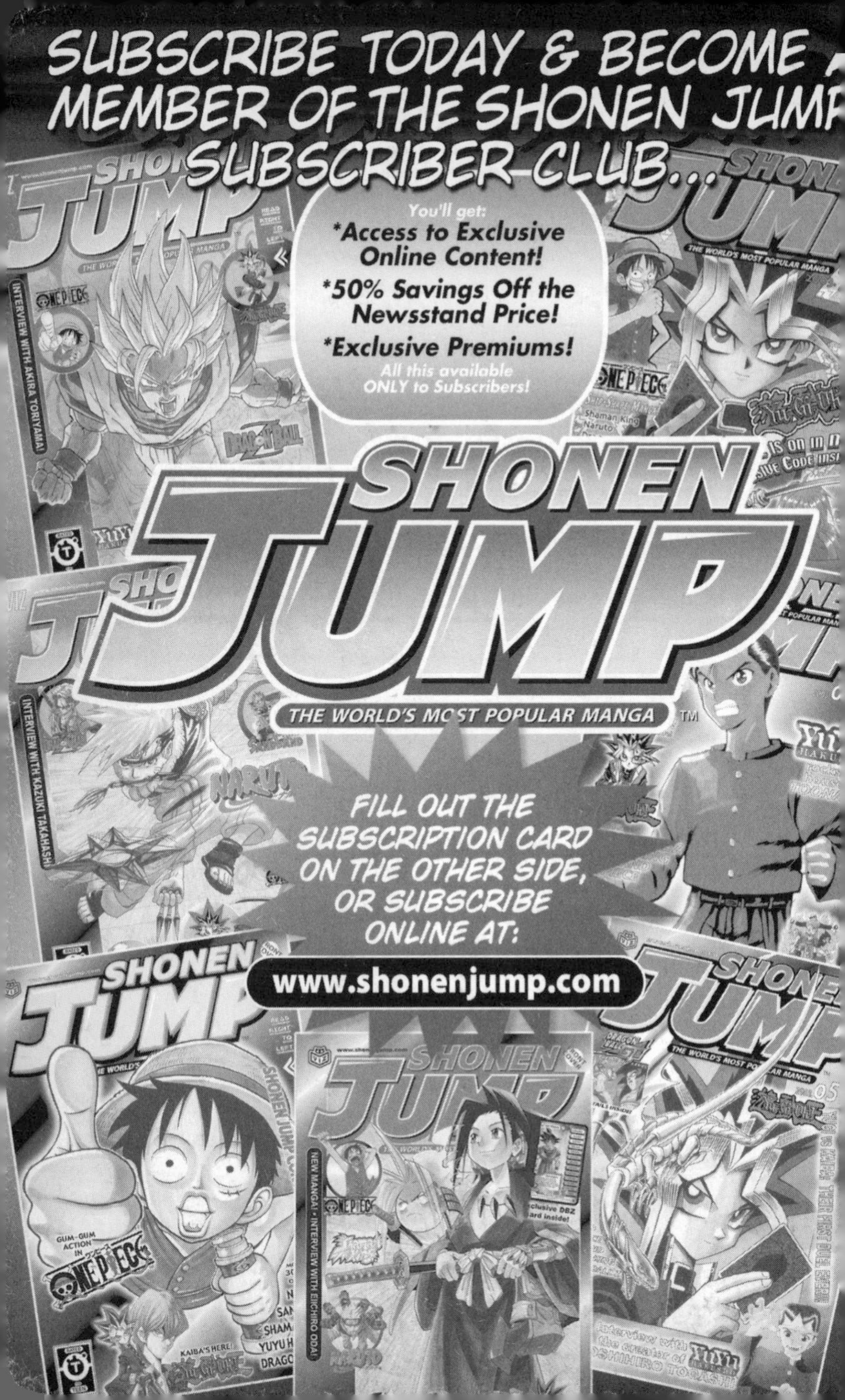
SUBSCRIBE TODAY & BECOME A MEMBER OF THE SHONEN JUMP SUBSCRIBER CLUB...
You'll get:
*Access to Exclusive Online Content!
*50% Savings Off the Newsstand Price!
*Exclusive Premiums!
All this available ONLY to Subscribers!
SHONEN JUMP
THE WORLD'S MOST POPULAR MANGA
FILL OUT THE SUBSCRIPTION CARD ON THE OTHER SIDE, OR SUBSCRIBE ONLINE AT:
www.shonenjump.com